The AGE of DIVISION

*Christendom from the Great Schism
to the Protestant Reformation*

John Strickland

PARADISE AND UTOPIA

The Rise and Fall of What the West Once Was

VOLUME 2

ANCIENT FAITH PUBLISHING ✠ CHESTERTON, INDIANA

Published by:
  Ancient Faith Publishing
  A Division of Ancient Faith Ministries
  P.O. Box 748
  Chesterton, IN 46304

Unless otherwise specified, Scripture quotations are from the New King James
Version of the Bible, © 1982 by Thomas Nelson, Inc., and are used by permission.

ISBN: 978-1-944967-86-4

Library of Congress Control Number: 2020947161

Printed in the United States of America

Contents

PROLOGUE: A Pope in Captivity   9

PART I: THE GREAT DIVISION

CHAPTER ONE: The Parting of the Ways   17
Christendom at the First Millennium   19
The Problem of the Proprietary Church   29
The Fading Influence of the East   32
An Augustinian Solution   36
Return of the Heroic Papacy   40
The Eastern Question   47
Excommunication   51

CHAPTER TWO: The Papal Reformation   59
Supremacy   60
A Diplomatic Revolution   67
Jihad Again   70
"The Great Innovator"   77
Crusades   90
Ecclesiastical Colonialism   99
Reaching the Limits in Russia   107

PART II: THE NEW CHRISTENDOM AND THE OLD

CHAPTER THREE: Popes, Kings, Monks, and Doctors   117
The Papal Mystique   118
Testing the Limits of Papal Supremacy   128
A Confusion of Orders   139
The Itinerants   146

Knowing God   151
Hesychasm   158

CHAPTER FOUR: The Patterns of Piety   167

The Bane of Clericalism   168
Filling the Eucharistic Void   174
From Heaven to Earth . . .   179
. . . and Back Again   186
Stavrocentrism   194
The Image of the Cross   205
"Joy-Making Mourning"   213

PART III: THE WITHERING OF WESTERN CULTURE

CHAPTER FIVE: Disintegration   223

A Case of Papal Eschatology   224
The Tragedy of Conciliarism   227
The Subversion of Doctrine   235
The Proliferation of Death   243
The Eleventh Hour   250
The Northern Thebaid   259
"Better a Fez than the Tiara"   267

CHAPTER SIX: The Fall of Paradise   275

The Curse of Penitential Pessimism   277
Martin Luther's Agony   285
The Protestant Counter-Reformation   289
The Labyrinth and the Abyss   291
"In Heaven and Not Here"   298
The Tower and the Kremlin   306
The Division of Russian Christianity 319
Pagans, Witches, and Heretics   323
"The Righteous Judgment of God"   326

EPILOGUE: Toward Utopian Horizons   335
INDEX   344
ABOUT THE AUTHOR   359

The comparison of the Church with Paradise shows us that men may indeed receive her baptism outside her pale, but that no one outside can either receive or retain the salvation of eternal happiness. For, as the words of Scripture testify, the streams from the fountain of Paradise flowed copiously even beyond its bounds. . . . Accordingly, though the waters of Paradise are found beyond its boundaries, yet its happiness is in Paradise alone.

—Augustine, *On Baptism*

PROLOGUE

A Pope in Captivity

POPE LEO IX STARED DOWN from the ramparts with horror. On the battlefield before him lay an army of corpses. Once vigorous men of war, they had marched under the papal banner at his command to this forsaken place in southern Italy, a town named Civitate.

The campaign of 1053 had had a simple purpose: to rid the land of its ruthless Norman occupants. Its rationale, however, was unprecedented. Never before had a pope—the successor to Saint Peter—organized, financed, and led an expedition of conquest. Leo was assuming the responsibilities and powers of a civil potentate. In his words, the expedition had been launched with the goal of "liberating Christendom."[1] Gazing ruefully upon the carnage below him, he now realized it had been a catastrophic failure.

Pope Leo's war was a first in history, yet it grew out of geopolitical tensions that had been simmering in Italy for centuries. Since the eighth century, the papacy had claimed territories at the center of the peninsula stretching between Ravenna and Rome. An attack on them such as the Normans threatened was considered an attack on the papacy. Equally pressing and more ancient were the interests of the Byzantine Empire. It had fought hard to recover the Italian peninsula during the sixth-century Gothic Wars,

---

[1]   Quoted in I. S. Robinson, editor, *The Papal Reform of the Eleventh Century* (Manchester: Manchester University Press, 2004), 150.

and the Greek-speaking population of the south still identified with the Christian East and looked to Constantinople for protection.

But early in the eleventh century, almost by accident, the land-hungry Normans had landed in the south during a pilgrimage to Jerusalem. They never left. In fact, they had exploited the region's political instability to launch a program of colonization, displacing the Byzantines and menacing the papacy. To end this peril, Leo had sent an appeal to the Byzantines for military aid. But relations with the patriarch of Constantinople were at a low point, and so, for the first time ever, he decided to raise his own army and lead it into battle against the enemy. He even persuaded the German emperor Henry III to contribute a battalion of knights, creating an international army of liberation.

After months of campaigning, this army had approached the Normans near Civitate. Though greatly outnumbered, the Normans decided on a preemptive attack. They had no desire to await the arrival of yet more forces rumored to be on the march from Byzantium. So on June 18, 1053, they acted. At first Leo's knights stood their ground. But though they fought tenaciously, an upstart Norman commander named Robert Guiscard—who during the day had been thrice unhorsed only to return to his saddle each time—finally managed to outflank them. As a result, the papal army was destroyed to a man as its commander watched helplessly from the battlements above. And as the cries of the dying faded with the sunset, Leo realized that a much greater plan was in danger of dying too.

THE BATTLE OF CIVITATE WAS fought to achieve more than the security of central Italy's Papal States. It was fought for the reform of Christendom.

The Normans of southern Italy were not just marauders, descendants of the Norse warlord Rollo who had agreed to baptism in exchange for the rich coastland of northern France. Leo regarded his enemy as an existential threat to Christian civilization. They represented all that was wrong about the past two centuries, when Viking invasions had brought much of Western Christendom to its knees. Merciless in war and rapacious in peace, their only faith was in the power of the sword. As long as they were allowed to roam through Europe freely, no churches or monasteries would be safe. Nor, of course, would the pope of Rome.

The Byzantines likewise represented more than a mere territorial rival to the papacy. Leo took his regnal name from Leo the Great, the fifth-century pope who had rejected the Fourth Ecumenical Council's Canon 28 recognizing Constantinople as "New Rome" with a jurisdictional stature equal to that of old Rome. As for his inspiration, that came from Pope Nicholas I. Two centuries earlier, it had been Nicholas who intervened in the election of Patriarch Photios of Constantinople and, after the latter refused to recognize his authority to do so, excommunicated him in an act best remembered as the Nicolaitan Schism.[2]

Leo IX was the most imperious pope since Nicholas, and he regarded Photios's current successor in the East with deep suspicion. Michael Cerularius claimed the title of "Ecumenical Patriarch," which in Latin translation appeared to imply a universal jurisdiction within the Church. Closer to home, Leo was suspicious of the Greek-speaking Christians of southern Italy, long ruled by Byzantium. In his judgment, their adherence to Eastern liturgical practices, such as using leavened bread for the Eucharist, represented a challenge to Rome, where unleavened wafers had recently been introduced for the sacrament. In his mind, liturgical diversity on the very doorstep of the Papal States could only undermine confidence in the papacy.

And if there was anything the papacy needed in the eleventh century, it was confidence. Leo's tenth-century predecessors had brought disgrace to the office, cowering before a Roman aristocracy that replaced them frequently and on a whim. Many popes obtained office through nepotism and bribery, and then misused it as a source of personal enrichment. To make matters worse, some were the cause of scandals so salacious as to earn for the period the ignoble label of *pornocracy*. The memory of John XII was a particularly painful example of this. The fact that he had assumed the Chair of Saint Peter through bribery only to die in the arms of his married lover was impossible to purge from the papacy's institutional memory. For Leo

2   Western historians customarily call the event the "Photian Schism," thus failing to acknowledge Nicholas's responsibility in causing it.

and those around him, the time had come for a wholesale reform. Only an assertive, self-confident, and energetic pope could address the multifarious problems confronting the West.

But little could be done as long as armed marauders had the freedom to pillage southern Italy and destabilize the Papal States. A holy war against the Normans, Leo concluded, would release the untapped powers of the papacy and direct them toward the reformation of all Christendom.

So the Battle of Civitate that ended so ignominiously for him was much more than a military defeat. It constituted the defeat of a nascent Papal Reformation.

THIS GRIEVOUS POSSIBILITY WAS ALREADY sinking in when, in the aftermath of the battle, the townspeople ejected Leo through their gates into the custody of the Normans. To be sure, matters could have been worse. His captors were, after all, fully Latinized Christians. They were members of the very Church to which he belonged and over which he claimed to rule. In fact, as he emerged from the town they actually received him with a sense of awe. One contemporary account has their commanders prostrating before him while their soldiers placed him under guard. In deference to his office, they gave him leave to walk among the bodies of his fallen soldiers. It would have made for a grim stroll, but the spectacle of gore did not break him. In fact, when he was done, he unilaterally pronounced—though church tradition gave him no authority to do so—that the warriors at his feet who had died fighting the Normans were nothing less than saints of God.

This charismatic act of canonization was an innovation, and it foretold the coming of many more at the hands of a papacy that was finally gaining a sense of its historic destiny. Saint Peter's successor had not only raised an army and led it to battle. He had consecrated its violence by equating combat with martyrdom. Dying beneath the papal banner had become, in this case at least, a path to salvation.

Leo remained in Norman captivity for nine long months. Relocated to the town of Benevento, he acclimated himself to prison the way a monk might settle into a cherished cell. He slept on the floor and maintained the sparest of diets. According to his biographer, his nights were spent in prayer and vigil and his days in fulfilling the petitions of the poor who flocked to him. He may even have welcomed captivity. This is certainly what his pious biographers claimed. But it is unlikely. For outside the involuntary cloister of Benevento, Christendom continued its slide into the abyss. The captive pope believed it was his responsibility to pull it back out.

One can imagine his relief, then, when on a certain day a familiar knock was heard on his door. It announced the arrival of Cardinal Humbert, a fellow French monastic whom Leo had brought to Rome from his native Alsace. This cleric was unquestionably the most zealous of all papal reformers, and his message was simple. Leo must dispatch a legation to Constantinople immediately or be eclipsed by Michael Cerularius. For, he reported, the usurper (Humbert claimed he had never been properly ordained) was again claiming primacy alongside Leo, as evidenced by his use of the title Ecumenical Patriarch. More appalling were reports that Michael had ordered the closure of Latin parishes in the Byzantine capital because they used unleavened bread at the Eucharist. What Humbert neglected to report was that the Normans had done something similar in southern Italy even earlier. They were completely ignorant of Eastern Christian practice and had therefore banned the Greeks' use of leavened bread. It was the Normans, therefore, who had precipitated the controversy, and they had done so under the very nose of Leo.

What made the situation impossible, Humbert insisted, was the widespread contempt for Latin liturgical practice in the East. This was a direct challenge to the primacy of Rome.

Such contempt was expressed by a provocative letter penned at Michael's urging by a Greek bishop named Leo of Ohrid. It actually accused the Latins of departing from the sacred traditions of the universal Church. The letter claimed, for instance, that the Latins were wrong not only in introducing unleavened bread but in insisting that priests shave their beards. It also took issue with the demand that priests practice celibacy. From time immemorial the majority of parish priests of the East had been married and with their wives had raised families. The seventh-century Council in Trullo had recognized this. But reformers in Rome—Humbert among them—had recently begun to demand complete celibacy by the parish clergy. Leo's letter was an attack on the perceived innovations of the West.

All of this was too much to bear for Benevento's revered but much beleaguered prisoner. Pope Leo soon assented to Humbert's demand. The bullish cardinal and two other stalwart advocates of reform were granted the powers of papal legates and dispatched to confront Patriarch Michael in the East.

The decision was everything for which ambitious reformers in the West had been hoping. By now, Pope Leo IX was terminally ill and would not live to hear the results of the legation. But as he presented Humbert with letters to bear to Constantinople, his final hope was that this move would persuade the patriarch to submit to the papacy, thereby giving a nascent papal reformation the free hand it needed in the West. Such, in any event, were likely the captive's thoughts as he lay alone on the floor of his prison cell in prayer after Humbert's departure.

The alternative result of the legation, he may have reflected, was that the East would not submit to papal supremacy and that Christendom, having reached its first millennium in unity, would enter a grievous and long-lasting age of division.

PART I

The Great Division

CHAPTER ONE

The Parting of the Ways

T HE DIVISION OF CHRISTENDOM DID not begin with an open conflict between the pope of Rome and the patriarch of Constantinople.
The spirit of division was more subtle than that. For centuries it had been
lurking in the background of church life, frequenting monasteries, expos-
ing itself only gradually, and, with one exception, avoiding detection in the
form of actual schism. Ultimately, it would join itself to the well-intentioned
efforts of a pope and his advisors as they undertook an ambitious reformation of the West.

During the first millennium there had been a slow uncoupling of Eastern
and Western views about the world (cosmology) and man's place within it
(anthropology).[1] The fact that Augustine (d. 430), virtually unknown in the
East, had after his death become the unrivalled theological authority of the
West meant that its culture was inseparably linked to him. Augustinianism,
as his posthumous influence can be called, assumed a decidedly pessimistic
character in comparison to the cosmologically and anthropologically affirmative legacies of Eastern fathers such as Basil the Great, Gregory of Nyssa,

---

1   The history summarized here is covered more broadly in this volume's predecessor, *The Age of Paradise*.

and Maximos the Confessor. On the implications of original sin in particular, East and West had begun to show significant differences in ethos within a very short period of time.

Also significant at an administrative level was the ninth-century rupture of communion caused by Pope Nicholas's intervention against Patriarch Photios. The Nicolaitan Schism (863–867) proved only temporary, but it revealed a growing ecclesiological divide in that the pope had now claimed the authority unilaterally to intervene in the affairs of another ancient patriarchate. This early assertion of what would be called papal supremacy was countered by the ancient principle of conciliarity, pushing the East and West further apart.

Finally, the Carolingian cultural revolution, motivated as it was by the Franks' effort to supplant Byzantium, created a model of Western culture that ostracized the Greeks. The Franks resorted to an almost exclusive reliance on Augustinianism, dismissing the hitherto fundamental influence of Eastern Christianity on the West.

The dissolution of Charlemagne's empire during the ninth century reduced the Frankish disruption to Christendom's cultural unity. A subsequent pope, John VIII (r. 872–882), improved relations with Constantinople and resumed his predecessors' resistance to that greatest symbol of estrangement, the Frankish addition to the Nicene Creed known as the *filioque*. But in 1014 a descendent of Charlemagne, the German emperor Henry II, overpowered papal opposition and ordered that the divisive creedal addition be placed within the very Mass celebrated at Saint Peter's Basilica in Rome.

But by this time the spirit of division was wandering freely in the formerly Frankish lands of France and Germany, where monasticism had been reduced to an intolerable condition. The spirit was borne by zealous ascetics seeking a restoration of what monasticism had once been, the fullest expression of Christendom's spiritual transformation.

Reform was in the air. Its effects were as yet tentative, lacking central organization and definitive leadership. But there were some who hoped that its cause might be taken up by a pious emperor whose authority transcended local interests. A few went even further. They saw the papacy, long preoccupied by the petty politics of the Roman aristocracy, as the institution needed for a reformation of Christendom.

Christendom at the First Millennium

CHRISTENDOM WAS A CIVILIZATION WITH a supporting culture that came into existence with the formation of the Church at Pentecost. It was not the product of the legalization of Christianity in the fourth century, though Emperor Constantine's embrace of the faith opened new opportunities for expansion. This culture was the product of the earliest Christians' way of living, which in the eyes of Roman pagandom deviated sharply from what was considered normal. The author of the second-century *Epistle to Diognetus* commented on the "wonderful and confessedly striking method of life" lived by Christians.

> *They dwell in their own countries, but simply as sojourners. As citizens, they share in all things with others, and yet endure all things as if foreigners. Every foreign land is to them as their native country, and every land of their birth as a land of strangers. . . . They pass their days on earth, but they are citizens of heaven.*[2]

From the start, the inhabitant of Christendom was one who lived in an incongruous union of earth and heaven, of world and paradise.

It might have seemed to those who read the Scriptures that the world has little in common with the ways of heaven. Jesus had declared that His kingdom is not of this world, and in the Sermon on the Mount He had sharply contrasted the values of each. Man's fulfillment—and that of the world in which he lives—lay not in this age but in the kingdom of heaven.

Yet there was more to the faith than this, and it was contained in the doctrine of the Incarnation. The "hypostatic union" (as theologians would call the joining of two natures in the person of Christ) was in fact the most

---

2   The Ante-Nicene Fathers, vol. 1, edited by Alexander Robert and James Donaldson (Grand Rapids, MI: Eerdmans, 1985), 26–27.

mysterious of the Christian doctrines and in a certain sense the key to them all. Whereas the Crucifixion brought special attention to Jesus' human nature and the Resurrection to His divine nature, the Incarnation magnified both. The doctrine was the profoundest of paradoxes. God was beyond His creation and transcendent from it. Yet because He had become human He was now immanent within it. How this could be was beyond human understanding. It was even said to confound the angels.

But that did not change the fact that heaven and earth had been united in Christ. And if this were so, then the world could now experience the kingdom of heaven. Early Christians likened this experience to paradise. Here they had in mind not only that primordial state enjoyed by Adam and Eve before the Fall but the eschatological one that awaited the blessed at the end of time. But while the latter could never be fully realized in the fallen world, the Second Coming was only one of two eschatological points of reference. The other was the Incarnation.

In his Epistle to the Ephesians, Paul emphasized that Christ had come down from heaven in order "that he might fill all things" with Himself (Eph. 4:10). His body the Church, established at Pentecost by the Holy Spirit, maintained this fullness. Members of that body were called to continue steadfastly in doctrinal integrity. By doing so they maintained "the unity of the Spirit in the bond of peace." The fullness of paradise thus depended upon this unity. For as Paul continued,

> There is one body and one Spirit, just as you were called in one hope of your calling; one Lord, one faith, one baptism; one God and Father of all, who is above all, and through all, and in you all. (Eph. 4:3–5)

The Church, like the Holy Trinity, was undivided and indivisible. And insofar as she was filled with the divine presence, she brought paradise into the world. Hence Paul's use of prepositions like "above," "through," and "in." The kingdom of heaven awaited eschatological fulfillment at the end of time. But until the Second Coming, the Church would bring the kingdom of heaven into the world, thereby transforming it.

And so a thousand years after Pentecost, Christendom remained a civilization with a supporting culture that directed its members toward the heavenly transformation of the world.

This was evident, for instance, in Constantinople, where the great cathedral of Hagia Sophia stood high on the hill overlooking Europe's maritime gateway to Asia. It drew the attention of all. The people who flooded into its vast interior every Sunday for the Divine Liturgy, the foreign dignitaries who caught sight of its glittering domes as they sailed into the Golden Horn on diplomatic missions, and even the Muslim potentates who dreamed of acquiring its treasures through conquest—all recognized the cathedral as a symbol of Christendom.

Hagia Sophia majestically declared the union of heaven and earth. The interior of its central dome was imprinted within by an icon of Christ Pantocrator, which proclaimed to those assembled for worship below—the largest place of Christian worship on earth—that God had come from heaven to dwell among them. The icons adorning its walls communicated the teaching of the Seventh Ecumenical Council, that humanity has been joined irreversibly to divinity. Any man or woman who experienced worship here could walk away with no other impression.

Hagia Sophia as it is today

In fact, when pagan visitors from Russia visited Hagia Sophia in the tenth century they exclaimed that they did not know whether they "were in heaven or on earth." Deciding to convert to Christianity, they returned to Grand Prince Vladimir (r. 980–1015) to urge him to join them. He did, and as Christendom entered its second millennium, the Russians became its newest members.

Grand Prince Vladimir

Neophyte Russia was a good example of Christendom's principle of heavenly transformation, the imperative to reconfigure life in the world according to the kingdom of heaven. Vladimir himself set the standard. A pagan warlord before his conversion, he had committed murder, rape, and idolatry. To judge by accounts recorded in the chronicles, however, baptism transformed his character. Once a prolific adulterer, he dismissed his mistresses and married a Byzantine princess, to whom he thereafter remained faithful. Once a notorious reveler, he converted court banquets into "agape meals" at which the poor were given a favored place. Once a ruthless tyrant, he responded to the Sermon on the Mount by ordering the suspension of capital punishment.

And when he died, his fellow-convert sons Boris and Gleb, favored by their father in the succession, voluntarily surrendered their power and their lives to another, spiritually untransformed brother because of their desire to participate in the Passion of Christ. These two princes were early witnesses to the experience of paradise in Russia. It is significant that they were the first Russians to be canonized as saints, demonstrating, among their fellow countrymen at least, the value placed on a moral transformation defined by the gospel.

They gave expression to an element in Christian culture that the historian George Fedotov called "kenoticism." It centered upon the extreme humility of Christ in becoming human, expressed by Paul's use of the word *kenosis*, or "emptying" (Phil. 2:5–8). This tendency had long been at the heart of Eastern asceticism. The fourth-century Makarios of Egypt, for instance, was renowned for sacrificing his will in order to obtain the grace of the Holy Spirit.[3] Among the many expressions of heavenly transformation, the Russians showed a particular capacity for this one.

The life of Feodosy (d. 1074) is another example of kenoticism. He was born soon after the millennium into a boyar (noble) family. As such, he was expected to exercise authority over those around him. He did, but only in extreme humility. His biographer, Nestor the Chronicler, documented a continuous Christlike inver-sion of power that manifested the principles of the Sermon on the Mount. We are told that as a youth on his parents' estate, Feodosy longed "to be identified with the poor." Deferential in almost every situation, he nevertheless demonstrated disobedience when enjoined by his mother to conform his life to the privileges of the boyar class. Nestor relates his habit of leaving the house daily to work in the fields alongside the family servants, welcoming the fact that doing so "would expose himself and his family to

Saint Feodosy of Kiev

---

3   In one of many examples, he did not resist the slander of a local girl who falsely accused him of seducing her, but instead accepted the scorn of villagers and even earned money to support her. Eventually she confessed his innocence, and he moved on to new acts of self-emptying.

disgrace." In defiance of his social status, he chose to wear poorly made and threadbare clothing. When the grand prince presented him with a new and handsome cloak, he gratefully accepted it but then passed it off to the first beggar he could find.

Feodosy eventually found his way to the Caves Monastery in Kiev and there under obedience to the abbot rose quickly in the esteem of its brotherhood. Soon he was selected by the monks to be the new abbot. But "even in the post of authority," we are told, he

> *did not alter his rule or his humble way of life, for he kept in mind the words of our Lord: "Whosoever will be the greater among you, let him be your minister." And so he humbled himself, and was the least of all, serving everyone and offering himself as an example.*[4]

The kenotic standard of extreme humility defined his every action as abbot.

When pilgrims visiting the monastery failed to recognize Feodosy and asked to see the abbot, for instance, his characteristic response was, "What do you want of him? He is a sinner." He regarded all of the monks under his authority as superior to him. In accordance with the Studite Rule (that used at the Studion Monastery in Constantinople), Feodosy made the rounds of each cell at night to enforce monastic decorum. But we are told that if he heard laughter or other signs of misbehavior inside a monk's cell, he would only tap lightly on the door. When the malefactor responded asking what the matter was, the abbot would reply meekly "You know" and move on.

Once, a particularly wayward brother violated one of the most basic rules of monasticism: he decided to forsake his vows and abandon the brotherhood. But then he returned, and when he did Feodosy scandalized the others by welcoming him back with tears of joy. When the monk violated the rules again in the same way, again Feodosy accepted him back without reproach. And so it continued, to the indignation of the self-righteous brotherhood: the abbot weeping copiously each time for his faithless brother, begging

---

4   "A Life of St. Theodosius," in *A Treasury of Russian Spirituality*, edited by G. P. Fedotov (London: Sheed and Ward, 1950), 15–48.

God to forgive him, and rejoicing like the father of the prodigal son every time he repented and came back.

Feodosy was meek before fellow monks, but to the powerful he could act imperiously. This was revealed in an incident in which the grand prince was betrayed by his brothers and exiled from Kiev. Feodosy, like Ambrose of Milan before him, condemned the act of violence and called the usurpers to repentance. When threatened with reprisals he merely scoffed, welcoming the opportunity to bear witness to the gospel and to be punished for its heavenly standard of prudence.

His attention to life beyond the monastery walls was also revealed in his efforts to comfort the sick and poor of Kiev. Whenever he saw a beggar he was said to weep as he personally gave him alms. He also built a shelter for the poor, assigning a tithe of the monastery income to alms and instituting in Kiev its first regularized distribution of food to the needy.

Through the lives of such saints, Russian Christendom distinguished itself with examples of heavenly transformation. So did Byzantium, though its better-documented historical record is replete with exceptions. The political system, for instance, was a centralized autocracy that generated a court culture of cruelty and deception. This culture had been transformed in certain ways since the time of Emperor Constantine, abolishing blood sports and establishing charities. But it continuously slid back into the spiritually untransformed habits of Roman pagandom, and with depressing consequences. One of these habits was the practice of blinding one's political enemies. The reign of Emperor Basil II (r. 976–1025) was an example of the political system's far-from-complete transformation. For it marked not only the successful defense of Christendom against the perpetual threat of Islam in the east, but the savage blinding of thousands of unarmed Bulgarian prisoners of war, all of them Christians.

Far from the Great Palace of Constantinople, where political power was concentrated, cathedrals and monasteries provided an environment for Byzantium's flowering intellectual life. The result of prayer and fasting, theology was a means toward communion with God. It was not an intellectual quest for knowledge about the truth so much as a means for communion with the

Truth, who according to the Gospel of John the Theologian was God Himself. Familiar with the rich legacy of pagan learning, theologians carefully circumscribed the influence of philosophy in their reflections, always favoring biblical and patristic inspiration.

A particularly important doctrine in the East was that of "deification" (*theosis*). Patristic teaching about human salvation emphasized the full range of Christ's actions, including the Crucifixion and Resurrection. But the Incarnation was at the center of a fascination with the divine participation of man. Fathers held the conviction that because man is made in the image of God, man now has the opportunity through the Person of Christ to participate in the very life of God. Athanasius had famously given expression to the principle with the aphorism "God became man so that men might become gods." Other fathers elaborated it. Maximos the Confessor, for instance, claimed that man,

> the image of God, becomes God by deification. He rejoices to the full in abandoning all that is his by nature . . . because the grace of the Spirit triumphs in him and because manifestly God alone is acting in him.[5]

In the East, then, reflection on human salvation (soteriology) was fundamentally optimistic. The grandeur of Byzantium and the zeal of neophyte Russia offered encouragement that history would continue to be an age of paradise.

Western Christendom at the millennium was, by contrast, a reminder of the world's inherent brokenness. Gone was the powerful Carolingian Empire Charlemagne had built in magnificent rivalry to Byzantium. The 843 Treaty of Verdun had dissolved it into three much weaker parts, just as a new power was looming in the north. The Vikings descended from their mountain-ringed fjords like a thunderbolt from Thor, brutally hammering the West into submission. Their swift longships and a ferocious fighting ethic made them nearly unstoppable. Coastal monasteries like Lindisfarne in Britain were the first to be wiped out. Then, as confidence grew, their marauding fleets ventured

---

5   Quoted in John Meyendorff, *St. Gregory Palamas and Orthodox Spirituality* (Crestwood, NY: St. Vladimir's Seminary Press, 1974), 40.

further inland by river, sacking all the towns and monasteries that lay in their path. In 885 they laid siege to Paris (then populated by no more than a few thousand citizens). The Christian townspeople, though starving and sickened by plague, ultimately managed to fight them off. But the raiders continued to conquer and pillage the West for more than a century yet.

The reign of terror began to ebb only when Viking leaders saw value in joining rather than obliterating Christendom. In 911 the warlord Rollo was granted the Duchy of Normandy on the northern French coast on condition he convert to Christianity and defend the region against further invasions by his still-pagan relatives. Back in Scandinavia a century later, conversions began apace under the boyhood convert King Olaf II of Norway (r. 1015–1028), who brought both Anglo-Saxon and Russian influences into a nascent Scandinavian Church. King Canute of England (r. 1016–1035) helped establish Christianity in his native Denmark.

As Scandinavian pagandom converted to Christianity, western Europe entered a new phase of its political history. This was marked by a system of government known as feudalism. In stark contrast to the system in Byzantium, feudalism featured a decentralized state in which local lords offered military service to a king or duke as subordinates, known as vassals. Taking an oath of fealty, these vassals would pledge their service in exchange for a nearly complete monopoly over the economic resources of the lands to which they were thereby entitled. Since the king rarely made an appearance, they were mostly free to do as they pleased.

Rollo of Normandy

As a result, feudalism exchanged the centralized power of a monarch or a metropolitan for the localized power of barons and bishops. Fragmentation was greatest in France, where the collapse of the Carolingian Empire had left local knights warring against each other for territories. Division was less extreme in Germany, where the long reign of Otto the Great (r. 936-973) led to comparative political stability.

The papacy also played a role. Following the precedent of Charlemagne's famous crowning at the hands of Pope Leo III in 800, tenth-century popes conferred legitimacy on Otto and his successors in exchange for military protection in Italy. However, by the end of the century, papal influence collapsed, at least in part because of the disturbing spectacle of what became known as the Cadaver Synod (897). Pope Stephen VI, in order to consolidate his power, ordered the body of his predecessor Formosus exhumed and, to the astonishment of all, posthumously placed on trial for perjury. The scene took place in the basilica of Saint John Lateran, the principal papal cathedral in Rome. Though defended by an archdeacon, poor Formosus had little chance of acquittal, and once found guilty, his corpse was unceremoniously cast into the Tiber River.

But in the aftermath of this spectacle, partisans of both popes waged such a divisive quarrel that the papacy as an institution became thoroughly discredited. In response, the Roman aristocracy moved in and during much of the tenth century succeeded in manipulating elections and dominating the papacy. What was worse, a string of unqualified popes began to show more interest in the vanities of court life, leading to wholesale demoralization. Pope John XII (r. 955–964), before dying in the arms of a married lover, was said to have turned the Lateran Palace into Christendom's most notorious brothel. Not for nothing has the papacy during this period been labeled a pornocracy.[6]

To escape aristocratic subjection, popes during the late tenth century began to look beyond the Alps to the Holy Roman Emperor, a self-styled successor to Charlemagne. By the turn of the millennium, the papacy's dependence on Germany had become so complete that in 1014 Pope Benedict VIII finally submitted to a longtime imperial demand dating from the time of Charlemagne—that the filioque be added to the Nicene Creed in Rome. Previous popes had condemned the divisive clause and refused to

6   See *Age of Paradise*, 259–260.

admit it south of the Alps. In fact, the very pope who crowned Charlemagne in Saint Peter's Basilica had placed over the relics of the first of the apostles silver shields on which the Creed was inscribed, both in Greek and in Latin, without the filioque. As we have seen, John VIII had likewise condemned the addition in the aftermath of the ninth-century Nicolaitan Schism.

But by the beginning of the eleventh century Benedict, desiring military assistance in southern Italy against the Byzantines and lacking legitimacy against his rival to the papal title, submitted to the emperor. He revised the Creed to include the filioque and placed it within the Mass celebrated at the coronation of Emperor Henry II (r. 1014–1024).

The event marked a turning point. By severing Rome from the hallowed creedal uniformity of East and West, the pope's action signaled a tendency toward division.

The Problem of the Proprietary Church

BUT THE GREATEST PROBLEM FACING Western Christendom at the millennium was not the demoralization and political captivity of the papacy. It was the disintegration of monasticism. The Vikings had plundered the wealth of the monasteries, but an even more baneful force descended on them afterward. Feudal rulers, only nominally Christian, gained possession of their properties and gradually subjected them to a totally profane and malignant system of management. It came to be known as the "proprietary church."

This system assigned proprietary ownership of ecclesiastical properties to local clerics and in many cases laymen. As Norsemen retreated back to the sea, the crumbling remnants of monasteries and parish churches were expropriated by petty Christian magnates for nothing more than personal wealth. Feudal lords acquired legal ownership of church properties by rescuing them from collapse or by erecting new buildings, and thereafter began to manage them as family assets. Church valuables were sold off to pay for warhorses and castle decorations. Monastery refectories were converted into mead halls in which debauched laymen passed their evenings in revelry. Many an "abbot" was in fact none other than the local knight, whose children received the monastery's assets through inheritance when he died. And if the monastic proprietor happened to appoint an actual monk as abbot, he did so only after exacting from him an assurance that spiritual matters would not interfere with secular ones.

The proprietary system also corrupted parish churches. Priests were totally dependent on the landlord for their appointment and income. This could severely compromise their pastoral ministry. Those who preached at the Mass—and not all did at this time—had to walk a fine line lest in deviating from it to the master's displeasure they find themselves begging in the street.

At the top of the clerical hierarchy, local bishops were sometimes compromised by the ruling magnate. But they themselves often enjoyed even greater access to church property than the feudal lords. These princes of the church vied with one another for the wealthiest dioceses and the treasuries they contained. It is no surprise that the practice arose of paying a fee for episcopal assignments, so lucrative were the highest levels of "ministry" within the proprietary church. Often it was financial gain and not pastoral calling that attracted a bishop to a benefice. "What a fine thing it would be to be archbishop of Rheims," one contender for the office was said to muse, "if only one did not have to sing mass!"[7] Needless to say these were impossible conditions for any sincere Christian influenced by the transformative power of the gospel.

So it was that a spiritual reaction to the proprietary church began to take shape during the tenth century. The first and most celebrated expression of this was in the monastery at Cluny, founded in 910 within the province of Burgundy in France. Its charter explicitly protected it from the feudal net that surrounded it. Its only lord was the pope of Rome, a unique distinction for a monastery north of the Alps.

Initially, papal affiliation had little practical importance because the papacy itself was in the grips of corruption. As we have seen, this was a period when the pope was the puppet of local Italian interests and often, due to his dubious origins, preoccupied with personal ambitions and even

---

7   Quoted in Marc Bloch, *Feudal Society*, translated by L. A. Manyon (Chicago: University of Chicago Press, 1961), 347.

carnal desires. The protection of a John XII did not mean much to advocates for a renewal of asceticism.

However, Cluny's autonomy could be useful even when the papacy was bankrupt. With it the monastery was free to establish additional chapters in other locations throughout the West. Cluny became an alternative center of church leadership. Within a century dozens of subordinate houses were in place. Within two centuries the figure grew to more than a thousand, stretching from England to Italy and from Spain to Germany. Some historians have described Cluny as a monastic empire.

It was in fact more of a network. Cluniac houses pledged adherence to the Rule of Saint Benedict and subordination to the mother house. The result was a level of uniformity and centralization not known in Christian monasticism before. Ironically, the original Rule had actually empowered each house to direct its own affairs. But the Cluniacs found a precedent for centralization in the religious policies of the Carolingian Empire. Charlemagne had been preoccupied, even obsessed, with the creation of a uniform political administration. It was the keynote of his policy of "correction," an effort to regulate and improve church life throughout his realm. This policy was extended by his heir, Louis the Pious, who in 817 called a council at Aachen that established a centralized administration for all Frankish monasteries. At the head of this project Louis placed Benedict of Aniane (d. 821).

Known as the "second Benedict," this most famous Frankish abbot had not always been Benedictine in his sympathies. Early in his life he had had a brief but passionate affair with the Rule of Basil the Great. However, concluding that the less regulated forms of Eastern monasticism were unsuitable for the Franks, he ultimately turned to the Rule of Saint Benedict of Nursia and dedicated his life to advancing it. As a complement to the centralizing policies of the Carolingian court, which included the demand for universal use of Latin and the political subordination of bishops, Benedict used the Rule to impose ascetical uniformity throughout the empire. No other rule was allowed, and monasteries were required to submit to periodic inspections to assure they were following it. Though this system collapsed with the Carolingian Empire at the end of the ninth century, its vision of a united monastic network ruled from a single source was reborn at Cluny.

Liberated from the proprietary system that was choking the life out of contemporary monasticism, Cluny could turn to the restoration of Benedictine monasticism. But it did not do so spontaneously. Its influence was the result of the leadership of a series of visionary abbots whose lengthy periods of governance elevated the network above all other reforming centers. Abbots like Odo (r. 927–942), Maiolus (r. 964–994), Odilo (r. 994–1049), and Hugh the Great (r. 1049–1109) labored tirelessly to restore the healthy ascetical practices that had, in centuries past, supported the union of heaven and earth. Cluny revived Western monasticism and became an equal to the spiritually transformative life of other cloisters in eleventh-century Christendom, such as Athos and the Caves in Kiev. Behind its walls one could once again hope to snatch "a glimpse of paradise."[8]

But outside those walls, Western Christendom was still in shambles. So great was the spiritual disorder of the world in which monastic reformers lived that they were forced to draw a line of division between the world, which in traditional Christian cosmology radiated God's presence, and the monastery. Only in a "world-weary monasticism," one historian of the reform movement has noted, could Cluniacs experience "a fulfillment of the first Pentecost, a return to man's original state and the actual beginning of his future glory."[9]

The Fading Influence of the East

AS VISIONARIES IN A TIME of decadence, monastic reformers looked to the past to chart the future. The vast spiritual wealth of Eastern Christendom was a possible source of inspiration, as the life of Benedict of Aniane had shown. In fact, historians have recently noted the continued and ironic influence of Eastern Christianity throughout the West on the eve of the Great Division.

---

8   Tom Holland, *The Forge of Christendom: The End of Days and the Epic Rise of the West* (New York: Doubleday, 2008), 164.

9   Bede K. Lackner, *The Eleventh-Century Background to Cîteaux* (Washington, D.C.: Cistercian Publications, 1972), 45.

Patterns of worship are a particularly good example of this influence. The principle of "orientation," by which a Christian temple was built so that the altar table was at its easternmost point, symbolizing paradise (which according to Genesis was located in the east), had historically been more consistently followed in Byzantium. The papal cathedral of Saint John Lateran in Rome, for instance, actually faced westward. Now orientation became a standard throughout the West as well.[10] The expansion and elaboration of liturgical services also continued to follow, as they had in the past, "essentially Byzantine characteristics."[11] One of the best-known features of Cluniac monasticism was an elaborate liturgical rite, undoubtedly influenced by the rites used in Jerusalem and Constantinople.

The East-to-West cultural exchange was also facilitated by the flow of Greek ascetics who stayed in Western monasteries and in some cases even built new ones. Southern Italy was a center of Eastern Christianity due to its Byzantine heritage and Greek-speaking population. There in Calabria monks had begun to revive the intensive prayer of the heart typical of Egypt's legendary desert fathers. One of these monks, Nilos of Rossano, left this "new Thebaid" and traveled northward up the peninsula to bring the Eastern practice to Latin monasteries. He helped reintroduce Monte Cassino to the Rule of Saint Basil, from which its founder Benedict had originally drawn elements of his own Rule. Nilos finally settled on the very outskirts of Rome, where in 1004 he founded the Greek-speaking monastery of Grottaferrata.[12]

Much more influential for the future of Western Christendom was Peter Damian (d. 1072), who though thoroughly Latin in his identity hailed from Ravenna, the former capital of western Byzantium when, in the time of Justinian, it included all of Italy within its borders. In the eleventh century the city was no longer Byzantine, but it was a reminder that Western culture

10 John Howe, *Before the Gregorian Reform: The Latin Church at the Turn of the First Millennium* (Ithaca, NY: Cornell University Press), 281.
11 Lackner, 59.
12 Andrew Louth, *Greek East and Latin West* (Crestwood, NY: St. Vladimir's Seminary Press, 2007), 280.

had once been Eastern. Its sixth-century basilicas were a complement to the much more famous Hagia Sophia of Constantinople. Ravenna had also been the home of Romuald, a monk heavily influenced by Eastern asceticism. Peter was his champion and biographer and communicated many of his ideals to the restless monastics of the eleventh century. Peter was also a contemporary of Nilos and visited the new centers of Eastern piety at Monte Cassino and Rome.

Peter Damian

Above all, Peter valued solitary prayer and strict asceticism. Practicing both with a zeal greater than that of perhaps any other monk of his time, he experienced the paradisiacal transformation of life known by eleventh-century predecessors like Romuald. Nor was it any different from that of the Greek Symeon the New Theologian, whose life was first written by Niketas Stethatos at precisely this time. Symeon had been emphatic about the monk's experience of paradise even now, in this world, equating it with tears of contrition and a vision of the divine light. Similarly, Peter, in a letter to a fellow monk, expressed the conviction that "holy men are able to look even now upon their Creator by the grace of contemplation."[13]

And yet Peter was less sure than his Eastern contemporaries that he really had a hold on paradise. Being filled as they were "by the shining rays of the Divine light," he was indeed impelled with longing to ascend ever higher toward heaven. Like Symeon, he used the analogy of a bird in flight. But unlike him, he considered his wings to be fundamentally flawed, incapable in their humanity of sustaining, at least in this age, contact with the divine presence. The body was too corruptible in his opinion to allow his spirit to soar for very long. In the end, he lamented, he was like a flying fish, whose wings might break the plane between the waters of the earth and the

---

13   Patricia McNulty, editor and translator, *St. Peter Damian: Selected Writings on the Spiritual Life* (New York: Harper Publishers, 1959), 29.

firmament of heaven momentarily, but which would soon plunge back into the dark abyss of the sinful world.[14]

Peter Damian's affinity with Eastern Christian cosmology and anthropology was therefore limited, and in his writings we can observe a striking shift away from its paradisiacal themes. He was not unique in this. His transalpine contemporary John of Fecamp (d. 1079) expressed consistently disparaging views on "this most unhappy life," and in a treatise entitled *On Contempt for the World,* Herman of Reichenau (d. 1054) simply grumbled "I am disgusted to live."[15]

Despite such sentiments, Eastern Christian influence in the eleventh-century West did not come to an end. Nor did it stop at the Alps. Numerous monasteries in France and Germany became homes to Greek monks such as those invited to reside at the episcopal palace of Toul, where, at the end of the tenth century, they celebrated divine services "as it was done in their native land."[16] All of this was a reminder that on the eve of the Great Schism, the West retained at least some of its ancient Eastern character.

But one must not make too much of Eastern influence at the millennium. Since the time of Charlemagne, the Franks and their descendants had done much to discredit the "Greeks." Polemicists like Theodulf of Orleans (d. 821) had attacked them as idolaters because of their claim, articulated by the Seventh Ecumenical Council, that icons did more than visually illustrate the Scriptures. The iconophobic Franks were unsettled by the Eastern assertion that icons proclaimed the doctrine of the Incarnation. And of course they impugned Eastern Christians for the refusal to adopt the filioque (which was, after all, a Frankish innovation). Ironically, they even claimed that by this refusal it was the Greeks who were deviating from the original Nicene Creed.

In short, while Eastern Christianity had not yet been driven completely out of Western Christendom, its reputation had been greatly diminished by the time the millennium arrived. The lands once ruled by the Franks—France and Germany—were now in the hands of their anti-Greek intellectual heirs.

---

14   Ibid., 29–30.
15   Lackner, *Eleventh-Century Background,* 142.
16   Ibid., 135.

Monastic reformers of Cluny and elsewhere were therefore predisposed to look no further than the West for answers to the problem of the proprietary system.

An Augustinian Solution

AND HERE, INEVITABLY, THEY SEIZED on Augustine of Hippo (d. 430). Like the reformers, this greatest of the Latin fathers had lived in a time of social and political disorder: Rome had fallen to the barbarians, and North Africa, where he was bishop, was being overrun as well. His greatest work, *The City of God*, was composed in response to this catastrophe. It was an effort to make sense of a world that may have been nominally Christian but showed little evidence of the kingdom of heaven within it.

The City of God was not the first reflection on Christian society. A century earlier, an Eastern bishop named Eusebius had written works celebrating the results of Emperor Constantine's conversion to Christianity. The Church, having long suffered political persecution, now included in her membership the very ruler of Rome. This development amplified an optimism already exhibited in the Christian subculture that had coexisted with pagandom. For Eusebius, the time had come for the emperor to contribute to the Church's sacramental ministry and bring the eschatological kingdom of heaven into this world. Christian statecraft, in his view, enabled men "to anticipate even here the commencement of [that] future existence."[17]

In contrast, *The City of God* asserted that there exists a fundamental incompatibility of heaven with earth. Paradise, understood as the experience of eschatological peace "even here" in the world (to paraphrase Eusebius), is therefore largely unattainable. "The Supreme Good of the City of God," Augustine wrote,

> *is everlasting and perfect peace, which is not the peace through which men pass in their mortality, in their journey from birth to death, but that peace*

---

17   Eusebius, *Oration in Praise of Constantine*, in Nicene and Post-Nicene Fathers, vol. 1, edited by Philip Schaff (Grand Rapids, MI: Eerdman's, 1887), 581–610.

in which they remain in their immortal state, experiencing no adversity at all. In view of this, can anyone deny that this is the supremely blessed life, or that the present life on earth, however full it may be of the greatest possible blessings of soul and body and of external circumstances, is, in comparison, most miserable?

Augustine of Hippo

There is an inherent pessimism about the world in this. For Augustine, misery is the inevitable and even normative condition of life for the Christian in this age. Even if occasional peace is experienced, it manifests itself "rather by future hope than in present reality."[18] Conceived in a state of unfamiliarity with Christendom's Eastern fathers, addressing the apocalyptic invasion of the barbarians, Augustine's vision of the world was strikingly different from that of Eusebius and other Eastern Christian writers.[19]

If the East produced a unitary vision of the world, Augustine's cosmology was decidedly dualistic. It divided Christendom into two opposing "cities." One was the community of the elect, the "city of God" (*civitas Dei*), defined by a love of God that detached it from any investment in the affairs of the world. The other was the community of the reprobate, the "city of the world" (*civitas terrena*), which was consumed by corrupted desires that the author collectively defined as "concupiscence."

---

18 Augustine, *City of God*, translated by Henry Bettenson (London: Penguin, 1972), 881.

19 A detailed comparison of these two visions of Christendom can be found in *Age of Paradise*, 119–127.

But as stark as its division of society was, Augustine's dualism did not set an unbridgeable chasm between the two cities. In fact, it was the city of God, with its heavenly orientation, that had the vocation and power to confront the world's unremitting tendency toward concupiscence. And it was the community of the elect that was called to redirect the world toward heaven. And to elaborate this dynamic, Augustine made use of a concept called "reformation."

As we have seen, traditional Christianity contained a transformational imperative that contrasted a sinfully disoriented life with one oriented toward the kingdom of heaven. One of its earliest expressions is found in Paul's admonition not to be "conformed to this world" but rather to be "transformed by the renewing of your mind" (Rom. 12:2). The root of the original Greek verb used here for "transformed" is *metamorphoo.* Its noun form is *metamorphosis,* which is easily recognizable to an English speaker. It happens to be this very word that Matthew and Mark use for Jesus' paradisiacal Transfiguration.

The Latin rendering of *metamorphoo* in Romans 12:2, however, is not as direct as the English. In the Vulgate, an edition of the Bible used almost exclusively in the West until the Protestant Reformation, the verb used for it is *reformare.* The noun form of this verb is *reformatio.* This is interesting in part because Latin has a word that means "transformation," and *reformatio* is not it. The verbal form of that word is *transformare.* But instead of this, *reformare* was used in the Vulgate. As in the case of the English word "reformation," the Latin *reformatio* lacked the sense of a complete transformation; instead, it suggested a "re-formation" of something that already had an established identity. It was in short not really a change in identity. It is possible to associate the more limited sense of change implicit in *reformatio* with the fact that Augustine did not seem to think it possible that a transformation of life in this world could bring one into a complete experience of the kingdom of heaven. His cosmology, in other words, did not quite reach the borderlands of paradise.

In a celebrated study of early Christianity, a Roman Catholic theologian named Gerhart Ladner argued a half-century ago that a fundamental difference existed between the way the Greek East and Latin West conceived of the transformational imperative. His characterization of Eastern fathers, unfortunately, was strangely one-sided.[20] His analysis of the Western fathers, on the contrary, was full of insight. When discussing Augustine, for instance, Ladner brought particular attention to the concept of individual spiritual progress indicated by Romans 12:2. Augustine called this progress "reform for the better" (*reformatio in melius*). Ladner went on to claim that whereas in the East "the progress of the new over the old dispensation . . . is conceived as ceaseless mystical progress" beginning in this age, in the case of Augustine it came to mean only "a greater grace toward perseverance in earthly sufferings and temptations and toward rest in God after terrestrial life." Accordingly, the transformational imperative led in the East to an immediate (though mystical) experience of paradise, whereas in the West it led to the moral capacity merely to endure suffering until, after death, one could hope to enjoy such an experience. In Augustine's concept of reform, then, the kingdom of heaven and the world were comparatively isolated realms of human experience.

It is not difficult to understand how centuries later monastic reformers at Cluny and elsewhere in the West would find Augustine's cosmology convincing as they shrank back in horror from the proprietary system that engulfed them. The eminent twentieth-century historian of Christendom Christopher Dawson once noted as much. "The Augustinian theology and philosophy of history," he stated,

---

20   "Strangely" because he was so very erudite. While his effort to characterize the Eastern fathers was commendable (they had yet to enter into the mainstream of modern Western theological reflection), he mistakenly claimed that they understood reform exclusively as a "return to paradise" in the sense of that enjoyed by Adam and Eve at the beginning of time. This primordial condition, however, is surely not the limit of Greek Christian thought. On the contrary, Eastern Christendom maintained a long fascination with an eschatological paradise that exceeded the state of Adam. To take just one ubiquitous example of this, the Divine Liturgy of John Chrysostom, served virtually every Sunday by clergy in front of the total population of the East, buoyantly thanked God for having "brought us up to heaven and . . . endowed us with thy kingdom which is to come."

with their intense realization of the burden of inherited evil under which the human race labored and their conception of divine grace as a continually renewed source of supernatural energy which transforms human nature and changes the course of history—all this had become part of the spiritual patrimony of the Western Church and, above all, of Western monasticism, and Christendom had only to return to this tradition to recover is dynamic energy.[21]

As advocates of traditional Christianity, everywhere monks looked they beheld a Church invaded by the world and its spiritually untransformed passions. For them the world was the nemesis of paradise, not its means of fulfillment. Life in such a world, it seemed, could only lead to estrangement from God.

Secure behind the walls of an autonomous monastery like Cluny, however, monks could live out the remainder of their lives in a state of personal reformation. Augustine may have been pessimistic about the capacity of man to experience the kingdom of heaven while living on earth, but reformed monasticism came pretty close.

As the Great Division drew near, then, the West still retained the paradisiacal culture it had inherited from the Christendom of the first millennium, and which, Carolingian ideology notwithstanding, it continued to share with the East. But to many it was like the failing wick of a neglected altar candle, flickering and guttering and on the verge of extinction.

What was needed for its revival was a person—or institution—that could carry the reformation beyond the walls of the cloister.

Return of the Heroic Papacy

THE HOLY ROMAN EMPEROR WAS one candidate. Heir to Otto the Great, Henry III (r. 1046–1056) had a complex relationship to the reformers. Through a firm hold on Germany and its newly acquired western territories (which included Burgundy, the home of Cluny), he kept some of the chaos

---

21   Christopher Dawson, *Religion and the Rise of Western Culture* (New York: Image Books, 1991), 122.

of feudalism at bay. But he could also be a cause of it. Like his ancestors, he controlled the appointment of all bishops and required of them an oath of fealty. This was formalized in a ceremony of investiture during which they received from him personally the symbols of their authority—the crosier and ring. The Church of Germany, Henry frequently declared, was *his* church, and no one but he had the right to appoint her bishops. Most reformers could live with this as it had been the custom since the time of Otto.

But this facet of German caesaropapism was beginning to rub others the wrong way. A century after the founding of Cluny, some were tiring of the proprietary status quo. A reformer named Abbo of Fleury (d. 1004) issued a particularly strong protest. "Let him who wishes the health of his soul," the abbot threatened, "beware of believing that the church belongs to any save God alone. For He said to Peter, the Prince of the Apostles: 'I will give thee My church'; 'Mine', not 'thine' . . . In truth, dear princes, we neither live nor speak as Catholics when I say 'this church is mine', and some other says 'that church is his'."[22]

Nevertheless, Henry was seen by reformers as a generally reliable patron for their cause. His empire was home to some of the

Holy Roman Emperor Henry III

---

22   Quoted in Geoffrey Barraclough, *The Medieval Papacy* (New York: W.W. Norton, 1968), 70.

most influential monasteries of the time. To those located at Reichenau, Gorze, and Brogne, Cluny itself had been added after the annexation of Burgundy under Henry's immediate predecessor. He showed sincere interest in the spiritual renewal of these monasteries and often consulted with their abbots. What is more, his personal piety was famous. He took as his wife the devout descendent of Cluny's founder, Agnes, and with her seemed to attend Mass more often than the clergy. Aware that the puppet papacy was a sore subject among reformers, Henry refused the customary crowning at Saint Peter's Basilica in Rome until a truly worthy pope ruled there.

That appeared to happen in 1045 when Pope Gregory VI replaced the latest puppet of the Roman aristocracy in Italy. Gregory's character seemed impeccable, and he was an advocate of reform. This thrilled the abbots of the north. From Cluny the chronicler Rudolfus Glaber presented the event as an historical turning point, declaring in his Augustinian vocabulary that the election had "reformed for the better" an institution long paralyzed by corruption.[23] Henry was satisfied and set off for Rome.

Then something unexpected happened. Upon his arrival he got wind of a rumor that Gregory was not, after all, as virtuous as he had been led to think. In fact, he was said to have paid a sizeable fee for his office. In the eyes of the reformers, this was unforgivable. It appeared no better than the corrupt practices of proprietary bishops. Therefore, at the Synod of Sutri in 1046, Henry declared the deposition of Gregory and two other papal contenders who were even more compromised. To make matters worse, the replacement Henry selected soon died, and more confusion followed. Only in 1048 was the Chair of Saint Peter vacant again. This time, Henry decided to place on it a monk who was not merely devoted to the reform agenda, but who hailed from the heartland of reform itself.

Bruno of Toul had distinguished himself as a committed reformer of the western region of Alsace. What is more, he was the nephew of Henry and as a young man had commanded his diocesan military levy—Germany's bishops, after all, were vassals of the ruler in every sense—in support of imperial forces. He was thus thoroughly enmeshed in the proprietary system.

---

23   Roger Collins, *Keepers of the Keys of Heaven* (New York: Basic Books, 2009), 200.

However, he was also a strict ascetic and had done much to advance reforms for two decades. Inclined to accept Henry's offer of the papacy, he nevertheless insisted that he observe canonical correctness and await election by the people of Rome. He thus made his way across the Alps in pilgrim's garb, and upon arrival at the Lateran Palace in 1049 became, by popular acclaim, Pope Leo IX.

Leo restored to the papacy its exalted character after two centuries of degradation. Throughout the history of the Church, the Chair of Saint Peter had been occupied at certain moments by men of deep piety and high ideals. They had used their powers heroically, opposing what they saw as existential threats to the Church. One of these had been Leo the Great (r. 440–461), a canonized saint in both the West and the East. It was his name that Bruno

Pope Leo IX

adopted upon election because he had been one of the earliest popes to claim a special role for the papacy in the leadership of the Church. At a time of disorder caused by barbarian conquest, the first Leo had opposed the heresy of monophysitism (which claimed that Jesus had only "one nature") and conducted diplomacy with the invading warlord Attila. What is more, he had challenged the Fourth Ecumenical Council's claim that the patriarch of Constantinople was the virtual equal of the pope. Leo had rejected this. He claimed that the papacy is without equal, possessing a primacy of "preeminence" (*principatus*) within the universal Church.

In fact there had never been any question of Rome's primacy within the Church after the first century. Everyone had acknowledged it. Beginning in the fourth century, it was even built into a model of authority consisting of five patriarchates: Rome, Constantinople, Alexandria, Antioch, and Jerusalem. In this pentarchy, as it became known, Rome was always honored as *primus,* from which the term "primacy" was derived. This status had been given to Saint Peter (Matt. 10:2), and though Peter had served as the bishop of Antioch early in his ministry, he eventually came to Rome and completed his life there as a martyr.

But nowhere in the New Testament is Peter's primacy defined in a jurisdictional sense. He is never shown to have had authority over the other apostles. On the contrary, Paul relates that Peter was actually subject to correction by them. In one case Paul had been compelled to confront Peter on the momentous issue of circumcision, "because he was to be blamed" (Gal. 2:11). Indeed, the only explicit indication in the Bible of jurisdictional authority among the apostles is the Council of Jerusalem, where, again, the issue of circumcision required resolution (Acts 15). In that case, the apostles came together and after deliberation (Peter having now clearly joined Paul in opposing the requirement) ruled together that the practice was not necessary. And the apostle to issue this ruling was not even Peter, but James. According to the Scriptures, then, jurisdictional authority within the Church was conciliar, not monocratic. It did not emanate from a single individual but was shared by the recognized episcopate, that is, the apostolic "overseers."

What eleventh-century reformers wanted, however, was a leader and a hero. This had already been indicated by the applause received by the apparently upstanding Gregory VI prior to his disgrace. Monasticism may have become the recruitment center for the struggle against the proprietary church, but its necessarily cloistered scope of "reform for the better" precluded a universal, let alone institutional, program. Even Emperor Henry III could not rise to the occasion with his investment in the system and the limited boundaries of his realm. But as a new pope freed from the control of Roman aristocrats, Leo IX could.

This is why he and the office he occupied became a magnet for reformers from the start of his pontificate. Three men in particular helped him define his policies around the reform agenda. They were Archdeacon Hildebrand, Cardinal Humbert, and Peter Damian. Together, they formed a cadre of activists dedicated to using the papacy as an instrument for long-awaited and far-reaching change. Indeed, what they sought was nothing less than a papal reformation.

CHAPTER ONE

All of that, however, was yet to come. For the time being, they did everything they could to support Leo's program of institutionalizing reform for the better. The new pope, they were pleased to discover, could not sit still. During the course of a five-year pontificate he spent a mere six months in Rome itself. The rest of the time he traveled far and wide across Europe to advance the reform agenda. His preferred method was to assemble local councils of bishops and present them with his demands for change.

One of these councils was held at Rheims the year of Leo's election. He used the gathering to assert his authority—the authority, that is, of Saint Peter— over prelates who were totally unaccustomed to a pope's presence in France.[24] All of them without exception recognized the principle of papal primacy, but none of them had ever been confronted by such an imperious assertion of it. Leo turned the council into a harangue against the purchase of episcopal office, an offense dubbed "simony" by the reformers after the example of the Simon rebuked by Peter for offering to pay for a ministry (Acts 8:18–20). Leo confronted each bishop with a direct question about whether he had paid for his office. One after another, the bishops brought before him admitted to the practice of simony. Those who performed penance in his presence he reinstated to their office on the spot. Those who did not, or avoided the council altogether, he deposed. The overall effect of the judgment was crippling. In a stroke, all of the local bishops were reduced to abject dependence upon the distant papacy, and not a few were humiliated in the process.

This was, of course, the intention. Leo's goal was not just to eliminate clerical corruption, it was to establish unassailable preeminence over the entire episcopate of the West.

But there was an Eastern corollary to the reform of episcopal primacy. Leo realized that his jurisdictional preeminence in the West hinged on his relationship to the East. There, the episcopate had always functioned in a conciliar way, according to apostolic precedent. Like their French counterparts, they recognized and affirmed the principle of papal primacy. But the intervention of the pope of Rome in Eastern affairs was mostly unprecedented and largely unthinkable.

---

24   No pope had set foot in France for 171 years. Holland, *Forge of Christendom*, 266.

Leo intended to change this. From the inception of his pontificate he had been listening to advisors such as Humbert as they broadened the theoretical powers of the papacy, extending them, in Tom Holland's words, "to ever more potent extremes."[25] They brought his attention especially to the fact that in Constantinople Michael Cerularius (r. 1043–1059) had taken to calling himself the Ecumenical Patriarch.

The title was not an innovation, but it had a controversial history. It was based on the Greek word *ecumene,* meaning "universal" in the sense of pertaining to the entire territory of the Byzantine Empire. Pope Gregory the Great had challenged the title in the sixth century, claiming that according to conciliar precedent no bishop—not even the pope of Rome—should assert his preeminence over all others. But the title had persisted, and as recently as 1024 the patriarch had sent emissaries to Rome requesting acknowledgement of the autonomy it implied. Leo's advisors all agreed that as long as such autonomy remained in place, the papacy would be unable to bring the wayward Western bishops to heel.

Patriarch Michael Cerularius and Pope Leo IX

As a result, there now arose what might be called the reform papacy's Eastern question: what to do about the persistence of Constantinopolitan jurisdictional autonomy.

---

25   Holland, *Forge of Christendom,* 268.

CHAPTER ONE

The Eastern Question

THIS BRINGS US BACK TO the melancholy scene at Benevento following the Battle of Civitate in 1053.[26] The conditions of Pope Leo's imprisonment may not have been harsh, but they were surely intolerable. For an active reformer like him these conditions must have caused a state of profound agitation. Though he practiced bodily mortifications such as sleeping on the floor of his cell, his mind did not cease to race with ideas on how to continue the program of reform. "We ourselves," he restlessly declared at the time, "shall not give up our intention of liberating Christendom nor shall we give any rest in our time, until holy Church, now so much in danger, is at rest."[27] The successor to Saint Peter would pursue his heroic ministry even when confined to prison.

One of his most frequent visitors was Cardinal Humbert, whom Leo had provocatively sought to make archbishop of Sicily (to the dismay of the Byzantines who claimed the island and the Greeks who lived there). As the months of Leo's confinement passed, both reformers came to realize that as long as the pope remained in prison, their agenda was in jeopardy. Councils such as Rheims were obviously out of the question for the time being. But correspondence and diplomacy were another question. Leo could turn his cell into a kind of command center, where, assisted by advisors such as Humbert, he could direct the reforms as effectively as if he were ruling from the Lateran.

And as it turned out, an opportunity arose for a vigorous assertion of papal power in the East. Several years earlier, in 1050, Leo had convened a reform council in the southern Italian town of Siponto. It was similar to others in advancing the reform agenda. However, in this case it went further. It ruled that the Greek practices of the local churches were to be abolished and that Latin practices must take their place. The decision was made while the Normans were expanding their control over the region. Wherever the conquerors went, they were demanding that the Latin practices with

---

26 See the prologue above.

27 Leo's letter is quoted at length in the contemporary Life of Pope Leo IX found in Robinson, *The Papal Reform of the Eleventh Century*, 150.

which they were familiar replace the native Eastern ones. Leo, though no friend of the Normans, gave his blessing to these changes and at the Council of Siponto even went so far as to codify them.

Getting wind of this development in Constantinople, Patriarch Michael Cerularius retaliated. He ordered that Latin churches long established in the eastern capital convert to Greek practice. And when he met with resistance during the course of 1053, he summarily shut those churches down.

These actions did not occur in a vacuum. Michael's interest in eliminating Latin practice in Constantinople was related, ironically, to an Eastern question of his own. Byzantium had annexed much of Armenia in 1024. This had brought into the empire an ancient Eastern church with customs different from those of the Greeks. One of these was the use of unleavened eucharistic bread.

Michael Cerularius possessed—or was possessed by—a limitless sense of his authority. He had once even been an aspirant to the imperial throne. A lifetime civil bureaucrat, he had only turned to a clerical career after imprisonment for conspiracy. His elevation to the patriarchate was due in no small part to his extraordinary ambition, but also to his connections. During his years in the political wilderness he befriended Constantine Monomachos, who was suddenly called to the throne in 1042 through marriage to the dowager empress Zoe. The following year, Michael was chosen by Constantine as the new patriarch. However, upon elevation to the patriarchate, Michael was accused of seeking the subordination of the emperor, thereby achieving through ecclesiastical means what he had failed to gain through politics. With time, he managed to win popular support in Constantinople against the emperor, assuring that he would play a role, and perhaps a decisive one, in the affairs of state. In any case, as patriarch he continued to act like a politician in church affairs, and a supremely insensitive one at that.

Michael's bureaucratic mind concluded that the monophysite Armenians could be assimilated to the Orthodox in part by forcing them to adopt the practice of using leavened bread. It was a foolish presumption. The only thing he achieved by it was the alienation of a proud Eastern Christian people, one that otherwise might have served in defending the empire against the threat

of the Muslim Turks farther east. This presumption also led Michael to perse-
cute the Latin Christians of Constantinople, alienating Pope Leo in the West.

For the equally imperious Leo, this was bad enough. But then the pope
received a letter that intensified the controversy over liturgical practices.
During his journey to visit Leo at Benevento, Humbert had passed through
the southern Italian town of Trani. There he had been hosted by the local
Archbishop John, who had recently been asked to forward the letter in question to Pope Leo. Its author was another Leo, the archbishop of Ohrid in Bulgaria, who had spent time in southern Italy and was familiar with the different rituals followed by Greeks and Latins there. This eastern Leo questioned
the Latin eucharistic practice being forced on the Greek populations of
southern Italy. The main issue was that the Latins offered unleavened bread at
the Mass. This, the letter declared, deviated from the Church's ancient practice of using normal leavened bread and called the sacrament into question.

The stark tone of this letter may have been unfortunate, but to Eastern
Christians in the West its author did have a point. The use of unleavened
bread was simply not of apostolic origin. Latin fathers such as Ambrose
and Augustine attest to the use of leavened bread for the Eucharist. At
some point that practice changed, though the change is not attested until
the time of Charlemagne (when so many other changes in liturgical practice occurred). First Alcuin, the leader of the Carolingian cultural revolution, and then Hrabanus Maurus speak of it. According to a leading Roman
Catholic authority on the Western liturgy, A. G. Martimort, the use of
unleavened bread was certainly not universal in the West until the eleventh
century.[28] Along with the filioque, the Franks may have promoted the practice as part of their efforts to define a Western culture distinct from Constantinople and even Rome (where it seems to have come into use only much
later). In any case, by the eleventh century the use of unleavened bread was
common within the Latin Church of Italy to which Pope Leo—a descendent

---

28   Or perhaps "a little earlier." Robert Cabié, *The Eucharist*, translated by Mat-
     thew J. O'Connell, vol. 2 of The Church at Prayer: An Introduction to the
     Liturgy, edited by Aime Georges Martimort (Collegeville, MN: The Liturgical
     Press, 1986), 132.

of the Franks himself—now hoped to assimilate the Greek population.

The letter of Leo of Ohrid therefore struck a nerve when Humbert, toward the end of 1053, placed it in the hands of the captive pope. Both seem to have read the document not as a polemic against unleavened bread, however, but as a challenge to their expanding concept of papal preeminence.

This explains the virulence of the pope's response, written, as much of his correspondence was, by the hand of Humbert. It is interesting that the reply declined to engage any of the arguments in favor of unleavened bread, as if that issue were not really the one in question. Rather, it went straight to the issue of papal authority. If the papacy endorsed the use of unleavened bread, Leo's reply asserted, then that was enough and the matter was settled. The Chair of Saint Peter was the final authority for any and all issues, liturgical or otherwise. This was demonstrated, the letter continued, by the fact that never in its history had Peter's chair been occupied by a heretic.

Here the theologically learned Humbert made a significant gaffe that betrayed a confusion about—or ignorance of—church history. For the Sixth Ecumenical Council had anathematized an occupant of that very chair, Honorius I, for his role in formulating the seventh-century monothelite heresy. Remarkably, in elaborating his argument for papal infallibility, the papal advisor actually held up Pope Honorius by name as an example of it!

Finally, the harsh and unreasonable response to Leo of Ohrid's letter was due, it seems, to the manner in which that letter had been addressed. The Eastern bishop wrote in a conciliar spirit, addressing not only the pope of Rome but all the bishops of the West. Such an ecclesiology, or understanding of authority within the Church, was sure to aggravate the reformers.

So, with a patriarch of Constantinople claiming ecumenical status and an obscure Bulgarian bishop standing in judgment over Western liturgical practice, the time had come to resolve Rome's Eastern question. Turning to the captive Leo, Cardinal Humbert insisted that a papal embassy be dispatched immediately to Constantinople.

CHAPTER ONE

Excommunication

THUS WE COME TO WHAT John Meyendorff called "without doubt the most tragic event in the history of the Church."[29] The Great Division did not result from the rising conflict between Pope Leo and Patriarch Michael Cerularius alone, or even primarily. It had had a long prehistory, as we have seen, and the mutual excommunications that were now imminent would not have remained in effect had this estrangement not occurred. Nevertheless, the decisions by pope and patriarch to sever communion did matter. However unwittingly, these agents of excommunication became the architects of a new—and divided—Christendom.

Tragically, even at the eleventh hour Pope Leo was given an opportunity for reconciliation. Before Humbert's provocative response to Leo of Ohrid could be dispatched, a courier arrived at Benevento with two more-important letters. One was from Emperor Constantine and one was from Patriarch Michael. The first was predictably conciliatory. This was typical, as the head of the Byzantine state had long shown himself eager to obtain papal support for his policies in the West, especially now when the Normans were overrunning Italy. Michael's letter was also conciliatory, but unpredictably so. Though known for his imperiousness, he now wrote assuring the pope of his friendship and goodwill, adding his own hopes for a Byzantine-papal alliance. He even offered to restore the pope's name to the Eastern diptychs, thus ending the division that arose after Rome's adoption of the filioque earlier in the century. His letter, in short, was an invitation to unity.

Nevertheless, it suffered from two glaring flaws in the eyes of its recipients. First, Michael addressed the pope as a "brother" in Christ and not, as was the custom in the West, as a "father." The latter title was an important symbol in the papacy's campaign against episcopal autonomy. The second issue was more accidental. In the Latin translation of the original—made, significantly, by Humbert himself—Michael identified himself as the patriarch of the "whole inhabited world." The original Greek for this phrase was

---

29   John Meyendorff, *The Orthodox Church* (Crestwood, NY: St. Vladimir's Seminary Press, 1996), 35.

ecumene, and as we saw above, it related to the now customary title of the Ecumenical Patriarchate.[30]

Historians customarily have been puzzled by this irenic letter and have largely ignored its significance in their account of what followed.[31] However, it is perhaps time to reconsider the patriarch's role in the ensuing schism. The historiography of the West has long been content to place much and even most of the blame at Patriarch Michael's feet.[32] It is certainly true that contemporaries considered his character deeply flawed. Michael Psellos, the author of a famous history of the Byzantine court, regarded him as truculent and vindictive. This all may be true. But in fact there is no evidence that he played a direct role in any further part of the sequence of events that unfolded at Constantinople in the fateful year of 1054. Those events, rather, seem to have been driven by the equally truculent but far more unbalanced Humbert.

Considering the great significance this embassy has come to have in our understanding of the Great Schism, it is ironic that the documents we possess speak of but three events leading up to it. Only one involves Michael, but all three were initiated by Humbert. In the first, the Western envoy and his fellow collaborators Frederick of Lorraine and Peter of Amalfi landed in Constantinople in early April and immediately visited the imperial palace. There they presented their credentials and delivered a letter to Constantine from Pope Leo. The meeting appears to have gone very well, with both parties eager to form an alliance against the Normans in Italy.

The second event was the legation's visit to the patriarchal chancery in order to deliver a papal response to Michael's letter of conciliation. Rather than welcome the restoration of the pope's name in the Liturgy at Hagia Sophia, it

---

30   Steven Runciman, *The Eastern Schism* (Eugene, OR: Wipf and Stock, 1955), 43.

31   It is usually attributed to an assumed deference on the part of Michael to Emperor Constantine, whose desire for amity with the West was unquestionably strong. But Michael was known for his attitude of superiority toward Constantine.

32   The Roman Catholic Aidan Nichols, for instance, introduces the event as "the schism of Michael Kerullarios." See his *Rome and the Eastern Churches: A Study in Schism,* second edition (San Francisco: Ignatius Press, 2010), 273.

declared the Constantinopolitan patriarchate to be a dependency of Rome.

What is more, it was here, in this letter, that a notorious document known as the *Donation of Constantine* first makes its vexing appearance in the history of Christian division. Composed most likely at the eighth-century court of Pope Stephen II to support negotiations with the Frankish king Pepin III, the document had languished in dusty dormancy until the middle of the eleventh century. The reformers brought it back to life, and now it was Humbert himself who became its earliest documented advocate.

In Pope Leo's name Humbert pressed the *Donation*'s legalistic (and false) claim for papal preeminence over every power in Christendom, whether imperial or episcopal. He and Leo both seem to have believed its fundamentally deceitful premise: that Emperor Constantine, on his deathbed, issued to the contemporary pope of Rome, Sylvester, a charter granting the latter and all of his successors absolute authority over both the political territories of the empire and every bishop found within them. It was a bold and categorical claim, and it was a complete forgery. Its spurious nature would not be discovered for four centuries, and until then it would be used time and again to advance the mischief of papal advocates against any and all defenders of conciliarity, whether in the East or the West. In this, its historical debut, the pope himself by the hand of Humbert demanded that Michael Cerularius renounce the title of Ecumenical Patriarch, claiming, without any foundation, that he had usurped his office against the canons of the Church.

This strange encounter was the only occasion when the ambassadors met with the patriarch. Since the papal letter was only read after their departure, its delivery was not marked by any significant disagreement. The only controversy was the petty objection of the Latins that their seating assignment in the chancery's meeting hall failed to acknowledge their superiority over Michael as legates of the successor to Saint Peter. This point is interesting in part because it revealed their disdain for the symbolism of Eastern ecclesiology (which seated the papal legates second to Michael, the local ruling bishop). More importantly, when they finally ceased complaining over the issue and actually sat themselves down, it appears they were, in fact, no longer even legates of the pope.

For Leo IX, having finally been freed by the Normans to return to Rome, had died at about the very time the legates landed in Constantinople. According to all interpretations of canon law, this meant that they had no further business being there, and, knowing of this development (as they undoubtedly did) they were obligated to suspend their activities immediately. They of course did no such thing. Driven by an institutionalized vision of reform for the better, they were becoming increasingly deaf to the voice of restraint.

The third documented event in the three-month drama at Constantinople was a confrontation with one of the city's leading scholars over the issue of eucharistic bread. Niketas Stethatos (d. 1090) was a monk at the Studion Monastery, from which much of the opposition to Byzantine caesaropapism had come during the ninth century. A disciple of Symeon the New Theologian, he had written the first and most definitive life of the saint. He was also an outspoken opponent of public immorality, particularly the adultery of Emperor Constantine, for which he earned his nickname (*stethatos* means "courageous" in Greek). But when he dared to author a defense of Greek liturgical practice that echoed Leo of Ohrid, Humbert turned on him and demanded a retraction.

It is significant that Niketas's theological interests mirrored those of Symeon, especially the experience of man's deification in Christ. He was, in short, a defender of Christendom's paradisiacal culture. "God is Wisdom," he declares in one treatise, "and by deifying through the spiritual knowledge of created beings those who live in the Logos and in Wisdom He unites them with Himself through light and makes them gods by adoption."[33] This statement was a classic expression of traditional Christianity's optimistic anthropology. It was supported by other theologians. Man is made by God with powers that, when exercised according to the divine will, "make him wholly godlike and divine."[34] Divine participation is in Niketas's understanding

---

33 "On Spiritual Knowledge, Love and the Perfection of Living," in *The Philokalia*, vol. 4, edited and translated by G.E.H. Palmer, Philip Sherrard, and Kallistos Ware (London: Faber and Faber, 1995), 153.

34 "On the Practice of the Virtues," *The Philokalia*, vol. 4, 82.

closely related to heavenly immanence. Because of the Incarnation, man now knows in this world the experience of "ascending to the Creator through the beauty of His creatures."[35]

Niketas began his defense of the Eastern position on the Eucharist by discussing the historical use of leaven. Leavened bread had always been used by the ancient Church in the Eucharist. It was true, of course, that the use of unleavened bread had been the precedent of the Jews in the Passover. But Christians, worshipping according to the New Covenant, should not try to replicate that precedent. In fact, it was arguable that the very bread used by Jesus at the Last Supper—the archetype of the Church's weekly eucharistic assembly—was not the unleavened bread of the Passover but in fact regular, leavened bread. The first three Gospels actually spoke of Jesus using normal "bread" (*artos* in Greek, as opposed to *azymes,* the word for unleavened bread).[36] The chronology of John, also, indicated that the Crucifixion occurred on the eve of the Passover—that is, prior to the feast of unleavened bread and not during it.[37] Finally, and most importantly to his argument, Niketas emphasized the meaning of leaven in the eucharistic bread. It symbolized the new life in Christ. To use unleavened bread was to ignore the Resurrection from the dead. It was to undermine the doctrine of deification. For "the living Holy Spirit," he claimed, "abides in his deified body, eating of which in the bread, changed by the Holy Spirit into the flesh of Christ, we live in him, since we have eaten of the living and deified flesh."[38]

The bellicose Humbert, upon learning of this treatise, responded with a polemic "full of screaming abuse" (Runciman).[39] He savaged the author as an enemy of the Church and a heretic. Niketas should not be called Stethatos, he sneered, but *Pectoratus,* that is, "one who crawls on his belly." He declared the Greek monk was not the product of a monastery but of a whorehouse. As in his reaction to Leo of Ohrid, the motivating animus of the diatribe was not so much the content of Niketas's critique of unleavened bread but

---

35   Ibid., 103.
36   See Matt. 26:26; Mark 14:22; Luke 22:19.
37   See John 19:14.
38   Quoted in Louth, *Greek East and Latin West,* 313.
39   Runciman, *The Eastern Schism,* 46–47.

the suggestion that the papacy was wrong to have adopted it.

The violence of Humbert's response was especially strange considering that Niketas, writing in the East where eucharistic bread had always been leavened, was nevertheless full of courtesy in his manner of addressing the Latin innovations. But this did not placate the insistent reformer from the West. By sustaining the argument of Leo of Ohrid, Niketas was in his judgment only serving the forces of darkness.

Since his arrival, Humbert had been on good terms with the emperor with his promises of an alliance against the Normans. He now demanded a good-faith deposit toward that alliance. Accordingly, the acquiescent Constantine ordered the burning of Niketas's offending treatise. All that remained for the legates to do was to obtain from Michael a statement of repentance for his association with this, the most egregious manifestation of the Eastern question.

This the patriarch never gave. He no doubt identified with the views of Leo of Ohrid and Niketas Stethatos, but in keeping his opinions to himself he denied Humbert the confrontation for which he longed.

Much has been written over the years about Michael's apparently provocative character. We can assume that most of it is true. Nevertheless, there is simply no evidence that it manifested itself during the three-month intervention of Pope Leo's emissaries. As Anthony Kaldellis has recently argued, Michael seems to have removed himself from the controversies the legates brought with them to Constantinople.[40] Rather than spurn an audience with them after the initial meeting at the chancery, as many historians assume, he seems to have chosen—whether for personal reasons or in obedience to the emperor—simply to avoid contact with them for the sake of amity. This was, after all, the sentiment expressed in his letter to Pope Leo prior to the dispatch of Humbert's embassy. That letter is real evidence of his disposition, and no other direct evidence exists.

---

40 Anthony Kaldellis, "Keroularios in 1054: Nonconfrontational to the Papal Legates and Loyal to the Emperor," in *Byzantium and the West: Perceptions and Reality*, edited by Nikolaos Chrissis, Athina Kolia-Dermitzaki, and Angeliki Papageorgiou (London: Routledge, 2019), 9–24.

Indeed, even Humbert himself, who clearly detested Michael, later accused the patriarch only of "avoiding" the delegates and not of confronting or otherwise disputing with them. It is true, however, that this in itself could have been interpreted by the Western reformers as an affront greater than direct confrontation. For if one considers the actions of the recalcitrant French episcopate in avoiding Pope Leo during the Council of Rheims, it is possible to conjecture that the reformist legates now interpreted Michael's evasion as an equivalent act of subversion. The first impression upon meeting Michael at the chancery, after all, was that the patriarch was asserting his episcopal autonomy against the claims of papal preeminence. Three months, then, had shown the papal legates that there was nothing more they could do to bring Patriarch Michael Cerularius into submission.

And so Humbert, flanked by his two accomplices, strode into Hagia Sophia before the Divine Liturgy on July 16 to bring his desperate and now illicit embassy to its completion. The "papal bull" he bore in his hands for the occasion was his own fabrication and lacked any canonical validity. It had been composed after the death of Leo in April and was therefore no more than the rant of a frustrated and impotent opponent of the patriarch. But in the absence of substantive negotiations—or even debates—with his adversary, there was nothing else he could do.

Humbert pushed his way through the crowds of faithful who had come to participate in the most fundamental of all activities in Christendom: the eucharistic assembly of the Lord's Day. Did he glance up at the Pantocrator gazing down majestically upon the assembled body of Christ from within the central dome? Did he pause to consider the vision of heavenly unity to which the cathedral's architecture bore witness? All that has been documented is that he forced his way into the sanctuary, and there, to the utter consternation of the assembled clergy, hurled his curse upon the altar.

What the bull of excommunication lacked in legitimacy it made up for with invective. Humbert accused Michael and his supporters of almost every blasphemy and heresy for which he had a name. The list was extensive, and it betrayed not only a fundamental misunderstanding of the East but an almost farcical ignorance of church history.

The words of Steven Runciman have been often quoted but remain the most eloquent assessment of its content. "Few important documents have been so full of demonstrable errors," the great English historian wrote.

It is indeed extraordinary that a man of Humbert's learning could have penned so lamentable a manifesto. It began by refusing to Cerularius, both personally and as Bishop of Constantinople, the title of Patriarch. It declared that there was nothing to be said against the citizens of the Empire of Constantinople, but that all those who supported Cerularius were guilty of simony (which, as Humbert well knew, was the dominant vice at the time of his own Church), of encouraging castration (a practice that was also followed at Rome), of insisting on rebaptizing of Latins (which, at the time, was untrue), of allowing priests to marry (which was incorrect; a married man could become a priest but no one who was already ordained could marry), of baptizing women in labor, even if they were dying (a good Early Christian practice), of jettisoning the Mosaic Law (which was untrue), of refusing communion to men who had shaved their beards (which was again untrue, though the Greeks disapproved of shaven priests), and, finally, of omitting a clause in the Creed (which was the exact reverse of the truth).

"After such accusations," Runciman concluded, "complaints about the closing of the Latin churches at Constantinople and of disobedience to the Papacy lost their effect."[41]

The deacons of Hagia Sophia, perceiving the terrible import of the act, pursued the legates as far as the square in front of the cathedral, bearing the bull in their hands and begging Humbert to reconsider. There, however, the proud reformer shook the dust from his feet and turned his face toward the west.

A few days later Michael Cerularius was compelled, with Emperor Constantine's approval, to respond to the excommunication in kind. Christendom's parting of the ways had finally arrived.

---

41   Runciman, *The Eastern Schism*, 48.

CHAPTER TWO

The Papal Reformation

THE EXCOMMUNICATIONS OF 1054 PROVED tragically permanent.
They need not have been. The Byzantines certainly did not desire a
break from Rome. For centuries to come their emperors would strongly
favor negotiations for the restoration of unity, if for no other reason than
to build an alliance against the forces of militant Islam. As for the papacy,
the actions of Humbert of course were not even valid according to canon
law. The way to reunion was therefore open to the first pope who sincerely
desired to pursue it.

But none did. Leo IX had started a reform movement that only grew in
strength after his death. Within a generation it had swelled to a full-scale
reformation that permanently altered the character of Western Christendom. The East, committed to the ways of the first millennium, could only
watch in dismay as the Papal Reformation progressively dismantled the
basis of past unity. By the end of the twelfth century, it was obvious that the
division of Christendom was permanent.

The division could only be reversed through one of two equally unlikely
scenarios: the abdication of the newly created Roman Catholic papal monarchy of the West, or the capitulation to it of the Orthodox East. Neither ever
occurred.

Supremacy

IN ROME TODAY STANDS ONE of the oldest monuments of Christendom—the Lateran Palace, which came into the possession of the Church during the fourth century. It had once belonged to Emperor Constantine, who conquered the city after the Battle of Milvian Bridge in 312. In the following year, when he issued the Edict of Milan granting Christians freedom, he bequeathed the building to the local bishop. As he did so, he gave orders that a large basilica dedicated to John the Evangelist be built next to it. For a thousand years, the complex of the Lateran Palace and the Saint John Lateran basilica would serve as the headquarters of the papacy and the place where decisions were made about the destiny of Western Christendom.

It was here that Cardinal Humbert would often have been found after his return from Constantinople in 1054. Pope Leo IX had made him the head of Rome's suburbicarian diocese of Silva-Candida—a largely nominal appointment. Because of the see's proximity to Rome, however, its occupant was permitted to frequent the Lateran and participate in papal administration there. It was an exciting time to do so. Popes would come and go, but the cardinals who conferred and prayed within the Lateran would, for decades to come, design the architecture of a new and very different Christendom. Along with the popes, they were the agents of a papal reformation.

Leo was now dead, and Emperor Henry III had delayed in naming a replacement. In fact a full year elapsed before a new pope was crowned at the Lateran. During this long hiatus in leadership, Humbert set to work on a treatise intended to guide what was now, after the excommunications of 1054, a self-consciously Roman Catholic Church. He was drawn especially toward the Augustinian language of "reform for the better," which, as we saw in the previous chapter, was a way of speaking of moral and spiritual improvement. Unlike Augustine, however, he applied this transformational imperative to institutions more than to persons. His contribution to the coming reformation would be largely one of indignation rather than repentance.

Humbert's treatise *Three Books against the Simoniacs* was a forceful and sometimes sarcastic attack on one of the most egregious problems of the proprietary system in the West. The treatise's target was the sale of clerical offices, or simony. It took Humbert four years to complete the work, but the reform it advocated was a necessary one. When the third and final volume was released in 1058, it provided a vision that was as uncompromising as it was radical. For instead of addressing the problem of simony itself, this volume proposed an entirely new way of defining the Church's relationship to the world. Christopher Dawson considered it "at once the earliest, the ablest, and the most extreme statement of the programme of the reformers."[1] The treatise presented a vision of a new Christendom in which the papacy as an institution would be a necessary mediator for the experience of the kingdom of heaven on earth. For the eminent German historian Gerd Tellenbach, it was nothing short of "a great revolution in world-history."[2]

As he strolled the halls of the Lateran Palace ruminating about the future, Humbert's thoughts would have extended toward broader problems in the proprietary system. One of the greatest was the role of Christian statecraft in a paradisiacal civilization. Ever since the conversion of Constantine, Christendom had accommodated and at times even depended on its faithful political rulers.

The Lateran complex that Humbert frequented was itself haunted by the memory of Christendom's first emperor. Not only had Constantine bestowed the property as a gift to the bishop of Rome, but legend spoke of him having been baptized in the adjacent basilica of Saint John. This latter point was not historically accurate; Constantine was actually baptized at the end of his life in Nicomedia on the Sea of Marmara. But patriotic Romans did not know this, or perhaps they simply did not want to acknowledge this fact.

Of more immediate concern to the cardinal was the famous mosaic of Constantine commissioned by Pope Leo III late in the eighth century. It was located in the papal assembly hall, an addition to the building modeled on the Golden Reception Hall of the Great Palace in Constantinople.[3] As such it

---

1   Dawson, *Religion and the Rise of Western Culture*, 130–131.
2   Gerd Tellenbach, *Church, State and Christian Society at the Time of the Investiture Contest*, translated by R. F. Bennett (Oxford: Blackwell and Mott, 1959), 111.
3   Charles B. McClendon, *The Origins of Medieval Architecture* (New Haven: Yale University Press, 2005), 126.

was another example of Eastern Christendom's foundational, if now fading, influence on the West. In this very room, Leo had discussed with Emperor Charlemagne the nature of Christian statecraft and the episcopate's role in it. The Western Empire that was created when the pope crowned the Frankish ruler on that occasion had in many ways modeled itself on the Christian statecraft of Byzantium.

Hence the mosaic set above the papal throne at the far end of the Lateran Palace's assembly hall. Humbert and all who beheld it saw Christ at the center, granting authority to His apostles. On either side of this were two additional mosaics. The one to the left depicted Christ again, this time bestowing authority on Pope Sylvester and Emperor Constantine during the fourth century. This was an image of what early Christendom called *symphony,* the harmonious cooperation between emperor and bishop to the glory of Christ. It was an image of a unitary Christendom.

But the mosaic to the right of the papal throne was different. It depicted the eighth-century successors to Sylvester and Constantine, Pope Leo III and Emperor Charlemagne. In this case, Christ was absent. In His place above them appeared Saint Peter, the first of the apostles and the mystical origin of the papacy. Was this not, Humbert might have thought as he ruminated upon the proprietary system, an image revealing not only the pope's succession from Peter but the emperor's as well? For both Pope Leo and Emperor Charlemagne receive their authority from Peter instead of from Christ. Was this not an image of a dualistic Christendom, in which clergy and laity were more clearly distinguished, even divided, under the ultimate authority of the first of the apostles?

The older, unitary cosmology expressed in the ideal of symphony still prevailed in Eastern Christendom. It also prevailed in the Holy Roman Empire, justifying Henry III's continued involvement in papal affairs. But after two centuries of degradation under the proprietary system, monastic reformers from the north like Humbert were no longer sympathetic to the ideal of symphony. For them, the reality was rather one of caesaropapism (though their vocabulary did not yet include such a word): one in which a government of the laity dominated the life of the Church to such an extent that even the clergy were caught up in secular concerns, and were corrupted as a result.

As he stared into the apse above the pope's throne, Humbert must have wondered why such an arrangement of power had ever been adopted. Was it not the case that as long as Christendom's princes corrupted clerical offices with their monetary interests, there would be no way of realizing the Church's vision of heaven on earth?

And as he pondered this question, a new belief about the Constantinian legacy may have formed in his mind. For Humbert was privy to a document about the primordial Christian emperor that had not yet been widely distributed in Christendom. History had seen its premiere only recently, in Humbert's disputes with Michael Cerularius prior to the excommunications of 1054. The document was known as the *Donation of Constantine*, and though it would prove totally spurious, it claimed to be the testament of Christendom's first ruler.

The *Donation of Constantine* was not composed in the fourth century, but in the eighth century when Pope Stephen II turned to the Franks for political and military support. Byzantium's emperors at that time were awash in the Eastern heresy of iconoclasm, but the papacy feared that its new allies in the West might prove no better. So the *Donation* was penned.[4] It claimed in the name of Constantine that all authority, both over the episcopate and over the state, was bestowed on the bishop of Rome. It was an absurd statement for anyone who had the slightest knowledge of history, but sadly at this time few did. As we saw in the previous chapter, for instance, Humbert himself held the erroneous conviction that the filioque was an original element in the creed.

The *Donation* sat in the papal archive for two centuries awaiting an occasion to be brought to light. The eleventh-century program of reform proved to be the occasion, and Humbert was the first among the reformers to make use of it. In his *Against the Simoniacs*—even more than in his letters in 1054 on behalf of Leo IX—he exploited the document's tendentious papalism to overwhelming effect. For him, Constantine was a perfect ruler because he had surrendered his authority over the bishops. He had recognized a radical

---

4   On the origins of the *Donation of Constantine*, see *Age of Paradise*, 191–192.

division between the clergy and the laity and had submitted to it. In Humbert's mind, it was on this division that the future of Christendom depended.

But such a future necessitated the fabrication of an imagined past. Like the sixteenth-century Protestant reformers, advocates for the Papal Reformation believed in a mythical golden age of church life. Upon greeting Leo IX's predecessor, for instance, fellow reformer Peter Damian had gushed, "Let the golden age of the apostles be renewed and, under your wise presidency, let the church's discipline blossom anew."[5]

The *Donation of Constantine* was only one of numerous sources that seemed to provide documentation of a past for which papal reformers longed. Another was a collection of legal precedents attributed to a monk named Isidorus Mercator. This too was a fabrication. Claiming to include the canons of early church fathers and councils, as well as letters from the first popes, the work was composed in the ninth century not long after the *Donation* (which it interpolated into its content for good measure). Isidorus's collection was, in fact, preoccupied with the assertion of papal prerogatives. Scholars place its composition at the Frankish monastery of Corbie, where defenders of episcopal autonomy were presenting the distant and still impotent papacy as a defense against the looming encroachments of the proprietary system. Because it was a forgery, the collection is known to historians as the *Pseudo-Isidorian Decretals*, but the eleventh-century reformers who landed on it had no doubt it was authentic. After all, by asserting papal supremacy, it provided them with everything they had been looking for.

In fact, they quickly assembled a new collection of canons that made liberal use of the *Decretals*. This work, entitled the *Collection in Seventy-Four Titles*, was composed at Rome—perhaps at the Lateran Palace itself—at about the same time Humbert was working on his treatise against simony. Indeed, some scholars have made the argument that Humbert himself was its author. In any case, of its 315 chapters, no fewer than 252 are direct interpolations from the *Pseudo-Isidorian Decretals*.[6]

---

5   Owen J. Blum, *St. Peter Damian: His Teachings on the Spiritual Life* (Washington, D.C.: Catholic University of America Press, 1947), 18.

6   John Gilchrist, editor and translator, *The Collection in Seventy-Four Titles: A*

Mural of the apostle Peter, Pope Leo III, and Charlemagne at the Lateran Palace in Rome

Canon law may not seem an exciting theme in the history of the West, but the *Collection of Seventy-Four Titles* represents a revolution in papal authority. It also announces a new, legalistic spirit connected to that authority. Within

Canon Law Manual of the Gregorian Reform (Toronto: Pontifical Institute of Medieval Studies, 1980), 15.

a century, for instance, some 1750 papal decretals were being issued every decade, compared to an average total of only 100 per decade during the entire length of the first millennium. The novel assertion of papal supremacy required the amassing of new resources, and the papal decretal was one of these. As one historian has noted, "it was precisely by exploiting this weapon of decretal legislation that the popes were able to make their authority felt throughout the length and breadth of Western Christendom."[7]

The new supremacy asserted by the papacy required a new word to give expression to it. This word was in fact "papacy" itself, or in Latin *papatus*. The word had never been used in history before. Andrew Louth is one historian who has drawn attention to the innovation, invisible as it is to the culture of modern Christendom, in which papal supremacy is taken as inevitable and timeless. In fact, the earliest recorded use of the word "papacy," as distinct from "pope" (which had been widely used since the fourth century), was not until 1047—the very dawn of the Papal Reformation. Louth speculates that the word was modeled on the ancient Latin word for bishop, *episcopatus*. As such, it expressed a new conception of the office of the bishop of Rome as "a further order of ministry in the Church, transcending the episcopate."[8]

By the time Humbert excommunicated the patriarch of Constantinople, then, and surely by the time he had completed his treatise on papal power five years later, the reformers that frequented the Lateran Palace had created a completely new understanding of the Church of Rome. Its bishop, the successor to Saint Peter, no longer claimed only primacy among other patriarchs and bishops. He did not limit his assertions, as Leo I had in the fifth century, to mere preeminence. Instead he possessed, as a legally established fact, ultimate and universal jurisdiction over them. This was the birth of papal supremacy.

---

7   Quoted in Atria A. Larson and Keith Sisson, "Papal Decretals," in *A Companion to the Medieval Papacy: Growth of an Ideology and Institution* (Leiden, Netherlands: Brill, 2016), 158–173.

8   Louth, *Greek East and Latin West*, 298.

A Diplomatic Revolution

SUCH A CLAIM WOULD NOT go unchallenged, and the papal reformers knew it. Their newly created conception of papacy was like a trebuchet against the walls of the old Christendom. And if its destructive force had already caused division when used against the East in 1054, it was now destined to do so within the West.

The papal reformers had until now been dependent on the common interests and goodwill of Emperor Henry III. It was he, after all, who had appointed Leo IX and watched with approbation as the reforming pope assembled northern Europe's most ambitious reformers in Rome. But in 1056, after filling the papal throne with yet another reformer, Stephen IX, following Leo's death, Henry died. The Western Empire was now in the hands of his son, who was a five-year-old boy. His regent mother Agnes proved unqualified to marshal the energy needed to manage papal nominations. In light of this situation, the reformers realized they had an opportunity.

In 1058 Pope Stephen IX died. In the absence of a vigorous ecclesiastical policy from the north, two parties in Rome contended for his replacement. The first to act was the local aristocracy, that very body that had ensnared the papacy in its net of intrigue during the tenth century and brought it to moral ruin. Having lost control of the nomination process during the reign of Henry III, these magnates leapt at the renewed opportunity to elevate one of their own. They did so in the person of Benedict X.

The second party was that of the reformers. It was now led by a monk named Hildebrand. He had worked side by side with other reformers, such as Cardinal Humbert and Peter Damian, since the days of Leo IX. Upon learning of Benedict's election during a visit to Germany (he had in fact been discussing papal affairs with Agnes there), he hastened back to Italy to find Benedict already enthroned in the Lateran. Undeterred by this, in December the reformers elected Nicholas II. Now two popes ruled the Roman Catholic Church.

No other patriarchate in Christendom has ever been subject to as many pretenders as the Roman papacy. These "antipopes," as they are known, tended to appear in times of crisis and uncertainty. The persecution-ridden third century was such a period, as was the pornocracy of the tenth. Now, as the Papal Reformation gained strength, two new duly elected but mutually exclusive claimants to the Chair of Saint Peter had appeared. It was never easy to resolve a contested pontificate. Often, the difference between a true pope and a false one was simply decided by the exercise of force.

And so Nicholas, backed by Hildebrand and other reformers, raised a small army and stormed the Lateran. He forced Benedict to flee and, for good measure, excommunicated him. But a schism dividing the partisans of each claimant now ensued. To end it, Nicholas sent Hildebrand on an errand to forge a military alliance strong enough to secure the reformers. This alliance represented one of the greatest diplomatic revolutions of the age.

The Normans, as we have seen, were the enemies papal reformers may very well have loved to hate. Not only had they wrought havoc on the southern borders of the Papal States, they had presumed to stand up to Leo IX's army at Civitate. In that self-proclaimed war of "liberating Christendom," the pope had declared the Normans to be worse even than the pagans. Now, as the Western Empire wavered and the Roman aristocracy reverted to its pernicious ways, Hildebrand visited the Norman camp to negotiate an alliance.

Its terms were astonishing. On behalf of Nicholas, Hildebrand offered the papacy's former enemy the right to all of southern Italy. This was the very territory Leo had fought and his soldiers had died to defend. What is more, it was territory the pope had no right to grant to anyone. It belonged, as we know, to Byzantium. But the excommunications of 1054 had brought an end to hopes of working with the Greeks in managing the West. In fact, with their new conception of papacy, the reformers wanted to free themselves from all former alliances, since all of them, implicitly or explicitly, compromised the claim to supremacy. The Normans were another matter. As upstarts lacking any legitimacy, they could be manipulated to serve the papacy's new mission. Indeed, in exchange for southern Italy, they showed themselves completely willing to take oaths of fealty to Pope Nicholas, and, what is more, to take up arms in his name. This latter pledge was soon redeemed.

Since his ejection from Rome, Benedict X had taken refuge among his partisans in the fortified town of Galeria. Nicholas ordered his new Norman vassals to attack the city and capture his rival. This they did, with their customary disregard for life and property. When the siege was over, Nicholas insisted not only on Benedict's formal abdication but on his trial and imprisonment. The former rival, proscribed as an antipope, died a decade later while still in captivity.

Because of the Norman-papal alliance, the leaders of the Papal Reformation were finally empowered. The ratification of the new order occurred at an Easter Synod held at the Lateran Palace in 1059. Sitting under the mosaics of the papal assembly hall, surrounded by reformers such as Hildebrand and Humbert, Nicholas declared that henceforth papal elections would be decided by neither the Roman aristocracy nor the emperors of Germany. No layman would ever again presume to interfere in the selection of a pope. Elections would now be decided by the college of cardinals, that body of the clergy chosen by the pope to uphold papal supremacy in perpetuity. Nicholas's decretal governs the papacy to this day.

The Normans, it turned out, had atoned for Civitate. Nor were their services to the papacy at an end. In 1066, as their northern leader William the Conqueror prepared for the invasion of England, they obtained from the pope the military banner that would lead them to victory on the field at Hastings. As a result, papal influence was ensured when the victorious Normans eliminated the Anglo-Saxon hierarchy and took control of the Church in England. They would subsequently do the same in Ireland, where heretofore Celtic monastics and not Latin bishops had governed the Church.

Closer to Rome, the Normans proved no less victorious when warring against the Byzantines and their allies in southern Italy. The elimination of this last vestige of Eastern Christendom in the West ensured papal supremacy there as well. News of the pope's grant of territories once ruled and long claimed by Constantinople must have enraged Emperor Romanos IV. There was, however, little he could do. Robert Guiscard, hero of Civitate and the new leader of the Italian Normans, proved unstoppable. Blessed by the papacy, he knocked out one Greek outpost after another, until all that remained was the city of Bari overlooking the Adriatic. During the early months of the siege, its defenders taunted the Normans by yelling insults at them from the ramparts and reflecting sunlight into their eyes with the use of the stronghold's abundant silver plate.[9] After three years, however, they had stopped laughing. In 1071, when a relief convoy from Constantinople failed to make it through the Norman naval blockade, the last symbol of a Roman Empire ruled from the East since the time of Constantine fell to Westerners.

By this time, however, Emperor Romanos scarcely noticed. For a far more existential threat had suddenly appeared at the opposite end of his empire, on the borderlands of Anatolia.

Jihad Again

THE ECCLESIASTICAL DIVISION OF CHRISTENDOM occurred at a particularly inauspicious time for the East. Beyond the Euphrates, in the distant reaches of the Anatolian plain, a new and menacing power was rising that would soon shatter the longstanding security of Byzantium. It would also enable the papacy, with its newfound powers, to launch the West into a totally unprecedented form of warfare known as the crusades.

The Turks were only one in a series of peoples from Central Asia that, over the course of history, subjected Western civilization to inexorable conquest. Like the Huns before them and the Mongols that followed, they obliterated everything that stood in their path. By the middle of the eleventh century they were ready to strike. Their Seljuk dynasty had overpowered the Abbasid Caliphate and captured Baghdad. And the Seljuks had embraced the Islamic civilization they now ruled. As recent converts, in fact, they would prove even more effective than the Arabs in spreading Islam through force of arms.

The Arab conquests of previous centuries had been motivated in part by the Muslim doctrine of *jihad*. That doctrine held that "submission" (the meaning of *Islam*) to the monotheistic deity preached by Muhammad could

---

9   John Julius Norwich, *The Normans in Sicily* (London: Penguin, 1970), 169.

be advanced through the conquest of nonbelieving populations. Such acts of violence were actually considered pleasing to the deity. For Muslims who died in jihad, the crown of martyrdom and a harem in heaven were promised. And for those who survived the wars of conquest, the good life of the colonial overlord was assured.

Islamic cosmology had a vision of conquest built into it. Its founder, Muhammad, himself had gone to war to unite the Arabs under the new religion. His successors went much further. They conquered all of southern Christendom. From the shores of Spain and across North Africa to the deserts of Syria, they annihilated every Christian army that stood in their way and sacked any city that dared to huddle behind its defensive walls. Through such conquest the Arabs created an empire in which Islam was enthroned in a code of law known as *sharia*, and Christians were stigmatized as *dhimmis*, second-class subjects compelled to convert to the new religion or pay a heavy tax instead. Churches were desecrated and evangelization punished by death. With time, the majority of what had been southern Christendom chose submission. For the minority, "dhimmitude Christendom" became, as it had been in Roman pagandom, a catacomb culture.

But Muslim expansion reached a limit at both the eastern and western boundaries of northern Christendom. In the West, the Franks stopped the Arab onslaught at the Battle of Tours in 732. In the East, the Byzantines repelled the Arabs from the walls of Constantinople in 718. As a result, the Arabs were forced to accept Christendom as a given reality in the world, attacking it in various places during the centuries ahead but never again seeking its complete destruction.

In the middle of the eleventh century, however, the Turks became the successors to the Arab empire in the east and canceled its accommodationist policy. Their militancy may be explained in part by their status as upstarts. Recent nomads of the Central Asian highlands, the Turks were unlikely heirs to the brilliant civilization of the Arabs. They were also relatively new to Islam, having converted only a century earlier. Their great rival was the Arab Fatimid Caliphate in North Africa and Palestine, home to Islam's holiest territories. To exercise vigorous Muslim leadership, Sultan Alp Arslan

(r. 1063–1072) decided he could not remain in the Fatimid shadow for long.

Indeed, the Fatimids offered the Turks a compelling example of Islamic rule. Under Caliph Al-Hakim (r. 996–1021), they had subjected "dhimmitude Christendom" to unrelenting persecution and, in many cases, outright violence. The unsubmissive population of dhimmis was purged from civil administration, and many were flayed to death for refusing to convert to Islam. In 1004 an effort was made to undermine the Christians' paradisiacal subculture by outlawing the celebration of Christ's Resurrection at Pascha.

Perhaps most dramatically, in 1009 Al-Hakim ordered Jerusalem's Anastasis, or Church of the Holy Sepulcher, torn down. The temple built by Emperor Constantine, which had long symbolized the union of heaven and earth—the very site where Christ had been buried and had risen from the dead—was gone. And with it disappeared the True Cross that had been the objective of pilgrims from throughout the East and West for hundreds of years.

Al-Hakim's campaign to eradicate Christendom quickly became a challenge and an inspiration at the Seljuk court. Alp Arslan was eager to put his people on the map of world empires. Jihad proved to be the means.

The Turks appropriated the mantle of righteous warriors fighting to extend Islam throughout the world. Their initial way of doing this was through raiding the Byzantine borderlands of Anatolia. Muhammad himself had established within Islam the image of the *ghazi*, or raider, who engages in armed incursions with the aim of acquiring personal wealth and the conversion of enemies. Self-proclaimed Turkish ghazis now carried out innumerable raids on the most vulnerable Christian towns of Georgia, Armenia, and Byzantium.

Alp Arslan harnessed the expansionist energy of the Turkish ghazis and directed it toward empire-building. He surrounded himself at court with advocates for westward military expansion in the name of holy war. According to the historian Alexander Beihammer, the doctrine of jihad thus became for the Seljuks "an essential expression of hegemonic self-awareness."[10] Gradually, it was extended beyond small-scale raiding to

---

10   Alexander Daniel Beihammer, *Byzantium and the Emergence of Muslim-Turkish*

include all-out assaults on Christian cities.

In 1064 Arslan attacked the Christian lands of Georgia and Armenia. Armenia, as we saw above, had become a protectorate of Byzantium following a treaty between its king and Emperor Basil II. In the meantime, however, the policy of religious assimilation favored by Patriarch Michael Cerularius had alienated the native population. What is more, from Constantinople came orders for the disbanding of an Armenian frontline guard and the introduction of heavy taxes. The harmful effects of Byzantine short-sightedness were about to be revealed.

Arslan invaded Armenia in 1064 and made straight for its capital. The city of Ani was known for its many stone churches and was home to nearly one hundred thousand people. After a siege of nearly a month, the Turks slaughtered them all. The act was so cruel that an Arab observer could not help but remark that "the dead bodies were so many that they blocked all the streets; one could not go anywhere without stepping over them."[11] Staggering from the blow, the city never recovered. After being sacked again in the fourteenth century by the Mongols, it faded into a kind of Christian ghost town, haunting the Anatolian landscape with hollow stone temples that still stand today.

But the Turks were not content with the insignificant territorial prizes of Transcaucasia. They soon turned their eyes toward the rich lands of Byzantine Anatolia. In 1067 Arslan launched an incursion that went to the very heart of Eastern Christendom. The city of Caesarea in Cappadocia had long been hallowed as a center of church life. Most famous among past residents was Basil the Great (d. 379), who on its outskirts had built a vast complex of charitable hospitals and poorhouses. Like Ani, the city was a crossroads between Europe and Asia and therefore possessed vast wealth. Totally unprepared for an attack so far into the Byzantine interior, the city was quickly overpowered by the Turks and its treasuries plundered. This brazen raid finally roused the emperor to action.

Anatolia (New York: Routledge, 2017), 112.

11   John Julius Norwich, *Byzantium: The Apogee* (New York: Alfred A. Knopf, 1994), 343.

Byzantine Christendom, however, was scarcely in a position to act. Romanos IV (r. 1068–1072) was the tragic hero of an empire on the brink of disaster. On the one hand, he was the courageous son of a military aristocrat whose dream—in the spirit of his illustrious predecessor Basil II—was to raise the empire's prestige high upon the shields of victorious soldiers. But to do this he needed political stability in Constantinople, and sadly he had none. He was surrounded at court by deception and conspiracy. His greatest enemies were the scholar-statesman Michael Psellos and his odious sidekick, John Doukas. Both had opposed the sudden marriage of Romanos to the dowager empress Eudoxia, which had elevated him to the throne. Doukas had his own designs on the throne and never stopped plotting until he saw them realized. With his court against him, the young emperor made the decision to rule from the battlefield.

Throughout his short reign, Romanos instituted policies designed to reverse a precipitous decline in the military situation. One problem was financial. Though Basil II had left a treasury bursting at the seams, half a century of shortsighted and wasteful spending had drained it. What was worse, a process by which poor peasants in Anatolia were progressively despoiled by the local aristocracy of what little land they owned not only deprived the state of tax revenue, but also alienated the majority of the population and inclined it, should a military crisis arise, toward profound apathy. To address these threats, the state had resorted to offering the empire's military recruitment districts—known as *themes*—the option of cash payments in the place of soldiers. It was a simple solution to the fiscal problem, but one that created a new and corresponding military problem.

As the themes opted to send taxes to the capital instead of soldiers, Romanos's standing army began to wither. He was forced to hire foreign mercenaries to build up the reduced ranks. But this introduced yet other problems. In addition to requiring substantial reserves to pay the mercenaries, it placed the empire's security in the hands of men who had little investment in its survival. Some forces, like the legendary Varangian Guard, were relatively reliable. But others, like those made up of Normans or even Turks, could hardly be relied upon if and when the empire found itself at war with their peoples.

This set the stage for the greatest military debacle in the history of Byzantium. Romanos, despite the grave situation at court and in the army, resolved to confront Arslan's unchecked raids on the interior. Two campaigns were launched in the years following the invasion of Caesarea, but as expected his army proved unmanageable. What is more, rumors of sedition that reached him from Constantinople caused him to return to the capital before a decisive confrontation with the enemy was possible.

Finally, in 1071 he put affairs at court in order as much as was possible and departed with a new and even larger army for the Anatolian borderlands of Armenia. There he intended to hunt down the Seljuk forces and limit their ability to do further damage. Arslan was at the time actually in the midst of a campaign against his Fatimid rivals. Learning of the long Byzantine march, he quickly reversed course and met his enemy north of Lake Van, near a fortress called Manzikert.

The sultan did not want to conduct a frontal attack on the Byzantine Empire. In fact he sent a delegation to Romanos proposing a truce. It was rejected. The emperor recognized a mortal threat when he saw one, and after waiting several years to corner his enemy, he had no intention of letting him slip away. That would only ensure continued Turkish incursions along his eastern frontier and the gradual reduction of its defensibility.

But despite its size, Romanos's army lacked a unified command. It depended too much on mercenaries. The stalwart Varangians were there, but so also were less devoted groups. There was a contingent of Normans and a contingent of Armenians. There was even, remarkably, a contingent of Turks. What is more, on the day he chose to fight, half of the army was scouting at such a distance from the battlefield as to be worthless. Finally, command of his reserve was in the hands of Andronikos Doukas, the son of the emperor's greatest enemy back at court, whose only thought was to usurp the throne for himself or another member of his scheming clan.

Soon after dawn, the Byzantines formed their line and marched toward the Turkish camp. But in an almost surreal way, they never reached the enemy. As they slowly moved forward, the Turks retreated just as slowly. All day long the Byzantines advanced, and all day long the Turks withdrew in good order. And as the strange maneuver played itself out, something ominous began to happen. The Byzantine line remained straight, but the Turkish line slowly and imperceptibly began to bend at the middle, creating a sort of vacuum. And the farther the Byzantines advanced, the farther they found themselves engulfed within it.

Then, when Arslan was satisfied he had sucked his enemy far enough into the vacuum, he gave the order to attack.

From all sides the Turkish archers began to rain arrows down upon Romanos's flanks. By now twilight was swiftly approaching, and the emperor concluded that the day would end with his men caught in a trap from which they could not easily escape. So he ordered his center to reverse its banners to signal an orderly retreat. This was the turning point. When his soldiers at the rear saw the reversed banners, they panicked and began to flee. However, all was not lost as long as the reserves played their part.

But the reserves were under the command of Andronikos, who now gave an order that would have brought a cunning smile to his father's face. He announced to his men that Romanos had fallen and the day was lost. A full retreat and the dissolution of the reserves ensued. As it did, the mercenaries occupying various positions among the remainder of the army also melted away. All that was left was the heroic Varangian Guard, surrounding the beleaguered emperor at the center of the battlefield as the carnage mounted around him. Finally, there were none left but a few of the bravest and luckiest of the Byzantines. For his part, Romanos was prepared to fight to the end; he had even had his horse shot out from underneath him. But an injury to his sword hand disabled him, and when the Turks finally reached the center, he stood virtually alone amid a pile of corpses.

The next day Emperor Romanos, lately known among his people as God's vice-regent on earth, lay prostrate beneath the boot of the sultan. Alp Arslan had, without planning it, defeated the greatest army in Christendom. Lifting his foot from the emperor's neck, he announced magnanimously that the prisoner was free to return to Constantinople with the understanding that he pay tribute to the Turks and allow them free rein in the East.

But Romanos must have known an even grimmer fate awaited him among his own people. In fact, before he even reached the Bosphorus he was ambushed by none other than Andronikos Doukas. The traitor of Manzikert had returned to the capital and there had been equipped with his own army by his father, John. His mission was to intercept and neutralize the dispossessed emperor.

What the magnanimous Turks had declined to do, the conspiratorial Greeks now did without hesitation. Captured by Andronikos's men, Romanos suffered the fate of so many victims of Byzantine intrigue: his eyes were gouged out. For days he lay in agony, near death from his wounds. As he finally reached the end, a cruel note arrived from Constantinople. In it his old enemy Psellos—accomplice to John Doukas—urged the dying emperor to rejoice in the loss of his physical sight, for, the author sarcastically gloated, it was the sure way to acquire celestial light.

Strangely, that same year, back at the opposite end of Anatolia, Romanos's far more honorable Muslim enemy also met an unexpected and violent end. In the aftermath of a skirmish among local Turkish warlords, Alp Arslan recklessly allowed a prisoner to approach him, and, when a dagger suddenly appeared from beneath the man's robe, failed to evade the fatal thrust that followed.

"The Great Innovator"

BACK IN WESTERN CHRISTENDOM, THE Papal Reformation was now in full swing. The papal election decree of 1059 had served as a point of departure for it. Composed largely by Humbert, the decree was a bold application of the theory of papal supremacy laid out in *Against the Simoniacs*. The heady events that were now moving forward were no longer in the hands of the excommunicator of Constantinople, however, for he died in 1061. The reformation was now directed by men we have so far scarcely met in our story. Cardinal Peter Damian of Ostia was one of them, and we shall learn more about him below. Another was Cardinal Hildebrand, described by one biographer as the "great innovator."

This most strident of all the reformers would eventually become Pope

Gregory VII (r. 1073–1085), and he would carry the reformation to its most extreme limits. He subscribed thoroughly to papal supremacy. In 1059, the year of the election decree, he had asked Peter Damian to compile a list of past papal decrees to help define the powers of the papacy. The occasion for this request is unclear. It could have occurred in connection with the project then underway at the Lateran to compile the *Seventy-Four Titles*. In any case, Hildebrand seems never to have received the requested list from Peter. So he decided to compose one himself. This was the origin of the most revolutionary statement of papal supremacy ever.

The document is known as the *Papal Dictate* (*Dictatus papae*). It dates to 1075, just two years after Hildebrand acceded to the Chair of Saint Peter and became Gregory VII. Since no explanation of its purpose is given in the papal register in which it appears, historians have long puzzled over its intent. Was it the table of contents of a planned treatise on papal supremacy by the pope? Was it designed as a manifesto for the upcoming struggle against the German emperor? Aristeides Papadakis has noted the remarkably close relationship of the document to issues raised during the excommunication of Michael Cerularius. Was the *Dictate*, therefore, a preliminary justification for the emerging schism that the papacy had done so much to provoke?[12]

Whatever his motivation, Gregory made one radical claim after another about the papacy. The pope "may be judged by no one." The pope "alone is rightly to be called universal." The pope alone shall have his name "spoken in the churches." The pope possesses the exclusive power, "according to the needs of the time, to make new laws." The pope "may depose and reinstate

---

12 "Presumably many of the prepositions of the Dictatus were also written with the Eastern Church in mind. The argument has actually been made that the Dictatus papae was a draft of the preliminary conditions for union, which Rome wished to impose on Constantinople after 1054. Apparently some twenty years later, when the text was composed, the papal embassy to Constantinople was still a live issue for its author." However, Papadakis admits that there is little scholarly support for the theory that the *Dictate* was written in direct response to the schism. *The Christian East and the Rise of the Papacy* (Crestwood, NY: St. Vladimir's Seminary Press, 1994), 57–58.

bishops without assembling a synod." The legate of the pope, even if inferior in rank to local bishops, "may render a sentence of deposition against them."

These were unprecedented claims. But they seemed mild beside others. The pope "may depose emperors." The pope "is the only one whose feet are to be kissed by all princes." The pope, if canonically ordained, "is undoubtedly made a saint by the merits of St. Peter." And the Church of Rome, over which the pope presides, "has never erred, nor ever, by the witness of Scripture, shall err to all

Alp Arslan humiliating Romanos IV

eternity." Here, in a list consisting of a mere twenty-seven sentences, papal authority was expressed in a voice never before heard.

Gregory intended to use the papacy to achieve what northern monastics never could, nor ever would have attempted. Using the newly defined powers of the papacy, he and his collaborators would transform Christendom from its current condition into, as Tellenbach put it, "the kingdom of God on earth."[13] Since the Christendom of the proprietary lords scarcely resembled that of the apostles, it was necessary to create a cadre of reform-minded leaders, and these of course must be members of the clergy. The result was a bifurcation of Christian society, that is, a division of it into two separate and unequal parts.

Historians have long been in agreement that Gregory's pontificate marked a sharp rise in clericalism. For centuries to come, the West would be a different society than it had ever been before. "The church of the twelfth and thirteenth centuries," Richard Southern noted, "was a society of disciplined and organized clergy directing the thoughts and activities of an obedient and receptive laity—kings, magnates, and peasants alike."[14] As we shall

---

13   This was Tellenbach's conclusion. *Church, State, and Christian Society*, 165.
14   R. W. Southern, *Western Society and the Church in the Middle Ages* (London:

see in chapter four, this development would have a profound effect on the culture of Christendom.

The spiritual bifurcation of society depended, in Christopher Dawson's analysis, on an application of "Augustinian dualism"—the same that monastic reformers had cultivated in places like Cluny.[15] Indeed, a young Hildebrand had spent time at that famed center of clerical reform during a period of transalpine exile. In flight from the malicious Roman aristocracy long before he became pope, he must have marveled at the sublime discipline of the monks there. Under their influence he came to see the world exclusively in proprietary terms—as rapacious, lustful, and corrupt. Such a world could never be a harbor to paradise.

This was a departure from the cosmology of the old Christendom. As a counterculture within Roman pagandom, it had assigned to the laity—to Christian women married to pagans, for instance—a cooperative and necessary role in the transformation of the world.[16]

And in the contemporary East, lay emperors like John II (r. 1118–1143) continued to rule by the principle of symphony; lay intellectuals such as Michael Psellos (d. 1079) continued to teach; and, on occasion, lay theologians like Nicholas Cabasilas (d. 1391) even continued to write books.[17]

Now, under the influence of the reformed papacy, the Western laity was reduced to a passive and increasingly abject role within the world. It was precisely at this time, and under these circumstances, that "the church" came to mean not the entire body of faithful,

Pope Gregory VII

Penguin, 1970), 38.

15 Dawson, *Religion and the Rise of Western Culture*, 132.

16 On the role of women in early Christendom, see *Age of Paradise*, 72f.

17 There is disagreement about whether Cabasilas was a layman or a priest at the end of his life. Papadakis indicates the former. *The Christian East and the Rise of the Papacy*, 315.

lay and clergy, but only the highest orders within the latter. Defined this way, the church came to be that organization or institution which, under the administrative direction of the papacy, determined the ideals of the culture. As for the laity, it "was obscured or forgotten."[18]

In short, the Papal Reformation produced a culture of clericalism, and nowhere was it more pronounced than in Christianity's first-ever campaign against priestly marriage. Until this time, certain canons of local councils (Elvira Canon 33 for instance) and letters of popes (such as Leo the Great) documented a desire for celibacy or at least continence for those priests already married at the time of their ordination. But no concerted effort had ever been made to enforce such guidelines categorically.

In the East, the ideal of clerical celibacy had always been balanced by an allowance for sexual relations within a preexisting marriage. In such cases, continued relations were approved, though a second marriage was not. In the fifth century, the Greek historian Socrates Skolastikos reported a famous statement by the Egyptian monk Paphnutios at the First Council of Nicaea, defending clerical marriage against rigorists who opposed it. This affirmative view of clerical marriage was ratified permanently in the East with Canon 13 of the Council of Trullo. This act actually forbade the separation of a priest from his wife and the denial to them of sexual relations on the pretense of piety, and it quoted scripture to that effect (Matt. 19:6; 1 Cor. 7:27).

In the West, on the other hand, various statements and an occasional canon against the practice of clerical marriage continued to appear up to the eleventh century. By many accounts, however, even at that time most priests were married and raised children with their wives. Others chose to live with concubines. The fact that at this late date marriage rituals in the West remained in a state of comparative underdevelopment (in the East the elaborate ceremony of crowning had long been in place) may explain this latter practice.

With characteristic extremism, Gregory ignored all ambiguity and declared that every priest must be celibate. In this he was not speaking alone.

---

18   Papadakis, *The Christian East and the Rise of the Papacy*, 50.

Virtually all reformers were of the same mind. As monks who had taken a vow of celibacy themselves, they saw no spiritual value in clerical marriage and the families that issued from it. Indeed, the demand for clerical celibacy represented an effort to monasticize the parish clergy, which formerly had been distinct from monastics. This had much to do with the reformers' Augustinian anthropology. As early as the tenth century, Abbot Odo of Cluny had claimed that all sexual activity is intrinsically evil, and that the child that results from relations even among married parents is stained with original sin and deserving of damnation due to the concupiscence responsible for its conception.[19]

Here it might be noted that reformers like Gregory insisted on celibacy not because they sought to release the clergy from the fetters of family obligations. This is a much later argument for clerical celibacy. The need for celibacy was ritualistic; even sexual activity within marriage was believed to stain the priest. He was above all the servant of the altar, and his hands must not be defiled by contact with the body of a woman.

Here Peter Damian offered the most insistent and extreme argument against clerical marriage. He considered the practice a heresy and duly assigned it the term "nicolaitanism." Appropriating the obscure account in Revelation of heretics known by that name, and connecting it without any justification to clerical marriage, he and other reformers asserted that even in the golden age of the apostles, such a relationship had been an abomination to God. This was another example of the reformers' fabrication of an imagined but useable past. And the reason for its invention was, of course, the sexual immorality endemic to the lay-dominated proprietary system of the current Western Church. The fact that many, if not the majority of, parish priests at the time were actually living in lawful wedlock with their wives mattered little. For Peter, clerical marriage was nothing more than fornication.

---

19   Phyllis G. Jestice, "Why Celibacy? Odo of Cluny and the Development of a New Sexual Morality," in *Medieval Purity and Piety: Essays on Medieval Clerical Celibacy and Religious Reform*, edited by Michael Frassetto (New York: Garland, 1998), 81–116.

In a belligerent letter addressed to the wives of priests, he used his formidable skill in rhetoric to reduce his audience to the status of prostitutes, or even worse:

> *And now, let me speak to you, you charmers of clerics, tasty tidbits of the devil, expulsion from paradise, venom of the mind, sword that kills souls, poison in the drink, toxin in the food, source of sinning, and occasion of damnation. I am talking to you, you female branch of the ancient enemy, hoopoes, screech owls, nighthawks, she-wolves, leeches . . . nymphs, sirens, witches . . . vile tigresses whose cruel jaws can be sated only on human blood . . . harpies flying about the sacrifice of the Lord to snatch those who are offered to God and cruelly devour them . . . lionesses . . . furious vipers [who] by the ardor of your impatient lust . . . dismember your lovers by cutting them off from Christ who is the head of the clergy.*[20]

Gregory wholeheartedly affirmed this point of view. In his many letters he not only attacked clerical marriage but equated it with fornication. Even a lawfully married wife was in his mind no more than a concubine.

Had the papacy not set itself against the practices of the Christian East, as it had done so fatefully in 1054, a more balanced approach to the problems of the proprietary system might have been found. As it was, papal reformers consistently denigrated clerical marriage, suggesting that ordination actually superseded and nullified it.

This had a baneful impact on the future of Western Christendom. First, it undermined its paradisiacal culture. The sacrament of marriage had been the basis for a sanctified society in which a man and a woman could experience the kingdom of heaven through their sacrificial love for one another. Paul had spoken of marriage as a "mystery" that united Christ with his Church (Eph. 5:32). It was therefore indissoluble and indelible. By declaring all clerical marriages null and void, however, papal reformers subverted the sacramentality of marriage in general. This of course was not their intent,

---

20 Quoted in Rachel Fulton, *From Judgement to Passion: Devotion to Christ and the Virgin Mary, 800–1200* (New York: Columbia University, 2002), 109.

and their successors in the Roman Catholic Church would ironically pay the price in modern times when fighting an heroic defense of marriage.

What is more, without questioning the sacramentality of marriage directly, the reformers implied by their statements condemning the conjugal act between a priest and his wife that divine participation—the heart of Christendom's anthropology—was fully experienced only through a life of celibacy. Frankish Augustinianism had done much to prepare the way for this with its overwhelmingly negative views of sexuality, but by instituting clerical celibacy in every parish community, the Papal Reformation now advanced such pessimism throughout the broader culture of the West.

Which brings us to a third outcome of the papacy's celibacy reforms. The celibate parish priest was now raised above the married layman. He was now required to live by the extraordinary standard of a monk, despite the experience of a millennium in which two paths of ministry—cloistered and public—had been kept distinct. Now, congregations of the laity related to a man who was visibly remote from their common experiences and emphatically superior to them. This served to divide Christian society even further into two separate categories: the clerical and the lay, the spiritual and the profane.

A fourth, unforeseen outcome of the innovation was that priests, now barred from the stabilizing support of a wife and family, were more susceptible than before to sexual temptations that could become a scandal to the faithful and an impediment to evangelical witness. The Protestant Reformation half a millennium hence would be fueled in part by a reaction against the hypocrisy and clericalism of mandatory clerical celibacy. And another half-millennium later, as twentieth-century Christendom entered an age of nihilism in which promiscuity became the popular standard of human fulfillment, celibacy would become an even greater burden than it had been when, within the eleventh century's culture of reform, it first became obligatory.

That clerical celibacy would prevail as the new standard was, however, by no means ensured even during the reign of Gregory VII. The innovative pope's relentless campaign to introduce celibacy actually met with stiff resistance throughout the West. Some bishops simply balked. Hubert of

Therouanne, for instance, ordered his priests to refuse baptism and burial to advocates of celibacy, so unreasonable and disruptive were their demands. In Constance, the local bishop Otto initially tried to satisfy the papal directives, only to give up in the face of overwhelming resistance. Infuriated by this, Gregory wrote an angry letter to the bishop accusing him in his characteristically harsh way of "unparalleled insolence." Gregory did not stop there. He actually called on the faithful of Constance to renounce their obedience to Otto until the apostate should repent of his dereliction and again enforce papal reform directives.[21]

Gregory's war against clerical marriage was particularly concentrated in a local upheaval that preceded his elevation to the papacy. One day, during the pontificate of Alexander II (r. 1061–1073), Cardinal Hildebrand received at the Lateran Palace a renegade knight from the city of Milan. His name was Erlembald, and he was the leader of a party of insurrectionists called the Patarenes. They were dedicated to the overthrow of the city's feudal archbishop Guido, who was infamous for his corruption. To advance their cause against this latest example of the proprietary order, they had aligned themselves with the Papal Reformation. Erlembald announced that he wanted to purify Milan of its corrupt clergy, whose abiding sins were simony and "nicolaitanism." Hildebrand supported Erlembald's cause, and he persuaded Pope Alexander to dispatch the rebel back to Milan with a papal military banner for use in a "holy insurrection." The outcome, of course, was bloody civil conflict.

Indeed, Pope Alexander called on the Milanese faithful to boycott all parishes in which a priest was rumored to have a wife. Armed uprisings followed, and eventually Guido was brought to his knees. However, before abdicating in 1070, he invited Emperor Henry IV to appoint his replacement in an effort to deny the papacy its victory. The result was the most divisive act in the high drama of Gregory's pontificate, an upheaval known as the investiture conflict.

This momentous development was also related to the Augustinian

---

21   Helen Parish, *Clerical Celibacy in the West, c. 1100–1700* (London: Routledge, 2010), 101.

conception of the world transmitted through Frankish learning. Inspired by *The City of God*, the reformers' dualistic cosmology permanently bifurcated Western Christendom's political order. Casting aside the ancient ideal of symphony, Gregory VII asserted supreme authority over the papacy's long-time partner and defender, the Holy Roman Empire.

Like the celibacy campaign, the investiture controversy arose from a desire to free the clergy from the corrupting influence of the proprietary system. The appropriation of church administration by lay feudal magnates had resulted in a dismal situation in which the gospel was often made of little effect. Parish priests were dependent for their family's livelihood on the goodwill of the local lord, who might prove uncomfortable with homilies challenging wealth and power. Though extreme, the plight of a ninth-century priest named Folcrad reveals how dangerous pastoral zeal could be under these circumstances. When he dared to confront his noble patroness for deserting her husband, she silenced him by having him castrated.[22]

At the highest level, bishops depended on the local prince for their appointment. This was true particularly in Germany, where the emperor bestowed office only on men he could be certain would put first the interests of his realm, and not necessarily those of the Church. To symbolize the German bishops' servitude, the empire had long used a ritual called investiture, whereby the bishop received both crosier and ring from the hand of the emperor. Within the context of feudalism, this act established a clear subordination of the clergy to the power of the lay ruler.

This Gregory intended to change. Ever since the papal election decree of 1059, based as it was upon Humbert's theory of papal supremacy, a showdown with the empire was inevitable. The decree's insistence that popes be selected by the college of cardinals and not by the emperor assured this. Henry III had had reason to be dismayed, for it had been his zeal for the good of the papacy that had led to the wresting of elections from the hands of the Roman aristocracy. But it was not until after his death that the first test of the new order arose.

---

22 Susan Wood, *The Proprietary Church in the Medieval West* (Oxford: Oxford University Press, 2006), 527.

The moment came after the resolution of conflict between Nicholas II and his rival antipope Benedict X. In 1061 Henry's widow Agnes gained enough resolve to back Honorius II against the reformers' choice for pope, Alexander II. Once again, schism resulted from papal reform. This particular division lasted three years, during which the contenders' armies fought in the field and within the walls of Rome, occupying sites such as Saint Peter's Basilica and the Castel Sant'Angelo. The battle was finally ended in favor of Alexander, bringing Hildebrand back into his role as the real power in the Lateran.

Therefore, it was he who was on the scene at the Lateran when the Patarene conflict finally resulted in Archbishop Guido's abdication. Guido, as we have seen, had arranged to have his replacement chosen by a young Henry IV. The Patarenes had their candidate too, and he naturally received the endorsement of the pope. In other words, schism threatened again. But this time the spirit of division spilled over the Alps into lands of the Holy Roman Empire.

In order to enforce their candidate in Milan, the reformers had resorted to an instrument rarely used before in political conflicts. Excommunication by a bishop was an ancient means of recognizing an unrepentant sinner's separation from the sacramental life of the Church. Prior to the eleventh century, it was limited to cases of personal moral or doctrinal deviation from the tradition of the Church. In the hands of the reformers, excommunication was weaponized.

Pope Gregory used it to punish Henry's candidate in Milan, along with the imperial legates who supported him. This infuriated the emperor and signaled to him that the decree of 1059 had now moved beyond the matter of papal elections alone. Indeed, the emperor was aware of the claims to supremacy made by Gregory in the *Papal Dictate*, especially its breathtaking assertion that the pope possessed the power to depose an emperor. When the pope wrote to Henry to threaten him with excommunication, therefore, the emperor interpreted the message as "an ultimatum from Gregory to strip him alike of his earthly kingdom and of his eternal salvation."[23] In 1076

---

23 H.E.J. Cowdrey, *Gregory VII* (Oxford: Clarendon Press, 1998), 135.

Henry gathered two dozen of his loyal vassal bishops to issue a preemptive rejection of the new doctrine of papal supremacy.

This Synod of Worms produced a scathing repudiation of the pope. After listing Gregory's crimes, this decree concluded with a categorical statement: "Accordingly, we renounce an obedience that we never promised you and will never show you. Because, as you have made publicly clear, none of us has hitherto been in your eyes a bishop, by the same token you will henceforth never be in any of our eyes the pope." To this Henry himself could not resist adding a renunciation of his own.

> *Hitherto I have looked to you for whatever befits a father and, to the great chagrin of our own subjects, I have obeyed you in all things. But by way of return, I have received from you what is to be expected of the deadliest enemy of our life and kingship. . . Every right to the papacy that you seem to have, I deny you; from the bishopric of the city whose patriciate is rightly mine by God's gift and by the sworn agreement of the Romans, I say—step down![24]*

When these letters were read at a synod of sympathetic reform bishops held in Saint John Lateran, they created an uproar that greatly encouraged the offended pope. Accordingly, he now issued his own rebuttal, strangely addressed not to Henry but to Saint Peter. Between an opening that protested Gregory's involuntary accession to the apostle's see and a closing that alluded to the Church built upon his person, Gregory solemnly declared Henry excommunicated and his millions of subjects bound to deny him obedience.

As it turned out, the ruler of the Holy Roman Empire was no match for the reformed papacy. Henry's greatest weakness was a simmering revolt in Saxony. The *Dictate* had declared the right to absolve subjects of loyalty to their prince—a particularly revolutionary assertion—and this was exploited by rebellious princes. Gregory thus became an accomplice to a civil war in which many thousands were killed. But the outcome was in his favor, and finally Henry capitulated.

---

24 Quoted in ibid., 137–138.

He did so in the winter of 1077. Learning of Gregory's presence at an Alpine castle at Canossa, he stood in the snow for three days until the pope appeared on the ramparts to absolve him. The humiliating act was not the end of the matter, however. He never forgot the outrage, and, once the Saxon uprising was contained, returned to the struggle with Gregory.

And so in 1084 Henry finally came to Rome itself at the head of the imperial army. He managed a breach in the walls and cornered Gregory in the Castel Sant'Angelo. But before the fortress fell, the situation suddenly changed. The Normans, the new defenders of the papacy, appeared out of nowhere at the behest of their lord. Their leader Robert Guiscard had received the papal summons, significantly, while campaigning against the Byzantine Empire with the encouragement of the pope. He now made haste for Rome and in no time at all was besieging its former besieger, Henry. The imperial army was soon overwhelmed and retreated. But the appalling end to the affair was yet to come.

The Normans, never known for clemency, now laid total waste to the City of Saint Peter. Thirty-seven thousand of them massacred unarmed citizens in the streets. They burned ancient churches to the ground. And those Romans who survived both butchery and inferno, they sold into slavery. Almost nothing was left. The entire city between the Tiber River and the Lateran Palace was reduced to a heap of smoldering ash.

The eloquent John Julius Norwich imagines how the scene may have affected the man whose relentless policies had, more than any other cause, placed the city in the hands of the terrible Normans.

What thoughts now, one wonders, must have occupied the mind of Pope Gregory as he surveyed the blackened ruins around him, the streets impassable with piles of fallen masonry, the corpses already putrefying in the heat of a Roman June? He had won his battle—after a fashion—but at what price? The heroic popes of the past had saved their city from the invaders—Leo I from Attila's Huns, his own namesake Gregory the Great from the conquering Lombards; he, though in many ways greater than either, had delivered it up to destruction. And yet . . . his conscience seems to have been astonishingly clear.

As he saw it, he had been fighting for a principle. . . . The present sufferings of his people were simply the inevitable retribution which by their faithlessness they had brought upon themselves. God's will had been done.[25]

The pontificate of Gregory VII could not survive this terrible event. The appalling costs of protecting him from his enemies finally dawned on the populace, and an elemental and visceral reaction ensued. Gregory was driven out of the city gates with threats against his life. Protected by Robert Guiscard, he huddled close to the retreating Norman army until, worn to the point of collapse, he died in exile the following year in the southern town of Salerno.

To the end Gregory considered the Papal Reformation to be the one great cause of his life, expressing in one of his final letters gratitude to God for being given leadership over it. He even expressed the restless and all-too-reformatory hope that the Church should one day "return to her true glory and stand free, chaste, and catholic."[26]

Crusades

BACK IN 1074, JUST BEFORE the investiture conflict with Henry IV exploded, Gregory VII shared a dream with those around him in the Lateran Palace. Perhaps he told of it while sitting beneath the images of Pope Leo and Emperor Charlemagne receiving their commissions from Saint Peter. He reported that recently he had received an unexpected and flattering letter from the Byzantine capital congratulating him on the inception of his pontificate. Its author was Emperor Michael VII, who came to power as result of the disaster at Manzikert and the subsequent fall of Romanos IV. Gregory was delighted to learn that the new emperor desired good relations with the papacy, something recent emperors had not been known to do. After all, only a score of years had passed since 1054. But what really got Gregory thinking was the idea that the Byzantines might finally be ready

25   John Julius Norwich, *The Normans of Sicily*, 241–242.
26   Quoted in Cowdrey, *Gregory VII*, 232.

to submit to what Patriarch Michael Cerularius had not: the absolute and universal jurisdiction of the Roman Church. This, he announced, could be assured if the armies of Western Christendom were to come to the defense of Byzantium in its struggle with the Turks.

The reform papacy already had a rudimentary concept of sanctified violence, having issued military standards to William the Conqueror and even having canonized soldiers fighting under Leo IX at Civitate. What better service to a divided Christendom could the successor to Saint Peter offer than leading a holy war against its great external enemy, Islam?

So Gregory impetuously announced to his cardinals the intention of raising an "army of Saint Peter" (*militia sancti Petri*) under his personal command to fight the invading Turkish hordes on the plains of Anatolia. Once the infidel had been defeated, he enthused, the churches of West and East would gather at his feet in New Rome and he would proclaim the end of what was becoming a schism greater than any in history.

Henry IV waiting for the pope at Canossa

It was a magnificent dream. And it came to absolutely nothing, because, apart from the largely delusional hope that the patriarchate of Constantinople would renounce its ancient ecclesiology and liturgical practice, the Holy Roman Emperor was at that very moment organizing with his German bishops the repudiation of Gregory's authority and the overthrow of his pontificate. The end result of this, as we have seen, was the sack of Old Rome.

But Pope Gregory's dream lived on, and it did so because it offered advocates of the Papal Reformation a means by which to sustain their cause beyond the cataclysm of 1084.

The new occupant of the Lateran Palace, moreover, was not the impractical prophet that Gregory had been. Pope Urban II (r. 1088–1099) was a bureaucrat. He was the product of Cluny, where he had learned not only the principles of monastic reform but the administration of a vast system of ecclesiastical institutions. It was under him that the papacy established a formal court, or *curia*, that would manage papal affairs for centuries to come. Staffed by a college of cardinals with largely administrative rather than pastoral assignments, the papal court took its place in the Lateran Palace and became the new command center of reformation.

After Gregory's humiliating death in exile, the reformers realized that a direct assault on princely prerogatives was untenable. However, the cause of reform could still go forward if the papacy could direct the feudal order, with its proprietary designs on church administration, toward a military movement with spiritual aspirations. The energies of feudal warlords could be channeled toward the recovery of Christian lands and thereby sanctified.

But could warfare be justified by the God of love? Jesus, after all, had never supported the use of violence and explicitly commanded His followers to love their enemies. When assaulted by them, He added, they must "turn the other cheek." Never in the course of the first millennium, in fact, had a "holy war" been declared by the clergy responsible for guiding the Church.[27]

---

27 In his wars for the recovery of Jerusalem against Persia, Byzantine Emperor Heraklios had used the language of holy war to inspire his soldiers. However, this was not done systematically and was never condoned by the clergy. Likewise, Emperor Charlemagne had conquered Saxony with statements about the conversion of its pagan population, but had been rebuked for doing so by

Christianity was not Islam. Ancient canons actually condemned armed conflict and imposed severe penalties, including excommunication, on Christians responsible for it. Nevertheless, this tradition of pacifism had in practice been ignored for centuries in the West under the proprietary system. Vassal bishops had been expected to bear arms and lead armies for feudal princes—most notably, as we saw in the case of the future pope Leo IX, the German emperor himself.

Papal advocates of holy war found support in the writings of Augustine. Or at least they claimed to do so. In fact, the great Western father regarded all forms of war as basically sinful and something the sincere Christian should resolutely avoid. However, fusing Aristotle's claim that the proper end of war was peace with the Christian concern with moral intentionality, he developed a rough concept of what can be called a "just war." The concept possessed what Christopher Tyerman has called "a convenient conceptual plasticity" that later theorists of Christian holy war could use.[28] One of them was Anselm of Lucca, a fervent advocate of reform during the pontificate of Gregory VII who produced a collection of canon law that laid out Augustine's theory.

Others went further, and by the end of the eleventh century an ideology of Christian militancy was sweeping through the Lateran Palace. Its advocates remembered how Leo IX had taken up arms against the Normans only a half-century earlier at Civitate, declaring after defeat that his fallen soldiers were saints. They remembered how Alexander II had bestowed a military banner on William the Conqueror, as if the invasion of Anglo-Saxon England in 1066 were a war against the enemies of the Church. And of course they could not forget Gregory VII. He had not only given his blessing to the Patarene insurgency, declaring its leader Erlembald a martyr after he fell in battle fighting the ecclesiastical establishment. He had also blessed the Normans to invade Orthodox Byzantium in 1080, promising their soldiers the remission of sins in a holy war against a people considered apostate.

---

monastic advisors such as Alcuin.

28   Christopher Tyerman, *God's War* (Cambridge, MA: Harvard University Press, 2006), 34–35.

Inspired by these examples, Pope Urban set out in 1095 to the French town of Clermont to bring Gregory VII's dream to realization. Along the way, he could not resist stopping at Cluny, where, as one of its former monks, he delighted in consecrating the newly built cathedral. In area, the edifice was larger than Constantinople's Hagia Sophia. Urban would have been touched by the comparison. As he stood beneath its dome, he must surely have imagined the impending reunion of East with West and the plan to proclaim it in Constantinople. He realized the declaration of war that would bring it about was nearly at hand. At a council in Spain earlier in the year, he had been approached by ambassadors from Byzantium. They had described in heartbreaking detail the Turkish advance through Christian Anatolia and conveyed the plea of their lord, Emperor Alexios Komnenos, for Western military support.

And so Urban left Cluny and continued on his momentous journey to the Council of Clermont. On the final day of its deliberations, he assembled the attendees in an open field and there called upon them to take up arms in a "crusade." Long after the event, this word was coined because combatants were sealed for their struggle by the sign of the cross (in Latin, *crux*, from which was formed the French word *croisade*). Only the papacy could authorize such a war, and no crusade could be called by the name without a pope's formal proclamation. Assuming leadership of this radical turn in clerical authority, Urban gave a speech at Clermont that established a new form of Christian homiletics designed not primarily to preach repentance but to stir indignation and direct it toward the achievement of a great common cause. In fact, the crusading homily would become a standard feature of Western culture for centuries. It would be issued forcefully by every rank of the clerical hierarchy, from pope to hermit. And it would be received with enthusiasm by every rank of layman, from king to peasant.

In the course of this, history's first call to crusade, Urban laid out the Augustinian argument justifying the war he had in mind by insisting that it must be fought with restraint and with the moral intention of liberating Christians from Muslim tyranny. But he went well beyond the doctrine of a just war. In a brilliant pitch to the sentiments of his feudal audience,

Pope Urban II

he presented the crusade as an armed pilgrimage that would bring participants the remission of penance due for their sins, a dispensation known as an "indulgence."

For the Christian knights arranged in front of him, whose memories were filled with the darkness of years of violence, such a promise must have been awesome. Their troubled consciences would be freed. And Urban promised even more than this. Those who gave their lives in the war, like Leo IX's soldier-saints at Civitate, would actually have their sins taken away. They could trust him in this, he asserted, for he was the successor to Saint Peter, in whose charge Christ Himself had placed the keys of the kingdom of heaven.

And the pope went yet further. Contrary to the needs expressed by the Byzantine emissaries, he called for an expedition to the center of the sanctified world, the geographical focal point of the Incarnation itself. The armed pilgrimage would target "the premier devotional destination in Christian cosmology," known as the Anastasis, or Church of the Holy Sepulcher in Jerusalem.[29] If victorious, it would bring combatants into the heavenly presence of the True Cross.

Pope Urban's appeal worked. Standing in the cold November air, thousands of bishops, knights, and peasants repeated the audacious words of Western Christendom's new clerical leader: "God wills it!" (*Deus volt*).

What followed was the First Crusade, and in 1099 it did in fact culminate in the capture of Jerusalem. This, of course, was of no help to the Byzantines,

---

29   Thomas Asbridge, *The First Crusade* (Oxford: Oxford University Press, 2004), 38.

who were being threatened by the Turks in the east and not the Arabs in the south. In fact, when Emperor Alexios learned that his ambassadors' request had apparently been used as a pretext for a very different kind of military operation, he grew cold to the whole endeavor. Crusading armies, as they passed through Constantinople on their way to Palestine, were treated with unveiled contempt and suspicion. The Latins themselves returned the sentiments, complaining that the Greeks were haughty in their sense of cultural superiority and cowardly in refusing to join wholeheartedly in the expedition. When cities like Antioch fell to the crusaders, therefore, they ignored the ancient claims of Byzantium and turned the region of the Levant into a confederation of Latin colonies. Before long, the Crusader States (known often as Outremer) occupied the eastern shores of the Mediterranean.

Despite significant colonization of the region, the Crusader States were highly vulnerable to attack. In 1144 the Turkish ruler Zengi captured the colony of Edessa, provoking Pope Eugene to launch the mostly unsuccessful Second Crusade. Its combatants now included royalty such as King Louis VII of France, who brought along his adventuresome queen Eleanor of Aquitaine (soon to be divorced and remarried to Henry II of England). In 1187 Jerusalem fell to the Arab sultan Saladin after he set a deadly trap for the crusaders at the Battle of Hattin.

Pope Gregory VIII now ordered the Third Crusade, which achieved better results than the second. It did not occur without mishaps, however. Along the way, Emperor Frederick Barbarossa drowned while crossing a river. King Philip II of France and King Richard the Lionheart of England both arrived in Palestine with their armies intact, and in 1191 succeeded in recapturing Acre from the Arabs. However, they soon fell afoul of each other, which led to the early departure of Philip. Richard, left on his own, was unable to recover Jerusalem. And so this war also failed in its primary objective. The king of England was even abducted by a German prince during his journey home and held for ransom. More crusades would follow during the course of the thirteenth century, but none would have the success of the first.

The violence of the crusades was naturally horrendous and would have made Augustine blanch. Even before the First Crusade began, recruitment efforts in the German Rhineland provoked ghastly mob violence against the Jews. When the ragtag army finally made its way through the Balkans, it treated the local Christian population to incessant brigandage. Once it crossed the Straits of Bosphorus, the assault on cities was particularly cruel. The citizens of Antioch—many of whom were Christian—were simply annihilated. When Jerusalem fell, it was said by contemporaries—with exaggeration no doubt, but ominously suggestive—that the streets flowed knee-high with blood.

Richard the Lionheart's actions at Acre are perhaps the most appalling. After the fall of the city to the crusaders, he negotiated an exchange of Arab prisoners for the True Cross. When Saladin appeared to stall, the "poet king" proceeded to massacre the three thousand unarmed men in his custody, all within sight of Saladin's camp. For this reason the crusaders never saw the True Cross again.

The crusades began as wars of reconquest in the face of militant Islam. However, the reformed papacy soon recognized a broader purpose for holy warfare. In 1209, Pope Innocent ordered a crusade to suppress the heretical Albigensians (also known as Cathars) in southern France. These were Christians who adhered to a gnostic heresy similar to others that had appeared in the East during earlier periods. It claimed that this world is fundamentally evil and bereft of God's presence. This heresy was by nature opposed to the sacraments at the heart of the paradisiacal culture that still flourished in the West. It also rejected the clerical hierarchy, which may have given it influence among those opposed to the reformers' clericalism. When a papal legate was murdered while preaching against the heresy, Innocent decided to send in an army and extirpate it by force. To promote this holy war, also deemed a crusade, he announced the same indulgence offered during wars against the Muslims. For the Albigensians, he stated, "are worse than them."[30]

The Albigensian Crusade lasted years, but the deadliest and most atrocious single battle was the sack of Beziers in 1209. The crusading commander was a member of the Roman Catholic clergy, an abbot by the name of Arnauld Aimery. He was asked how to distinguish heretics from

---

30   Tyerman, *God's War*, 583.

non-heretics during the battle. His reported response was to order his men to "kill them all, for God will know his own." Twenty thousand Christian civilians were thus slaughtered in this one action alone.

The Albigensian Crusade was launched by Innocent to exterminate a heresy, and eventually it succeeded. It thus served to alter the way in which heresy and religious heterogeneity was confronted in Western Christendom. For the first millennium of the Church, violence had not typically been the way bishops and rulers dealt with heresy. Arius, for instance, was the most notorious heresiarch in history, but as a result of his condemnation at the First Ecumenical Council, he was not subjected to torture or execution but mere banishment. In an exceptional case, a bishop named Priscillian was executed for sorcery in 385, but the ruling against him was issued by the state and not the clergy. Indeed, the clerical contemporaries Martin of Tours, Ambrose of Milan, and Pope Siricius all protested the judgment on religious grounds. Only in the eleventh century did heresy begin to be met with lethal punishment, with the reformed clergy playing the leading role. The earliest such case was the execution of a group of heretics in Orleans in 1022.

But the mass slaughter that was the Albigensian Crusade created a totally new precedent. Religious persecution became institutionalized. To formalize this, in 1233 Pope Gregory IX created the papal inquisition. This body came to regularize the process throughout the Roman Catholic Church. It possessed the powers of surveillance and punishment, and they were much greater than anything seen before. They were supported by the bureaucratization of the papal court and the expansion of religious legal codes. The inquisition, in short, would have been impossible without the rise of the Papal Reformation.

It is noteworthy that no institutional form of religious persecution was ever introduced in the Christian East. Because of Western historiographical ignorance of the Orthodox Church, however, the inquisition would come to represent, for secular intellectuals in modern times, the illegitimacy of any civilization grounded in Christianity, whether Western or Eastern.

Ecclesiastical Colonialism

ONE OF THE MOST DIVISIVE outcomes of the crusades was the Latinization of Eastern Christendom. The territories conquered by the crusades contained large populations of Christians. In the cities, these were mostly under the jurisdiction of one of the ancient Orthodox patriarchates. In rural areas, Christians tended to be a mix of the Orthodox and monophysite or Nestorian communities. However, the contempt for all forms of Eastern Christianity harbored by agents of the papacy since the time of Cardinal Humbert soon translated into a more or less explicit policy of what Aristeides Papadakis has called "ecclesiastical colonialism."

It took a few years for this policy to be fully implemented, particularly because Urban II initially intended to allow the Orthodox hierarchy to remain in place. After the fall of Antioch, however, the Norman and French conquerors wrote him to propose a new strategy. It resonated with the ideology of the Papal Reformation and demonstrated how the conquest of the East was intended to result in the extension of papal supremacy there.

"What," they asked the pope, "would be more proper than for 'the father and head of the Christian religion'" to travel to the city once ruled by St. Peter (Antioch) and to enforce, as the apostle's successor, true Christianity there?

> For we have beaten the Turks and the heathen, but we do not know how to defeat the heretics, the Greeks and the Armenians and Syrian Jacobites. We therefore continually entreat you, our dearest father, that you, our father and ruler, will come to the city which is yours, and that you, who are the vicar of St Peter, will sit on his throne and then you will find in us obedient sons, acting rightly in all things, and you will be able to root out and destroy all heresies, of whatever kind they are, by your authority and our strength.

This, as Papadakis observes, was an extraordinary statement. For it reveals that as far as the crusaders were concerned, "Christendom was synonymous exclusively with their own version of Latin, Western, Christianity."[31]

---

31   Papadakis, *The Christian East and the Rise of the Papacy*, 92–93.

Despite Urban's initial misgivings, such ecclesiastical colonialism ultimately prevailed. In the case of Antioch, the Orthodox Patriarch John IV was sent into exile and a Latin bishop put in his place. The same occurred with the ancient patriarchal throne of Jerusalem. One after another, the Orthodox centers of church administration were first disrupted and then usurped by Roman Catholic crusaders. What is more, Eastern liturgical practices were restricted and even replaced. In this way, the goals of the papal legates of 1054 were closer than ever to being achieved. But such developments, rather than fostering the old unity of the first millennium, could only result in the further division of Christendom.

The final act in this tragedy was perhaps the most devastating. It occurred under one of the most ambitious popes of the Papal Reformation, Innocent III (r. 1198–1216).

It was he who brought to completion a century and a half of institutional reform. This was evident at a momentous council he hosted at the Lateran Palace in 1215. Nearly fifteen hundred bishops and abbots attended at his command and endorsed his reform program. Since the time of Leo IX, papal reformers had been using councils to advance their cause. At this, the most authoritative council ever held in the West, the three principal changes demanded since the time of Gregory VII were placed above all others. Thus, simony was abolished (Canon 63), clerical celibacy was instituted (Canon 14), and a ban on lay investiture (the appointment of bishops by secular rulers) was imposed (Canon 43). The universal jurisdiction of the papacy was again asserted, signified by the conferral of a vestment called a *pallium* that the pope would bestow on other bishops (Canon 5).

Yet Innocent went further than even Gregory VII, if this were possible. The title Vicar of Saint Peter had long been accorded to the pope to emphasize his episcopal succession from the first of the apostles. This was not enough for Innocent. He now introduced a more daring designation. He claimed to be nothing less than the "Vicar of Christ." Though the distinction may have seemed slight, like so much of the reformation it served to undermine the paradisiacal culture of the West.

At the dawn of Christendom, traditional Christianity had declared that

God is present in this world by virtue of the Incarnation. Jesus Christ, having formed His Church, continues by the Holy Spirit to be present within her life, especially in the sacraments. As a result, Christian culture possessed a principle of heavenly immanence, which nourished the civilization to which it gave rise.

The presence of Christ in the sacramental life of His Church was assured by the episcopate, those successors to the original apostles who received the Holy Spirit at Pentecost. Christ had foretold that event, stating that He would send the Holy Spirit from the Father, and that the Holy Spirit "proceeds from the Father" (John 15:26). This latter point is what prevented the Eastern fathers from endorsing the Frankish innovation of the filioque when it became a controversial issue in the ninth century.

In union with the East, the papacy had at that time likewise condemned the alteration of the Creed. As we have seen, however, the papacy's position on the issue was reversed after the millennium, when German imperial pressure—the same forces that on a smaller scale had been at work within the hated proprietary system—was brought to bear on the vulnerable pontificate of Benedict VIII. The filioque now came to be said within the Mass at Rome. And with the northern influx inaugurated by Leo IX, the papacy solidified its adherence to the Frankish innovation. As Leo's legate, Cardinal Humbert himself (who hailed from France) not only insisted that Constantinople embrace the filioque, but in his ignorance of church history actually expressed acute scorn that the Greeks had "removed" it from the original Creed.

As Innocent now imposed a new title asserting the pope's unique association with Christ, the filioque again cast its divisive shadow. For if he was the vicar or "substitute" of Christ and not just of Peter—who was after all only one of the numerous apostles—then he alone became the source of all episcopal authority on earth. This, of course, had been the most basic claim of the Papal Reformation. And if the pope alone is the source of episcopal authority, then he alone, as the Vicar of Christ, is the source of all sacramental grace.

In the East, traditional Christianity continued to assign to every bishop (and, by extension, to every priest under his rule) equality in grace, making Christ present in every diocese and parish community. Papal supremacy, on the other hand, now made Christ's presence contingent on the person of the pope. And since the Holy Spirit was now understood (because of the filioque) to proceed from Christ, the pope, as his vicar, regulated or controlled the distribution of the sacramental gifts that bring paradise into the world.

What is more, the result of this was that the Church, which had now become highly clericalist as a result of the Papal Reformation, was understood more and more as an institution that regulates sacraments rather than a mystical body that receives grace in an unmediated way from the Holy Spirit. Rather than being the presence of the kingdom of heaven in the world, as she continued to be in the East, the Church was increasingly seen as a clerical organization with the task of transforming the world. In Augustinian terminology, she was the city of God whose ministry is to reform the city of man "for the better." Western Christendom, as it struggled to preserve the transformational imperative, was thus beginning to lose its experience of heavenly immanence.[32]

But for the time being, Pope Innocent III was far more concerned with fighting crusades. He would in fact be credited with three of the greatest. The war against the Albigensians we have already considered. At the end of his pontificate he would also call for the Fifth Crusade. But it was the Fourth Crusade, conceived almost immediately upon Innocent's election, that would, more than any other action of the papacy, seal forever the Great Division of Christendom.

Less than a year after becoming the Vicar of Christ, Innocent issued a papal bull calling for another armed pilgrimage to Jerusalem. At the time he did so, the Orthodox, who were presumed as always to benefit from the war, were in fact outcasts in Latin Christian opinion. About a generation earlier, in 1182, a mob of Byzantines had attacked the mostly Venetian colony of Roman Catholics in Constantinople, destroying their shops and setting fire

---

32 For a reflection on the relationship between papal supremacy and the filioque, see Philip Sherrard, *The Greek East and the Latin West: A Study in the Christian Tradition* (Limni, Greece: Denise Harvey, 2002), 83–90.

to their houses. The death toll of the outrage rose to the thousands, so great had Greek resentment of the Latin population in the city grown. But now the Latins had much to resent, especially those of Venice.

Innocent's call for the Fourth Crusade in 1198 was not realized for four years, and when it was, it went terribly off course. From the start, its mercenary interests outweighed any spiritual purpose. French leaders were

Pope Innocent III

dependent on Venetian transport to carry them overseas to the Holy Land, and when they ran out of money they decided to sack the city of Zara on the Adriatic to pay the Venetians. This defied one of Innocent's few prohibitions, that no Christian lands be despoiled (the residents of Zara were in fact Roman Catholics).

A strongly worded excommunication followed. "Behold," the pope wrote,

> *your gold has turned into base metal and your silver has almost completely rusted since, departing from the purity of your plan . . . you have, so to speak, withdrawn your hand from the plough . . . for when . . . you should have hastened to the land flowing with milk and honey, you turned away, going astray in the direction of the desert.*[33]

These were poetic words full of biblical allusions, but they were little more than that. Eager to get the stalled crusaders moving again, Innocent soon lifted the sentence and urged them forward. Yet the expedition's insolvency persisted, despite large hauls of booty from the defeated Zadarians. While the crusaders were considering their dilemma, a new opportunity unexpectedly presented itself.

The crusaders were notified that a claimant to the Byzantine throne named Alexios Angelos was willing to pay them whatever they needed if they would help him in his cause. He was the son of a recently deposed emperor who had been overthrown and blinded by his own brother, confusingly named Alexios III. The usurper's nephew and namesake convinced the

---

33   Quoted in Jonathan Phillips, *The Fourth Crusade and the Sack of Constantinople* (New York: Penguin, 2004), 124.

crusaders to assemble their men and sail for the Queen of Cities, where he promised money would be paid to the Venetians to continue the journey on to Jerusalem. As it turned out, the diversion became the final destination of the Fourth Crusade.

After landing near Constantinople in 1203, the crusaders realized they had been duped. The pretender did succeed in reclaiming the throne as Alexios IV, but once he did, he repudiated his debt. This enraged the crusaders, whose threats of retaliation provoked another palace revolt, during which the new emperor was murdered. His assassin and successor, yet another Alexios (this time, the Fifth), felt no obligation to the crusaders and indicated as much.

When the crusaders held a council in the spring of 1204 to decide what to do next, the clergy that were with them urged them to attack Constantinople. These clerics even went so far as to assure them that the bloodletting ahead would be forgiven because the people of Constantinople were now complicit in regicide. The indulgence offered by the Vicar of Christ would be valid in the conquest too. After all, they observed, the Greeks were renegades from the Church of Rome. As one contemporary account reported, the crusaders were thus assured by the clergy that "if you fight to conquer this land with the right intention of bringing it under the authority of Rome, all those of you who die after making confession shall benefit from the indulgence granted by the pope."[34] After days of siege, during which the crusaders battered the city's sea walls from their ships (a vessel in the lead was named the *Paradiso*), the city defenses were finally breached.

And they were breached by . . . a Roman Catholic priest. Alleumes of Clari was one of the innumerable warrior-priests of the contemporary West. He had joined the crusade to save his soul, intending to drive the Muslims out of Jerusalem and plant his feet in the Church of the Holy Sepulcher. However, schismatic Constantinople with its rich spiritual treasurers now proved equally attractive to his pilgrim sensibilities. When a postern gate was discovered in the wall, he leapt through it with haste, and then, discovering a crowd of Greek defenders on the other side, drew his sword and

---

34   Quoted in Tyerman, *God's War*, 551.

rushed at them with a war cry. So fierce was the countenance of Father Alleumes that the area was quickly evacuated, and he was free to return to the gate. There he loosed the crusading army on a city that had never, in her nine hundred years of existence, fallen to a foreign power.

The day was April 12, 1204, which happened to be Great and Holy Monday. The crusaders passed the first three days of Passion Week slaughtering unarmed civilians, raping women, and robbing the city of its wealth. The most symbolic sacrilege occurred at Hagia Sophia. There, the invaders smashed the holy altar to pieces, hoping to pocket a gemstone or a shard of its exquisite marble to keep as a trophy. Icons were looted or smashed. Reliquaries were desecrated. And when the soldiers began loading their plunder onto the backs of mules, someone brought in a French camp follower and placed her on the patriarchal throne. As the demonic spectacle continued, she danced, waved a wine bottle in the air, and sang songs to the bawdy amusement of all.

Historians often characterize Pope Innocent's response to the news of the sack of Constantinople as one of outrage. It is true that a full year after the event he did send a letter to one crusader lamenting the fact that now the Greeks would regard the Latins as blasphemers who had subjected fellow Christians to "the works of hell." And it is certainly possible to take this at face value and conclude that the pope was truly appalled by the reports of violence and greed he had by then received. How could any Christian bishop react otherwise?

However, there can be no doubt that such an advocate for papal supremacy as he was also welcomed the opportunity of establishing one more ecclesiastical colony in the East. And what a colony it was. In fact, Innocent's earliest documented communications to the conquerors—which deserve to be viewed as the most spontaneous and therefore telling—speak of the event as a "miracle" of God. The city of Constantine and the cradle of Christian statecraft had been transferred, he gloated, from "the proud to the humble, from the disobedient to the obedient, from schismatics to Catholics."[35] As Jonathan Phillips argues, only after a year had passed and the crusaders

---

35   Quoted in Phillips, *The Fourth Crusade*, 299.

decided to abandon the expedition to Jerusalem did the pope change his opinion and express dissatisfaction with the outcome. It is very significant that at no point did Innocent, whose supreme authority was responsible for the crusade, issue an order to withdraw from the conquered Christian land. He did not even excommunicate those who had wetted their swords with Christian blood.

What he did do is place the patriarchate of Constantinople under the jurisdiction of Rome. A Venetian nobleman named Thomas Morosini was elected by the crusaders to replace the exiled Orthodox patriarch John X, as the Orthodox patriarchs of Antioch and Jerusalem had earlier been replaced. As a result, the very throne from which Michael Cerularius had claimed ecumenical status and had defied the excommunications of Cardinal Humbert now belonged to the Roman Catholic Church. The Great Schism, it seemed, had finally ended.

The Latin Empire of Constantinople would only last half a century. Immediately, a Byzantine government in exile arose in Nicaea and bided its time until it could reclaim the capital. But until it did, Latin colonists systematically despoiled the wealthiest city in the world of almost everything of value it contained. Much of this was the ordinary spoils of war. Most notoriously, the Venetian doge Enrico Dandolo—the mastermind of the conquest—arranged to have a famous quartet of bronze horses removed from the hippodrome and relocated to his native Saint Mark's Square. Though replaced with replicas at the end of the twentieth century, they long symbolized Venetian power and influence within Western Christendom.

Far more debilitating to the paradisiacal culture of the East was the theft of the city's holy objects. Thousands of relics, icons, and items of liturgical plate were removed from the city's temples and monasteries by greedy bishops and abbots eager to endow their homeland with spiritual treasure. Western Christendom therefore became the destination of what one scholar has called "a great holy diaspora" of saints' relics.[36] Ironically, then, even when colonized, Eastern Christendom exercised an influence on the formation of the West.

---

36   David M. Perry, *Sacred Plunder: Venice and the Aftermath of the Fourth Crusade* (University Park, PA: Pennsylvania State University Press, 2016), 3.

The sack of Constantinople, 1204

Reaching the Limits in Russia

THE STORY OF THE CRUSADES against the Orthodox was not yet complete, however. In the Baltic borderlands between Russia and Germany lived a diverse population of pagans. German knights, eager for new territory, regarded them as fit subjects for an expanded Holy Roman Empire. A Wendish Crusade in 1147 resulted, bringing the Germans ever deeper into eastern Europe. Popes such as Innocent III, always looking for new crusading opportunities, encouraged further expansion to the east in the decades that followed. In fact, almost every year the German knights and their supportive clergy fought campaigns against their neighbors. In these missionary wars, territorial conquest and spiritual conversion merged, revealing, as one historian has put it, "how far a positive ideology of legitimate religious violence had penetrated the western Christian world and how far cultural and territorial acquisitiveness marched with spiritual imperialism."[37]

But not all of the populations targeted by the Germans were pagans. Beyond the Wends were the Russians, and they, as we know, had embraced Christianity following the conversion of Grand Prince Vladimir in 988. During the reign of one of his many sons, Yaroslav the Wise (r. 1016–1054), Christianity transformed nearly every element of Russian statecraft. The

---

37 Tyerman, *God's War*, 679.

state began to collect taxes to support the clergy. It built churches such as Saint Sophia Cathedral in Kiev, which as its name implies was inspired by Hagia Sophia in Constantinople, and like its namesake was intended as a monument to heavenly immanence. The government established an academy to facilitate the translation of patristic texts and the foundation of theological education.

Finally and most symbolically, Yaroslav appointed the first native primate of Russia. Little is known of Metropolitan Ilarion of Kiev, but he left behind a widely disseminated composition entitled *Sermon on the Law and Grace*, which emphatically defined Russia as a Christian nation that participated fully with all other Christian nations in the life of Christendom. This vision was further elaborated in the twelfth century by Grand Prince Vladimir Monomakh (r. 1113–1125), whose *Testament* called on successors to embrace transformative principles from the Sermon on the Mount such as care for the poor and the forgiveness of enemies.

A very different personality was Grand Prince Andrey Bogolyubsky (r. 1157–1174). One of Kievan Russia's most bellicose rulers, he bore little resemblance to meek predecessors like Boris and Gleb, whose canonization as passion-bearers had established the kenotic principle within the official political culture. This is ironic, for Andrey maintained a strong love for Russia's first saints and kept the sword of Boris, left unused at the time of this voluntary death, over his bed as a kind of relic.

Andrey came from a rapacious line of warlords. His father was Yury Dologoruky, whose sobriquet means "long-arms" because of his neverending seizure of other princes' lands. One of his most prized acquisitions, for instance, was a small hunting settlement named Moscow. For his part, Andrey's political ambition was insatiable. As prince of the town of Vladimir, he waged a series of ruthless wars against other Russian principalities. Among his enemies was mighty Novgorod, which nearly fell to his siege. A campaign against Kiev, on the other hand, was successful. In its aftermath he sacked the city, appropriating its valuables and shipping its holy objects off to Vladimir. One icon of the Virgin Mary embracing Christ in affection came thereafter to be known by the name of his capital. This Vladimir

Icon of the Mother of God became one of the greatest treasures of Russian Christendom.

Andrey realized that the Kievan state was chronically weakened by its decentralization and a political culture that encouraged the kind of internecine war he himself was so skilled at fighting. Therefore, he did something bold. He began to model his government on that of Byzantium. His goal was to impose a centralized monarchy comparable to if not actually as absolute as autocracy. He established a new court at the town of Bogolyubovo (hence his sobriquet, which means "God-loving") near Vladimir and lobbied the ecumenical patriarch to elevate the bishop there to the status of metropolitan. He failed in this, but that did not prevent him from building the greatest churches in Kievan Russia. In Vladimir these included Dormition Cathedral and Saint Dimitry Church, and at Bogolyubovo the famous Church of the Protection of the Birthgiver of God. He also instituted what became one of the most widely observed holidays in Russian Christendom by the same name, celebrated with great solemnity on October 1 ever since.

Andrey was ruthless, and he provoked the same ruthlessness in his enemies. These were chiefly the boyars of his capital, who risked losing their aristocratic powers if the Russian state moved in an autocratic direction. So, one night while Andrey was sleeping, twenty members of his court crept into his bedchamber and ran him through with their swords. The scene was ghastly. Andrey might have defended himself with the sword of Boris kept over his bed, but it had been removed in preparation for the regicide. Unarmed, he nevertheless fought desperately against his assailants. But after much resistance, he finally succumbed to their blows. Taking him for dead, the boyars returned down the palace staircase and prepared to depart. But suddenly they again heard his groans. Amazingly, having survived the initial pummeling, he had somehow managed to crawl to the base of the staircase. There they now finished him off for good, while he vainly cried out for help from the loyal servants who never came—possibly because none of his servants were actually loyal.

Though Andrey's rule had been marked by an implacable ambition and an insatiable desire for conquest, the pathetic helplessness of his death reminded Russians of Boris and Gleb, and he was eventually canonized with them with the unique national designation of "passion-bearer." One of Andrey's pious biographers even places the words of the dying Boris—modeled on Christ's words from the cross—on his lips. Fedotov considered this a "religiously tactless" statement.[38] With our modern aversion for political hagiography, we might agree. But that does not change the fact that the canonization of Andrey represented another example of traditional Christianity's cultural transformation. The official culture of Russia defined as virtuous the purported piety of the prince, and not his ambition.

As it turned out, Andrey Bogolyubsky was ahead of his time. His efforts to unite Kievan Russia by imposing autocratic policies imported from Byzantium proved a failure, though they would one day be taken up more successfully by his Muscovite heirs. For now, the decentralized state with its propensity for civil war prevented a unified political and military resolve when it mattered most.

In the south, Russian principalities had long been used to military incursions from the steppe frontier with Asia. But their leaders, divided by petty interests, lacked the entire strength of Russia to deal with the threat. In 1185, Igor of Novgorod-Seversk unilaterally led a doomed campaign against the fierce nomads from the steppes known as the Polovtsy. Not long afterward, the Russians were amazed to find these enemies seeking an alliance with them against a much more menacing power coming from the east.

At the Battle of the Kalka River in 1223, they met these new enemies. They were the Mongols, and the engagement did not go well for the Russians. The few princes who survived it were bound together, and a platform was placed on top of them. While the Mongol generals feasted on this platform, their prisoners were slowly crushed to death below.

The Mongol juggernaut wiped out nearly every principality of Russia. Their method of war relied on terror. Any town that resisted conquest was reduced to ashes and its unarmed residents massacred. Toward the end of

---

38   George P. Fedotov, *The Russian Religious Mind, Volume I: Kievan Christianity* (Belmont, MA: Nordland Publishing, 1975), 109.

1237 Ryazan, one of the easternmost towns, was the first to go. Its residents did not really know what hit it, but a chronicler later recounted the experience of the siege.

> On the dawn of the sixth day the pagan warriors began to storm the city. . . . And the Tatars [Mongols] came to the Cathedral of the Assumption of the Blessed Virgin, and they cut to pieces the Great Princess Agrippina, her daughters-in-law, and other princesses. They burned to death the bishops and the priests and put the torch to the holy church. And the Tatars cut down many people, including women and children. Still others were drowned in the river. And they killed without exception all monks and priests. And they burned this holy city with all its beauty and wealth, and they captured the relatives of the Ryazan princes, the princes of Kiev and Chernigov. And churches of God were destroyed, and much blood was spilled on the holy altars. And not one man remained alive in the city. All were dead. . . . And there was not even anyone to mourn the dead. Neither father nor mother could mourn their dead children, nor the children their fathers and mothers. Nor could a brother

Church of the Protection of the Theotokos, Bogolyubovo
Shutterstock @ Sergei Sokolnikov

mourn the death of his brother, nor relatives their relatives. All were dead. *And this happened for our sins.*[39]

The culminating sentence of this agonizing statement is interesting and significant. Things might be changing in the West, but the old Christendom to which Russia belonged had, after all, cultivated in its members an abiding instinct toward repentance, not indignation.

The chronicler of Ryazan's fall spoke of bloodshed on the altar. This was apparently no hyperbole. The town of Vladimir was the scene of a particularly heinous act of savagery. Once the conquerors had smashed their way through the city's defenses, they trapped a large number of residents in Dormition Cathedral, built by Andrey Bogolyubsky, where his body was buried. After a desperate resistance, the church's heavy doors were knocked down and the pagans rushed in to kill every last Christian, some of whom had taken refuge around the altar table.

The only large towns to evade destruction were Novgorod and Pskov. Otherwise, all that remained of Kievan Russia after three years of Mongol destruction was Kiev itself. And in 1240 it too was laid waste. A papal envoy to the Mongols later reported, after traveling through what had once been Russia's capital city, that virtually nothing remained of it but charred ruins and the half-buried skeletons of its doomed Christian defenders. Almost all of Russia now lay prostrate beneath the Mongol yoke.

Yet the scourge of foreign invasion was not yet at an end. For in 1240, the very year Kiev fell to the pagans from the east, the pope of Rome ordered that Roman Catholic armies attack Russia from the west.

Gregory IX, founder of the papal inquisition, assigned to the crusading order known as the Teutonic Knights the responsibility for carrying out the operation. The Germans had long eyed Novgorod and Pskov hungrily, and now that they were isolated from the rest of Russia and vulnerable to attack, they believed the time had come to strike. Gregory's papal

---

39 "Tale of the Destruction of Riazan," in *Medieval Russia's Epics, Chronicles, and Tales*, edited and translated by Serge A. Zenkovsky (New York: Meridian Books, 1974), 198–207.

legate William of Sabina, when he arrived on the scene from Rome, agreed with them. Novgorod and Pskov were leading powers in the region and had been engaged in Orthodox missionary activities among the local pagans for decades. Conquest would not only clear the way for Roman Catholic evangelization among pagans, it could also result in the colonization of another center of Eastern Christendom.

In 1242 the Teutonic Knights met the army of the Russians on the frozen surface of Lake Peipus. Though the crusaders took the initiative with a cavalry charge, the Russians under Grand Prince Alexander Nevsky (r. 1236–1252) withstood the assault. Then, as the heavily armed crusaders tired of battle, Alexander ordered a counterattack that drove them across the lake. Those who were not killed fled in disarray back to the West.

The Battle on the Ice was the turning point in the Northern Crusades. Starting with a campaign against pagans, the conflict inevitably brought the armies of Rome against those of the Orthodox. But unlike the Greeks, the Russians managed to stave off colonization. According to one Russian chronicler, this was due to heavenly intercession. The army of Alexander Nevsky, he claimed, had been saved from foreign aggression by the saintly passion-bearers Boris and Gleb.[40]

What was certain was that the division of Christendom would not be healed by force of arms.

The Battle on the Ice

---

40   Eric Christiansen, *The Northern Crusades* (London: Penguin, 1997), 134.

PART II

The New Christendom and the Old

CHAPTER THREE

Popes, Kings, Monks, and Doctors

T HE PAPAL REFORMATION HAD ALTERED forever the character of
the West. Not even the Carolingian epoch, in which the very concept
of the West was invented, was as formative as the generation that spanned
the election of Pope Leo IX and the death of Pope Gregory VII. The century
that followed, as we have seen, only consolidated the changes. Like the Protestant Reformation yet to come (and toward which, as we will see, it inevitably led), the Papal Reformation marked a turning point in the rise and fall
of what the West once was.

Some historians have called it the "Gregorian Revolution," but its radical
effects were by no means limited to the papacy. Nearly every constituent
element of Western culture and civilization was affected. In the next chapter
we will consider the cultural effects of the Papal Reformation, from clericalism to penitential pessimism. In this one we will explore the institutions
that constituted civilization.

These include, in the first place, the papacy itself, which had been transformed during the eleventh century from one of several ancient patriarchates into the mystical heart of a self-consciously *Roman* Catholic Church.
As we have seen, the very word *papatus* was first coined at this time. Other
institutions were introduced to support the papacy's revolutionary designs.
In Rome, the newly created papal court served as its administration and was

supported by a greatly augmented body of canon law. Kings were ordered on pain of deposition to uphold and defend the papacy. Soldiers were mobilized and wars fought to extend its jurisdiction in all directions, especially to the east. Monks were enlisted as its advocates. Universities were founded and professional theologians recruited to support its clerical hierarchy. A newly created inquisition monitored fidelity to it, and deviations could bring torture and execution on those guilty of them.

The Papal Reformation had been at once the cause and consequence of the Great Division, permanently separating the West from Orthodoxy. It produced a Christian civilization unlike that which had existed during the first millennium. The old Christendom—whose civilization continued uninterrupted in the East—had risen in a largely organic way. Its transformational imperative was driven by humility and repentance, key virtues of traditional Christianity. But if this imperative had revealed the presence of paradise in this world, now, in the West, a vast gulf seemed to yawn between the two. Indignation provided the bridge, becoming the virtue and motivation for an institutionalized "pursuit of paradise." Christianity became, in its indignant mode, an instrument for the engineering of a new order, a kind of proto-utopia.

This was not, to be sure, a secular utopia. As we shall see, the kingdom of heaven remained its standard of cultural integrity. But with its instrumental approach to Christianity, it set the West on a course toward modernity.

In the meantime, paradise became increasingly institutionalized by the popes, kings, monks, and doctors who led it there. This was both the genius and the tragedy of the new Christendom.

The Papal Mystique

FROM ITS INCEPTION, THE NEW Christendom was defined by reform. In this it was the offspring of the old Christendom, and in many ways it brought the transformational imperative of traditional Christianity to a kind of fulfillment. But as we have already seen, it did so by distorting that imperative. Though the new Christendom claimed to be the successor to the civilization born of Pentecost, it came into being as much by revolution as by inheritance.

The Papal Reformation had introduced a concept of reform that was as different from its predecessor as it was dynamic. In fact, its restless ambition betrayed this difference. Reform came from on high rather than from within. It was no longer gentle, no longer voluntary. It was insistent and at times violent. The street fighting of the Patarenes and the civil war of the Saxons were only its most visible expressions. This reform was not spontaneous but carefully planned and methodically conceived.

Reform issued from the Lateran Palace, but it was formulated by something that can, with caution, be called Augustinianism. As we have seen, Augustine was a dualist. He posited two distinct societies in the world, which he called the "city of man" and the "city of God." He also placed great emphasis on the imperative of "reform for the better," though he had limited its application to the personal experience of repentance and spiritual transformation.

Augustinianism, on the other hand, went further. Lagging behind the saint's own writings by centuries, this vast intellectual resource became Christendom's first-ever "system of thought." In the West, where early theological output was comparatively small, Augustine towered over all other authorities. The East, by contrast, generated a wide range of theologians, which had prevented any single one of them from overshadowing the others. The fourth century, into which Augustine was born, produced no other Western intellectual of equal stature, while in the East flourished such theological heavyweights as Athanasius of Alexandria, Basil the Great, Gregory of Nyssa, and Gregory the Theologian.

It was not until the eighth century that Western Christendom produced an equivalent intellectual flowering. This flowering came through the agency of the Carolingians. And it came at a time when the proprietary system was beginning to choke the life out of the Church. For Frankish theologians, Augustinianism provided a remedy. First, it had the virtue of originating with a Latin father (the Franks detested the Greek East). More importantly, it could be traced to one who had also been confronted by encroachments on the Church. Of course, Augustine himself had lived in a world in which the forces of pagandom seemed as strong as those of Christendom. Not so the Franks. For them, the world was not divided between pagandom and Christendom; the world *was* Christendom.

So the Franks applied Augustinian dualism to a unitary society in which existed two spiritually defined poles, the elect and the reprobate. For the monastic reformers that followed in their footsteps, this paralleled the difference between the cloister and the castle. But when a monastic definition of the elect was taken beyond the walls of the cloister and, in the time of Leo IX, placed on the throne of Saint Peter, a new attitude toward the world became inevitable. Armed with this dualistic concept of Christian society, papal reformers undertook an evangelization greater than that of the apostles—whose primate, they were quick to point out, was the mystical source of their authority.

Peter and the other apostles had preached repentance. The new clerical elite professed indignation. They were set not on personal but on institutional transformation.

Ironically, this resulted in a marked secularization of the world. Prior to the eleventh century, the unitary model of Christian society, formulated first by Eusebius in the fourth century, continued to characterize the cosmology of East and West. But the Papal Reformation changed this. With its bifurcation of society, it subverted one of Christendom's most important sources: heavenly immanence.

As Hans Boersma has noted, the Gregorian Revolution led to a "desacramentalizing of the cosmos." Citing the twentieth-century Roman Catholic theologian Yves Congar, Boersma has argued that the manner in which Leo IX and those who followed in his footsteps approached ecclesiastical authority was momentously counterproductive to a spiritually healthy society. The papacy may have wanted to reform what it considered a society of reprobates, but the way in which it pursued evangelization caused long-term harm to Christian ecclesiology. By removing authority from a Church defined broadly as the body of Christ and relocating it to a "church" now defined narrowly as the ordained clergy, it deprived Christendom of its ancient culture of heavenly immanence. According to Boersma's summary of the first millennium,

> *people had believed that God was at work in the church in a rather direct fash-*
> *ion. God, according to this view, made his active presence felt in the church*
> *in a quite immediate way. There had been little need for careful reflection on*
> *the exact delimitations of the church's juridical powers, because people had*
> *regarded authority not so much as a bureaucratic or juridical structure, but*
> *more as God working actively in the life of the church.*[1]

The reformation papacy, he continues, changed all of this. Eager to impose good order on Christendom, it introduced a juridical understanding of divine presence. Only canonically ordained priests who were free of avarice (that is, not tainted by simony) and ritually pure (that is, practicing clerical celibacy) could mediate between God and man. And, of course, such priests must perform their sacerdotal actions in communion with and submission to the pope, without whom there could be no valid sacraments. An ecclesiological culture thus arose in which heavenly immanence was no longer intrinsic to the divine-human body of Christ. It was now extrinsically mediated through the clerical—that is, human—establishment.

What Boersma is talking about here, in part, is the rise of clericalism. By imposing the high standard of celibacy on priests and forestalling imperial interference in episcopal appointments, the newly conceived papacy set the clergy above the laity in a radically different way than it had existed during the first millennium. The result was the bifurcation of society that we discussed in the previous chapter. Two exclusive spiritual classes, the clergy and the laity, now existed. And without a doubt it was the clergy that, as an extension of the papacy, exercised sacramental preeminence.

Particularly ominous for the future of Christendom was the way in which the sacramental presence of Christ came to be restricted by this new clericalism. The Roman Catholic Church was careful not to fall into the errors

---

1   Hans Boersma, *Heavenly Participation: The Weaving of a Sacramental Tapestry*
     (Grand Rapids, MI: Eerdmans, 2011), 54–55.

of Donatism, according to which the validity of sacraments depends on the virtue of the priest. But this did not obviate a tendency to regard the priest as the spiritual superior of his flock and the conduit of divine grace. Scholasticism helped introduce a new way of expressing the priest's place within the liturgical assembly by declaring he stood "in the person of Christ" (*in persona Christi*). With time this understanding could rival the traditional one in which Christ as Head of the Church is present everywhere within her. Accordingly, the priest could come to be seen as the mediator between God and man, and, what is of even graver significance, as the vicar or stand-in for an otherwise absent Christ. And this troublesome possibility was only amplified by the practice of popes, beginning as we saw with Innocent III, assuming the title Vicar of Christ.

What is more, as an order set apart from the rest of lay society, the clergy actually came to be equated with the Church herself. And in turn, the Church became the clergy. Traditional Christianity's doctrine of the body of Christ, in which sacramental communion with God occurred and through which the cosmos experienced heavenly transformation, was in practice greatly distorted. To be sure, this new tendency existed at an informal level and never officially supplanted the old ecclesiology. But in patterns of speech and even in popular conceptions, "the Church" (*ecclesia*) was now the society of clerics set apart from the society of believers in an ecclesiological dualism.

Nowhere was this more in evidence than in the custom of speaking, beginning with the investiture controversy, of a distinction "between church and state." The expression is an absurdity. All members of the state were members of the Church, and all members of the Church within a given geographical place were members of the same state. Never before had Christendom harbored a sense of the Christian ruler and his government being somehow outside of the Church, nor of bishops and priests being divided from the state. This mutilation of the old ecclesiology was an inevitable consequence of the papacy's institutional transformation of society.

The new papal ecclesiology was reinforced by various new papal institutions and practices and was designed to advance them. For instance, the expansion of the papal court under Urban II continued during the twelfth century. The Lateran Palace was now the final tribunal for all of Western Christendom. The pope assumed the status of "universal ordinary," meaning in the vocabulary of legalists that he was the highest appellate judge with jurisdiction over all courts everywhere. It is hard to tell whether he welcomed the flood of cases that now flowed to Rome.

On the one hand, the West now submitted to the pope's juridical authority. His powers reached into the furthest recesses of Europe, enabling him to resolve property disputes in Poland and marital disputes in Spain. A stream of suppliants and penitents flocked to Rome, seeking redress and absolution. In 1200, for example, a parish priest came to the Lateran from England after accidentally killing an infant while riding his horse. The tragedy occurred because he had been fighting a case of insomnia, but he had suspended himself from performing the Mass, according to canon law. Innocent III issued a judgment that was as mild as it was reasonable: in light of his honorable intentions, the priest was restored to his ministry and sent home with only a minor penance.[2]

On the other hand, the pope and his growing staff were simply inundated with legal cases. Alexander III was said to have spent five days a week adjudicating them. Under such circumstances, the popes' time and attention for traditional archpastoral care was greatly limited. Bernard of Clairvaux was only the most famous critic of this development, chastening Pope Eugene III with impunity—as only he could do—for turning the Lateran Palace into a brawling courthouse. What kind of care can the head of the Church provide, the abbot asked sarcastically, if all he does is "litigate or listen to litigants from morning to night"?[3]

But the papal machinery kept churning, aided by the new college of cardinals, whose members effectively became the heads of an ever-widening network of administrative departments. Support for the papal monarchy was also provided by canon lawyers. This was, after all, the era of the "lawyer popes." When a papal vacancy occurred, cardinals showed a decided

---

2   Collins, *Keepers of the Keys of Heaven: A History of the Papacy* (New York: Basic Books, 2009), 251.

3   Barraclough, *Medieval Papacy*, 106.

preference for law professors. Gregory IX (r. 1227–1241) was one of these. Trained at the most celebrated law school of the time, the University of Bologna, he went on as pope to create the legal apparatus of the papal inquisition.

More significant for the exercise of papal supremacy was Gregory's compilation of canon law. Known as the *Decretals,* it was designed to bring together the overwhelming number of legal decrees issued by the popes in recent times. It was in many ways the completion of a process already under way since the time of Gregory VII, whose *Papal Dictate,* as we noted in the previous chapter, asserted papal supremacy in the matter of law. Since that time, a canon lawyer named Gratian had provided a comprehensive legal codification of papal supremacy, establishing the principle that papal decretals take precedence over the canons even of ecumenical councils. There was, as one contemporary remarked, "a new canon law" being elaborated at Rome, and Pope Gregory IX was responsible for consolidating it.[4]

As papal ecclesiology assumed legal and institutional form, it inevitably provoked a reaction from conservatives. Traditional Christianity had always, of course, assigned to the episcopate a position of great authority within the life of the Church. Saint Paul was very outspoken about this, and early fathers followed suit. An early Greek father such as Ignatius of Antioch was really no different in this from early Latin fathers such as Cyprian of Carthage. Both stressed that the liturgical assembly surrounding a local bishop—not any regional metropolitan, let alone patriarch or pope—was the locus of sacramental life. Christ, the "great high priest" (Heb. 4:14), was fully present wherever the local church assembled with her bishop. With the ecclesiological revolution that accompanied the Papal Reformation, however, this changed. And as it did, conservative defenders of the old ecclesiology began to voice their opposition.

Before the end of the eleventh century, for instance, a local bishop in England decried Gregory VII's assertions of supremacy. He is known to scholars as Anonymous of York because he declined to sign his tracts out of apparent fear of retribution. Interestingly, these tracts presented views very

---

4   Ibid., 105.

similar to those of the Orthodox East. They include a defense of royal authority and the principle of ecclesiopolitical symphony. They also defended the institution of priestly marriage, evidently considering it of ancient origin. Perhaps most striking, though, was the defense of the local bishop against the encroachments of a newly defined imperial papacy.

Anonymous of York was a conservative opposed to papal radicalism, the sign for one historian of "a vast shift of the spirit in the medieval West."[5] Another scholar considered him a representative of "pre-Reformation Anglicanism," associating him with English Protestants.[6] Considering our narrative, however, he would seem rather a representative of pre-Reformation Orthodoxy, if the word "reformation" here is taken to refer not to the Protestantism of the sixteenth century but to the papism of the eleventh. In any case, Anonymous of York's ecclesiological vision at this moment of historical crisis, when the old Christendom was giving way to the new, has been characterized as asserting "the goodness of the created world and a repudiation of that debilitating dualism of which the abnormal tensions between marriage and celibacy, *regnum* and *sacerdotium*, earth and heaven were all sorry manifestations."[7]

Such views were rarely expressed during the heady process of papal reform. This was due to the fact that, unlike the Eastern patriarchs, the diocesan bishops of the West lacked any historical tradition of rivaling the pope of Rome. Undergoing evangelization and conversion through a more rural than urban process, they knew only one great and venerable patriarchal metropolis. This explains, for instance, why Celtic bishops so quickly capitulated to Latin missionaries at the Synod of Whitby in the seventh century.[8] Nevertheless, the new ecclesiology would cause division for centuries to come.

---

5   George Hunston Williams, *The Norman Anonymous of 1100 A.D.: Toward the Identification and Evaluation of the So-Called Anonymous of York* (Eugene, OR: Wipf and Stock, 2008), 10.

6   Ibid., 23.

7   Ibid., 13.

8   For the background to this important Western council, see *Age of Paradise*, 221–222.

An example is the protest made by William Durand, the early fourteenth-century bishop of Mende in France. He was a canon lawyer and therefore knew something of the legal revolution that followed in the wake of Gregory VII. In preparation for the Council of Vienne, he was asked by Pope Clement V to present views about the course of reform in recent times. Like the other Roman Catholic councils that followed the Great Division, this one was programmatic in that it was designed not to address any particular heresy (as early ecumenical councils had done), but to support continued reformation.

William was not sanguine about the course of reform to date. In his report, he attacked papal ecclesiology and called for a return to the conciliar ecclesiology of the ancient Church. In the face of the radicalism of the papal reformers, who advocated progress through institutional reform, he favored the ancient historical record and the writings of church fathers. Like Anonymous of York, he objected categorically to the reduction of the diocesan bishop to the status of mere vicar of the pope. Since the time of Gregory VII (as attested in his *Papal Dictate*), any legate of the pope—even a low-ranking subdeacon—possessed the power to preside over a council of local bishops. This was a violation of tradition and a scandal to good order. If reform was needed, William suggested, it should focus on the extravagant demands of the papacy.

William was clearly suspicious of the powers now amassed by the reformation papacy. With its juridical supremacy, many bishops and abbots were required to travel to Rome on their election to office. The reasons for this were not merely ecclesiastical. In many cases the holder of office was required to pay a "service tax" for confirmation. In 1257, for instance, the new abbot of Bury St. Edmunds in England was forced to pay two thousand pounds before being blessed to return to his assignment.[9] Did not such practices constitute the very simony that reformers like Gregory VII had condemned, asked William? And now the sin was being committed by the pope himself! Needless to say, Clement V did not respond well to William's report. The counter-reforming bishop was thrown into prison and languished there for seven years.[10]

---

9   Collins, *Keepers of the Keys of Heaven*, 252.
10   William's story is told in Barraclough, *Medieval Papacy*, 138.

The new papal ecclesiology was perhaps most visible in relations with the Orthodox Church. After the excommunications of 1054, various efforts at healing the division had been made. Some of these were auspicious, but none were successful. One of the most interesting was an exchange between Metropolitan Niketas of Nicomedia and Archbishop Anselm of Havelberg. In it Anselm presented the papacy's new ecclesiology. The conservative Niketas responded with a remarkably gracious response. Nevertheless, in addressing Anselm as a "dear brother" he observed that the Roman Church, though holding "the first place of honor,"

> has separated herself from the rest by her pretensions. She has appropriated to herself the monarchy which is not contained in her office and which has divided the bishops and the churches of the East and the West since the partition of the Empire. . . . If the Roman Pontiff, seated upon his sublime throne of glory, wishes to fulminate against us and to launch his orders from the height of his sublime dignity, if he wishes to sit in judgment on our Churches with a total disregard for our advice and solely according to his own will, as he seems to wish, what brotherhood and what fatherhood can we have in such a course of action? Who could ever accept such a situation? In such circumstances we could not be called nor would we really be any longer sons of the Church but truly its slaves.[11]

This statement expresses the profound dismay caused by the rise of papal supremacy. And with few exceptions, the Orthodox would hold to this position as long as Rome failed to return to the old ecclesiology.

This was evident in 1274 at the Second Council of Lyons, when Pope Gregory X orchestrated a reunion of the Orthodox with Roman Catholics. In the intervening century, the Great Division had been irreversibly solidified by the Fourth Crusade. But the Latin Empire had now been overthrown, and the Byzantine emperor Michael VIII (r. 1261–1282) was prepared to let bygones be bygones in exchange for renewed promises of military aid against

---

11   Quoted in Francis Dvornik, *Byzantium and the Roman Primacy* (New York: Fordham University, 1966), 145–146.

the Turks. As it turned out, he did not have the support of his bishops in this. In true caesaropapist fashion, he deposed a patriarch to make the union happen, but the man he chose as a replacement completely failed to win over the Orthodox. Under Michael's pressure, a union treaty was signed by the Eastern bishops in attendance, but in Byzantium it came to nothing.

Testing the Limits of Papal Supremacy

THE PONTIFICATE OF GREGORY VII marked a turning point in the political history of the West. After that time, rulers no longer enjoyed uncontested influence in the religious policies of their realms. The investiture controversy with Henry IV had been alleviated at Canossa, but as the siege of Rome that marked the end of Gregory's pontificate (and life) shows, it remained a major point of contention. Only in 1122 with the concordat issued by the Council of Worms was agreement between a new emperor and a new pope reached. This agreement recognized the legal principle of papal supremacy throughout Roman Catholic Christendom, while conceding to the emperor the right to nominate (though not invest ceremonially) the bishops of Germany.

But from the start, tensions arose that threatened to divide the political order anew. One was the ambition of the English monarchy to establish centralized rule. As we know, the Anglo-Saxon state was overthrown by William the Conqueror in 1066. The Norman state that replaced it initially enjoyed papal approval. Indeed, William's armies had fought under a papal military banner at the Battle of Hastings. Along with the nobility, the old Anglo-Saxon episcopate was swept aside and replaced by a people who had become staunch allies of the papacy.

Soon, however, the Norman establishment in England began to deviate from Rome's standard of ecclesiastical good order. In the person of King Henry II (r. 1154–1189), deviation became defiance. Henry had come to power as the Duke of Normandy and heir to the conquest of his predecessor William. Before seizing the English throne for himself, he had amassed a large fiefdom in northern France. To this he added the holdings of his wife, Eleanor of Aquitaine (d. 1204), who had obtained a divorce from his territorial rival, King Louis VII of France. Known for an explosive temper and restless temperament, the red-haired Henry was ambitious and energetic, like few other European rulers. He worked to unite England into a powerful national monarchy. To this end he was continually at war with France, an ominous development that opened the way to centuries of Anglo-French conflict, which would include the Hundred Years' War (1337–1453). Henry was also the first to send forces to Ireland in an effort to subjugate that otherwise peaceful Christian neighbor. In this he was encouraged by the pope, for this move promised to subject the native Celtic clergy to the new papal ecclesiology.

Henry, however, regarded the centralized policies of the papacy as an obstacle to English national expansion. He therefore sought ways to lessen the English Church's dependence on Rome. The most provocative of these ways was a legal reform under which the clergy would be subject to royal courts and not, as stipulated by the new canon law, those of the pope. To execute this policy, he recruited as archbishop of Canterbury—the highest ecclesiastical office in the land—one of his most trusted court advisors. Thomas Becket was his former chancellor and a trusted drinking companion to boot. To Henry he seemed the perfect man for the job, ready to tolerate encroachments on clerical privilege and eager to keep the pope at bay. Becket's appointment was a grave miscalculation that resulted in one of the greatest setbacks to royal prerogatives in church life since Canossa.

For it turned out that after his ordination to the episcopate, Archbishop Thomas refused to be a puppet of the monarchy. No one had expected this; no one thought it possible. One contemporary chronicler likened the transformation to a baptismal experience: "He put off the old man who is created according to the world, and strove to put on the new man who is created according to God." Another remarked: "This is the transformation of the hand of the Almighty."[12]

In 1164 Henry enacted his legal reform, and the archbishop refused to obey it. When Henry convened a court of nobles to confront him, Thomas stated simply that he was a loyal servant of the king and would obey him in

---

12   Quoted in Dan Jones, *The Plantagenets* (New York: Penguin Books, 2012), 62.

all matters—with the one exception. That, he said, was "saving the honor of God." In other words, his loyalty was not unconditional but was determined by a power higher than the king.

This, of course, was the legacy of ecclesiopolitical symphony. Elaborated by Eusebius in the time of Emperor Constantine, this principle assigned to Christian rulers the responsibility of working in harmony with bishops for the good of the Church. But it could be violated if the ruler placed earthly priorities before those of the Church. Symphony had been applied most dramatically in Ambrose's censure of Theodosius during the fourth century, after the emperor brutally mistreated his citizens. It was a recognition that unlike the emperor-worship of Roman pagandom, Christendom looked beyond the exigencies of earthly power to the evangelical values of the kingdom of heaven.

Henry did not much appreciate this principle. Said to pace nervously around the nave during the Mass, thinking only of ways to advance the power of the monarchy, he showed little interest in the kingdom of heaven. Confronted by Archbishop Thomas's principled refusal to compromise the supremacy of ecclesiastical courts, Henry threatened him with the capital charge of high treason. Thomas fled England to take refuge in the lands of

The murder of Thomas Becket

Henry's rival, King Louis VII. Thereafter he visited Rome to consult with the pope. Only after five long years did Thomas again set foot on English soil. And less than a month after that, he was dead.

This, one of the most infamous assassinations in the history of Christendom, took place on the indirect orders of Henry. The king was reported to have exclaimed indignantly to a quartet of knights attending his Christmas court, "Will no one rid me of this troublesome priest?" Those very men thereupon marched to Canterbury Cathedral and, on December 29, smashed their way through the door to confront Thomas. The archbishop was preparing for the divine office. Cornering him, the knights slew him and then trod contemptuously on his corpse.

The response was swift. Henry immediately found himself a pariah, and was able to recover a semblance of his former authority only after submitting to a public flogging on the streets of Canterbury. He lived long enough to see Thomas canonized as a saint and the place of his assassination turned into one of the most popular pilgrimage sites in the West. Clearly, Christendom's rulers transgressed the principle of symphony only at great cost.

As for the assassins, they traveled to Rome and received as a penance from the pope the obligation to join the crusades. Warren Carroll, in a lively retelling of the whole episode, piously imagined them standing at the head of their column facing the infidel before Jerusalem with the same swords they used against Becket, and, contrite to the end, giving their lives in defense of a place of martyrdom even holier than Canterbury.[13]

Indeed, the ultimate measure of papal supremacy in the political sphere was not the maintenance of a legal jurisdiction over the clergy but the recruitment of monarchies to fight papally directed holy wars. Pope Gregory VII had never had the time or attention to put this into practice, but his crusading dream was fulfilled by the next great advocate of supremacy, Urban II.

As we saw in the previous chapter, the First Crusade was designed above all as a means of unifying Christendom under the leadership of the pope.

---

13   Warren H. Carroll, *The Glory of Christendom* (Front Royal, VA: Christendom Press, 1993), 108.

This is why the initial justification for the crusade—relieving the Byzantines from the onslaught of the Turks—became quickly and permanently obscured. During the twelfth century, the crusades continued to bring the armies of the West together under papal command. They became in a real sense the military expression of papal ecclesiology. The pontificate of Innocent III was the culmination of this development. At the command of the self-styled Vicar of Christ, crusaders now warred against Albigensians and Orthodox, both of whom rejected papal supremacy. Innocent died while planning the Fifth Crusade against the Muslims. But his successor, Honorius III, regarded the project as a sacred legacy and saw it through to completion. Like the Fourth Crusade, the Fifth was a fiasco.

It had begun with much promise. The ambitious titular king of Jerusalem, John of Brienne, led a large army toward the strategic Egyptian city of Damietta. But soon after he arrived to begin a siege, he was forced to cede command to the papal legate, Pelagius. The latter was a member of the college of cardinals and a fanatical advocate for papal supremacy. When serving as ambassador to Latin-occupied Constantinople years earlier, he had forcibly closed Orthodox churches there and thrown some of their clergy into prison. This was too much even for the Latin emperor, and Pelagius was sent back to Rome.

Placed by the pope at the head of the present crusade, Pelagius made another rash and incomprehensible blunder. When the frightened sultan Malik al-Kamil offered to cede Jerusalem without a fight in exchange for the crusaders' withdrawal from Egypt, Pelagius, "determined to shed as much blood as possible," rejected the proposal out of hand.[14] War was his preference. However, while he captured both Damietta and Cairo, he ultimately became bogged down in the Nile Delta and was forced to surrender in 1221. Jerusalem remained in Muslim hands.

But holy war was taken up again by the next pope. We already know Gregory IX as the founder of the papal inquisition and the compiler of Rome's new body of canon law. He was, in short, another steadfast advocate of papal supremacy. It was also he that issued the call for a crusade against

---

14   John Julius Norwich, *Absolute Monarchs* (New York: Random House, 2011), 181.

the Orthodox of Russia. On an even grander scale, he organized the Sixth Crusade to take back Jerusalem. With long experience at the papal curia, Gregory concluded that the latest debacle had been caused not by the attack on Egypt nor by the placement of armies in the hands of the fanatically militant Cardinal Pelagius. The failure of the Fifth Crusade, he was convinced, had been due to the nonparticipation of Western Christendom's greatest military power, the Holy Roman Empire. Its ruler had refused to obey the pope's call to arms.

Emperor Frederick II (r. 1220–1250) had been crowned in Rome in the presence of Gregory and had at that time promised to lead a crusade. But as the years passed, he did nothing about it. By the standards of the period he was characteristically belligerent, spending years fighting for territories in Italy. But when it came to holy warfare, he proved himself uncharacteristically peaceable, almost pacifistic.

This may have been the result of his upbringing in Sicily, which, along with much of Italy, belonged to his extensive empire. The island had become one of the most culturally diverse places in Christendom. Greek Orthodox mixed with Latin Roman Catholics. Arab colonists, who had long ago seized the island from Byzantium, had in turn been conquered by the Normans under Robert Guiscard.

Holy Roman Emperor Frederick II

A monument to all of this was the glorious twelfth-century cathedral of Monreale near the city of Palermo. A Roman Catholic church, it represented the union of Norman architecture and Byzantine iconography. Accordingly, its nave was designed as a standard Western basilica, but its apse contained mosaics of Christ Pantocrator and other standard Eastern images. Particularly striking is an icon in the nave depicting the expulsion of Adam from Paradise. Despite the tragic narrative, this icon expresses like few equivalents in all of Christendom the anthropological optimism of traditional Christianity. The face of the downcast Adam possesses features identical to those of the glorified Christ standing next to him. The icon expresses perfectly Christendom's conviction that man is made in the image of God and, despite his sins, continues to possess that image.

The young Frederick would have been impressed with the Christian diversity so well exemplified at Monreale Cathedral. He was also influenced by Arabic culture. Arab scholars contributed to his education, and he developed a respect for Islam. He learned Arabic and was said to speak it fluently. The young emperor was said to have lived the life of a caliph and kept a harem. However, none of this was auspicious for a future of crusading.

As a result of the Papal Reformation, it was considered the obligation of a Christian emperor to raise armies upon appeals from the pope. As Frederick continued to vacillate about his crusader vows, Gregory decided to use force. He threatened the emperor with excommunication if he did not launch a crusade in the immediate future, and to avoid any ambiguity he set a deadline of the Feast of the Ascension in 1227. Frederick seems to have genuinely tried to comply. An army was mustered and galleys sent toward the Holy Land from his home port of Brindisi in southern Italy early that year. But when an outbreak of influenza incapacitated him, Frederick was forced to turn back and plead for another postponement. Gregory would have none of it.

Frederick's failure to fulfill the demands of the pope became, as Christopher Tyerman has noted, "the pivot around which the crusade was transformed from an enterprise of Christian solidarity into one of confrontation and division."[15] Resorting to the weapon of choice of his eleventh-century namesake, Pope Gregory excommunicated the emperor. Once again, the loyalty of millions of imperial subjects was subverted and the prospect of civil war chillingly raised.

Strangely, it was exactly at this moment that Frederick's long-slumbering crusading resolve awoke. In the following year, he landed at the port city

---

15   Tyerman, *God's War*, 747.

of Acre and prepared for an attack on Jerusalem. But Sultan al-Kamil was ready with a new offer to maintain the peace. Again he offered Jerusalem, this time in exchange for nothing more than a promise to keep the city demilitarized and the Muslim shrines in Arab hands. The Christians could even take possession of the holy cities of Nazareth and Bethlehem. Never a crusading zealot, Frederick avoided the mistakes of Cardinal Pelagius and signed the treaty. Jerusalem was again a Christian city.

The modern historian is dumbfounded at the reaction this provoked among the clergy. Peace had been preserved and the holiest place in all of Christendom recovered. But the pope was incensed. Frederick may have succeeded where previous kings like Richard the Lionheart had failed, but he had done so as an excommunicate, an enemy of the Church. The Latin patriarch of Jerusalem, appointed by Rome as part of the ecclesiastical colonization of the East, immediately placed the city under papal interdict, thereby banning all sacraments. Thus the incongruous scene at the Church of the Holy Sepulcher when Frederick, wearing his imperial crown and proclaiming an end to Muslim control of the city, was all but shunned by the attending Christian clergy. The ambivalent crusader would obviously have nothing more to do with such folly, and shaking the dust from his feet he hastily made arrangements to return to Italy.

But the divisive specter of papal supremacy followed him there too. Upon arrival at the port town of Brindisi, he was informed that his Italian territories were in a state of rebellion, and that Gregory was responsible. While the emperor had been away on crusade, the pope had used his status as an excommunicate to justify nothing short of another crusade against him. Gregory had even recalled Cardinal Pelagius from retirement to lead the campaign in southern Italy. And not only Italy, but Germany too was engulfed in civil war. There Gregory had appointed a rival claimant to the throne and had raised a fortune to overthrow the German emperor.

But the pope proved a less successful warlord than Frederick, and by the end of 1229 the papal invasion had been routed. The following year, defeated in battle and realizing there was no advantage to maintaining his ban on Christendom's most powerful ruler, Gregory lifted the excommunication.

Tensions continued to smolder for years, however, and twice more they flared up with excommunications until finally, during yet another war against papal forces, Christendom's most ambiguous ruler finally died.

During the latter stages of this struggle, another ruler entered the drama of papal politics. King Louis IX (r. 1226–1270) of France, however, was no Frederick II. He was the devoted son of the papacy and did everything in his power to defend its supremacy over Europe's political order. This began in 1245, when he hosted in the city of Lyons a church council designed to deal with Frederick's dissent. At that very council Louis pledged to wage a new war against the Muslims, a conflict that became the Seventh Crusade. Pope Innocent IV offered his full support, and his legate began a preaching tour to promote it.

In 1249 Louis's ships landed at the Egyptian port of Damietta, the same point of invasion the Fifth Crusade had chosen. Louis himself hastily led an assault on its fortress and was rewarded with a stunning victory. However, when the crusaders ventured out into the open in subsequent campaigns, they were not so fortunate. At the Battle of Al-Mansurah in 1250 they were almost totally wiped out, and after one final and desperate effort to retreat to Damietta, the remnant of the expeditionary force was surrounded and

King Louis IX of France

killed. Only Louis and a handful of attendants were spared and taken prisoner. Eventually they were released, and Louis returned to France after an extended tour of the Crusader States. Imprisonment and the annihilation of his entire army had not quenched his zeal for crusading.

Back in France, he began to plan the Eighth Crusade. Before it could take place, however, he was compelled to call his brother, the adventurer Charles of Anjou, away from the East. With the recent collapse of the Latin Empire, the deposed emperor Baldwin was seeking military support to reenact the conquest of Constantinople. Charles promised a large army for this, but happily for King Louis—and Orthodox Byzantium—the plan ultimately came to nothing.

Since the time of Urban IV (r. 1261–1264), the papacy had been actively interested in reestablishing control over Constantinople. Indeed, it continued to recognize a titular Roman Catholic patriarch in exile, appointing replacements throughout the centuries to come. It was not until 1964, in fact, that the office was finally dissolved as a preparation for the rescinding of the excommunications by Pope Paul VI and Patriarch Athenagoras. However, the age of division was decidedly lacking in such ecumenism, and the decision not to attack Constantinople was based on the simple realization that it would not succeed. Putting the plan on hold, the pope reassigned Charles to support a crusade against the Muslims instead.

The advance force of the Eighth Crusade landed near Tunis and, awaiting Charles's forces to join them, was soon bogged down. The Arabs proved resilient and the summer heat stifling. Then cholera broke out. One by one, the crusaders succumbed to the arrows of the Muslims or the even greater agony of a slow death caused by vomiting and thirst. As the crusade finally collapsed, Louis himself fell ill, dying on the very day his brother Charles finally arrived with an army of now useless reinforcements.

Louis IX, soon to be canonized by the pope, died a faithful servant of the papacy. But his grandson Philip the Fair would defy this legacy, bringing papal supremacy to the point of crisis.

The Papal Reformation had been a mighty force. Yet as the fourteenth century dawned, it was showing signs of having run its course. The pontificate of Boniface VIII (r. 1294–1303) was at once a recapitulation of its achievements and a sign of its limits. Like so many of his predecessors, the new pope was a lawyer. And like some of his fellow lawyer-popes, he issued a new collection of canon law designed to consolidate the powers of the papacy. In fact, he endowed the institution with a nearly unrestricted political authority. Kings as well as bishops were now to be the pope's vassals.

King Philip the Fair (r. 1285–1314), like Frederick, was more concerned with monarchy than sainthood. His military objectives were directed not

Pope Boniface VIII

toward ecclesiastical colonialism in the East but toward national struggles in the West. England was now ruled by Henry II's Plantagenet heir, Edward Longshanks, and a contest erupted over possession of territories in Normandy and Aquitaine. Philip settled on war. But to fight the English, he needed to raise money. His customary tax revenue proved insufficient, and after manipulating the currency he turned on different privileged sectors of the French population. Among his targets were the Knights Templar, to whom he was in considerable debt. So Philip ordered the dissolution of the military order and, for good measure, burned a handful of its members at the stake. He also turned on the Jews, banishing them from France and confiscating their wealth. But it was his effort to tax the clergy that provoked a fateful confrontation with Boniface.

The pope, heir to Gregory VII in both ambition and temperament, reacted without restraint. He thundered against Philip's taxation scheme in a bull denouncing lay interference in clerical affairs. The bull not only cited the legal terms of papal supremacy but presented an exaggerated picture of what the pope considered a history of lay interference in the spiritual affairs of the clergy. It was in this sense both a clerical indictment of the laity and a cause for the further division of society into opposing spiritual classes. Eventually the pope was forced to back down, but this did not mollify Philip. Intent on war with England, the king demanded that in addition to paying taxes for the war, the French clergy should also pledge loyalty to their monarch over the pope. A new investiture controversy like that between Henry IV and Gregory VII was developing.

Philip acted first. To make a statement, he arrested one of the bishops, something the new canon law also forbade. Boniface reacted swiftly. He called all of France's bishops to Rome for a council in 1302, though only about half dared to defy Philip and come. Those who did were presented with a manifesto that has gone down in history as the most extreme assertion of papal supremacy of all time. The bull *Unam sanctam* repeated the claims made by various popes, from Gregory VII to Urban II to Innocent III. But, with Philip supposedly in mind, it goes so far as to declare that "it is necessary for salvation that *every human being* be subject to the Roman Pontiff" (italics added). A more perfect expression of papal ecclesiology has never been issued before or since.

For the period of high-handed defiance of royal power was over. Gregory VII had succeeded in subduing Emperor Henry IV by excommunicating him and placing his realm under interdict. Now Boniface prepared to do the same. By choking off the flow of sacramental life to an entire nation as if by turning a spigot (for such was his power as Vicar of Christ), he provoked Philip to do what his German predecessor had been unable to do. The king of France sent a band of mercenaries to the town of Anagni in Italy, where Boniface was residing. These men fought their way into the papal palace and, seizing the pope, demanded his immediate abdication. When he refused, they beat him within an inch of his life. One of the men actually intended to kill him, but his accomplices talked him out of it. It mattered little, though, for within weeks Boniface died from the shock and injuries.

The principle of papal supremacy did not die with him, but it never fully recovered. The proto-utopian civilization's cornerstone was beginning to crack.

A Confusion of Orders

BACK WHEN INNOCENT III WAS bringing the Papal Reformation to completion at the Fourth Lateran Council, a revolutionary change was occurring in the West. As we have seen, papal supremacy had originated in the monasteries as a reaction against the proprietary system. By the middle of the eleventh century, indignation over systemic corruption had swelled to a sufficient size in France to burst the banks of the cloisters. It flooded first into the policies of German emperor Henry III and then, with his support, found a course to Rome. And once it had accumulated at the Lateran Palace, the principle of "reform for the better"—limited since the time of Augustine to personal transformation—became institutionalized. It created the pastoral machinery of the papal court and began the systematic transformation of the world.

But it is important to realize that having equipped the papacy with its uniquely dynamic understanding of the transformational imperative, monastic reformers continued to agonize over the gulf they perceived between the paradisiacal life of the apostles and their own realities. So great was the dissatisfaction of some that they began to alter traditional monasticism.

Monasticism arose in the fourth century as a way of living out the heavenly values of the gospel at a level that did not seem possible in regular society after the mass conversion of the population. When Anthony the Great unexpectedly heard the reading about the rich young man giving away his goods to the poor and following Christ, he himself did exactly that. He became the father of monasticism. The life of the hermit and later the cenobitic (a monk who lives in a community of fellow monks) was designed to offer more freedom to live by the precepts of Christ than any other way of life this side of paradise. Indeed, monasticism was soon regarded as a way of life comparable to sacramental marriage that established paradise in this world. The penultimate step in the sixth-century monastic guidebook called the *Ladder of Divine Ascent* (known in some editions as the *Ladder of Paradise*) was entitled "Concerning heaven on earth, or Godlike dispassion and perfection, and the resurrection of the soul before the general resurrection."

Until the second millennium there was little substantive difference between monasticism in the East and in the West. Both Basil the Great (d. 379) and Benedict of Nursia (d. 547)—the two most influential fathers of monasticism in each respective half of first-millennium Christendom—taught more or less the same thing: that a cloister separated from the affairs of normal society is the best environment for a life oriented toward the kingdom of heaven. Such a life was grounded in thoroughgoing repentance. Benedict called the formalized act of repentance a "conversion of manners" (*conversatio morum*). Basil was content with "change of heart" (*metanoia*), the Greek used by the evangelists for the word *repentance* in the New Testament. Both meant the same thing: the monastic would be transformed by a way of life profoundly at odds with the culture of the fallen world. His or her way of life would be defined by paradise.

In the East, monasticism continued beyond the first millennium to have a predominantly penitential character. In Byzantium, the Studion Monastery outside Constantinople had become the leading center of asceticism, particularly after Saint Katherine Monastery on Mount Sinai was forced into isolation by the Arab conquests. With its proximity to the imperial capital, Studion also became a center for intellectual life. As we saw in chapter one, for instance, it was from this cloister that Niketas Stethatos had defended Eastern liturgical practice against the attacks of Cardinal Humbert.

At a greater distance from the capital, the monastic network of Mount Athos had also become an important center of spiritual life. By the beginning of the second millennium, the peninsula on which the Holy Mountain was situated was already bejeweled with dozens of monasteries and hermitages, fulfilling a prophecy of the Virgin Mary in the first century that its mountainous coastland would become a "paradise" to monks. But it was only after Athanasios of Athos (d. 1000) erected the Great Lavra there that Athos became one of the major monastic centers in all of Christendom. The highly inclusive terms of its charter fostered contacts with many non-Greek

Great Lavra, Mount Athos

monastics, including a Benedictine community that came from Italy to settle on the mountain.

After the Great Division, of course, the influence of Athos was restricted mainly to the East. But it was extensive and affected the Christian culture not only of Byzantium but of the Slavic lands of Bulgaria, Serbia, and Russia as well. Historians have even spoken of an "Athonite Commonwealth" that united Eastern Christendom as a civilization founded on the ideals of traditional Christian asceticism.

The Kiev Caves Monastery, for instance, was said by an eleventh-century contemporary to have "issued from the Holy Mountain."[16] It was founded by a monk named Antony (d. 1073) after he had visited Athos and been tonsured there. Following the example of his namesake, Anthony of Egypt, he sought spiritual transformation through living as a hermit in a cave in the hillside on the west bank of the Dnieper River. He is said by his biographer to have been particularly drawn toward hesychastic prayer of the heart. Like the founder of monasticism, this Antony was soon pursued by numerous would-be disciples and withdrew into further seclusion, leaving the monastery in the hands of successors. One of these was Feodosy, whose kenotic way of life we considered in chapter one. Under him, the Caves Monastery adopted the Studite Rule and became the main transmission point of monasticism in the Russia of its time. From here a dozen or so monasteries were planted in Kiev and more than twenty in distant Novgorod.

Meanwhile, Athonite monasticism also penetrated the Balkans. In the case of Serbia, it flowered brilliantly in the person and work of Sava (d. 1236). The son of Grand Prince Stephan Nemanja (who was later known by his monastic name, Simeon), Sava fled political entanglements at home and settled at Vatopedi Monastery on the Holy Mountain. Here his father joined him after abdicating and being tonsured. Together, they established Hilandar Monastery as a refuge for Serbians seeking monastic solitude and as a center for the production of Serbian manuscripts. Sava later reflected on his experience on the Holy Mountain: "I saw angels here on earth, and I

---

16   Quoted in John Fennell, *A History of the Russian Church to 1448* (Harlow, England: Longman, 1995), 65.

saw men who belonged in heaven."[17] Eventually, he brought this paradisiacal experience back to Serbia, where he contributed actively to the expansion of other Athonite satellites. Among them were monasteries at Gracanica, Decani, and Studenica. What is more, in 1219 Sava obtained from Constantinople autocephalous status for the Serbian Church and became its first archbishop.

In Russia and Serbia, as on Athos, monastic piety continued in the tradition of Christendom's earliest ascetics. This

Saint Sava of Serbia

piety was centered on repentance and the personal transformation of life it brought. In this it was no different from the Benedictine monasticism of the first-millennium West.

But monastics lived in the world, and in the West they were profoundly aware that the cloister did not automatically shield them from the corrupting influences of the proprietary system. A monastery free of feudal avarice had been, as we have seen, the dream of Cluny. Yet despite vigorous efforts to resist worldly entanglements, that first and most famous center of reform had, by the end of the eleventh century, accumulated enormous riches in the form of donations. Its grand church—the largest in all Christendom—was an expression of heaven on earth but also, for some, a monument to the vanity of the feudal lords who had endowed it.

It was also a reminder that Cluny had developed an order of divine worship so elaborate and time-consuming that monks were prevented from

17   Graham Speake, *A History of the Athonite Commonwealth: The Spiritual and Cultural Diaspora of Mount Athos* (Cambridge: Cambridge University Press, 2018), 83.

fulfilling one of the most basic requirements of the Benedictine Rule: manual labor. This became the responsibility of a subordinate class of laborers known as *conversi,* or lay brothers. Many of these were serfs who had obtained liberty from their feudal lords, but they were barred from taking monastic vows and joining the monks in their common life. In other words, the arrangement mirrored the same worldly divisions as existed in the feudal order, thereby subverting monasticism's paradisiacal culture.

But division was in the air, and a group of monks called the Cistercians decided to break from the Cluniac network in order to reform monasticism for the better. As Christopher Bellitto has noted, "it is hard to understand the Cistercians apart from Cluny."[18] Both were driven by the spirit of reform, and both sought to escape the decadent present by returning to a pristine and in many cases imagined past. Like Cluny's founders two centuries earlier, the Cistercians claimed to be retreating to the original Rule of Saint Benedict. They expressed this in a founding constitution called the *Charter of Love* (*Carta caritatis*). In 1119 Pope Calixtus II gave his formal authorization to this charter, and with that a new age in Christian monasticism began.

This papal endorsement represents the beginning of "orders" within monasticism, a phenomenon unique to the new Christendom. Until this time, every monastery in both East and West was largely in charge of its community life and in this sense represented a counterpart to the conciliar ecclesiology of the early Church. Even the Rule of Saint Benedict, adopted so widely throughout the West, explicitly prescribed local autonomy. Cluny, with its hierarchical network, had tested this principle without formally breaking it. But by having their charter recognized by the pope, the Cistercians "introduced tensions and rivalries that were unknown in early medieval monasticism."[19] Indignant at the shortcomings of Cluny, the leaders of the new order actually turned on fellow monastics outside it.

Cluny proved an irresistible target. The most famous spokesman of the

---

18 Christopher M. Bellitto, *Renewing Christianity: A History of Church Reform from Day One to Vatican II* (New York: Paulist Press, 2001), 74.

19 Giles Constable, *The Reformation of the Twelfth Century* (Cambridge: Cambridge University Press, 1996), 124.

Cistercians, Bernard of Clairvaux (d. 1153), seems to have had Cluny's richly decorated temple in mind when he rhetorically asked whether it would produce repentance or vanity.

Bernard of Clairvaux

What is this show or splendor intended to produce? Tears of contrition or gasps of admiration? O vanity of vanity, but above all insanity! The walls of the church are ablaze with light and color, while the poor of the church go hungry. . . . The money for feeding the destitute goes to feast the eyes of the rich. . . . What possible bearing can this have on the life of monks, who are poor men and spiritual?[20]

He also attacked the pomp of Cluniac abbots. "What evidence is there of humility," he again asked rhetorically, "when one solitary abbot travels with a parade of horseflesh and a retinue of lay-servants that would do honor to two bishops? . . . If you saw them passing, you would take them for lords with dominions over castles and countries, not for fathers of monks and shepherds of souls."[21]

Against such polemics the Cluniacs responded in kind. Their abbot Peter the Venerable (d. 1156) decried Bernard and others as a divisive "new breed of pharisees . . . who separate themselves from others."[22] And when the Cistercians followed the lead of the Cluniacs and began to employ lay brothers to manage their vast, lucrative granges (the acquisition of which often

---

20 Quoted in Bellitto, *Renewing Christianity*, 76.
21 Quoted in ibid., 77.
22 Quoted in Constable, *Reformation*, 33.

resulted in the expulsion of their peasant inhabitants), they too fell victim to charges of hypocrisy.

But the Cistercians were only the first of the orders. Other reformers went further, abandoning altogether the traditional standard of cloistered stability. The apostles, after whom all monastics modeled their common life, were active in their ministries, going from place to place in their fulfillment of the gospel. The increasingly frenetic need to reform Christendom redirected the attention of some who might otherwise have withdrawn from society in order to change themselves for the better. Instead, they established orders designed to change others for the better. Entering the heart of society, they pioneered what had formerly been a contradiction in terms: itinerant monasticism.

The Itinerants

FRANCIS OF ASSISI WAS THE most influential of the itinerant monks. A repentant young feudal nobleman, one day he had a vision of Christ speaking to him from the mouth of an icon at an abandoned temple. Christ commanded Francis to "rebuild" His Church, and Francis set about repairing the temple until he realized the command applied to all of Christendom. Such was the scale of reformation then in effect. Francis ultimately carried a charter to Rome, where in 1210 Pope Innocent III approved it. It was said that the pope did so only after he too had had a vision of a temple in collapse—in this case Saint John Lateran—with Francis repairing it.

The mission of Francis's Order of Friars Minor was largely urban. During the twelfth century, historians believe, a dramatic increase in population and wealth resulted in "Europe's first and authentic autonomous urbanization."[23] This far exceeded anything the Roman Empire had accomplished, especially in the north. The Franciscans, as the friars were known, fanned out across the West and settled particularly in cities. There they cared for the poor (they were by definition beggars themselves) and the sick. Under such circumstances, it is hard to imagine a more dynamic expression of

---

23   R. I. Moore, *The First European Revolution* (Malden, MA: Blackwell, 2000), 31.

Christendom's paradisiacal cosmology at work.

The Franciscans became a model to the other great mendicant order, the Dominicans. This order came into existence in 1216, when Pope Honorius III approved Dominic's plea for an order that would address the rise of heresy in the West. The Albigensian Crusade was fully mobilized at this time, and Dominic himself had earlier been involved in preaching against heresy in southern France. His Order of Preachers, as the Dominicans were formally known, were a variant of the Franciscans; they forsook monastic withdrawal in order to bring the gospel to society. Where the Franciscans offered care to the poor, however, the Dominicans offered doctrinal integrity. They were dedicated to preaching traditional Christianity among heretics such as the Cathars. They also came to assume leadership in the emerging university system due to their commitment to theological study. For this reason, they would make up a large percentage of the personnel of the inquisition as its scope expanded in the centuries ahead.

Service to the papacy was also offered by another, more dubious exception to the traditional principle of cloistered stability. As we have seen, the crusades had originated with and were fought under the direction of the reformed papacy. As monastic vocations became itinerant, it was perhaps inevitable that asceticism and holy warfare would eventually be combined. Early signs of this were seen in methods of crusader recruitment.

Immediately after the Council of Clermont, Urban II had ordered the clergy of the West—including monastics—to begin preaching the First Crusade. By all accounts its most celebrated preacher was a wandering ascetic named Peter the Hermit. He traveled throughout France and Germany to raise an army, and then personally led it all the way to the walls of Jerusalem. Other monks likewise played significant roles. We have already met Arnauld Aimery. It was he who gave the order to slaughter the townspeople of Beziers, whether heretic or Roman Catholic. Prior to the massacre he had been the abbot of Citeaux, the mother house of the Cistercians. Innocent III enlisted him as the Albigensian Crusade's principal recruitment officer, and it was at his famous monastery that the crusade was first preached on the Feast of the Holy Cross in 1208.

Perhaps the grandest act of crusade recruitment was played out at Vezelay in 1146. Pope Eugene III, who ordered the Second Crusade, was a Cistercian and turned for support to his spiritual father, Bernard of Clairvaux. The results were stunning. With King Louis VII and Queen Eleanor standing on either side of him, Christendom's most famous abbot stirred up such enthusiasm for the enterprise that when he was finished speaking, the throngs of recruits quickly exhausted the supply of woolen crosses he had brought with him for distribution. He was compelled to shred the habit he was wearing to provide more.

What is most remarkable is that it was not only individual monks who recruited soldiers and even fought in the crusades. In fact, new orders were actually established to conduct the fighting. The three most important were the Knights Hospitaller (1113), the Knights Templar (1129), and the Teutonic Knights (1198). Each of these were itinerant orders formally approved by a pope and dedicated to conducting military service under the direction of the papacy. Each was given an ascetic rule by which to live.

The Templar Rule set the tone for all others and was notable for being written by Bernard of Clairvaux himself. The new Christendom's most famous monk fell in love with the knights after meeting their leader. He persuaded the warriors to accept a strict ascetic way of life. The Templars became "military Cistercians" and did almost everything their cloistered counterparts did: they fasted vigorously (though due to their vocation meat was allowed on certain days); they were expected to keep silence when possible; they followed the daily cycle of divine services (at which readings from Joshua and Maccabees were emphasized due to their military content); and they wore a hooded white habit in imitation of their cloistered brothers.[24]

Following the example of other monastic advocates of holy war, Bernard did not stop with the Templar Rule. He went as far as writing a treatise entitled *In Praise of the New Knighthood*. In it he declared without hesitation that "the knights of Christ may safely do battle in the battles of their Lord, fearing neither the sin of smiting the enemy nor the danger of their own downfall, inasmuch as death for Christ, inflicted or endured, bears no taint

---

24   Desmond Seward, *The Monks of War* (London: Penguin, 1995), 32.

of sin, but deserves abundant glory."[25] Perfectly aligned with the new papal doctrine of indulgences, such a claim encouraged Christians to do what traditional Christianity had always taught them never to do: to kill their enemies, with an assurance that doing so would open to them the kingdom of heaven. The commandment to love their enemies, to say nothing of turning the other cheek when smitten by them, was thus reversed. The reformation of Western Christendom was undermining doctrinal integrity, and with it the culture of paradise.

Not everyone joined Bernard in praising the "monks of war," however. A fellow Cistercian living in England at the same time observed that

> this dreadful new military order that someone has rather pleasantly called the order of the fifth gospel was founded for the purpose of forcing infidels to accept the faith at the point of the sword. Its members consider that they have every right to attack anyone not confessing Christ's name, leaving him destitute, whereas if they themselves are killed while thus unjustly attacking the pagans, they are called martyrs for the faith. . . . We do not maintain that all they do is wrong, but we do insist that what they are doing can be an occasion of many future evils.[26]

With the establishment of orders, a new monasticism had come into being—an itinerant monasticism that ceased to have its roots in the cloister. As such it served as an adjunct to the Papal Reformation. In the West, Dominican and Franciscan friars helped build a new Christendom in which preaching, charity, university education, and even the elimination of heresy all occurred under the direct supervision of the papacy. In the East, the monks of war conquered territories within the old Christendom and imposed papal supremacy upon them. Papadakis called them the "shock troops" of the reformation.[27]

---

25 Bernard of Clairvaux, *In Praise of the New Knighthood* (Trappist, KY: Cistercian Publications, 2000), 39.
26 Quoted in Seward, *Monks of War*, 36.
27 Papadakis, *The Christian East and the Rise of the Papacy*, 67.

Indeed, Christopher Dawson noted how itinerant monastics became a "disciplined *corps d'elite* under the direct command of the Papacy."

> *An international body of this kind, detached from the local territorial obli-gations and private interests, had always been a great need of the reformed Papacy, and therefore the creation of the Mendicant Orders together with the foundation of the universities marks the culmination of the movement towards international and superpolitical unity which was the ideal of medie-val Christendom.*[28]

The great Roman Catholic historian spoke here of unity. But surely the unity achieved through the new monasticism came through division.

The monastic reformation that began with the Cluniacs of the eleventh century and became openly polemical among the Cistercians of the twelfth century was, in the end, fundamentally divisive. It contributed to a fragmen-tation of Christendom. Nowhere was this more evident than in the tendency of monasteries like Citeaux to break from their parent houses and form new orders. There is something proto-Protestant in Bernard's indignation at the Cluniacs and his eloquent polemics against them. It was the same approach to reformation that would later characterize the implacable Luther.

And in fact the tendency toward fragmentation was evident from the start. Pope Urban II had noted it when conceding the establishment of the Cistercian order. He spoke ominously at that time of a "dreadful schism in the house of God" that might result from a heterogeneity of orders. A cen-tury later, the Fourth Lateran Council actually issued a moratorium on new orders, "lest an excessive diversity of religions should introduce serious con-fusion into the church of God." Such contemporary assessments of the new monasticism led one historian to consider titling his study of the period "the schism of the twelfth century."[29]

In the new monasticism of the West, the Great Division had bred only further division.

---

28 Dawson, *Religion and the Rise of Western Culture*, 215.
29 Constable, *Reformation*, 2.

CHAPTER THREE

Knowing God

IN THE WEST, THE TWELFTH-CENTURY transition away from cloistered monasticism had its parallel in theology. The "queen of the sciences," as it came to be known, had until the Great Division typically been in the hands of bishops and monks. Irenaeus of Lyons, Athanasius of Alexandria, Gregory of Nyssa, Gregory the Theologian, Augustine of Hippo, Cyril of Alexandria, Leo the Great, Maximos the Confessor, John of Damascus, Theodulf of Orleans, Alcuin of York, Photios of Constantinople, Symeon the New Theologian—that is, the great majority of church fathers from the first century to the eleventh—had all shared in the accountability and stability of the cathedral or cloister. And in the East, as we shall see, this feature of the old Christendom continued into the second millennium. In the West, however, papal supremacy and monastic itinerancy combined with developments in the social and economic order to produce a new approach to theological inquiry. All of this resulted in a new theology which, in the words of Papadakis, was "no longer liturgical, contemplative, or traditional."[30]

The formation of the university system through which learning was entrusted to a professional intellectual, known by virtue of his training as a "doctor," created a need the Dominican and Franciscan orders were especially well suited to fill. They were both dedicated to learning (the explicit ministry of the Dominicans was to teach against heresy). They were both capable of sending their friars just about anywhere in the West. And they both had the formal papal authority to do so.

This last element was important. The university system became universal, with subjects and curricula recognized from one end of Western Christendom to the other. Only the papacy claimed a universal jurisdiction over this territory, and papal charters became standard prerequisites for the great universities of Bologna, Paris, and Oxford. Since professors and their resident students were often treated with suspicion by locals, the papacy frequently intervened to grant them privileges and exemptions. In 1231, for instance, Gregory IX issued a bull in defense of scholarly autonomy,

---

30   Papadakis, *The Christian East and the Rise of the Papacy*, 168.

granting the university of Paris the right to determine its curricula without interference from the bishops. He even went so far as to place the institution directly under his own protection.

The most distinctive mark of the new academic theology, however, was its method. Known as scholasticism, this approach to understanding departed significantly from the theology of the old Christendom. It was fundamentally rationalistic. It did not merely pass on the first millennium's doctrinal tradition (*paradosis* in Greek and *traditio* in Latin literally mean "that which is handed down"). It subjected it to rigorous logical and semantic tests with the assumption that a higher understanding of the faith would result. But as we shall see in a later chapter, such a method could also result in a departure from tradition.

The scholastics were all strongly influenced by Augustinianism. Augustine had made wide use of pagan learning in his writings and had gone through a phase in his pre-Christian intellectual formation that depended on Plato. What is interesting is that Augustinianism in its scholastic form was not, however, always faithful to Augustine. For the fourth-century father had emphasized that while philosophical reason can be used to clarify Christian doctrine, an absolute priority must be assigned to faith. Along with the Greek fathers, he was awestruck at the mysteries of Christian revelation and in many cases was content to leave it at that. As he put it, "If you are not able to understand, believe that you might understand. Faith precedes; understanding follows."[31] With such a principle in place, human reason took a subordinate place in the mystery of knowing God, and intellectual humility was assured.

The new Christendom of the Latin doctors began to turn this principle on its head. The earliest case was that of Anselm of Canterbury (d. 1109), who made formative contributions to scholasticism while still at the French monastery of Bec. It is true that as a monk (rather than professor) he bucked the trend toward professional theology. The university system was only in its infancy, and there was little question of him participating in it. He has been

---

31   Quoted in John W. Baldwin, *The Scholastic Culture of the Middle Ages* (Prospect Heights, IL: Waveland Press, 1971), 87.

Anselm of Canterbury

called the last of the fathers and the first of the scholastics.

It is significant that Anselm's tentative departure from the priority of faith over reason took place in the aftermath of a controversy over the Eucharist. The Greek fathers had always called the sacrament a "mystery" (*mysterion*), and with their Latin counterparts they had accepted the traditional doctrine that after the consecration, the bread and wine are also the very body and blood of Christ. How this happened was . . . a mystery.

But in the eleventh century a disagreement arose that resulted in a more specific hypothesis about how the mystery occurs. This disagreement occurred between Lanfanc, Anselm's predecessor as abbot of Bec, and an adversary named Berengar. The latter questioned an earlier Frankish theologian's claim that the consecrated Body of Christ is one and the same as his deified body in heaven. Lanfranc challenged this using the logic of Aristotle. Lanfranc seized on his logical distinction between a thing's "accidents" and its "substance" to claim that while the consecrated Eucharist seemed to remain bread according to its accidents, it had within the liturgy been transformed in substance into the Body of Christ. As John Baldwin put it, "the significance of this controversy was that for the first time two theologians argued about a mystery of the faith purely in terms of grammar and dialectics."[32] It was a revolutionary moment in a revolutionary century.

In 1059 Berengar was called to the Lateran Palace by the pope and forced to sign a retraction of his views. The document, interestingly, was authored

---

32   Baldwin, *The Scholastic Culture of the Middle Ages*, 88.

for the occasion by none other than Cardinal Humbert. The act had the effect of endorsing Lanfranc's Aristotelian rationalism. As a result, the term "transubstantiation," never used before for the Eucharist, entered the theological vocabulary of the West.

Studying under his teacher and succeeding him as abbot, Anselm spent his time learning Aristotelian logic and grammar. One of the theologian's first treatises was actually entitled *On Grammar*. More famous was his *Proslogion,* in which he put forward a famous dictum: "Faith seeking understanding." While faith remains the starting point as it was with Augustine, it is now reason (or understanding) that represents the ultimate goal. Indeed, Anselm's famous treatise was an effort at demonstrating the existence of God on purely rational grounds. Not on a single page, not in a single sentence does the name of Jesus Christ ever appear. It is purely an argument for the existence of a deity *sola ratio,* through reason alone.

A half-century later, scholasticism had gained the upper hand in much of Western theology. Perhaps the most audacious exponent of it was the wandering French teacher Peter Abelard (d. 1142). After a youth spent in various schools (he had an early fascination with Anselm and briefly studied under him), he settled in Paris to teach at a school he founded himself. He was notorious for his reliance on Aristotle and his arrogant manner toward traditional teaching authorities. At the inception of Western civilization's university system, he was an academic celebrity sought out by curious intellectuals. In fact, he was even something of a "campus radical" long before that persona was established in the 1960s.

For in addition to his academic provocations, he found time to seduce the intellectually talented niece of a local priest, a girl named Heloise. After making her pregnant, he was forced to marry her secretly, but then in turn forced her to join a convent so that he could continue his teaching, unhindered by scandal. In the meantime, after the birth, he sent his infant son away to an orphanage and appears to have given no more thought to him. His anti-establishment behavior enraged Heloise's uncle, who hired thugs to attack the young scholar one day and castrate him. He spent most of the rest of his life in a monastery, forced to endure its sober environment but defiantly seeking to change the traditional culture of Christendom. Toward the end of his life he was nearly excommunicated, and his books were burned by order of the pope.

Abelard's most important work was *Yes and No*, a dialectical reflection on the Christian faith. It consists of a series of 158 statements by the fathers and their logical negation. It was intended as an intellectual exercise for his students, relying heavily on Aristotle. But it encouraged a highly cerebral approach to theology, making the "queen of the sciences" much more a form of science in the modern sense indeed.

Abelard's intellectual radicalism did not go unchallenged. He faced the censure of Bernard of Clairvaux, who relentlessly attacked the scholastic method whenever he encountered it. It was Bernard, more than any other, who precipitated papal intervention. He was responsible for the threat of excommunication that hung over the beleaguered Abelard at the end of his life. Nevertheless, in seeking to rescue faith from the imperiousness of reason, Bernard was forced to distinguish sharply between the two, suggesting that each had a separate scope of relevance in Christianity. But this intuitive reaction to Abelard would not be formalized for another century.

Scholasticism was brought to the summit of its influence during the thirteenth century in the work of Thomas Aquinas (d. 1274). A member of the Order of Preachers, he was the student of another famous Dominican named Albert Magnus and settled at the University of Paris to learn from him. Albert was the West's master of Aristotelianism, having domesticated it in ways Abelard had been incapable of doing and integrated it into just about every branch of knowledge.

As Thomas carried on Albert's Aristotelian project, he was forced to defend "the Philosopher"—as he deferentially called Aristotle—against the continued suspicions of theological traditionalists. By this time, the opposition once offered by Bernard had been taken up by the Franciscans. One of these, Bonaventure, even taught side by side with Thomas. Bonaventure (d. 1274) was in fact the head of the Friars Minor, and because of his vast learning he also served as a professor in Paris. Along with other Franciscans, Bonaventure took his theological stand on Augustinianism, especially its claim that reason can only spring from faith. It cannot function autonomously without it. Philosophy, therefore, must be subordinate to but at the same time united with theology. Thomas rejected Bonaventure's position. He believed that the Philosopher, though pagan, had given to Christians a system of reasoning that illuminated and clarified the faith.

Writing with a highly technical vocabulary accessible only to professional philosophers, Thomas Aquinas laid out the entire range of theological categories and subjects in a massive exposition of the Christian faith entitled the *Summa theologica* (or "summation of theology").

Thomas Aquinas

In one sense the work represents a struggle against the divisive effects of scholasticism, which, since the time of Anselm, had pitted reason against faith. Thomas admitted that some revealed dogmas, such as the Trinity and the Incarnation, were beyond the scope of natural reason. But he claimed others were not. The existence of God, for instance, and the immortality of the soul were both subject to the methods of philosophy. Had not the papacy itself already endorsed the eucharistic doctrine of transubstantiation, which shared the concepts of substance and accidents with Aristotle? Those forms of knowledge subject to reason came to be known as *natural theology*, and those that defied reason were reserved for the academic discipline of *revealed theology*.

An example of Thomas's use of natural reason in the *Summa* is his discussion of the filioque. In dialectical fashion, he presents a series of questions about this late addition to the Creed and follows each with hypothetical objections. Interestingly, unlike Cardinal Humbert, he accepts that the phrase "and the son" was not part of the original Creed. And he takes up the Orthodox argument against it by recognizing that the Scriptures only speak of the Spirit proceeding from the Father (John 15:26). But then Aristotelian logic takes over.

The theologian implicitly calls on the Philosopher to explain how it would be impossible for the Spirit not to proceed from the Son, since the "order of nature" reveals that the Son and the Spirit cannot have the same relationship with the Father without one of them taking precedence over the other in the sequence of that relationship. Curiously, this causes Thomas to acknowledge that it could therefore logically be true that instead of the Spirit proceeding from the Father and the Son, the Son proceeds from the Father and the Spirit. He seems on the verge of entertaining a theoretical *spiritoque*. But, he happily notes, "no one" teaches this. Finally, to supplement his argument against "Greek" objections to the filioque that were based on conciliar precedent, he asserts the claim, then unassailable in the wake of the reformation, that even ecumenical councils are subordinate to the Roman pontiff.

The *Summa theologica* was an ambitious project, exuding optimism about natural reason. The West was still a long way from modern times, but as the historian Steven Ozment has shown, scholasticism represented a step toward "secularization." Its *epistemology* (or theory of knowledge) departed radically from that of Augustine and, for that matter, that of the Greek fathers.

> For Augustine, to speak of reason was to speak of the mind of man illumined by the mind of God. For Aquinas, to speak of reason was to speak of the mind of man naturally exercising its own innate talents.[33]

In other words, human knowledge—even about God—was becoming autonomous. For Papadakis, this development (along with the Papal Reformation) represented yet another "alarming symptom of the disintegration of the common Christian tradition."[34]

But that was not all. Scholasticism was also a departure from the

---

33 Steven Ozment, *The Age of Reform, 1250–1550: An Intellectual and Religious History of Late Medieval and Reformation Europe* (New Haven: Yale University Press, 1980), 51–52.

34 Papadakis, *The Christian East and the Rise of the Papacy*, 167.

paradisiacal culture of the old Christendom. In the West, mystical knowledge *of* God was being exchanged for a rationalistic knowledge *about* God.

Hesychasm

THIS BRINGS US TO ONE of the truly definitive contrasts between the new Christendom and the old. At the height of the scholastic movement, a controversy arose in Byzantium over the question of how, exactly, man can know God. Its background included the long-term familiarity of the Greeks with their pagan intellectual ancestors, such as Plato and Aristotle. However, the immediate cause of the controversy was a reaction to the epistemologically optimistic claims of Thomas Aquinas. The great scholastic had made provocative claims about the potential of autonomous human reason. But reactions often result in overcompensation and extremes. In this case, a theologian with a foot in both the scholastic West and the patristic East tried to resolve the widening gulf with a form of epistemological agnosticism. But it proved to blind him to the presence of God in this world—both figuratively and, in the matter of what was called the Uncreated Light, quite literally.

Barlaam of Calabria (d. 1348) was an Orthodox theologian when he arrived in Constantinople in about 1330. He came from southern Italy, where, as we saw earlier, Eastern Christianity had an ancient presence (though it had been suppressed since the eleventh century). There are two theories about his initially fierce identification with Orthodoxy. One is that he was raised Orthodox despite the Latin persecution of his homeland, and that he fled to the East as soon as he could arrange a life for himself there. The other is that he was raised Roman Catholic but then converted to Orthodoxy as part of his reaction against scholasticism. Strangely, there is no definitive evidence to confirm either theory.

What is certain is that soon after his emigration, Barlaam began teaching theology at the academy in Constantinople. His erudition was so great that he was asked by the emperor to lead a delegation to the papal court to discuss reunion, and in connection with this assignment he produced a series of treatises against papal supremacy and the filioque.

In these treatises he made extensive reference to Dionysios the Areopagite. This mysterious writer claimed to be the first-century Athenian convert of Paul mentioned in Acts, but modern scholarship is unanimous in claiming he was most likely a pseudonymous theologian of the fifth century. By now works such as his *Mystical Theology* had become famous for a method known as *apophaticism*, which emphasizes the unknowability of God. Accordingly, a true understanding of divinity begins in a state of silent astonishment, with the realization that God transcends any human category of understanding. Dionysios's works had been used by Greek fathers such as Maximos the Confessor and John of Damascus. They were also much beloved and quoted by Thomas Aquinas, which is a paradox because the greatest of the scholastics was known for his ambitious project of explaining divine mysteries, not consigning them to unknowability.

It was exactly Dionysios's doctrine of the unknowability of God that attracted Barlaam. He used the apophatic method to call scholasticism into question. In particular, he used it to challenge Thomas's argument in defense of the filioque. "Thomas and everyone who reasons as he does," Barlaam complained, "thinks that there is nothing inaccessible to the human mind; [but] we believe that this opinion comes from a soul of demoniacal and evil pride; for most divine things transcend human knowledge."[35]

So far, so good, at least as far as Byzantine opponents of the West's new theology were concerned. However, one Greek theologian who was following Barlaam's polemics from a remote hermitage on Mount Athos began to see a problem with the argument, especially with its use of Dionysian apophaticism. He countered that man could indeed know God, and could do so directly.

The monk's name was Gregory Palamas (d. 1359). As a seasoned ascetic, he could not accept Barlaam's categorical rejection of the possibility of knowing God. He too admired the writings of Dionysios and clearly had little sympathy for the scholastic project. However, as an Athonite monk he shared in a rich and ancient tradition of what was called *hesychasm*, an approach

---

35   Quoted in Meyendorff, *St Gregory Palamas and Orthodox Spirituality*, 84.

to the knowledge of God centered on prayer rather than reasoning. It was in some ways the opposite of scholasticism, which tended to seek knowledge *about* God, not knowledge *of* God. For the hesychasts, the fundamental theological faculty of man was not the mind but the heart (*nous*).

Gregory's place within the larger context of Eastern Christendom was masterfully presented in a study by John Meyendorff. He noted that since its beginnings in the fourth century, monasticism had always culti-

Saint Gregory Palamas

vated the experience of God's immediate communion with man. This was due to its commitment to living out the consequences of the Incarnation. It was a way of life in which the whole man—mind as well as body—participated in the life of Christ by the baptismal grace of the Holy Spirit.

An early example of this anthropological unity was found in the person of Makarios the Great (d. 391). His *Spiritual Homilies* (which many believe were composed by disciples rather than by the saint himself) provide a corrective to other early ascetics who leaned toward a Neoplatonic disdain for the body and the material world. "Macarian mysticism," Meyendorff wrote,

is entirely based on the Incarnation of the Word. . . . It allows man even here below to enter into eschatological reality, the Kingdom of God, which embraces him, his spirit and his body, in a divine communion. The whole man, body and soul, was created in the image of God and the whole man is called to divine glory.[36]

Springing from the positive asceticism of the desert fathers, the *Homilies* exude the heavenly immanence of Christendom's paradisiacal culture.

The glory that the saints possess in their souls even today will (on the Day of Resurrection) clothe their naked bodies again and raise them up to the heavens. Then our body and our soul will rest eternally with the Lord in the Kingdom. When God created Adam he did not give him bodily wings like the birds but prepared for him in advance the wings of the Holy Spirit. . . . Saintly souls receive these wings even now when they take flight in the spirit toward heavenly thoughts.[37]

"Even now"—in this age—Makarios insists, the experience of heaven awaits those who desire it.

For this to happen, a transformational imperative is required. It takes hold of a Christian's life from within at the moment of baptism. Renewed by a lifetime of repentance, it changes the world the Christian inhabits into a paradise in which salvation is experienced even now, as a present reality. "Christians live in a different world," Makarios explains, using the present tense. "They have a table that belongs to them alone, a delight, a communion, a way of thinking uniquely theirs. That is why they are the strongest of men."[38]

This is not the institutional reform for the better that the Papal Reformation advanced throughout the new Christendom of the West. It was not external. It was concealed from the world, hidden within the heart of a repentant believer who, according to the ascetic practices of traditional Christianity, spent his days in prayer of the heart.

---

36   Ibid., 20.
37   Quoted in ibid., 22.
38   Quoted in ibid., 23.

Such a believer came to be known as a hesychast, one whose life was directed toward an experience of communion with God so immediate he entered a state of *hesychia,* or "stillness." Anxiety and fear—to say nothing of anger or pride—were foreign to this state. It was achieved only by acquiring an evangelical purity of heart—something only repentance and continuous prayer could bring. Of particular importance here was the Jesus Prayer: "Lord Jesus Christ, Son of God, have mercy on me, a sinner." Having origins in the Gospel (see Mark 10:46–47), the prayer provided a channel for a continuous stream of hesychastic asceticism from the fourth century to the fourteenth, when it was taken up by Athonite monks like Gregory Palamas.

But Barlaam was suspicious of hesychasm. He contested the possibility of really knowing God as directly as Gregory and other Athonite monks claimed to experience Him. Emboldened by success in teaching and diplomacy, Barlaam decided to venture into a study of Byzantine asceticism in order to match his opponent. He visited Thessaloniki, where a group of hesychasts discussed their experience of prayer with him. He learned that some of those practicing the Jesus Prayer did so while controlling their breathing and focusing their attention on the belly. This seemed to him excessively physical. The consummate rationalist was even more dismayed, however, when he learned that some hesychasts reported that during prayer they beheld God Himself in the form of Uncreated Light. He voiced his objections to this in a series of broadsides against the monks, mocking them as "navel-gazers" and charging them with the heresy of pantheism.[39]

Along the way, Barlaam struck a direct blow at one of Christendom's most fundamental principles. His agnosticism about knowing God subverted the culture of divine participation and even called into question the reality of the Incarnation. When in 1338 Gregory learned of this attack, he decided his life as a hermit on Mount Athos had to end. It was necessary to return to the world and undertake a defense of hesychasm.

Gregory's contribution to Christian culture was to demonstrate that man's participation in the life of God is real and not symbolic or otherwise

---

39 The specific charge was Messalianism, whose adherents claimed to see God with their physical eyes through intensive prayer rituals.

merely figurative. His demonstration was made in a work called *Triads for the Defense of the Holy Hesychasts* and another entitled the *Hagiorite Tome*. In them he argued consistently and effectively against Barlaam's agnostic claim that God's transcendent "divine simplicity" bars man from direct communion with Him.

With Thomas Aquinas and even Augustine, Gregory affirmed that God in His *essence* is indeed totally transcendent over man. But in His *energies*, He fully communicates Himself. This is the meaning of the apostle Peter's mystical statement about becoming "partakers of the divine nature" (2 Peter 1:4). God does not remain aloof from human experience but immediately—without any mediating created grace—fills the creation with His presence. "God," Gregory writes in the *Triads*,

> in His overflowing goodness to us, being transcendent to all things, incomprehensible and ineffable, consents to allow our intelligence to participate in Him and becomes invisibly visible in His superessential and inseparable power.[40]

Because of the Incarnation, the transcendent God has become immanent within the world through His Son, who possesses a deified material body, and by his Holy Spirit, who dwells in men through the holy mysteries (or sacraments) of the Church.

Barlaam had been committing the same spiritualizing error as early Neoplatonists who deviated from the Christocentric asceticism of Makarios. His argument implied that an unapproachable God had merely given man knowledge about salvation, but in no real way did He participate in the human experience. At best this tendency had provided between heaven and earth a realm of divine ideas that man could aspire toward but never really achieve. The Neoplatonists' God was one that man could imitate but never fully assimilate in this life. Man's calling was therefore to escape the prison house of the body and return to the realm of pure spirituality. The body, human history, and even the world itself ceased to have any intrinsic value. A way thus opened toward secularization, whereby the world would be

---

40   Quoted in ibid., 123

consigned to ultimate meaninglessness and only a transcendent heaven came to have any eschatological value.

This was an extreme, but it was the direction of Barlaam's attack on hesychasm as Gregory Palamas perceived it. His distinction between essence and energies precluded such an anti-incarnational doctrine once and for all.

Pending, that is, conciliar confirmation. The hesychast controversy sparked by Barlaam was not confined to an exchange of letters or a flurry of treatises. It drew in all of the Byzantine establishment. Among the highest clergy, it was immediately obvious that the attacks on hesychasm and the counterattacks by Gregory required episcopal intervention. This was all the more the case in that the intellectual issues ran deep within the Greek Church. As noted, any use of pagan thought within theology was controversial in the East.

This is not to say that Plato and Aristotle were novel there. Just the opposite was actually the case. They were so well known, and for the most part noncontroversial at a purely philosophical level, that the basic education of any Byzantine nobleman included them as authorities. Beyond this, court circles had included advocates for a kind of secular proto-humanism inspired by the pagan Greeks since the ninth century, and this trend peaked during the reorganization of the imperial academy at Constantinople during the eleventh century. Michael Psellos was the most famous of these advocates.

Psellos had been succeeded at the academy by John Italos, who, as his name suggests, was an emigré from the West. Three centuries before Barlaam, he had also come from Calabria in southern Italy and had taken up leadership of the academy. And like Barlaam, he soon became the center of theological controversy. John had advanced pagan thought within the field of Christian theology to such a degree that he was charged with a series of heresies. These included a Platonic belief in the preexistence of souls and a rejection of the bodily resurrection. Psellos was accused of harboring a preference for Aristotle and Plato over the Scriptures and the fathers. The result was anathematization and his public retraction. But so subversive were his efforts to supplement traditional Christianity with pagan philosophy that the Synodikon against heresiarchs in use since the victory over iconoclasm was augmented to include anathemas against him personally.

So it was inevitable that Barlaam's philosophically inspired attack on hesychasm would provoke concerns among the bishops. They were supported in their inquiry by Emperor John VI, though a Byzantine civil war then raging prolonged the process and complicated its resolution. In 1341 both emperor and patriarch were present at a council that condemned Barlaam's position and demanded he recant. He departed from Constantinople soon after. His place in the leadership of the proto-humanist faction opposed to hesychasm was taken by Gregory Akindynos, a former student of Gregory Palamas. Because of the chaos caused by civil war and the political fortunes of the patriarchate, a series of additional councils was convened during the decade that followed, with the result that now Akindynos also found himself excommunicated for his theological position. Finally, in 1351 a council in the capital repeated the conclusions of a decade before, and hesychasm was confirmed.

The vindication of Gregory Palamas was a second "triumph of Orthodoxy." The first had been the definitive recovery of iconographical worship after the Seventh Ecumenical Council. This had been the occasion for the formulation of the Synodikon of Orthodoxy, solemnly read every year on the first Sunday of the Great Fast (known as the Sunday of Orthodoxy). Now, to its anathemas on iconoclasm and the teachings of John Italos was added an affirmation of hesychasm. The Synodikon in universal use has not been augmented since.

The victory of hesychasm was a victory for the paradisiacal culture of the old Christendom. At a time when scholasticism had altered theological inquiry by imposing rationalism on it, and when an incipient humanism questioned the very possibility of knowing God, Gregory Palamas and the Byzantine ecclesiastical establishment reaffirmed traditional Christianity's principle of divine participation. This was no small achievement.

For Barlaam's attack on hesychasm, while motivated by the scholasticism of the West, had been supported by a latent humanism in the East. This element was largely confined to the court and academy in Constantinople. It had been firmly resisted by the monks for centuries, but because of the hesychast council of 1351 it was now permanently defeated. The empire only had a century of life left in it, but this eleventh-hour defense of divine participation assured Byzantium that it would pass on to its Slavic successors and those beyond them a truly paradisiacal culture. Only in seventeenth-century Russia would Western scholasticism once again sing its siren song to the intellectuals of the old Christendom.

In the meantime, secular humanism became a compelling alternative to traditional Christianity in the West. Its origin lay in the same fourteenth-century Italy to which Barlaam, defeated by the council of 1341, returned. Its earliest advocate was Petrarch, who is often called the "father of humanism." If this is so, then perhaps its grandfather—or great uncle—is Barlaam. For the defeated enemy of hesychasm, having renounced Orthodoxy and converted to Roman Catholicism to become an advocate for the papacy in Calabria, lived long enough to provide tutelage in the Greek language to Petrarch himself. Under his mentorship, the father of humanism became ever more enthralled by the Greeks. And it was not their church fathers he came to love, but their pagan philosophers.

CHAPTER FOUR

The Patterns of Piety

T HE DEPARTURE OF BARLAAM FROM Constantinople in 1341 was rich
in the symbolism of division. In many ways it resembled the actions of
Cardinal Humbert in 1054. The Calabrian theologian had been drawn to
the New Rome no less urgently than was the father of papal supremacy. He
too attacked there the Eastern Christianity he did not recognize. That the
practices in question were in fact ancient—unlike many of those in the new
Christendom to which he unfavorably contrasted them—seems to have been
lost on his factional mind, just as it was on Humbert's.

Barlaam's actions are similar to Humbert's in another sense: they symbolized a state of excommunication. Like his predecessor, he stormed away
from the ecumenical patriarchate in a state of defiance. The emerging Western "virtue" of indignation led him to renounce Orthodox Christianity
rather than repent and learn from it. His subsequent actions are evidence
of this. Just as Humbert's return to Italy was marked by the composition
of the reformational treatise *Against the Simoniacs*, Barlaam's was marked by
conversion to Roman Catholicism and service to the papacy.

But most importantly, Barlaam's rejection of the East signaled the growing desiccation of Western culture. His defiant stand against hesychasm
represented how very little his thought and that of the scholastics generally
was being irrigated by those twin sources of the old Christendom, heavenly

immanence and divine participation.[1] Below the surface of the civilization to which he returned—with its emerging institutions of reformist papacy, national monarchy, itinerant monasticism, and scholastic theology—the experience of paradise was being slowly choked off.

This was an ominous development for the West. There, a new culture was forming that had less and less contact with the paradisiacal values of the old Christendom. The day would come when its values were almost completely secular. For now, during the age of division, Western culture maintained a self-consciously Christian standard of integrity. But its sources were drying up. This can be seen most vividly in new—and old—patterns of piety.

The Bane of Clericalism

THE MOST IMPORTANT DISTINCTIONS IN piety, perhaps, were the ways in which West and East adapted to the one really ominous threat to paradisiacal culture. The laity had for centuries been growing more and more secondary to the eucharistic assembly. For after the mass conversion of the fourth century, Holy Communion had been served less and less frequently. And by the end of the first millennium, it was positively rare.

The reasons for this were twofold. On the one hand, the laity seems to have felt itself less and less worthy of approaching the chalice. Communion was reserved only for special occasions such as the annual season of Great Lent. On the other hand, the clergy saw itself as guardian of the altar's holy gifts and actually encouraged lay withdrawal from them.

Both tendencies opened the way to the bane of clericalism. It had always been a temptation to assign to the clergy primary responsibility for living out the transformational imperative. The lure, ironically, often acted first upon the laity. Imposing the cross on others was easier than taking it up oneself. Idealizing the piety of one's pastor also helped ease the responsibility of living out the high moral standards of the Sermon on the Mount. And the clergy were often all too happy to oblige.

But the abiding temptation toward clericalism became particularly

---

1   On these, see *Age of Paradise*, 40–50.

strong in the West after the first millennium, when papal reformers consciously attacked the structure of lay participation (and in the case of the proprietary system, interference) in church life. As we have noted in previous chapters, a bifurcation of Western society into two unequal spiritual classes was a consequence of the Papal Reformation.

This is not to say the East was cheerfully free of clericalism. The temptation toward it was always felt there too. This is documented in Constantinople during the eleventh century. Niketas Stethatos, the Studite monk who defended Eastern practices against agents of the Papal Reformation, wrote the following:

> *Know that the place of the laity in the assembly of the faithful during the anaphora is far from the divine altar. The interior of the sanctuary is reserved to the priests, deacons, and subdeacons. . . . How then from [their] distance can the laymen, to whom it is not allowed, contemplate the mysteries of God accomplished with trembling hands by his priests?*

Nothing is said here about lay reception of the Eucharist, but the sense of division between two classes of worshippers is sharp. Niketas may actually have had the emperor in mind when generalizing about "laymen," as he had been a public critic of Constantine Monomachos's adultery. And as a disciple of Symeon the New Theologian Niketas was certainly no stranger to criticisms of the clergy.[2] But a generalization is still a generalization. In his judgment, laymen were simply unworthy even of looking on the sacrament because of their "unsanctified glance."[3] It would be hard to find words stronger than these to document the temptation toward clericalism in Byzantium.

However, the same Divine Liturgy of which Niketas spoke contains an eloquently anti-clericalistic (though not *anticlerical*) prayer about the total unworthiness of the clergy to glance upon—let alone handle—the Eucharist.

---

2 Symeon was notorious for his attacks on clerical hypocrisy and his accommodation of lay leadership in spiritual direction.

3 Hugh Wybrew, *The Orthodox Liturgy: The Development of the Eucharistic Liturgy in the Byzantine Rite* (Crestwood, NY: St. Vladimir's Seminary Press, 1991), 134.

It occurs at the Great Entrance, when the clergy carry the gifts to the altar after passing through the assembled laity.

> *No one who is bound by the desires and pleasures of the flesh is worthy to approach, or draw near, or to worship thee, O King of glory, for to serve thee is great and awesome, even to the heavenly powers. Nevertheless, through thine ineffable and boundless love for mankind thou didst become man, yet without change or alteration, and become our high priest.*

The emphatic "nevertheless" in this statement is a reminder of the paradox of the Incarnation. No one on earth is worthy to draw near to the awesome God. Not even the angels in heaven are worthy. The only true priest is Christ. Through His ministry alone the transcendent God has become immanent in creation, establishing communion with all men. Seen from this heavenly perspective, the difference between clergy and laity is minimized, even negated. The priest is a sinner called to acknowledge an unworthiness equal to (if not greater than) that of the layman standing outside the sanctuary. Such a prayer precludes even the slightest opportunity for clericalism.

Furthermore, having made this plea to the heavenly High Priest, the earthly priest is required by the rite to face the assembled laity and, bowing before them, to ask them as brothers and sisters for forgiveness. Any potential for division between the two classes of worshipper is, at least in the context of the Divine Liturgy, nullified.

Finally, the priest bears up the bread and wine in a procession that takes him out of the sanctuary to stand among the laity and, along with them, sing the Cherubic Hymn, which proclaims a transformative union of heaven and earth:

> *Let us who mystically represent the cherubim and who sing the thrice-holy hymn to the life-creating Trinity now lay aside all earthly cares, that we may receive the King of all who comes invisibly upborne by the angelic hosts. Alleluia, alleluia, alleluia.*

The Orthodox experience of liturgy, like its experience of salvation, was a paradox. It was clerical, but not by nature clericalistic.

The same had undoubtedly been true of Western piety prior to the eleventh century. But the Mass had fewer liturgical fail-safes against ecclesial bifurcation. What is more, the institutional agenda of papal reformation had required a distinguished leadership to be set apart from the lay masses. It was from the clergy, after all, that the shock troops of the Gregorian Revolution had been recruited. In comparison to the East, there were simply far fewer mechanisms in place to protect against clericalism. As a result, the laity became increasingly superfluous.

For instance, the papal reform of eucharistic bread (manifested, as we saw, by Cardinal Humbert's attack on a tradition to which the East still adhered) introduced unleavened wafers that could no longer be baked by parishioners. The common leavened bread formerly used in the West had represented the principal offering of the laity at the Mass. It had been formalized in a procession called the Offertory, the Western equivalent of the Great Entrance. In this liturgical gift of leavened bread, Theodor Klauser once noted, the layman "gave something of his own substance, something fundamental to his very existence and by doing this represented the giving of himself."[4] In other words, the layman thus participated in the divine sacrifice of God and was deified by it.

Such piety continued in the East, even after the withdrawal of the laity from frequent eucharistic communion. Leavened loaves of bread continued to be the material offering of the people to God. Even when a more formalized preparation of liturgical bread came into use, by which the statement "Jesus Christ the Victor" was carefully stamped in abbreviated form into the loaves, the laity maintained a close relationship to the offering. Called a *prosphoron* (literally, "offering"), each loaf was used to provide small particles of bread representing various loved ones the laity kept in mind during the eucharistic assembly. After the Eucharist had been consecrated from a distinct loaf and consumed during communion, these particles were then

---

4   Theodor Klauser, *A Short History of the Western Liturgy* (Oxford: Oxford University Press, 1979), 109.

added to the chalice to symbolize the unity of those commemorated with the sacramental Body of Christ.

The novel unleavened wafers that were now used in the West, however, prevented any such commemorative use. They were not intended for common hands and were baked by specialists—probably monks or lower clergy. For this reason the people's actual contribution of bread to the Offertory of the Mass ceased, and with it their material participation in Christ's sacrifice.

Liturgical participation by the Western laity was also undermined by another, more momentous change. The monastic reformation that preceded the Papal Reformation had resulted in an inflation of ordinations to the priesthood. As a result, by the eleventh century, most monks were not merely repentant Christians seeking salvation at a distance from society, as had been the case with Benedict of Nursia (who was never ordained); they were now ordained clergy with an obligation to serve the divine services on a regular basis. Since a traditional monastery or cathedral had only one altar for the whole liturgical assembly, the multiplication of priests required a reform in architecture in which additional altars were installed in side chapels separate from the main altar. These became the nexus for a rotation of Masses scheduled throughout the week to allow the multitude of otherwise superfluous priests to fulfill their sacerdotal duties.

The result was the rise of the private Mass. On a daily basis, priests said the eucharistic rite simply, silently, and swiftly—in many cases no doubt with a glance over their shoulder at the next priest waiting in line to use the altar. Traditional Christianity's original vision of an entire congregation of God's people assembled on the Lord's Day, documented so radiantly in early centuries by Ignatius of Antioch in the East and Justin Martyr in the West, was now clouded by a sequence of almost covert services performed by a priest with a sole acolyte in a shadowy side chapel. Gone was the participation or even presence of the people at such private Masses.

As with clerical celibacy, this innovation was not free of controversy, and it took a reformer with the stature of Peter Damian to justify it. His short treatise *Dominus vobiscum* was written to explain how a priest could use the traditionally plural forms of liturgical address (such as the phrase "the Lord be with you," which is the English translation of the book's title) even when serving alone. It was something of a legal fiction, but it satisfied the concerns of a growing class of self-sufficient liturgical celebrants. The result was a growing division of the clergy from the people, as priests were expected to perform such services on a daily basis. For the clerical elite of Western Christendom, liturgical piety was becoming privatized. And as the laity looked on in silence, new forms of piety began to emerge for them as well.

A matching tendency to privatize liturgical experience was one of them. The most respected pious laymen came to be those who frequented the daily private Masses, and moreover who ordered them with intentions that were entirely personal. In addition to bringing rich and poor together in the weekly assembly of unity that was the Sunday Solemn Mass (*Missa solemnis*), the liturgical culture encouraged individuals to attend separate Votive Masses (*Missae votivae*) in which only they and a priest prayed for a closed circle of loved ones. This, to be sure, offered new opportunities for the expansion of Christendom's liturgical piety. But it was a sword that cut both ways. It could also, in light of the comparatively passive experience of the Solemn Mass, become an engaging alternative to it.

The privatization of liturgical piety was closely related to another outcome of the new clericalism. Since the time of Charlemagne, divine services in the West had come to be performed exclusively in an incomprehensible language. The Franks had been the first to insist—with the reformist papacy eventually agreeing—that only Latin be tolerated in divine services. The innovation had been vigorously challenged by Eastern missionaries such as Cyril and Methodios, who transmitted the faith to the Slavs in their own vernacular. But in the West, linguistic pluralism was eventually suppressed.

As a result, by the second millennium very few people understood the content of the Mass. In lands with Romance (or "Roman-like") languages, such as Italy, Spain, and France, the vernacular used by common people no longer resembled the Latin of earlier centuries. And when it came to Germans, Anglo-Saxons, Celts, Hungarians, or Poles, the linguistic division between liturgical celebrant and layman was even more absolute.

Only the educated clergy could now make sense of the prayers and scripture readings that were, after all, the heart of Christendom's transformational imperative. What is more, prayers such as those accompanying the consecration of the Eucharist were increasingly spoken softly or in complete silence (something also found in the East).

Under these conditions, as modern liturgists have noted, the laity was reduced to a passive and largely subjective role. "Deprived of frequent communion and with a liturgy in Latin," Gregory Dix observed, "private adoration was all that was left to the unlettered layfolk, even the most devout of them, with which to exercise their piety."[5]

Filling the Eucharistic Void

GIVEN CHRISTENDOM'S PARADISIACAL VALUES, AN elitist approach to communion could not sustain itself forever. In response, the clergy introduced practices designed to remind congregations of Christ's real presence in the eucharistic assembly. In the West the most notable of these was the elevation of the Host at the Mass. With time a bell was also rung to announce its consecration. The effect on a spiritually hungry laity was tremendous. Accounts are given of latecomers flooding into the temple at that moment, craning their necks to see the Host and training their ears to hear the signal that the greatest of miracles had, on the very ground they stood on, been accomplished.

The consecration of the Eucharist became a moment of intense piety. One observer commented that the laity "come when they hear the bell, entering to see the elevation, and when it is over they leave, running and fleeing, as if they have seen the devil."[6] Some laypeople claimed to see light radiating from the Host held in the priest's hands. Others reported it appearing as the infant Jesus. The elevation of the consecrated Host thus became, according

---

5   Gregory Dix, *The Shape of the Liturgy* (London: Bloomsbury T&T Clark, 2005), 249.

6   Quoted in Richard Kieckhefer, "Major Currents in Late Medieval Devotion," in *Christian Spirituality: High Middle Ages and Reformation*, edited by Jill Rait (New York: Crossroad Publishing, 1987), 75–108.

to Joseph Jungmann, "the new pivot and center of the canon of the Mass." For a non-communing laity, seeing it raised in the air over the altar table was in itself "a sort of Communion."[7]

Another opportunity for venerating the Eucharist without actually partaking of it was provided by the establishment of the feast of Corpus Christi. After a consecrated Host was miraculously seen issuing blood on the altar table of a local church, Pope Urban IV (r. 1261–1264) issued a papal bull authorizing the holiday in 1264. It thereafter spread slowly but persistently throughout the West.[8] Eventually it would become one of the most characteristically Roman Catholic of divine services, especially in the face of sacramental conflicts during the Protestant Reformation. By presenting the consecrated Host within an ornate monstrance and singing hymns of adoration, clerics enabled laymen to participate with them in the experience of heavenly immanence.

Thus the liturgical reforms that issued from the Papal Reformation provided the medium for a far-reaching shift in piety. As Colin Morris has noted, "scarcely any of these reforms increased the sense of community within the local churches. Indeed, the whole tendency was to diminish the sense of community." Instead, a new eucharistic piety emerged with a marked tendency toward individualism.

> *The Eucharist had been, for the early Church, the supreme expression of its unity. . . . The new practices which arose in the celebration of the Mass, such as the elevation of the Host, were directed, not towards the restoration of community, but towards the kindling of personal devotion.*[9]

---

7 Joseph A. Jungmann, *The Mass of the Roman Rite: Its Origins and Development*, vol. 2, translated by Francis A. Brunner (Notre Dame: Christian Classics, 1951), 208.

8 Eucharistic adoration was never introduced in the East as a liturgical end in itself, though the consecrated Lamb had long been venerated at the Presanctified Liturgy prior to communion.

9 Colin Morris, *The Discovery of the Individual, 1050–1200* (Toronto: University of Toronto Press, 1972), 12.

For Gregory Dix also, the "old corporate worship" of the first millennium now gave way to a "mere focus for the subjective devotion of each separate worshipper in the isolation of his own mind."[10]

Such piety was the liturgical outcome of an age of division, the byproduct of ecclesial bifurcation. As the clerical elite absconded with the Mass to side chapels and performed the services in an incomprehensible language, the layman ceased participating actively in liturgy and was reduced to merely seeing and hearing it.

And, to an extent, thinking about it. For one of the most important efforts to bridge the gap between the old piety and the new was to reconceive it mentally. During the first half of the second millennium, descriptions of the liturgy began to flourish, especially in the West. Liturgical interpretation was as old as the practice of infrequent communion. Whether it was consciously intended as compensation for eucharistic nonparticipation or not is impossible to tell. Its origin was in the East, where lay withdrawal occurred first. According to Robert Taft, the shift was marked by the reconstruction of Hagia Sophia in 537. That huge edifice inspired a new way of envisioning worship, one in which communion with God was accomplished as much through liturgy as through sacrament. In a sense, then, Constantinople's Great Church (as it came to be known) was the first *temple* of Christendom. Until this time, churches were largely utilitarian structures—modeled usually on the classical Roman basilica—which proved suitable for gathering the eucharistic assembly. Now churches helped determine how that assembly was liturgically experienced.[11]

The East developed two distinct tendencies in liturgical interpretation. One approached liturgy as a reflection on, and participation in, the life of Christ. This approach was basically historical. Each unit of the service was viewed as an allegory related to a discrete earthly event. Early examples of such interpretation included works by Dionysios the Areopagite and Maximos the Confessor, but the first full-scale expression of it was the

---

10 Dix, *The Shape of the Liturgy*, 599–600.
11 Robert F. Taft, *The Byzantine Rite: A Short History* (Collegeville, MN: Liturgical Press, 1992), 35–36.

work of Patriarch Germanos of Constantinople (d. 740). "The church," he claimed,

> is an earthly heaven in which the super-celestial God dwells and walks about. It represents [literally icon-ifies] the crucifixion, burial, and resurrection of Christ. . . . The holy table corresponds to the spot in the tomb where Christ was placed. . . . [it] is also the throne of God, on which, borne by the Cherubim, He rested in the body.[12]

As an opponent of iconoclasm, Germanos was highly esteemed in the West and exercised wide influence there.

The most obvious evidence of his influence was the liturgical commentary of the Frankish bishop Amalar of Metz (d. 850). He seized on the allegorical element in Germanos's writing to present a rich and complex meditation on how the Mass communicates the actions of Christ during His life in the world. Later commentators built on Amalar's work, turning the Mass into "a comprehensive representation of the Passion of Jesus."[13] As they did so, they fostered a new approach to Christian worship that sustained at least one element of the old paradisiacal piety: divine participation. However, it did not require eucharistic communion. It did not even require the active engagement of anyone but the clergy. The layman was free to listen and as he did so to ponder Christ's historical presence in the world. Once participants in the Mass, the laity now became a veritable audience for it. The expression "hearing Mass" eventually cemented this development.

One outcome of this development was the dramatization of the Western liturgy. Going beyond the Mass, the offices of certain feast days became saturated with dramaturgy. Passion Week provided the annual peak in this tendency, with its visual commemoration of the Savior's betrayal and death. Beginning possibly in England, Palm Sunday worshippers assembled to watch the clergy read the Passion Gospel in multiple parts, as if

---

12 Germanus of Constantinople, *On the Divine Liturgy*, translated by Paul Meyendorff (Crestwood, NY: St. Vladimir's Seminary Press, 1984), 57–59.

13 Jungmann, *The Mass of the Roman Rite*, vol. 1, 177.

acting out the event. While this had the potential to emphasize performance rather than proclamation, it created an engaging effect, one that served as compensation for the assembly's otherwise largely passive role. A similar approach to reading the Gospel on Good Friday was also introduced at this time.

The rise of a distinctively dramaturgical approach to the liturgy in the West was not lost to contemporaries. In the eleventh century, Honorius of Autun observed how

> it is known that those [ancients] who recited tragedies in theaters presented the actions of opponents by gestures before the people. In the same way our tragic author [i.e., the liturgical celebrant] represents by his gestures in the theater of the Church before the Christian people the struggle of Christ and teaches to them the victory of His redemption.[14]

Not all contemporaries approved of this. Liturgical traditionalists, as well as those advocating the clergy-oriented principles of the Papal Reformation, lamented what they considered a mawkish appeal to popular piety. To compensate the laity for infrequent communion and linguistic obfuscation, liturgical celebrants were resorting to devices such as audible sighing, agonized cries, and "histrionic gestures" with their bodies.[15]

The dramatic flowering of the Western liturgy resulted in yet another innovation, the introduction of designated vestment colors for the various holidays of the year. This was done by Pope Innocent III. Within the new liturgical environment, it quickly caught on.

It has been argued that with the appearance of such practices, the Mass served to preserve the dramatic arts in the West, providing a bridge between the closing of theaters by Justinian in the sixth century and the reopening of them to Shakespeare in the sixteenth. It is certainly true that liturgical dramaturgy facilitated the emergence of a new genre of performance art in the

---

14   Quoted in O. B. Hardison, *Christian Rite and Christian Drama in the Middle Ages* (Baltimore: Johns Hopkins University Press, 1965), 39–40.
15   Quoted in ibid., 79.

West, known as the mystery play. The famous fifteenth-century *Everyman* was a late example of this.

But of more interest here is the fact that, organized and performed by the laity, such paraliturgical dramas represented an alternative way of participating in a mystery of salvation that otherwise seemed more and more the affair of clerics.

From Heaven to Earth . . .

AS WE HAVE NOTED, INTERPRETING the Mass as an allegory on the historical life of Christ was an invention of the East. Amalar and others who wrote in this vein were borrowing from earlier liturgical commentaries such as that of Patriarch Germanos. But their approach was only one of two that had appeared in Byzantium. The other was in fact much more prominent there. Its focus was the presence of the kingdom of heaven in this world. According to Robert Cabié,

> the Eastern allegorical interpretations differ clearly from those of the Latin Middle Ages. They are built around a basic symbolism: the "Divine Liturgy" is, in a sense, heaven come down to earth and the focal point of a cosmic vision of reality. Here the entire universe is transfigured by the Holy Spirit in the offering of the sacred gifts.[16]

This quintessentially Eastern approach to liturgy did not contemplate Christ's presence on earth in the past so much as his ongoing presence, or *present-ness*. It placed eschatology before historicity.

The effect was cosmic transformation. Cabié's use of verbs is appropriate. The world is "transfigured" by the divine presence. In the New Testament, the Greek word *metamorphoo* is used for both the Transfiguration of Christ (Matt. 17:2) and the transformation of the Christian in Christ (Rom. 12:2). It

16   Robert Cabié, *The Eucharist*, translated by Matthew J. O'Connell, vol. 2 of The Church at Prayer: An Introduction to the Liturgy, edited by Aime Georges Martimort (Collegeville, MN: The Liturgical Press, 1986), 148.

can be said, then, that Eastern liturgical piety was predominantly transfigurational, or metamorphic. What is more, such an understanding of liturgy was *anagogical* in character; that is, it revealed heavenly realities not otherwise discernible in the natural world. It might therefore be distinguished from the *allegorical* approach of Amalar, in which liturgy communicated events in this world, namely the salvific actions of Christ in history.

Maximos the Confessor was the first to bring systematic attention to how the church building mystically transfigures the world. In the *Ecclesiastical Mystagogy,* which was inspired in part by Dionysios the Areopagite, he equated the Divine Liturgy that took place in temples on earth with a heavenly liturgy taking place eternally in heaven. This anagogical interpretation was elaborated by later theologians.

One of these was Germanos, whose use of allegory, as we have seen, had appealed strongly to Amalar. However, the patriarch of Constantinople also applied anagogy in his treatise on the Divine Liturgy. In fact, the work both opens and closes with it. We have already quoted his initial statement that the church is an "earthly heaven." In his final paragraph he returns to the theme, declaring that in the Divine Liturgy "we are no longer on earth but standing by the royal throne of God in heaven, where Christ is."[17]

Not all Byzantine commentators were satisfied with either an anagogical or an allegorical interpretation of the liturgy alone. In fact, the most respected among them, Nicholas Cabasilas (d. 1391), gave priority to its eucharistic function. At the beginning of his treatise, he states simply that "the essential act in the celebration of the holy mysteries is the transformation of the elements into the Divine Body and Blood; its aim is the sanctification of the faithful, who through these mysteries receive the remission of their sins and the inheritance of the kingdom of heaven."[18] Perhaps Nicholas intended his commentary as a call to return to frequent communion. This did not happen, however, and other theologians continued

17 Germanus, *On the Divine Liturgy,* 101.
18 Nicholas Cabasilas, *A Commentary on the Divine Liturgy,* translated by J. M. Hussey and P. A. McNulty (Crestwood, NY: St. Vladimir's Seminary Press, 1998), 25.

to use a combination of anagogy and allegory to fill the eucharistic void.

One of these was Symeon of Thessaloniki (d. 1421). The liturgical scholar Hans-Joachim Schulz considered his work to be "the first complete literary counterpart to the iconography of the heavenly liturgy."[19] Symeon declared that the church building "is an image of the whole world, for God is everywhere and above everything." Though transcendent, God has through the Incarnation become immanent on earth, filling the world with His presence through the Church's liturgical life. Symeon asserts that "there is only one Church, above and below, since God came down and lived among us, doing what he was sent to do on our behalf." Heaven enters this world and is experienced through the arrangement of liturgical architecture and the actions of liturgical celebrants. The liturgical transformation of the world "is carried out both above and here below, but with this difference: above it is done without any veils and symbols, but here it is accomplished through symbols."[20]

Symeon used the word "icon" for the church building. According to the fathers of the Seventh Ecumenical Council, icons were not only useful for communicating to an illiterate society the historical realities recorded in the Bible. Indeed, a narrative purpose was not even the primary one. What true icons did was proclaim the reality of the Incarnation. They showed forth the presence of God in this world. Icons of Christ did so most explicitly, but those of saints did likewise because, as traditional Christianity held, Christ is present in the saints. By applying the technical word "icon" to the church temple, Symeon and others were assigning a similar function to the material space dedicated to Christ's communion with His people.

What is more, Eastern churches were built with iconographical programs designed to enhance such symbolism. This not only provided a counterpart to the liturgical commentaries we considered above, it brought heaven-on-earth anagogy directly into the lives of the laity. As such it can be seen as another mechanism to protect against clericalism.

---

19   Hans-Joachim Schulz, *The Byzantine Liturgy*, translated by Matthew J. O'Connell (New York: Pueblo Publishing, 1986), 119.
20   Taft, *The Byzantine Rite*, 69.

Following the ninth-century restoration of icons—an event known in the Orthodox Church as the "triumph of Orthodoxy"—increasing attention was placed on the programmatic arrangement of temple iconography. Patriarch Photios had inaugurated the placement of an icon of the Theotokos in the apse of Hagia Sophia directly above the altar table. It depicted Mary with Christ as an infant enthroned on her lap. As an expression of the Incarnation, its location above the altar, where during the Liturgy the Holy Spirit transformed the eucharistic gifts, brought even more attention to the theme of heavenly immanence.

In the eleventh-century church of Hosios Loukas in Greece, this incarnational theme was powerfully amplified for all who entered the temple, clerical or lay. Directly over the doors leading from the narthex into the nave was an icon of Christ. The head of the Church, He greeted the worshipper, as it were, with a Gospel Book opened to the declaration that He is the light of the world (John 8:12). This entryway was organized so that even before passing through it, one would see in the distance the apse containing the Theotokos with the God-Man enthroned on her lap. And as one moved eastward toward the altar, he would become immediately conscious of the vast space

Icon of Christ Pantocrator in Hosias Loukas

opening up above him, drawing his glance upward toward the central dome. There he would see Christ again in the iconographic form of the Pantocrator, this time being made present to His assembled people by the dome's visual effect of heaven descending on earth.

By the end of the thirteenth century, Orthodox iconography began to add yet more emphasis on the liturgical transformation of the world. In the Serbian monastery of Saint Sophia in Ohrid, for instance, the apse was now centered upon a vivid representation of the Incarnation, the icon of the Theotokos of the Sign. Along the wall below (that is, directly behind the altar table), a scene called the Communion of the Apostles was painted. This mural shows Christ, vested as the heavenly High Priest, distributing consecrated bread to His people. As He does so, He is surrounded by angels vested as liturgical celebrants. This scene is not merely historical; it is not a depiction of the Last Supper. It represents an event that goes beyond what took place in the past. Paul, though absent from the historical Last Supper, is depicted there. And Christ Himself distributes communion not from a common table (as in icons of the Last Supper) but from an altar. For the art historian Hans Belting, such a liturgical image "created its own experience of time, which embraced both the revelation of God in the past and the fulfillment of time in the future."[21] In other words, the ritual actions observed within the temple were an eschatological experience, uniting the world to heaven.

And what worshippers beheld in front of them in the apse they also saw above them in the central dome. At another Serbian monastery, Hilandar on Mount Athos, the icon of Christ Pantocrator was surrounded by angels vested for the Divine Liturgy. They bore in their hands various liturgical articles such as processional candles. Furthermore, like the faithful in this world beneath them, they were oriented, that is, they faced the eastern side of the dome, where the heavenly altar was represented.

By this point in history, a solid iconostasis was typically placed between the altar and the nave, where the laity stood. Some see this as a move toward

---

21   Hans Belting, *Likeness and Presence: A History of the Image before the Era of Art,* translated by Edmund Jephcott (Chicago: University of Chicago, 1994), 174.

clericalism, accentuating the dictum of Niketas Stethatos that the altar should be shielded from the "unsanctified glance" of the layman. And perhaps at some level it was such a move. However, the design of the iconostasis reveals how it can just as easily be interpreted as a statement about divine presence and a fail-safe *against* clericalism. For on its nave side numerous icons are placed, proclaiming the presence of Christ in this world and the unity of worshippers with His saints. The layman facing the iconstasis during services beholds an image of paradise. And the doors at its center, known as the Royal Gates, support the experience. They are often likened to the gates of paradise. For though they are sometimes closed, indicating the tragic reality of the Fall, they are opened to the laity at key moments during the Divine Liturgy. One such moment is when the clergy bring the Gospel into the nave to proclaim the kingdom of heaven. Another is when the clergy bring the chalice to the laity, joining the nave to the altar and making the entire temple an image of paradise.

The liturgical piety of the old Christendom was designed, as one historian has noted, to transform the liturgical participant and "to remake his or her reality."[22] Those who attended divine services were not so much witnesses to cosmic transformation as participants in it.

As we have seen, in the new Christendom, heaven-on-earth piety began to wane after the Great Division. Architecture, however, was initially slow to adjust. This is readily visible in the features of the prevailing aesthetic known as the Romanesque. This style originated in Frankish lands, where rulers claimed to reign over the true empire of Christendom and imitated the old empire to prove it. Charlemagne's Palatine Chapel in Aachen (805), for instance, appropriated elements from Constantinople such as the central dome.

A fascination for all things Byzantine also marked the western empire under its Ottonian dynasty, especially during the short reign of Otto III (r. 996–1002). The son of a Byzantine princess, he intended to take another Greek for his bride. Had he done so (he died suddenly while the girl was

---

22   Carolyn L. Connor, *Saints and Spectacle: Byzantine Mosaics in Their Cultural Setting* (Oxford: Oxford University Press, 2016), 142.

en route from Constantinople), the effect on modern culture might have been spectacular. As the art historian Otto Demus speculated, "an emperor three-quarters Greek and only one-quarter Saxon" would have subsequently ruled the mightiest state in Christendom, offering the possibility of a real reconciliation between East and West. The Eastern problem of Pope Leo IX and the excommunication of Cardinal Humbert might have been obviated. Alas, this did not happen. Otto's heirs, as we saw in chapter one, preferred popes whose militancy for reform ultimately led to the departure of the West from the East.

But Byzantine influence in the West persisted for a time, as monuments of the Romanesque show. The entire interior of churches was frequently covered with murals, as in the East. Rare examples that have survived time and Protestant iconoclasm include the biblical scenes lining the nave vault at Saint Savin in France and the remarkably Byzantine Christ Pantocrator within each of the apses of the Doppelkirche in Bonn, Germany.

The most important work of Romanesque architecture was the third renovation of the main abbey church of Cluny. Consecrated by Pope Urban II during his crusade tour in 1095, Cluny III (as art historians call it) was the largest church on earth and the greatest example of contemporary Western design. Many of its elements were purely northern European, such as its

Reconstruction of Cluny III

elongated nave and spire-like bell towers. It was very tall, at nearly one hundred feet. Yet other elements originated in the Christian East. Most significant in this respect were the church's semicircular apse, in which the altar was located, and its central dome. Viewed from its eastern end, the edifice would probably have looked as familiar to the occasional Greek pilgrim as any church in his native Constantinople.[23]

In fact, Cluny III was also oriented; that is, its apse was located at the easternmost point of the church. This placed the altar table symbolically in the direction of paradise, toward which Christians prayed. This symbolism had originated in the East, and by the end of the eleventh century it had become standard in the West as well. Entering the narthex from the west, the faithful passed into a space set apart from the world, which at the same time transformed the world.

From the eleventh century to the thirteenth, then, the symbolism of Romanesque and Byzantine temple architecture was largely the same: an oriented tripartite design of narthex-nave-sanctuary/choir representing, with the rich use of interior iconography, the kingdom of heaven on earth.

. . . *and Back Again*

BY THE END OF THE twelfth century, however, Eastern influence on Western liturgical architecture was coming to an end. By that time, a new vision of the temple's role in the liturgy had appeared, embodied in a new architectural style. This style has come to be known as the Gothic, though originally it was named "Frankish" because of its origins in France. In fact, it has been observed that one can trace the outlines of the Gothic's geographical cradle by drawing a circle with a one-hundred-mile radius around the city of Paris. But once the style established dominance within this region—known as the Ile-de-France—it soon conquered all of Western Christendom.

---

23 Sadly, modern historians will never really know exactly how the magnificent church looked. During the height of the French Revolution's assault on Christianity, vandals destroyed it almost entirely. Only a small section was saved, and to that archeologists have been able to add conjectures about its appearance.

Historians of art contrast the Gothic style with the Romanesque. Many textbooks, while noting differences between the two, treat the relationship as an organic transition from one to the other. There are in fact certain elements that both share, such as an elongated cruciform basilica with a prominent transept. However, as Otto von Simson argued long ago, the relationship is not one of continuity. It is rather one of fracture and even of revolutionary innovation.

> No misconception has proved a greater obstacle to our understanding of Gothic architecture than its interpretation as the "logical" sequel to Romanesque, as the consistent development of stylistic principles and technical methods evolved during the preceding period. In point of fact, Gothic architecture is not the heir but the rival of Romanesque, created as its emphatic antithesis.[24]

And the most antithetical element of it, when considering a paradisiacal culture, was the rejection of heaven-on-earth anagogy. Gothic architecture subverted Christendom's principle of heavenly immanence, and in this sense it can be seen as the aesthetic symbol of the age of division.

This can be seen in the three principal developments that gave rise to the Gothic style during the twelfth century. Each had a direct impact on its inventive mastermind, Abbot Suger (d. 1151), whose reconstruction of the abbey church of St. Denis is an early example of the West's new piety.

The first development was the rise of national monarchies. Suger was dedicated to the interests of the king of France, Louis the Fat (r. 1109–1137), who distinguished himself by building a strong centralized state. Suger served as Louis's political advisor and firmly supported efforts to elevate

Abbot Suger

---

24   Otto von Simson, *The Gothic Cathedral: Origins of Gothic Architecture and the Medieval Concept of Order* (Princeton: Princeton University Press, 1988), 61.

France above England and other rivals. He advocated the construction of monumental churches that would display national power and attract pilgrims from throughout Europe to the French capital.

A second development was the rise of monastic rivalry. As we have seen, the origin of disparate monastic orders dates to this period. The first was the Cistercian Order, and its leader Bernard of Clairvaux helped redefine Western piety against what he considered the decadence of the Cluniac network. His programmatic attack on Cluny III, in fact, was the context for developing a new style of architecture rivaling the Romanesque. To communicate heavenly immanence, Cluny and its Byzantine equivalents had, as we have seen, made rich use of images. Bernard rejected this. He wrote an iconophobic reflection entitled *Apologia to Abbot William* in which he claimed that the true ascetic should have little or no interest in the delight that results from liturgical art. Heaven was transcendent, he argued, not immanent. According to von Simson, "Bernard's insistence that religious art be admitted only inasmuch as it was able to guide the beholder to the transcendental source of all beauty, appealed profoundly to Suger."[25]

Much more valuable than iconography was nonsensual austerity, the kind idealized in what Bernard called the "paradise of the cloister" (*paradisus claustralis*). The experience of the kingdom of heaven thus became a purely intellectual one, lacking icons and other images altogether. Bernard actually banned their use, though he agreed to allow painted crucifixes to satisfy the visual needs of the cloister's inmates. Otherwise, the Cistercian cloister was as bare as a mosque.

Bernard's piety was reminiscent of the Byzantine iconoclasts, or, closer to home, the Frankish semi-iconoclasts who reacted with hostile incomprehension to the incarnational doctrine of the Seventh Ecumenical Council. Because of this trait, some have seen in him a kind of proto-puritan, a Calvinist before his time. But his bifurcated conception of Christendom made him willing to concede painted imagery to the laity, who occupied a subordinate status of spiritual dignity. As he bluntly put it, "since the devotion of the carnal populace cannot be incited with spiritual ornaments, it is

---

25   von Simson, *The Gothic Cathedral*, 113.

necessary to employ material ones."[26] A new, antimaterial piety was emerging in the West in the thought of its most renowned and influential ascetic.

Which brings us to the third important development in the rise of the Gothic style: scholasticism. If Cistercian piety had laid an ascetical basis for the dematerialization of paradise, the university doctors laid a theological one. The renowned Abelard was a Parisian like Suger and helped make the French capital a center of the nascent university system. He was an Aristotelian, but other minds—especially those assembled at the cathedral school in nearby Chartres—were with equal force attracted to Plato. Scholastics blended this other great pagan authority with Augustinianism to produce a model of beauty that stressed mathematical harmony over physical imagery.

One of this model's most perfect expressions was geometry. As we have seen, Romanesque churches—like Byzantine ones—featured extensive representations of Christ and the saints. They also contained extensive statuary (something not found in the East). Under the influence of Plato, much of this was now rejected as coarse at best and impious at worst. As we shall soon see, the scholastic aesthetic, combined with Bernard's iconophobia, favored a new vision of paradise that had little connection with this world.

The result of these three developments was the Gothic cathedral. Abbot Suger, placed by circumstances at the center of cultural convergence that was the Ile-de-France, was the first to give expression to it. In 1144 he completed the reconstruction of the west facade and choir of the abbey church of St. Denis, located some five miles north of Paris.

The facade is of interest because of its central portal and the tympanum that surmounts it. The sculpture there symbolizes the soul's entrance into paradise. However, the emphasis is not on a paradise experienced in this world. In fact, judgment is

The west portal of the Abbey Church of St. Denis

26 Ibid., 43.

the portal's main theme. Above the doorway in the tympanum is the Last Judgment, and on either side of the doorposts are sculpted images of the five wise and five foolish virgins. As a result, the worshipper's contact with paradise is intentionally ambiguous. What is more, along the bronze doors themselves Suger had inscribed a statement warning those entering that the material images they see before them are in fact of no ultimate importance. Such images of paradise are, in Platonic fashion, only shadows. The contrast to the entrance of Hosios Loukas could not be more sharply defined. For as one steps across the threshold of St. Denis, he leaves the material world behind.

What meets him inside is also very different from the interiors of Byzantine and Romanesque churches. For St. Denis is free of what Bernard decried as coarse imagery suitable only for the unspiritual glances of the laity. The interior walls are completely bare. Their stone surfaces are exquisitely dressed and rise to breathtaking heights, guiding the eye upward along their smooth, rarefied planes, away from the corrupted world. They terminate in ribbed vaults that likewise are devoid of any iconography.

This was truly an aesthetic revolution. As we have seen, the churches of the old Christendom were mostly filled with murals depicting the salvation of man. The Gothic aesthetic was inspired not by heavenly immanence, however, but by earthly transcendence; it was not a vision of heaven on earth but of a heavenly escape from earth. It was grounded not in the doctrine of the Incarnation, but in the scholastic conviction that the material creation is inferior to the spiritual creation and that true beauty must therefore transcend the material world.

This determined the one iconographical concession of the Gothic interior, and it was a magnificent one. Stained glass took the place of murals. But these windows constituted a unique form of iconography. They were totally determined by geometry, which, because of its mathematical precision, was regarded by the scholastics as a symbol of immaterial divinity. And only within a vast and elaborate arrangement of geometric shapes are incarnational images of Christ and His saints even visible. Looking upward into the windows of St. Denis, the worshipper might wonder whether he is more attracted to the historical scenes of human salvation or the dazzling arrangement of their chromatic background.

The cathedrals that sprang from the cultural soil of the Ile-de-France during the century that followed Suger's reconstruction of St. Denis were monuments to the new aesthetic. Interior surfaces were freed of earthly images and covered with vast geometric spectacles. The multiple colonnades that ascend to the vault of Chartres (begun in 1194) are an example. The carefully measured square bays of each side aisle in the nave of Amiens (begun 1220) are equally perfect in their proportions. But perhaps the most emphatically mathematical feature of the early Gothic cathedrals of France was the rose window.

Each great cathedral came to feature a rose window above its western facade and at opposing ends of its north-south transept. The northern transept of Notre Dame in Paris (begun in 1163) contains a good example of the Gothic style's rationalization of heavenly beauty. The rose window is centered on an image of the Virgin Mary. Surrounding her image, three concentric circles of stained glass images radiate outward. Each of these circles is composed of ensembles of images arranged within elongated isosceles triangles whose acute corners point toward the Virgin Mary. The first circle is made of sixteen such triangles, each of which features a prophet from the Old Testament. The second circle, being larger, is made of thirty-two triangles (the number of prophets times two) featuring Old Testament kings, judges, and patriarchs. The third, outer circle is composed of another thirty-two shapes—not isosceles triangles but equilateral triangles formed by intersecting circles known as trefoils. These contain images of additional Old Testament kings and priests. The narrative effect of this magnificent composition is to show how the Virgin Mary, mother of the Son of God, is herself the culmination of Old Testament history. The aesthetic effect, however, is primarily rational. The window's intricacy and mathematical sophistication produce intellectual delight.[27]

The rose window was not, of course, the only use of stained glass in Gothic

---

27   And happily still do. When the venerable cathedral burned in 2019, nearly all of its artistic treasures were saved, including the rose windows.

The vault of the cathedral at Chartres

Icon of Christ Pantocrator in the central dome of St. Sophia in Kiev
(photo from culture.ru)

Apse icon of the Theotokos of the Sign above the Communion of the Apostles in St. Sophia Church in Ohrid
shutterstock by marcovarro

The Vladimir icon of the Theotokos
shutterstock by Prosto Records

The north rose window in Notre Dame Cathedral, Paris
shutterstock by Iren Key

Interior of Sainte Chapelle, Paris
shutterstock by Songquan Deng

The Pisano Crucifix in Bologna, Italy
shutterstock by Zvonimir Atletic

Icon of the expulsion of Adam and Eve from Paradise, in Palermo
WIKICOMMONS

The Lamentation by Giotto, in Padua, Italy
shutterstock by Mirages

The Isenheim Altarpiece
WIKICOMMONS

The Dance of Death, in Hrastovlje Church, Slovenia
WIKICOMMONS

Interior Frescoes of the Theotokos by Dionisy at Ferapontov Monastery, Russia
Shutterstock

Icon of Christ Pantocrator by Andrei Rublev

Icon of the Hospitality of Abraham (also called Old Testament Trinity) by Andrei Rublev
WIKICOMMONS

architecture. Supported by technical innovations like the flying buttress and the pointed arch, walls made way for vast spaces of stained glass. Indeed, it can be said that the walls of the Gothic cathedral were made of glass, supported here and there by the absolute minimum of stonework. A particularly awe-inspiring example of this effect is Sainte Chapelle in central Paris (1238), where the entire church seems to consist of nothing but glass (thin piers between the sections of window provide the only vertical strength for most of the building). Nothing like this had ever been seen in the world before, and the piety of the new Christendom was what inspired it.

The turn from transfiguration to transcendence was expressed by Suger himself in the treatise he wrote on the occasion of Saint Denis's consecration. It was read publicly in the presence of King Louis the Fat himself. None of it makes easy reading, but a few phrases are worth quoting. It opens by equating God to a "supreme reason," a trope as typical of the Parisian literary salons of the eighteenth century as of the monastic audiences of the twelfth. "The admirable power of one unique and supreme reason," it asserts, "equalizes by proper composition the disparity between things human and divine; and what seems mutually to conflict by inferiority of origin and contrariety of nature is conjoined by the single, delightful concordance of one superior, well-tempered harmony."[28]

This complicated sentence is a restatement of the Incarnation. But it is not one in which the two natures of the God-Man Jesus Christ are proclaimed, as in the iconography of the past. Now, the rational and antimaterial principles of "reason," "concordance," and "harmony" form the link between heaven and earth. And, as the Gothic spires that began to surmount churches throughout the West suggested, in order to reach heaven, one must, using reason alone, repudiate the earth.

It was this that Otto von Simson seems to have had in mind when he concluded that "the creation of Gothic cathedrals marks and reflects an epoch in the history of Christian thought, the change from the mystical to the rational approach to truth, the dawn of metaphysics." Indeed, the rationalization of Christian culture was now clearly underway.

---

28 Ibid., 124.

And though this rationalization started off in confidence, it would end in confusion. The bright "dawn of metaphysics" that occurred in the twelfth century would eventually fade into darkness during the nineteenth. It was a demise that Friedrich Nietzsche called the "twilight of the idols." And when it happened, an age of nihilism was quick to follow.

Stavrocentrism

THE SUBJECTIVE EXPERIENCE OF LITURGY that we discussed above was cultivated within the walls of the new Gothic churches. But it did not remain within them. During the same twelfth century that produced St. Denis, a new way of organizing the believer's relationship with God appeared. It emphasized an affective or emotionally driven response to salvation. Its origins have always been obscure, though many historians have traced them to the Benedictine custom of meditative scripture reading known as "divine reading" (*lectio divina*). Others have located them in a psychological response to fears about an impending judgment of the world by Christ.

Traditional Christian piety did not encourage emotional subjectivity because it was largely shaped by the liturgy. Regulated by scripture, hymns, architecture, and eventually iconography, corporate worship cultivated an objective experience of salvation. Christ was presented above all as the victor over sin and death. His Resurrection was almost always the center of attention.

The Byzantine pattern of worship is an expression of this emphasis. Its allusions to the Resurrection are innumerable. The annual celebration of Pascha, which the West shared with the East from the earliest times, is the most obvious example. Byzantine hymnography not only commemorates Christ's victory over death; it celebrates the spiritual transformation of the human race that resulted. For the entire forty-day season of Pascha, Orthodox Christians declare at divine services:

This is the day of Resurrection. Let us be illumined by the feast. Let us embrace each other. Let us call brothers even those that hate us, and forgive all by the Resurrection. And so, let us cry: Christ is risen from the dead,

trampling down death by death, and upon those in the tombs bestowing life.
("Let God Arise")

And Pascha is not the only occasion for allusions to the Resurrection. Even
Passion Week, with its focus on the suffering and death of Christ, exudes
confidence in the coming Resurrection. Here there is less of the drama that
had begun to alter the Western liturgy, where priests and in some cases the
laity were called on to enact the Passion and actually proclaim the demonic
words "Crucify Him!" In the East, on the contrary, any meditation on the
Passion is also a meditation on the Resurrection. On Great and Holy Friday,
for instance, the Orthodox sing:

> *Today he who hung the earth upon the waters is hung upon the tree.*
> *The King of the angels is decked with a crown of thorns.*
> *He who wraps the heavens with clouds is wrapped in the purple of mockery.*
> *He who freed Adam in the Jordan is slapped on the face.*
> *The Bridegroom of the Church is affixed to the cross with nails.*
> *The Son of the Virgin is pierced by a spear.*
> *We worship thy Passion, O Christ.*
> *We worship thy Passion, O Christ.*
> *We worship thy Passion, O Christ.*
> *Show us also thy glorious Resurrection.*

On Great and Holy Saturday, the empty tomb—the symbol of victory—is
already foreseen in several hymns about the myrrhbearing women. One
hymn speaks of the triumph of joy over sorrow.

> *Very early in the morning the myrrhbearing women ran with sorrow to thy*
> *tomb. But the angel came to them and said: The time for sorrow has come to*
> *an end; do not weep, but announce the Resurrection to the apostles.*

This victory is perhaps most beautifully expressed in a hymn from the canon
for the day attributed to the ninth-century nun Cassiani.

Do not lament me, O mother, seeing me in the tomb—the Son conceived in the womb without seed—for I shall arise and be glorified with eternal glory as God. I shall exalt all who magnify thee in faith and in love.

In fact, it is at the very tomb of Christ—a piece of liturgical furniture placed in the middle of the nave for veneration at the end of Passion Week—that the Gospel of the Resurrection is proclaimed on Holy Saturday.

Throughout the entire year, the Resurrection fills the services of the Lord's Day, Sunday. The Resurrectional Vigil served on Saturday evenings was modeled on worship at the Anastasis (known in the West as the Holy Sepulcher) in Jerusalem. It included several hymns taken from Passion Week and Pascha. It also featured the proclamation of the Resurrection in the Gospels. One canon actually forbade penitential prostrations on Sundays in order to honor Christ's victory over sin.

In medieval Russia, too, the Resurrection was the most prominent element in piety, contributing to the same transformative culture that influenced Feodosy of the Kiev Caves. A sermon for the first Sunday following Pascha by Kirill of Turov (d. 1182) captured the sense of transformation cultivated by a heaven-on-earth piety. "Last week there was a change in all things," he declared,

for the earth was opened up by heaven, having been purified from its satanic impurities. . . . All creation was renewed. . . . Today the newborn lambs and calves frisk and leap about joyfully and returning to their mothers gambol about, so that the shepherds, playing on their reeds, praise Christ in joy. . . . Today there is a feast of regeneration for the people who are made new by the Resurrection of Christ, and all new things are brought to God.[29]

During the first millennium, the Latin West shared this emphasis with the East. The Resurrection was commemorated often and remembered everywhere. One example was the funerary decoration of Christian tombs. The burial of a seventh-century bishop named Agilbert near Paris, for instance,

---

29   *Medieval Russia's Epics, Chronicles, and Tales,* 90–91.

appears to have occurred with joy and optimism. His tomb depicted Christ in majesty, like the Eastern icon of the Pantocrator. Philippe Aries described the icon in detail.

> On a large panel adjoining it we find the resurrection of the dead on the last day. The elect, with arms upraised, acclaim the returning Christ, who holds in his hands a scroll, no doubt the Book of Life. No judgment or condemnation is in evidence. This image is in keeping with the general eschatology of the early centuries of Christendom. The dead who belonged to the Church and who had entrusted their bodies to its care . . . were at rest until the day of the Second Coming, of the great return, when they would awaken in the heavenly Jerusalem, in other words in Paradise.

But after the eleventh century, Aries continues, "the scene changed." First Romanesque and then Gothic churches began depicting the Resurrection with an emphasis on the separation of the just and the damned. By the thirteenth century, the triumphant victory of Christ over death became "almost blotted out." Now "the idea of judgment won out and the scene became a court of justice."[30]

What had happened? According to Rachel Fulton, a fundamental shift in piety related to the person of Christ had taken place. Beginning with Peter Damian in the middle of the eleventh century—the very moment Rome became sacramentally divided from Constantinople—an element of dread began to characterize the Western believer's attitude toward Christ. No longer influenced on a large scale by Eastern piety, Latin writers began more and more to fall back on an Augustinian anthropological inheritance, emphasizing the guilt of original sin and man's inability to will a salvific desire for communion with God on his own.

Peter Damian himself was terrified by Christ. But in his state of fear he also adored Him because, as an ascetic, he had learned how to atone for his

---

30   Philippe Aries, *Western Attitudes toward Death: From the Middle Ages to the Present*, translated by Patricia M. Ranum (Baltimore: Johns Hopkins University Press, 1974), 29–32.

many sins. The zealous ally of the reform papacy introduced on a systematic level—and urgently advocated—the practice of self-flagellation. Intentionally causing bodily pain was not unknown in the history of Christian asceticism. The early Syrian hermit Symeon the Stylite had resorted to it. But it was rare and never became a standard practice until the eleventh century. Then, in the monastic reforms advocated by Peter, it was legitimized and widely disseminated as "the discipline." And when conservatives expressed consternation, Peter wrote a short treatise entitled *In Praise of Flagellation* to defend it. We will consider flagellation within the context of penitential piety below. Here it helps shed light on the momentous transition from an objective piety centered on Christ's Resurrection to a subjective one centered on His Crucifixion.

As noted above, Peter believed that the imminent judgment of the world would be unbearable for those who had not shared actively in Christ's physical suffering. He was convinced that bodily pain was necessary for the expiation of one's personal sins. Christ's death was the center of attention in his thinking, but it was not only the Savior's suffering that effected salvation. The penitent sinner must also undertake his own self-inflicted passion. The entire life of the model monk, he argued, "was for him a Good Friday Crucifixion."[31] For such a life would enable him to share in the "stigmata of Jesus."

Peter Damian occasionally had visions of Christ looking down with benevolence on the self-torture of the penitent. As the monastic reformer's attention became fixated on the Crucifixion, he pleaded in one passage that Christ would grant him a share in it through the use of his own imagination.

> Grant, most pious Lord, as if at the very moment of your passion that I might see you hanging in the torment of the cross. Grant that I might receive blood of highest price dripping in my mouth. O blessed sacrifice that breaks asunder the walls of hell, and opens the door of the heavenly kingdom to the faithful! . . . I see you with my internal eyes, my Redeemer, affixed with the nails of the cross. I see you wounded with new wounds. . . . Lord, sign me with the

31   Fulton, *From Judgment to Passion*, 101.

impression of this holy cross, purify me with this virtue. Thus through this
[sign] deliver me wholly and entirely from your justice, so that there may be
found in me no share whatsoever in the adversary, and so that when you are
coming in judgment . . . I shall be signed with this mark [stigma].[32]

Here we see that individual imagination ("I see you with my internal eyes")
had become a key to Western soteriology, the doctrine of salvation.

Indeed, a soteriological revolution was just getting underway. Most historians recognize Anselm of Canterbury as the first writer to express the
new affective piety in all its force. Benedicta Ward considered that "the
approach to prayer that he himself experienced and communicated to others formed a bridge between the patristic and medieval ways of devotion
in the West."[33] The author of the *Prosologion*, an effort to prove God's existence through purely rational means, Anselm also devised a completely new
way of understanding salvation. In his *Why God Became Man*, he argued that
the soteriological mystery (which no theologian had formerly undertaken to
explain systematically) was entirely reducible to the Crucifixion. And from
this moment, Western piety became increasingly *stavrocentric,* or "cross-
centered," rather than *metamorphocentric,* or "transformation-centered."

Drawing upon the principles of honor and legal satisfaction current in
Western feudalism, Anselm argued that Christ's death had not been so
much a victory over the devil as an act of satisfying the implacable justice of
the infinite God. Gone was Athanasius's emphasis upon the deifying effects
of the Incarnation, and barely remembered was the glorious outcome of
the Resurrection. From this point forward, Western concepts of salvation
were preoccupied with—and sometimes limited exclusively to—the suffering and death of Christ. The events that most emphasized transformation—
the Incarnation, Transfiguration, Resurrection, and Ascension—became
obscured by this singular act of His Passion.

---

32   Ibid., 105.
33   Benedicta Ward, "Anselm of Canterbury and His Influence," in *Christian*
     Spirituality: Origins to the Twelfth Century, edited by Bernard McGinn and John
     Meyendorff (New York: Crossroad Publishing, 1986), 196–204.

And this too contributed to a new piety. Not surprisingly, Anselm was the first to give full expression to it. His *Prayers and Meditations* were a counterpart to his satisfaction soteriology, being caught up in a grateful meditation on the Passion. A "Prayer to Christ" from the work is beautifully touching but also intensely individualistic, emphasizing an emotive response to the Crucifixion. "So, as much as I can," it opens, "though not as much as I ought, I am mindful of your passion, your buffeting, your scourging, your cross, your wounds, how you were slain for me, how prepared for burial and buried, and also I remember your glorious Resurrection, and wonderful Ascension."[34] Here traditional Christianity is still in evidence; not only the Passion but the Resurrection and Ascension are brought to mind. But Anselm's preoccupation is the Passion, and, what is more, the emotions that result from an imaginative contemplation of it.

This affective and stavrocentric piety was developed further by Bernard of Clairvaux. In fact, the influential Cistercian abbot is responsible for what many historians consider a radical shift in the christological piety of the West.

There now arose a practice of "devotion" to the humanity of Christ. The Latin word *devotio*, emerging into wide circulation at this time, designated a form of piety that was extraliturgical and conducted mostly within private practices such as prayer and contemplation. It was Bernard who helped navigate the transition. Because of it, Western culture began to develop in new ways the ancient Christian virtue of *sympathy* (literally, "to suffer with" another).

Bernard asserted that "our hearts are attracted most toward the humanity of Christ in the events of his life." Christ became human because "he wanted to recapture the affections of carnal men who were unable to love in any other way, by first drawing them to the salutary love of his own humanity, and then gradually to raise them to a spiritual love."[35] This is a fascinating statement. According to it the Incarnation is not about God's assimilation

---

34 *The Prayers and Meditations of St Anselm with Prosologion*, translated by Benedicta Ward (London: Penguin, 1973), 95.
35 Ewert Cousins, "The Humanity and Passion of Christ," in *Christian Spirituality: High Middle Ages and Reformation*, 375–391.

of humanity to His divinity, resulting in the prospect of man's deification. It is about creating the basis for man's emotional relationship to God. The fourth-century Athanasius had stated that God became man so that man might become God. It seems that for Bernard, God became man so that man might sympathize with God.

This is not to say that Bernard ignored Christ's divine nature. In his *Sermons on the Song of Songs,* he spoke explicitly about how in Christ "the conjoining of natures unites the human with the divine and makes peace between earth and heaven." He "who makes himself our Mediator with God is the Son of God and is himself God." But Bernard asks, "Where am I to find the faith to dare to trust in such majesty? How, I say, shall I, who am dust and ashes, presume to think that God cares about me?" This agonizing question is answered only by meditating on Christ's humanity, which God deigns to share with man.

> When I know that the Mediator who is the Son of God is mine, then I shall accept him trustingly. Then there can be no mistrust. For he is brother to my flesh.[36]

For Bernard, then, between the two natures of Christ it is the human and not the divine that primarily attracts his devotion.

Bernard and Anselm were cloistered monks, and their stavrocentric piety would have been destined to circulate only within the walls of monasteries were it not for the rise of itinerant monasticism in the thirteenth century. Here especially the work of Francis was crucial. In the words of Cousins, it was he who "more than any other saint or spiritual writer . . . transformed religious sensibility in the direction of devotion to the humanity of Christ."[37] Francis embraced the new piety and instilled it in the Order of the Friars Minor. His emphasis in the Rule on extreme poverty was inspired by his meditation on the historical life of Christ. The Franciscan manner of living

---

36 Bernard of Clairvaux, "On the Kiss," in *Selected Works,* edited by Emilie Griffin, translated by G. R. Evans (San Francisco: Harper, 2005), 97–104.

37 Cousins, "Humanity and Passion."

was likewise an imitation of Christ's humanity. In all cases Franciscan piety was centered on the Gospels' record of Christ's earthly life.

One of the West's most enduring cultural institutions, Christmas, was shaped in part by this. The Nativity never rivaled the Passion in the annual liturgical calendar of the West until modern times, but as another event in the Gospels it offered a focus for the new piety. To enhance this focus, Francis designed the first-ever outdoor crèche scene in a cave near the Italian town of Greccio in 1223. Having visited the shrine of the Nativity in Bethlehem during his pilgrimage to the Holy Land, he used actors for each of the figures represented, including an infant for Jesus. This was his contribution to the emerging liturgical dramaturgy of the time.

Also famous was Francis's reception of the stigmata, the physical marks of Jesus' wounds on the cross. Peter Damian had spoken of such marks of piety in figurative terms, but this was different. For the first time in history such wounds actually appeared on a Christian's body. The stavrocentric piety of the West was the inescapable context for this unprecedented event. In fact, as more and more Roman Catholic saints likewise received these mystical marks of the cross, the stigmata can be seen as the ultimate symbol of Western stavrocentrism.

By contrast, it could be said that in the East the ultimate symbol of metamorphocentrism was the illumined face of one who had seen the Uncreated Light. Many saints experienced this condition. The earliest was Moses, whose encounters with God in the wilderness prefigured the Transfiguration (Ex. 34:33–35). Later, Francis's Eastern contemporaries the hesychasts also claimed to experience the divine energies as light.[38]

Moreover, when Eastern piety did emphasize suffering, it did so as an act of extreme humility, or kenoticism, rather than self-affliction. A good example is an anonymous twelfth-century Russian work entitled *The Descent of the Virgin into Hell*. It was one of many imaginative literary works of pilgrimage

---

38 Though Gregory Palamas lived a century and a half after the Western friar, in his discussion of the Uncreated Light he was simply documenting the experiences of ascetics for centuries. Symeon the New Theologian lived two centuries prior to Francis and wrote frequently of seeing the Uncreated Light.

through hell that appeared throughout Christendom, the most famous being the first volume of Dante's *Divine Comedy*. A good two centuries earlier, *The Descent of the Virgin* recounted a similar adventure undertaken by the Mother of God and guided, not by a pagan poet as was Dante, but by the Archangel Michael. It opens with Mary in heaven declaring that she desires to behold the sufferings of those consigned to eternal torment. As Michael leads her from place to place within hell ("Take me farther" she insists at one point), she never stops weeping at what she sees. She does this not out of horror but out of compassion. Her great humility enables her to identify completely with those whose lives fell far short of her holiness. It impels her to abandon the delights of paradise and enter, as Christ did through the Incarnation, into the depths of human darkness. It enables her to suffer with others and even to forgo the blessings of heaven. At one point she actually begs God to allow her to take the place of the condemned. By these acts of kenotic intercession, her Son Jesus Christ at last grants a reprieve to the damned every year from Holy Thursday to Pentecost.[39]

The metamorphocentric piety of neophyte Russia was marked by sharp moral contrasts. Grand Prince Vladimir had been a pagan warlord but was transformed by the gospel to oppose capital punishment. Boris and Gleb were heirs to fratricidal conflict but accepted death rather than raise arms against their brother. Feodosy was born a boyar but spent his life in menial labor. So also, *The Descent of the Virgin into Hell* brought the most luminous of all saints into direct and voluntary contact with the most degraded of all sinners. Such contrasts highlighted the potential of the paradisiacal culture of Christendom, from the moment Paul admonished the Roman Christians not to be "conformed to this world" but rather to be "transformed" by baptismal renewal (Rom. 12:2).

The stavrocentric piety of the West, by contrast, was something new. It represented a cultural watershed. According to Ewert Cousins,

---

39 *The Descent of the Virgin into Hell*, in *Medieval Russia's Epics, Chronicles, and Tales*, edited and translated by Serge A. Zenkovsky (New York: Penguin, 1974), 153–160.

in the first millennium of Christianity there did not develop anything compa-
rable to the widespread devotion to the humanity of Christ of the High Middle
Ages—with the use of the imagination in a specific method of meditation, with
its extensive cultivation of human emotions, especially compassion, with its
almost exclusive emphasis on the passion, and with its ramification into art
and its proliferation of devotional forms in hymns, prayers, and penances.[40]

It was a development that brought real problems.

First, for both Orthodox and Roman Catholic Christians, Jesus Christ,
the Son of God, is one person. He is the God-Man. This is what Cyril of
Alexandria tirelessly asserted in the face of the fifth-century heresy of
Nestorianism, in which a sharp distinction was made between the divinity of Christ and the humanity of Jesus. In addition, the Savior possesses
two distinct natures, one divine and one human. This was the teaching of
Pope Leo the Great, upheld at the Fourth Ecumenical Council. To practice
a devotion to one or the other of these two natures was dubious at best. At
worst it threatened the doctrinal integrity of the faith.

Vladimir Lossky considered the emergence of a distinct devotion to the
humanity of Christ, in which His divinity is somehow obscured by a heightened focus on His Passion, to be a departure from the piety of the old Christendom. "The cult of the humanity of Christ," he wrote,

is foreign to Eastern tradition; or, rather, this deified humanity always
assumes for the Orthodox Christian that same glorious form under which it
appeared to the disciples on Mount Tabor: the humanity of the Son, manifest-
ing forth that deity which is common to the Father and the Sprit. No saint of
the Eastern Church has ever borne the stigmata, those outward marks which
have made certain great Western saints and mystics as it were living patterns
of the suffering Christ. But, by contrast, Eastern saints have very frequently
been transfigured by the inward light of uncreated grace, and have appeared
resplendent, like Christ on the mount of Transfiguration.[41]

---

40   Cousins, "Humanity and Passion."
41   Vladimir Lossky, *The Mystical Theology of the Eastern Church* (Crestwood, NY:

Here we see contrasted the new, stavrocentric piety of the West and the old, metamorphocentric piety of the East. But it is a fact—suggested by the funerary imagery discussed above—that the West had once, before the first millennium, owned a share in this legacy of the old Christendom.

A second problem was latent in the new piety, but it would manifest itself only later. As the culture of Western Christendom became preoccupied with the Passion, introducing new forms of liturgy such as the stations of the cross to commemorate it, other elements in traditional Christianity eventually became obscured. Again, Cousins provides insights into the matter. "From a psychological point of view," he observes, the

> late medieval devotion to the passion of Christ is one of the most problematic phenomena in the history of Christian spirituality. It is also problematic from a doctrinal and spiritual point of view. For attraction to the suffering and death of Christ became so intense in some cases that Christians lost sight of the other aspects of the Christian mysteries and of their organic interrelatedness. Emphasis on the passion led to forgetfulness of the resurrection. Focus on the suffering humanity of Christ overshadowed the Trinity and its outpouring of divine love in creation.[42]

The Image of the Cross

THE CULTURAL SHIFT TOWARD STAVROCENTRISM can also be traced in the history of that most pervasive of all symbols of Christendom, the cross. The place of the cross in piety began to change after the Great Division, especially the representation of Christ on the cross. That image was in fact of relatively recent provenance. As in so many other cases, the East was the source of influence. It produced an archetypal icon of the cross that historians often label Christ the Victor (*Christus victor*).

One of the earliest examples of this icon happens to demonstrate the westward flow of influence. The icon was located in the chapel of the

---

St. Vladimir's Seminary Press, 1998), 243.
42   Cousins, "Humanity and Passion."

Archiepiscopal Palace in Ravenna, where the Byzantine Empire had established its western headquarters. In the apse was depicted an early sixth-century image of Christ with the cross. But at this early stage in iconography, He carries the instrument of his death over his shoulder like a weapon. And indeed, Christ is depicted as a strong young man dressed as a soldier. Symbolically, His feet rest on the heads of a lion and a serpent (fulfilling the messianic prophecy in Psalm 90:13). It was a vivid proclamation of Christ's victory over death through the cross.

Images of Christ's actual death on the cross only became standard somewhat later. Christendom was reluctant to endorse them, it seems, until it could do so without subverting the joyful optimism that characterized its paradisiacal culture. What is more, to depict Jesus' death as a merely historical event accompanied by blood and the harrowing pain of suffocation had the potential of subverting a Christology in which He was not only a man but also God. The Crucifixion could be depicted only if it was an icon, that is, a pictorial representation proclaiming a heavenly reality beyond the natural appearances of this world.

In this case the reality proclaimed was Christ's divinity. As Theodore the Studite (d. 826) had declared in opposing iconoclasm, "the representation of Christ is not in the likeness of a corruptible man, which is disapproved of by the apostles, but as He Himself had said earlier, it is in the likeness of the incorruptible man, but incorruptible precisely because He is not simply a man, but God who became man."[43]

Accordingly, the earliest images of the Crucifixion depicted Christ standing on, rather than hanging from, the cross, demonstrating the voluntary character of His death and His power, even through death, of destroying the power of death. They depicted Him without pain in His expression, gazing forward at the viewer with serenity and dignity. His eyes were open, in communication with the Christian standing before the image. In this icon, all the events in Christ's earthly ministry were synchronically made present to the believer: the Incarnation, Crucifixion, Resurrection, and Ascension.

---

43 Quoted in Leonid Ouspensky, *Theology of the Icon*, vol. 1, translated by Anthony Gythiel (Crestwood, NY: St. Vladimir's Seminary Press, 1978), 161.

Even the Second Coming was suggested by Christ's majestic gaze toward the viewer.

Byzantine iconography of the Crucifixion remained steadfast in its commitment to Christ the Victor. But in the aftermath of iconoclasm, it began to depict Christ with His eyes closed, in contrast to earlier archetypes. This was not a concession to any kind of naturalism. It was to combat the arguments of heretics (such as the recent iconoclasts) that compromised Orthodox Christology by minimizing Christ's complete humanity. The new detail

Mosaic of Christ the Victor in the Archiepiscopal Chapel at Ravenna

affirmed that Christ really died on the cross. But to assert the power of His divinity over death, iconography simultaneously used light and color to depict His crucified body as resplendent and beautiful.

This symbolism reinforced the doctrinal conviction that Christ's divine nature remained inseparable from His human nature. It was an iconographical counterpart to the liturgical prayer taken from the Byzantine celebration of the Resurrection at Pascha:

> *In the tomb with the body; in hades with the soul; in paradise with the thief; and on the throne with the Father and the Holy Spirit wast thou, O Christ our God, filling all things.*

At this stage in the history of Christian culture, there was no difference between the christological piety of East and West. Latin piety about the Crucifixion before the millennium was likewise victorious in character. It is seen in works such as the sixth-century hymn *Pange Lingua* (still sung on Good Friday in the Roman Catholic Church), whose opening stanza declares:

> *Sing, my tongue, of the battle of the glorious struggle, and over the trophy of the cross proclaim the noble triumph by which the sacrificed redeemer of the world conquered.*

The eighth-century Anglo-Saxon poem *The Dream of the Rood* is another example of the victorious depiction of the cross in the West.

So strong was this piety that a bishop of ninth-century Turin was shocked at the appearance of a different kind of image of the cross. Instead of a painted icon, it was a crucifix—that is, a sculpted three-dimensional image. This made a much more naturalistic impression on the believer. To the bishop the innovation was problematic because it seemed to do no more than commemorate "the disgrace of the passion and the degradation of death." He even criticized those who venerated it as little different from nonbelievers who deny the Resurrection. Such "cannot think of him

Icon of the Crucifixion in Dormition Church in Daphne, Greece

except as suffering and dead; and they believe in him and hold him in their hearts permanently undergoing his passion."[44] There was an element of Frankish iconophobia in the complaint. But there was also the suggestion that any iconography that did not unambiguously proclaim the Resurrection subverted Christian culture.

But with the emergence of a new Christendom, Christ the Victor began to be displaced by Christ the Sufferer (*Christus patiens*). The earliest example of this was the tenth-century Gero Crucifix, depicting the Savior with His eyes closed and head slumped forward. This crucifix established a uniquely Western archetype for an image suitable to the new devotion to the humanity of Christ. And with it the conditions were laid for the rise of artistic naturalism.

We have observed how Romanesque churches maintained a close aesthetic affiliation with their Byzantine equivalents. The same was true of the cross, and with the rise of the Gothic style, iconography of the Crucifixion likewise changed. In his fascinating study of the history of the crucifix,

---

44 Richard Viladesau, *The Beauty of the Cross: The Passion of Christ in Theology and the Arts, from the Catacombs to the Eve of the Renaissance* (Oxford: Oxford University Press, 2006), 63.

Richard Viladesau observes that when piety shifted from heaven-on-earth eschatology to life-of-Christ historicity, a revolution in art began to occur.

> *In the Romanesque period, the cross is primarily portrayed not merely as an element in the earthly story of Jesus but in the light of his resurrection and his divinity. In the Gothic crucifix, by contrast, we see an increasing emphasis on the human story of Jesus, and on a particular moment in that story. This means that we are dealing with a different kind of art: an art whose idea of "representation" is more naturalistic.*[45]

An example of this is an icon painted in Bologna by Giunta Pisano during the first half of the thirteenth century. Interestingly, the artist was a student of Byzantine iconography. The work therefore possesses a close affinity with the majestic image of Christ the Victor even while depicting Him hanging from the cross. The body forms a graceful curve. The feet are side by side on a footrest rather than nailed together, creating the impression of standing with authority. The hands are gracefully uplifted in the "orans" posture of prayer to the Father, reminding the believer that the one crucified is the Son of God. The color and muscular tone of the body are lively and vigorous. All of these features—typical of the Byzantine iconographical canon—symbolized Christ's victory over death even at the moment when death was setting in.[46]

Nevertheless, Pisano's crucifix was intended to be an object of devotion to Christ the Sufferer. In this it drew as much on the new piety as the old. The head is slumped forward and to one side. The eyes are closed. And the brows are lowered in pain as the mouth frowns. Pisano was commissioned to

---

45 Viladesau, *Beauty of the Cross*, 114.

46 It is a paradox that the earliest images of Christ dead on the cross, rather than alive, were executed in Byzantium. All authorities agree that the affective piety that led to the Western emphasis on Christ's suffering and death never established itself in the East. Yet the innovation of depicting Him with eyes closed and a slumped body can be documented in Constantinople as early as the eleventh century and probably occurred even earlier. Psellos defended it against an apparently suspicious public. And Cardinal Humbert cited the practice as one of the many things deserving excommunication in 1054.

The Gero Crucifix

paint a similar representation of the Passion for the main church of Assisi, where it would have served as a monument to Franciscan stavrocentrism and a means of disseminating it among the thousands of laity who came on pilgrimage from throughout Western Christendom.

But Pisano's Bologna crucifix was still an icon. Its pictorial design, based on Byzantine archetypes, was still intended to make the reality of heaven present in this world. Its use of naturalism was therefore subordinate to this anagogic purpose.

With the paintings of Giotto (d. 1337), however, naturalism begins to assume a purpose of its own. It becomes the perfect aesthetic, or theory of beauty, for the West's new affective piety. This new aesthetic is found in a series of images on the life of Christ that Giotto executed within a private chapel in Padua whose use, apart from divine services, was for the performance of paraliturgical mystery plays.

The private and the dramatic are both clear themes in the paintings. The Crucifixion, for instance, depicts a cadaverous Christ hanging from the cross as a multitude of people and angels react to the appalling sight. A brawl is taking place among the soldiers to apportion His garments. On the opposite side of the corpse are the women disciples, who support the Virgin Mary as she swoons in horror. Above this, a host of angels scatters in all directions like hornets from a disturbed nest. In the foreground, at the foot of the cross, Mary Magdalene sobs as she seizes hold of the Savior's lifeless feet. In an adjacent image of the Lamentation, the scene is similar. The human creation weeps while the angelical creation writhes in horror as the dead body of Jesus is brought to the tomb.

In both of these paintings Giotto emphasized the natural, empirical experience of these historical events. There are as yet no real shadows (consistent with Byzantine iconography's use of a heavenly light source), but the physical space is organized three-dimensionally. The garments worn are not like those of a conventional icon; they are not afterthoughts of mere symbolical significance. Here they are real clothing, and their weight can be perceived in draping caused by gravity. Even more revolutionary are the faces of the figures. They all have expressions—mostly of grief—that are extremely emotional. The angels have ceased to be purely spiritual beings in that they are wringing their hands and contorting their faces. Such emotional intensity was unprecedented, but it served the new affective piety well.

Giotto also used naturalism to heighten the dramatic effect of the scenes. What resembles a cast of characters in a play is arranged in each scene so that some are upstage from others, creating the illusion of depth. Dramaturgy is particularly strong in the Lamentation, as all secondary characters surround the dead protagonist, Christ, in such a way as to draw the viewer's eyes to Him. Giotto acts as the director, as it were, cuing his audience to suffer with the disciples. Cleverly, those in the foreground present their backs to the viewer, serving as models for his own act of devotional lamentation.

According to one art historian, Giotto "decisively broke the iconic bonds of Italian art." Those bonds, as we have seen, had been forged during the first millennium to anchor the Crucifixion in the Resurrection. They were based largely on Byzantine precedent. Iconography since that time had introduced natural elements into the imagery of Christ's death, but in doing so never resorted to naturalism. By employing symbolism, Byzantine iconographers always emphasized Christ's victorious divinity.

The affective piety of the West now changed that. The goal of the image was no longer the communication of divine presence in the crucified body of the Lord. Now, the goal was to provoke—sometimes dramatically—an emotional response to the historical event of the Passion. This was seen to enhance the viewer's experience of communion with Christ, which had, in the increasingly dematerialized, clerically dominated culture of the West with its practice of very infrequent Communion, fallen into sharp decline.

Rarely again would Western painting look to the iconographical tradition of the first millennium for its archetypes. The aesthetic threshold to modernity had now been passed, and even Giotto's Italian contemporaries realized it. They looked on the Padua paintings and saw something unprecedented, even revolutionary. Their way of describing it, significantly, was as something called "modern art" (*ars moderna*).

"Joy-Making Mourning"

THE CULT OF CHRIST THE Sufferer contributed to far more than art history, however. The naturalistic images of Giotto, like the emotive treatises of Bernard, were only part of a broader cultural development in which guilt became a predominant virtue. Sympathetic devotion to the suffering of Christ was one means to attain it. Another was penance. Long a source of joy in the old Christendom, penitential piety became increasingly juridical and inconclusive in the new.

The sinner of the first millennium would have had a similar experience of penance whether he lived in the East or the West. For centuries, only grave public sins such as apostasy, murder, or adultery were typically subject to a formalized ritual of correction known as canonical penance. That ritual was liturgical. Penitents would be barred from eucharistic communion and were required to stand at the back of the church (if admitted to it at all) until their penance was lifted. This could take months or even years. There was a strongly corporate emphasis in this: Grave sin was not only an offense against God; it was an affront to the body of Christ.

But through reconciliation to the community, the penitent was also expected to undergo a very individual experience of spiritual transformation similar to his original baptism. Indeed, as James Dallen has so well emphasized, penance in its original canonical form was an act of "postbaptismal conversion."[47] Indeed, in the seventh century John of the Ladder lik-

---

47   The understanding of penance as a kind of postbaptismal conversion originated among the desert fathers, but was also held by Augustine. James Dallen, *The Reconciling Community: The Rite of Penance* (Collegeville, MN: Liturgical Press, 1991), 62.

ened it to a second baptism.[48] This is why penitents came to be associated with the catechumenate preparing for baptism. Like the catechumens, they fasted and prayed during the Great Fast, and when it was completed at Pascha those deemed worthy were readmitted to communion along with the newly baptized. Eventually, the entire Church joined catechumens and penitents to make Lent an annual season of repentance for all of Christendom.

Nevertheless, canonical penance was difficult to endure, and it eventually fell into disuse. It was ultimately replaced by private confession, which came to be applied differently in the East and the West. As a result, two distinct approaches to private penance emerged.

In the East, private penance assumed a largely therapeutic form. John Chrysostom was one of the earliest Greek fathers to speak of it this way. He likened the church building to a physician's office, and the priest to whom one confessed his sins to a doctor rather than a judge.[49] Formal penances were intended as spiritual medicine, designed to cure the sinner of his passions and enable him to live the life of the Church more fully.

Indeed, Christendom's paradisiacal culture was contingent on the therapy of repentance, for repentance enabled people to turn from a spiritually untransformed world toward the kingdom of heaven. The Greek word for repentance was *metanoia*, meaning literally a "change of heart." Healing entailed transformation.

As we saw in the previous chapter, monasticism formalized the process of repentance. It drew upon the paradisiacal experience of early desert fathers such as Abba Joseph, whose life of spiritual transformation was observed by a disciple.

> *Abba Lot went to see Abba Joseph and said to him, "Abba, as far as I can I say my little office, I fast a little, I pray and meditate, I live in peace and as far as I can, I purify my thoughts. What else can I do?"*
> *Then the old man stood up and stretched his hands towards heaven. His*

---

48 John Climacus, *The Ladder of Divine Ascent* (Boston: Holy Transfiguration Monastery, 2001), 71.

49 Dallen, *Reconciling Community*, 75.

fingers became like ten lamps of fire and he said to him, "If you will, you can become all flame."[50]

It was this transformation of human life—bringing to mind Christ's Transfiguration—that captured the hearts of early monks and led them through a lifelong journey of formalized repentance. Penance became a journey toward paradise.

The West originally shared in a therapeutic vision of penance. John Cassian (d. 435), who traveled among the desert fathers of Egypt, had cultivated such a vision in the monasteries he founded in southern France. There sorrow for one's sins was what it had been back in Egypt: what John of the Ladder had called "joy-making mourning."[51] Like so much of traditional Christianity, this feature of penance was a paradox. Sorrow was necessary to it, but so was joy. The two could not be divided. Paul had indicated this when distinguishing between "godly sorrow," on the one hand, and a "sorrow of the world" that leads to despair on the other (2 Cor. 7:10). It is "godly sorrow," Cassian declared, that "nourishes the soul through the hope engendered by repentance, and it is mingled with joy."[52]

Nevertheless, a more juridical model of penance was beginning to appear in the West on the eve of the Great Division. This was due in part to the assimilation of Celtic practices by the Franks. During the first millennium, Ireland was a land of monasteries rather than dioceses, and monks rather than bishops played the leading role in shaping penitential practice there. From an early point the Celts had drawn directly on the Eastern piety of southern France and regarded the Christian life as one of continuous transformation. An intimate therapeutic relationship between the penitent and his confessor had therefore arisen along lines similar to the practice of the desert fathers.

But since this relationship was centered on the monastery and not the

---

50 *The Sayings of the Desert Fathers*, translated by Benedicta Ward (Kalamazoo, MI: Cistercian Publications, 1975), 103.

51 John Climacus, *Ladder*, 70.

52 John Cassian, "On the Eight Vices," *The Philokalia*, vol. 1, 88.

cathedral, restoration within a liturgical community was absent. Repentance was almost exclusively an individual experience. What is more, the system came to make use of penitential manuals in which nearly every type of sin was listed with a corresponding medicine of penance useful in healing it. But when these penitentials (as the manuals were called) were introduced outside the personal monastic context in which they arose, they could appear more like punishment codes than instruments of spiritual renewal.

This is what happened in France and Germany when the penitentials were taken there by Celtic missionaries such as Columbanus. Frankish theologians were in fact suspicious of such individualized forms of penance, but they found it impossible to resist the tariff system, as it has been called (due to the imposition of penalties according to each sin), especially since it was perfectly designed to support their ambitious reforming project of centralizing penance within a single, universal order of church life. The result was a tendency toward penitential legalism on the eve of the first millennium.

Even so, the Frankish authority Alcuin (d. 804) would write a treatise on confession that combined both the therapeutic and the juridical elements of the earlier tradition. A century later, the Frankish canonist Regino of Pruem did the same. He regarded the priestly confessor as a sympathetic healer rather than a rigorous judge, instructing him "to exhort affectionately the penitent" by calling him his "brother" and declaring that "I also am a sinner and perhaps I have done worse deeds than you have done." In this sense, according to one historian, "penance and confession were done for and with the penitent, not to her."[53] It is significant that prior to the eleventh century, Western priests always pronounced absolution in the invocative mood, calling on God to forgive, rather than the declarative mood in which the priest himself grants forgiveness.

All of this began to change in the wake of the Papal Reformation. On the one hand, the rise of clericalism altered the relationship between priest and

---

53 Karen Wagner, "Cum aliquis venerit ad sacerdotem: Penitential Experience in the Central Middle Ages," in *A New History of Penance*, edited by Abigail Firey (Leiden, Netherlands: Brill, 2008), 201–218.

penitent. In some ways the one became a judge and the other the judged. The sudden expansion of canon law, marked by the appearance of Gratian's *Decretum* in the middle of the twelfth century, also caused a shift in priorities from pastoral discretion to legal precision in determining penance. At the same time, early scholasticism began to classify confession as a formal sacrament that was necessary for forgiveness to take place. The canonist Peter Lombard, a contemporary of Gratian, was the first to number confession as one in a list of seven official sacraments. The clergy were now assigned preeminence in overseeing its institution. Under Pope Innocent III, the Fourth Lateran Council in 1215 mandated that every member of Roman Catholic Christendom make a sacramental confession to a duly ordained parish priest at least once a year. Formalized repentance had never before been a legal requirement.

This served to circumscribe what had formerly been the liberating and transformative power of penance. Until this time, the contrition of the penitent and not the authority of the confessor was seen as the essential element in confession. Thomas Aquinas regarded contrition as a necessary element in confession but made the sacerdotal role of the priest even more indispensable. He claimed, in his highly technical way, that forgiveness was the result not of the work of the penitent (*ex opere operantis*), but of the work accomplished by the sacramental action itself (*ex opere operanto*). And this, of course, required a priest. Later scholastics would even bring rational analysis to the limitations of the penitent's actual contrition. They discounted it by introducing the concept of "attrition," a state of imperfect repentance that requires additional sacerdotal grace through a priest to become truly effective. In any case, as scholasticism reached its peak of influence at the end of the thirteenth century, Duns Scotus (d. 1308) came to argue that the priest's role in working absolution was in the end the only truly necessary one. By this time, then, a juridical conception of penance had come into being that subverted the therapeutic experience of postbaptismal conversion.

And as a result, penance became punitive rather than medicinal. A priest might grant absolution and thereby save the sinner from hell, but a requisite act of "satisfaction" was still imposed and must be completed to avoid the pains of purgatorial punishment after death. This commonly included prayer, fasting, and almsgiving.

It also included pilgrimage. With the rise of tariff penance, confessors began to impose journeys to specific shrines that were said to have redemptive powers. The most renowned of these was of course Jerusalem. Participating in the "armed pilgrimage" of a crusade to the site of Christ's Passion was considered incomparably effective in evading postmortem punishment. Other sites were centered on saints' relics, such as those of the Apostle James at Santiago de Compostela in Spain and of Thomas Becket at Canterbury Cathedral in England. But the default for every pious pilgrim was the city of Saint Peter, where four great basilicas (Saint John Lateran, Saint Peter's, Saint Paul outside the Walls, and Saint Mary Maggiore) provided enormous purgatorial capital.

That such acts of penance would become mechanical rather than spiritually transformative was inevitable, and reformist clergy were quick to address the problem. The most famous guidebook to Compostela, for instance, urged pilgrims to practice true penance by giving whatever money they might carry with them to the poor. For "the pilgrim who dies on the road with money in his pocket," it warned, "is permanently excluded from the kingdom of heaven." Upon his return, the pilgrim must show true amendment of life if he is to hope in the efficacy of his penance.

> *If he was previously a spoliator, he must become an almsgiver; if he was boastful he must be forever modest; if greedy, generous; if a fornicator or adulterer, chaste; if drunk, sober. That is to say that from every sin which he committed before his pilgrimage, he must afterwards abstain completely.*[54]

Clearly, penitential pilgrimage in this case was thoroughly therapeutic. But given the fear of purgatory, good works were often undertaken mechanically for their postmortem benefits alone, not for spiritual transformation. This abuse would later provide fuel for the Protestant Reformation.

---

54 Quoted in Jonathan Sumption, *The Age of Pilgrimage: The Medieval Journey to God* (Mahwah, NJ: Hidden Spring, 2003), 176–177.

But for now a therapeutic approach to penance continued to be found in the new Christendom as in the old. The best comparative example, perhaps, was found in the rituals of the Great Fast. Both halves of Christendom observed forty days of fasting prior to the annual celebration of Pascha. This period was regarded as one of repentance during which both the Roman Catholic and the Orthodox Churches meditated on the tragedy of sin. Both looked to the parable of the prodigal son as the ultimate model of godly sorrow, whereby the sinner's resolve to return from self-imposed exile is met with abundant love and forgiveness by God.

Another biblical image was paradise. In the West, people followed the example of penitents in the early Church who had ashes imposed on them at the beginning of the Fast, a day that came to be called Ash Wednesday. The imagery of the expulsion from paradise was vivid. As the priest imposed the ashes, he repeated the words of God Himself when casting out Adam: "For dust thou art, and unto dust thou shalt return" (Gen. 3:19). The Western ritual was, in short, a meditation on death.

In the East, the experience was one of forgiveness. It also made use of the imagery of exile from paradise. The day before the Fast came to be known as the Sunday of the Expulsion of Adam from Paradise. But it was also called Forgiveness Sunday. It featured hymns that combined the sorrow of sin with the joy of forgiveness. One from Vespers for the day suffices:

> O precious paradise, unsurpassed in beauty, tabernacle built by God, unending gladness and delight, glory of the righteous, joy of the prophets, and dwelling of the saints, with the sound of thy leaves pray to the Maker of all: may He open unto me the gates which I closed by my transgression, and may He count me worthy to partake of the Tree of Life and of the joy which was mine when I dwelt in thee before.

And even before this hymn is sung, for two weeks Eastern Christians preparing for the Fast had been singing another hymn whose text was Psalm 136 (137) about the Babylonian Jews' exile from the glory of Jerusalem. Avoiding any sense of despondency, the hymn interpolates into every stanza the biblical word expressing hope and joy: "Alleluia."

But perhaps the most vivid experience of penitential transformation in the East was the rite of mutual forgiveness prescribed for the first day of the Great Fast. It called on every member of every parish community to ask forgiveness of every other member of that community. What is more, it prescribed that each offer forgiveness to the other according to the Gospel read that day from the Sermon on the Mount. In it Jesus states that those who forgive will be forgiven, and those who refuse to do so will not be (Matt. 6:14–15).

Through this liturgical act of spiritual transformation, the whole world was thus offered an experience of evangelical transformation. And as the rite was enacted, it became customary for the people to sing the hymns of Pascha to enhance that experience. One, cited above, included one of the most paradisiacal phrases in all of Christendom:

Let us call brothers even those that hate us, and forgive all by the Resurrection.

PART III

The Withering of Western Culture

CHAPTER FIVE

Disintegration

T HE AGE OF DIVISION BEGAN with an heroic effort to preserve the
integrity of Christendom. The papacy brought an end to the proprietary system, and in doing so placed the laity firmly under the magisterial
authority of the clergy.

Heroic actions, however, often have tragic consequences. By the time the
Papal Reformation had spent itself during the thirteenth century, it had
rent a once unitary Christendom in two. The West, now estranged from the
old Christendom, was losing contact with the paradisiacal streams of its former culture.

Centuries before, Augustine had compared the catholic Church—what
the Orthodox had always claimed to be—to paradise. In a passage quoted
in the epigraph of this book, the Latin father reflected on how it is possible
to participate in the paradisiacal life of the Church while still being separated by schism from her. He observed that "though the waters of Paradise
are found beyond its boundaries, yet its happiness is in Paradise alone."[1] The
West could not remain separated indefinitely from "the fountain of Paradise" without suffering a cultural disintegration.

---

1   *On Baptism: Against the Donatists*, in Nicene and Post-Nicene Fathers, vol. 4,
     782.

Seen in this light, the Papal Reformation had an outcome that was decidedly unheroic. A civilization was altered, but its culture was thereby deprived of the mystical experience that had filled the lives and fired the hearts of its members since the Day of Pentecost. In many ways traditional Christianity became a mere instrument of reform for the better. Its heroically countercultural imperative toward the heavenly transformation of the world became institutionalized in such a way as to alter that imperative. Indignation had replaced repentance, and with the rise of clericalism, submission and obedience were often all that was demanded of a penitent.

In chapter one, we discussed the Pauline call to an unfettered *metamorphosis* (Rom. 12:2). This had now given way to a papally regulated *anamorphosis*, or mere "reform." To use the Latin in which Romans 12:2 was communicated to Western Christendom, *transformatio* became *reformatio*. In the end, the reformation directed from Rome did not so much incarnate the kingdom of heaven as domesticate it. And the unintended consequence was the withering of Western culture.

As the fourteenth century dawned, more than one advocate of papal supremacy pacing the corridors of the Lateran Palace realized how elusive paradise had become. Few, however, had the courage to admit it.

A Case of Papal Eschatology

AN EXCEPTION TO THIS WAS Pope Celestine V (r. 1294). His strange pontificate lasted only five months, but this was enough time to reveal a deep dissatisfaction with the culture and civilization of the new Christendom. Before his election, Celestine had been a recluse living an ascetic life on a mountain in Italy. One day, out of the blue, a delegation from the college of cardinals came for him and dragged him back into the world to place him on the papal throne. He was not happy with this, but he was a monk and he submitted to it.

Nevertheless, he brought an awkwardly paradisiacal vision of Christendom to the now thoroughly bureaucratic papal court. Like his predecessors, Celestine was not very confident in the world as it was. But unlike them, he was convinced that a spiritual renewal was just over the horizon. He was a millennialist, finding inspiration in the writings of a mystic named Joachim of Fiore (d. 1202).

Joachim had been the first person in history to read the Scriptures as a prophecy of the future. Christianity contained definite teachings about the end of history and certain signs that would accompany it. But not until this time had someone appropriated the Bible to make predictions about the future. For Joachim Scripture was the key to understanding why paradise seemed so elusive to his contemporaries.

As he pored through some of its most mysterious sections (such as the Book of Revelation, which in the East had never been integrated into the liturgical lectionary), Joachim became convinced that history moves in an upward, progressive direction. This was something new. Historians have in fact noted an optimistic spirit in the piety of the twelfth century. It sprang not so much from a sense that all was well with Christendom—the opposite was actually the case—but from a sense that solutions would come through reforms for the better. If contemporaries were lamenting an absence of heavenly immanence, Joachim prophesied that the end of such disappointment was near. He sought to restore to the old Christendom the principles of heavenly immanence and divine participation. As Jon Sweeney notes, he rejected the idea prevalent among contemporaries of his such as Peter Lombard "that the Godhead, in the purest and most ideal sense, couldn't ever possibly be known in this world."[2]

But paradise remained elusive. Joachim believed that the Scriptures revealed three stages of world history that had to occur before the manifestation of paradise. The first was that of the Israelites, which he designated the Age of the Father. The second was that of the Church, which he designated the Age of the Son. Significantly, Joachim considered this age to be under the direction of a "clerical order" (*ordo clericorum*). The third he designated the Age of the Spirit. Though it had ironically been precipitated by the Papal Reformation, this age would bring an end to the papacy and all forms of clericalism. It would initiate all men into an equal

---

2   Jon M. Sweeney, *The Pope Who Quit* (New York: Image Books, 2012), 134.

ministry of the Spirit. Then paradise would be manifest in the world.

Pope Celestine drank deeply from the well of Joachimite apocalypticism. But he was not alone in a civilization losing its moorings in the old Christendom. Other Joachimites were actually opponents of papal supremacy. They included partisans of the thrice-excommunicated Frederick II, who declared the "third age" would commence under the emperor in AD 1260. The death of Frederick and the date's passing without consequence actually had little impact on their expectations. As one historian put it, the disappointment "merely invalidated their calculations, not Joachim."[3] The Franciscan Spirituals were another group with strong sympathies for the mystic. Soon after Francis's death, they separated themselves from the mainline friars by demanding absolute poverty.

But it was Pope Celestine who most brought Joachim's vision into the mainstream of Western Christendom. During his tenure, the Franciscan Spirituals looked to him as their advocate, and they were not disappointed. When he promised them a privileged place of leadership, they saw the age of the Spirit beginning to open. For them, Celestine was the promised "angelic pope" who would lead Christendom into its final, consummating glory.

But within six months of his election, Celestine became, as Sweeney entitled his biography, "the pope who quit." It proved impossible to bring about the mystical experience of paradise the ascetic pope had apparently hoped to inaugurate. Why he reached this conclusion is hard to tell. But it surely had something to do with his model of the pontificate, which, inspired by an eremitical monasticism similar to that of the East, looked to personal transformation more than institutional reformation. His successor, Boniface VIII, brought a swift end to his idealism. He annulled many of Celestine's edicts. For good measure he then threw him into prison, where the mystical and impractical pope emeritus soon died in obscurity.

Boniface, as we saw in chapter three, was by contrast no zealot for the kingdom. He was a bureaucrat—a lawyer by training, a politician by preference, and a diplomat by necessity. He believed that the kingdom of heaven

---

3   R. N. Swanson, *Religion and Devotion in Europe, c. 1215–c. 1515* (Cambridge: Cambridge University Press, 1995), 204.

had become institutionalized in the papacy, and that all Christendom needed to do was to accept that fact. The likes of King Philip the Fair had no intention of doing so, and the result was a crisis of papal supremacy that never really ended.

The Tragedy of Conciliarism

AMONG THE MANY INNOVATIONS OF the Papal Reformation was the claim that the papacy, and not councils of bishops, was the supreme authority within the life of the Church. This had been the sixteenth assertion of that "great innovator" Gregory VII when he issued his *Papal Dictate*: no council of bishops can be designated ecumenical without the pope's authority. Indeed, when the Roman Catholic Church began, almost immediately after her separation from the Orthodox Church, to assemble councils, she did so under the direct supervision of the popes.

In the century from 1123 to 1215, it was popes who called together synods of bishops that were thereby declared ecumenical. And they did so with the principal goal of reforming the Church. Historically, ecumenical councils had been called to address great heresies, such as Arianism, Nestorianism, or iconoclasm. Not so those designated ecumenical by the reform papacy. In less than one century, no fewer than four such councils were called at the papal headquarters at the Lateran Palace. Each made a contribution to the reform agenda, issuing legislation that banned lay investiture, simony, and clerical marriage. The last, known as Lateran IV, was as we have seen the most ambitious and the most effective in bringing the Papal Reformation to completion.

In these and subsequent cases, an ecumenical council for the Roman Catholic Church was understood as an adjunct to the papacy and little more than a useful legislative body. Along with the college of cardinals and the staff of the papal court, such a council was, in effect, no more than another part of the ever-expanding papal bureaucracy.

This could not be further from the doctrine of conciliarity (or synodality) as it was understood in the East. From the time of Nicaea I (which addressed

Arianism and issued the Nicene Creed), an assembly of bishops was understood to be an act as much of God as of man. Indeed, the words of the apostles at the Jerusalem Council recorded in Acts 15 were often repeated in ancient conciliar legislation: "It seemed good to the Holy Spirit and to us . . ." Councils in general, and ecumenical councils in particular, were understood as the presence of God in this world, securing the Church in her doctrinal integrity. As such they were an elemental part of Christendom's experience of heavenly immanence.

When papal ecclesiology subverted traditional conciliarity, however, this changed. The pope was now a necessary intermediary between the Holy Spirit and the world. It has been argued that the filioque played a role in this, for if the Spirit proceeds from Christ the Son, the pope, as the Vicar of Christ, can be seen as the dispenser of the Spirit's sacramental grace. It is certainly true that canon law now declared unambiguously that the Vicar of Christ was the necessary source of a bishop's ministry (and that of all the lower clergy). The pope was the effective head of the entire clerical establishment in the way Christ had always, in traditional ecclesiology, been the true Head of the Church. The local bishop was no more than an extension of the pope's authority, a regional agent in his universal jurisdiction.

This, as historians such as Richard Southern have noted, added considerably to the local bishop's absolute influence. With such power behind him, he could contribute as never before to the institutionalization of a Christian society. But this power came at the cost of his relative influence—he was no longer the center of the local church as the autonomous bishops in the time of Ignatius of Antioch had been. What is more, his role in manifesting the presence of Christ in the world was hereby diminished. The local bishop, like the assembled council, no longer manifested heavenly immanence directly.

However, at a purely practical level, the new papal ecclesiology also had a fundamental weakness. Boniface had declared in *Unam sanctam* that "it is necessary for salvation that every human being be subject to the Roman Pontiff." Because the office of the papacy was now the central principle of ecclesial identity (and not the mystical presence of the Holy Spirit in the sacramental life of the local church), doubts about his legitimacy could be ruinous. The unity of the Roman Catholic Church had come to depend—as the Eastern Church never had—on confidence in the successor to Saint Peter.

A blow to this confidence was now struck in the wake of Boniface's downfall. It is known as the "Avignon papacy," a period of more than half a century when the successor to Saint Peter no longer inhabited the city in which the apostle died and in which his sacred relics lay. Instead, from 1309 to 1376 he ruled Western Christendom from the French city of Avignon. To many, the shock of this break from tradition was so great it became dubbed a second "Babylonian captivity."

It is no coincidence that the disgraced Boniface had been kidnapped and beaten while living at a distance from Rome. In fact, the traditional papal capital was at this time a very unsafe place for anyone, especially a pope. Two political factions known as the Guelfs and the Ghibellines warred with one another over the question of papal authority and imperial power. The city was often the flashpoint in their conflict. With the fall of Boniface, Philip the Fair gained the upper hand in papal elections. When one of his candidates, Clement V (r. 1305–1314), became pope, the papal court was moved from Rome to Avignon. There it remained for sixty-seven years.

The papal palace in Avignon

During this time the papacy lost much of the prestige it had accumulated under the vigorous reformers of recent centuries. Some of its independence was forfeited by close proximity to the French king. Clement packed the college of cardinals with Frenchmen, causing Italians to fall into the minority and setting the conditions for a future conflict over the papacy's national affiliations. He also clouded the French papal court with controversy. He raised taxes and substantially increased papal income, but then he used the treasury as his own private fortune to distribute at whim to favorites and family members.

The next pope, John XXII (r. 1316–1334), caused scandal with his theological policies. Suspicious of the Franciscan Spirituals, he ordered their suppression. When some resisted, calling him a heretic, he had the inquisition burn them at the stake. In fact, the apocalyptic views of the Spirituals were at odds with those of John. Their inspired prophet, Joachim, had claimed against the views of many scholastics that God could be known immediately in this life—an expression of traditional Christianity's doctrine of divine participation. John rejected this, but he went further. He claimed in a series of homilies that even after death and before the resurrection it is impossible for the elect to experience paradise, what was called the "beatific vision" of God. This was indeed a heresy, and he only escaped posthumous judgment for it by renouncing it on his deathbed. Finally, John's alienation of the emperor (whom he excommunicated) provoked the latter to support theologians with conciliar rather than papal views of ecclesiology. This conciliar party would feature prominently in the decades to come.

Another milestone of decline was the pontificate of Clement VI (r. 1342–1352). Even more than his predecessors, he was committed to keeping the king of France happy. As a result, the college of cardinals grew ever more Francophilic. Particularly demoralizing was the atmosphere of the papal court. Modeled on the royal court of Paris, it exceeded that court in extravagance. Clement lived, in the words of John Julius Norwich, "less like a pope than an oriental potentate." At his coronation feast, for instance, three thousand guests joined the new pontiff in consuming 1,023 sheep, 118 head of cattle, 101 calves, 914 kids, 60 pigs, 10,471 hens, 1,440 geese, 300 pike, 46,856 cheeses, 50,000 tarts, and 200 casks of wine.[4] Clement's governing slogan, appropriately, was "a pontiff should make his subjects happy."[5]

The Avignon papacy came to an end in 1377 when Gregory XI finally returned the papal court to Rome. For decades, forces of division had been gathering within the college of cardinals and among the various political powers of the West. When Gregory died a year later, these forces all came into the open. The result was the greatest test of the papacy since the start of the reformation.

Within weeks of Gregory's death, the Italian cardinals on scene in Rome elected an Italian replacement who took the name Urban VI. This provoked a reaction by the French cardinals, who proceeded to elect a French replacement named Clement VII. Their rather audacious choice was the king's cousin. As he returned to Avignon, Urban called on the powers of the West to launch a crusade against his rival. But nothing came of it. Clement, himself a former military commander known for massacring thousands of civilians in battle, unleashed an Italian ally named Joanna of Naples on Urban. Though her armies were ultimately defeated (and she herself imprisoned and murdered), Urban was unable to marshal the forces necessary for his crusade. As a result, Western Christendom was forced to live with two popes.

This was the beginning of a period known as the Papal Schism. Other names for the division include "Western Schism" and even "Great Schism," so traumatic was it. It surely does not deserve the latter title, rival as such a title is to the division marked by the excommunications of 1054. It was neither as consequential nor as long-lasting as the schism of 1054. But the Papal Schism was undoubtedly a disaster for the new Christendom and contributed substantially to its disintegration. Its effects on papal supremacy would never be reversed completely, and for this reason the traumas it caused can be seen as the birth pains of the modern papacy.[6]

The schism's sequence of events need not detain us much. In the past, antipopes had occasionally troubled the history of the papacy. But not until

---

4   Norwich, *Absolute Monarchs*, 213.

5   Barraclough, *Medieval Papacy*, 153.

6   Ibid., 164.

the Papal Reformation elevated the institution to supreme authority was schism on this scale possible. The Chair of Saint Peter was now so necessary to the functioning of Western civilization that under the immediate circumstances, new divisions were inevitable. Popes Urban and Clement had entrenched themselves. Now the various political powers of Europe took sides. And they did so for almost entirely political reasons. France, of course, was invested in Clement. England, France's emerging enemy, was therefore convinced Urban was the true pope. That ensured that Scotland, at odds with England, sided with Clement. And so on. In the end, the division of the papacy divided the powers of the West into two camps.

This system proved remarkably resistant to correction. Both Urban and Clement had, strictly speaking, been elected according to the new canon law of the period. Therefore, according to the new ecclesiology, which asserted that a duly elected pope could be judged by no one, neither could be deposed. And when they died, they left behind rival successors who continued to preside from their separate courts in Avignon and Rome. Proposals for negotiation always foundered on the stubborn refusal of either pope to cede power. Finally, at the Council of Pisa in 1409, both were deposed by the bishops—something not strictly allowed under the new canon law—and a new pope was elected. However, this only created a third papacy, as both rivals refused to comply. Western Christendom was now divided by three competing popes!

Finally, at the Council of Constance (1414–1418), the Papal Schism was brought to an end. The gathered bishops obtained the resignation of two of the contenders and declared the deposition of the third. Furthermore, a conciliar decree declared what every opponent of papal supremacy since the time of Anonymous of York had been waiting to hear:

> *This holy Council of Constance . . . declares, first, that it is lawfully assembled in the Holy Spirit, that it constitutes a General Council, representing the Catholic Church, and that therefore it has its authority immediately from Christ; and that all men, of every rank and condition, including the pope himself, are bound to obey it in matters concerning the Faith, the abolition*

of the schism, and the reformation of the Church of God in its head and members.[7]

The language was nearly that of the Orthodox Church. What this remarkable document did was reestablish, after centuries of papal supremacy, the principle of conciliar supremacy.

The Papal Schism was over. However, a new conflict about papal supremacy was about to begin.

The appalling spectacle of rival popes maintaining independent courts and being kept in power by nothing more than the military force of rival governments had taken its toll on Western Christendom. Papal supremacy may once have rescued it from the proprietary system, but now, three centuries later, the system of papal supremacy on which the reformation had depended itself cried out for reformation. Theologians began to look for alternatives. As they did so, they might have looked to Western Christendom's past and to the East that continued to keep its tradition. But as we shall see, they did not. Too much had changed during those three centuries.

In the aftermath of Constance, a movement arose that assigned ultimate earthly authority not to the pope, or even to the cardinals, but to the entire Church. It was in some ways the product of necessity for, according to the new ecclesiology of Gregory VII, the pope could be judged by no one on earth. Clearly, someone had to stand as judge over Gregory's rival successors, elected as they were according to the new canon law, and so another ecclesiological reform was needed.

What is tragic, though, is that as theologians at the University of Paris began to formulate the solutions that came to be known to historians as "conciliarism," they paid virtually no attention to the entire first millennium record of Christendom. They were historically blind. Even Jean Gerson (d. 1429), one of the most subtle and open-minded advocates of conciliarism, was so ignorant of history that he took something as patently

---

7   Quoted in Ozment, *The Age of Reform*, 156.

fraudulent as the *Donation of Constantine* "at face value."[8]

For Western conciliarists, Aristotelianism, not the historical record of thirteen hundred years of Orthodox history, was the chosen weapon against division. Regarded as a breakthrough in the papal problem by one of the earliest conciliarists, the Parisian theologian Conrad of Gelnhausen, was the Aristotelian principle of "equity" (*epikeia*). In this view, legal decrees such as those contained in the new law books were interpreted according to their original *intent* and not as absolute principles in themselves.[9] This principle proved revolutionary in the struggle against an absolute papal supremacy. As Gerson, the leading theorist of conciliarism and an organizer of the councils of Pisa and Constance, put it,

> *The pope can be removed by a general council celebrated without his consent and against his will. Normally, a council is not legally . . . celebrated without papal calling and approval. . . . But, as in grammar and in morals, general rules have exceptions—and especially when the infinite number of special circumstances surrounding a particular case are taken into account. Because of these exceptions a superior law has been ordained to interpret the law. This is what Aristotle called equity.[10]*

Division from the East thus left the resolution of the crisis in the hands of scholastics for whom Aristotelian rationalism, not church tradition, provided answers.

Even more poignantly, the final outcome of conciliarism played out against the backdrop of efforts to establish Orthodox union with Rome. In 1431, Pope Eugene IV convened a council in Basel. The bishops who attended were still under the spell of Constance, however, and the pope soon lost

---

8   Francis Oakley, "Gerson as Conciliarist," in *A Companion to Jean Gerson*, edited by Brian Patrick McGuire (Leiden, Netherlands: Brill, 2006), 179–204.

9   Gerald Christianson, "Introduction: The Conciliar Tradition and Ecumenical Dialogue," in *The Church, the Councils, and Reform: The Legacy of the Fifteenth Century*, edited by Gerald Christianson, Thomas M. Izbicki, and Christopher M. Bellitto (Washington, D.C.: Catholic University of America, 2008), 1–24.

10   Quoted in Ozment, *Age of Reform*, 163.

confidence in them. He therefore ordered the council dissolved, claiming papal supremacy in doing so. Political upheaval in Italy intervened, during which the conciliarist bishops held fast in Basel. In 1439, they declared Eugene deposed and elected their own pope, citing Constance's principle of conciliar supremacy as justification.

However, by now Eugene had assembled a new council in Florence, and there he declared his intention of establishing reunion with the Orthodox. It would be the last such effort before Byzantium was finally lost to the Turks. And, if played correctly, it would give Eugene the means of reestablishing papal supremacy against the bishops of Basel. For no achievement would be of greater consequence for a papacy seeking to reassert itself than the end to the Great Division.

The tragedy of Western conciliarism was about to reach its denouement. So was its theological parallel.

The Subversion of Doctrine

AS WE SAW IN CHAPTER three, a decisive shift in theological reflection occurred after the Great Division of 1054. First Berengar and Lanfranc disputed over the doctrine of the Eucharist using nothing but grammar and logic. Then, more fatefully, Anselm of Canterbury—Lanfranc's student—wrote a treatise on the existence of God using logic alone. Anselm famously announced that the scholastic project was "faith seeking understanding" (*fides quaerens intellectum*).

This principle fundamentally reconstituted the role played in theology by philosophy, long appropriated by church fathers but kept subordinate to the Church's doctrinal tradition. Western patristics had not been much different from those in the East in this sense, and Augustine spoke for the entire first millennium when he declared that "faith precedes; understanding follows." But the Anselmian shift away from tradition had now been made, and the doctors of subsequent centuries could not resist the siren song of rationalism.

Bernard of Clairvaux, known sometimes as "the last of the Western fathers," had made one final, lonely challenge to scholastic rationalism. He attacked the most audacious scholastic of his time, Abelard, for placing theology in the thrall of mere philosophical reasoning. In doing so he echoed the same criticisms made in the East by a long line of fathers, from Basil the Great to Gregory Palamas.[11] But as Bernard made his defense, he too crossed a portentous line. As John Baldwin observed,

> Bernard's chief objection to Abelard and [other scholastics] seemed to have been that they were confusing the legitimate boundaries between faith and reason. In letter after letter he protested the introduction of reason and logic into the realms of faith. Reason has its appropriate sphere of operation, but it cannot be used to profane the sanctuary of divine mystery.

So far, Bernard seems to sound very Eastern. But Baldwin continued by observing something new in the dispute with Abelard. What Bernard "seemed to have been proposing," the historian noted, "was a division of knowledge into two realms, the one investigated by faith, the other by reason. In effect Bernard introduced a breach into Anselm's unity of faith seeking understanding."[12] This breach was the theological hallmark of theology in an age of division. It had found fullest expression in the optimistic intellectual system of Thomas Aquinas, which, as we have seen, distinguished between "natural theology" and "revealed theology." But during the fourteenth century such dualism began to disintegrate.

The scholastic division of faith and reason found its completion in the theology of William of Occam (d. 1350). The scholastic movement had inspired the appearance of a multiplicity of schools—an intellectual counterpart to the diversification of monastic orders—and Occam, a Franciscan, was the champion of what came to be known as *nominalism*. It represented

---

11   Basil defended the use of secular philosophy in his "Address to Young Men on the Right Use of Greek Literature," but insisted it be strictly subordinated to holy tradition. A millennium later, Gregory Palamas likewise supported the use of pagan philosophy in certain areas of knowledge, but dismissed its application to Christian doctrine.

12   Baldwin, *The Scholastic Culture of the Middle Ages*, 91.

for the West a radical reassessment of knowledge, beginning with theology. Theologians like Aquinas, in their ambitious effort to summarize all knowledge, had spoken frequently of "universals," categories of explaining the form or nature of things. Cats, for instance, all shared in common universal features such as mammalian-ness, four-leggedness, and furriness.

William of Occam

But Occam objected to this. Using an intellectual tool that came to be known as "Occam's Razor," he cut away all such universals and claimed the only knowledge man can really have is of things in their individuality. He did this by making use of semantics and logic, two powerful intellectual disciplines inherited from the philosophy of the pagan Greeks. Two cats might look similar and this might suggest a common nature, he admitted, but such unity of form is nothing more than an abstraction, a name. Nominalism, from the Latin word for "name" (*nomen*), thus rejected universals and claimed that only particulars have any reality. And once it did, the entire edifice of Western theology began to crumble.

For according to nominalism, God could not be known, either through the mystical Eastern sense of *theoria* or the rationalistic Western sense of cognition. In Him one could only have faith. Occam was a sincere believer himself and defended Christianity against other religions and against non-belief. But the God of his belief was utterly transcendent and unknowable to human reason. He had created a covenant the individual could choose to enter into, but the moral laws of this covenant were purely arbitrary. Their observance did not lead to any kind of holiness defined objectively by God Himself, and even less to any participation in the divine nature. Indeed, such a nature could never be known and in fact technically did not even exist. Instead, God and man were radically separated by their unbridgeable individuality. Salvation consisted in men believing in God and submitting to His moral order. And once again, this order was totally arbitrary. God had ordained that men avoid committing murder or adultery for the sake of their own salvation, but Occam claimed He just as easily might have ordained the opposite. In fact, the rationalist liked to remark mischievously that Christ could have been incarnate as a donkey as much as a man. Since God was absolutely sovereign, the believer is saved or damned by an absolutely arbitrary act of divine will and not by a life of virtuous growth in an objective divine grace or participation in divinity. Accordingly, deification was impossible.

The rise of nominalism had a profound and permanent impact on Western Christendom. One noteworthy effect was its weakening of traditional Christology. We have already seen how a shift in piety altered the believer's relationship to Christ by emphasizing His human suffering at the expense of His divine omnipotence. Nominalism reinforced this tendency by reducing reasoned knowledge of Christ to the particulars of His earthly ministry—especially His Passion—and dismissing as unknowable their objective significance. According to nominalist ontology, or theory of being, the believer could no longer be assured of an objective communion with the divine nature. Even a universal human nature was now suspect. By rejecting the reality of universals, nominalism threw the actual effects of the Incarnation into question. Occam had asserted, after all, that while he believed that God had become man because of the Scriptures, God might just well have become a donkey. Because of the doctrinal integrity of both East and West during the first millennium, Christ had been understood to unite within His one "person" (*hypostasis*) two very definite natures, the divine and the human. This was the proclamation of the Fourth Ecumenical Council and the basis for its doctrine of what was called the "hypostatic union." It was the basis of traditional Christianity's belief in man's capacity for communion with God and even for deification.

But now, nominalism challenged this. It called into question the very idea that there was really such thing as a universal human nature that the Son of

God had assumed and in which all men shared.[13] The effect was to undermine the principle of divine participation, one of the most fundamental of Christendom's paradisiacal values.

Nominalism also undermined the principle of heavenly immanence. The union of heaven and earth at the heart of traditional Christian cosmology could not survive the wounds inflicted by Occam's Razor. The razor had severed the world from God, and under nominalist influence the new Christendom would cultivate a new cosmology in what Charles Taylor has called "the great mechanization of the scientific world picture."[14]

Nominalism was so radical when it appeared in the thirteenth century that, like the art of Giotto, it was recognized as totally different from what had existed in the first millennium. Theologians called it the "modern way" (*via moderna*) and distinguished it from the "old way" (*via antiqua*). Even so, on the eve of the Protestant Reformation it would become the leading school of Western thought.

In the meantime, the new Christendom continued to disintegrate. Theologians reacted to the erosion of scholastic epistemology, or theory of knowledge, by turning to a more subjective and intuitive approach to divine communion. Because it claimed only the particular is real, nominalism brought greater attention to the experience of the individual believer. Intuition took the place of reason when contemplating God. And since reason and faith were radically separated—the one limited to earthly particulars and the other to heavenly things—the way of faith was increasingly nonrational. The result was a wave of mysticism that further undermined the cultural edifice of the West.

Jean Gerson, the chancellor of the University of Paris, was acutely sensitive to the threat from both nominalism and mysticism. In fact, he was

---

13 Occam (also spelled Ockham) appears to have evaded the charge of heresy on this point by conceding a human nature in the case of Christ, but he did so as an exception. Richard Cross, "Nominalism and the Christology of William of Ockham," *Recherches de theologie ancienne et medievale* 58 (January–February, 1991), 126–156.

14 Charles Taylor, *Sources of the Self: The Making of the Modern Identity* (Cambridge: Cambridge University Press, 1989), 160.

a man surrounded by threats. As we have seen, he was a conciliarist who helped organize the early fifteenth-century councils seeking a resolution to the Papal Schism. He was also something of a nominalist. In promoting conciliarism he was in a sense continuing the work of Occam, who had taken a stand against papal supremacy during the previous century. Perceiving an impending crisis in theology, Gerson composed a work entitled *On Mystical Theology,* in which he used the nominalist preference for intuition to argue that true faith is borne not by reason but by the believer's emotional experience. In his critique of scholasticism, he emphasized the mystic's attention to "internal" manifestations of the divine presence rather than merely "external" ones. Though the head of the most prestigious university of the new Christendom, he cast a nostalgic glance back to the first millennium, when theologians were fathers and not doctors, pastors and not professionals.

Gerson was a voice of moderation in a time of misgivings. A greater disquietude gripped the theologians of Germany. One was a Dominican named Meister Eckhart (d. 1328). He was the product of the university system, having studied in Paris and returned to his native land as a professor and a spiritual guide of both professed nuns and a group of laywomen called beguines. As we shall soon see, the latter would eventually be condemned for their belief that even in this life one can experience the kingdom of heaven. Like them, Eckhart emphasized that all believers, not just trained theologians, can experience the mystical wonders of paradise. And like some of them, he would end his life in front of the papal inquisition.

Eckhart was certainly no moderate. A trained theologian, he spoke the language of the scholastics, but he preferred the utterances of the mystics. This is demonstrated by his preference for compositions in the German vernacular rather than in university Latin. He coined terms like the "ground of the soul" for the center of man's being, and "breakthrough" for the soul's ascent to divine communion.

To evade the restrictions of scholasticism, Eckhart fell back on the neoplatonism of Origen. This seems to have put him in the orbit of Eastern Christianity. For he showed a much greater interest than his Augustinian predecessors in the matter of deification. Unlike the Greek fathers, however, he gave man's participation in divinity only an emotional aspect. The results could be quite touching. "I became man for you," he has his interlocutor Christ complain. "If you do not become God for me, you do me wrong."[15] In such passages, piety has become intensely subjective and almost sentimental in its intimacy. An equivalent expression of deification would be hard to find in Eckhart's Byzantine contemporary Gregory Palamas. It was certainly not to be found in Origen. But like the great Alexandrian and unlike Palamas, Eckhart denigrated the material body. Even more problematically, he seemed to indicate a belief that the soul is, like God, preexistent. These are some of the reasons Pope John XXII called him to Avignon and, after his death while awaiting judgment, condemned his teaching.

But Meister Eckhart had provoked a generation of Germans grown weary of the cerebral impotence of scholasticism. A charismatic and inspirational preacher (especially when speaking in the vernacular), he was followed by a throng of disciples. One of the most articulate was his fellow Dominican Johannes Tauler (d. 1361). In sermon after sermon—delivered in the language of the people—Tauler developed the Meister's argument for mystical rather than rational experiences of God. These experiences, typically gained in a state of ecstasy, were presented as the goal of the individual's life. Another Dominican follower of the Meister, Heinrich Suso (d. 1366), laid out the mystical life in a voluminous series of vernacular sermons and treatises, and even composed an autobiography to reveal how very real and personal communion with God could be.

Such communion was centered on an asceticism of pain. We noted that as early as the eleventh century Peter Damian had turned to self-flagellation as a means of appeasing the wrath of God. For that papal reformer, sanctified self-harm was a way of avoiding punishment after death. Suso went further. He described in his autobiography a series of disciplines he devised to inflict as much pain as possible without actually killing himself.

Some were quite inventive. For instance, in order not to pass the nights in comfort and rest, he made a kind of nightshirt pierced with 150 inward-facing nails. This caused such pain while he lay on his bed that he would

---

15   Quoted in Evelyn Underhill, *Mysticism* (New York: Image Books, 1990), 420.

squirm about "as a worm does when run through with a pointed needle."[16] To prevent himself from involuntarily relieving the agony in his sleep, if ever that should come, he designed mittens that likewise featured embedded nails facing outward so that if he should try to adjust the nightshirt it would cause even greater bleeding. Finally, he had leather straps designed that would harness both arms tightly against his body, not only preventing relief from the pain but actually increasing it by causing his limbs to cramp. Thus bound and bleeding, he passed sixteen years of his life in nocturnal vigil, writhing in pain and grimacing as vermin crawled over his back to feed on the suppurating issue of his wounds.

Suso's most important work was the *Little Book of Eternal Wisdom*, written in the vernacular with an accessible style that could not have been more unlike the impenetrable Latin of the schoolmen. The work was widely copied, and, based on the number of manuscripts in existence, appears to have been one of the most popular works of the period. It instructs the reader in how to ascend to ever higher levels of union with Christ by meditating on His Passion. However, the meditation does not extend beyond His death and burial. Turning to the Mother of God, the author closes by conveying her imagined words of agony in being separated from Christ by the tomb.

> *For when they separated me from my Beloved, the separating wrestled with my heart like bitter death. Supported by their hands who led me away, I walked with tottering steps, for I was robbed of all consolation, my heart longed woefully to return to my Love, my confidence was wholly set in Him, I rendered Him alone of all mankind entire fidelity and true attachment, even to the grave.*[17]

The Resurrection from this grave is never mentioned, so intent was Suso on breaking his readers' hearts with pious lamentation.

---

16 Henry Suso, *The Life of Blessed Henry Suso by Himself*, translated by Thomas Francis Knox (London: Burns, Lambert, and Oates, 1865), 58.
17 Henry Suso, *A Little Book of Eternal Wisdom* (London: Burns Oates and Washbourne, 1910), 110–111.

In a paradox, then, the effort to achieve a mystical experience of Christ's presence in this world depended on an emotional exercise in imagining His absence from it. It was an epitome of piety in the age of division.

The Proliferation of Death

FEW GENERATIONS OF CHRISTIANS WERE as consoled by the death of Christ as the one that lived—and died—in the middle of the fourteenth century. In 1347 the Black Death came to Europe. Carried from Central Asia by the Mongols, it was a second, and even more deadly, scourge brought on Western Civilization by that murdering horde of conquerors. One theory suggests the plague was transmitted to Europeans first during the Mongol siege of a town in the Crimea, during which the assailants hurled infected corpses over the walls. From there, merchant vessels brought the disease to Italy, whence it spread throughout Christendom. The Arabs were also devastated by it. Within a few years, about half the population of Europe had perished. While the mortality rate was less in the north, along the Mediterranean coast as many as eighty percent of townspeople died. And the death they died was unforgettable for those who survived to tell of it. In the space of days, buboes appeared in the armpits and groin of victims that could swell as large as apples, in many cases to the point of bursting. But victims rarely lived long enough for the disease to reach that stage.

For Christians, the cause of this most dreadful pestilence in history was

inevitably perceived to be the wrath of God. In the West, a culture of dread in the face of divine displeasure had already been cultivated in Gothic architecture. Beginning with the cathedral of St. Denis, entrance into the

The Black Death

liturgical assembly was no longer marked by images of paradise (as in the East) but by a Last Judgment sculpted within the central tympanum of the western entrance.

The musical counterpart to this liturgical experience was the *Dies irae* ("Day of Wrath"), composed by the Franciscan Thomas of Celano (d. 1260). It opened with a paralyzing cry:

> *Day of wrath and doom impending.*
> *David's word with Sybil's blending,*
> *Heaven and earth in ashes ending.*

It then continued to bring attention to the terror sinners would experience before the awful face of Christ in judgment:

> *Oh, what fear man's bosom rendeth,*
> *When from heaven the judge descendeth,*
> *On whose sentence all dependeth.*

The majesty of the heavenly judge is so great that only terrified repentance can withstand it.

> *Low I kneel, with heart's submission,*
> *See, like ashes, my contrition,*
> *Help me in my last condition.*

It is significant that the *Dies irae* came to be included within the Requiem Mass, a service in much use during the plague years. Survivors of the pestilence might have found themselves standing within the temple and staring at the corpse that was once their loved one (though the bodies of many victims were taken directly from deathbed to cemetery and tossed into mass graves). In such a situation Christians, though baptized into the death and Resurrection of Christ, might be more inclined to contemplate His death alone.

This, after all, was what the pattern of the new Christendom's piety had become. As we have seen, Heinrich Suso had placed meditation on the Crucifixion at the center of mystical experience. He used visual imagery to focus it. In one passage from the *Little Book*, he compares the comforting image of the rainbow with that of Christ's crucified body.

> *Remember, heavenly Father, how Thou didst swear of old to Noah, and didst say: I will stretch My bow in the sky; I will look upon it, and it shall be a sign of reconciliation between Me and the earth. O look now upon it, tender Father, how cruelly stretched out it is, so that its bones and ribs can be numbered; look how red, how green, how yellow, love has made it! Look, O heavenly Father, through the hands, the arms, and the feet, so woefully distended, of Thy tender and only-begotten Son. Look at his beautiful body, all rose colour with wounds, and forget Thy anger against me.*[18]

We noted above the emergence of naturalism in the paintings of Giotto, particularly those depicting the Passion. A half-century after his Padua paintings, other artists were going even further in the naturalistic depiction of Christ's death. This new, "modern" style was better equipped than traditional iconography to sustain the new piety. Now empathy and the emotional experience of grief were considered necessary for true communion with the crucified. A popular guide to contemplation declared that its readers "must imagine that they are present at the very time of the passion and must feel grief as if the Lord were suffering before their very eyes."[19]

Naturalism enabled this. It also supported the shift toward nominalism by its enhancement of the concrete and historical elements of Christ's humanity, leaving the symbolism of His divinity (such as was still to be found in the iconography of the East) to faith alone.

Finally, graphic imagery of Christ's suffering supported the new soteriology, or theory of salvation, that Anselm had introduced in the wake of the Great Division. Christ's death was a horrifying act of satisfaction offered to

---

18   Ibid., 40.
19   Quoted in Viladesau, *Beauty of the Cross*, 157.

an offended God the Father. For as Anselm had claimed in *Why God Became Man*, "either the honour which has been taken away [from God by man's sin] should be repaid, or punishment should follow."[20] In either case, Christ now stood in His Crucifixion as the substitute for the sinner, and every Christian was encouraged to look on the event with a profound sense of gratitude, responsibility, and guilt.

The Crucifixion paintings that now proliferated within this unique historical context were unprecedented in their ghastliness. An anonymous Bohemian work known as the Kaufmann Crucifixion, painted in 1360 as an altarpiece, is particularly graphic. It depicts blood from Christ's pierced hands pouring down upon the rocks below Him (where it has begun to pool), and also running down his forearms to the elbow, where gravity causes it to drip. More shocking, perhaps, are the bodies of the thieves on either side of the Savior. They are convulsed in death agonies, their mouths gaping and their limbs mangled. Their wrists and shins have been slashed, and from these wounds yet more blood gushes. Such imagery became commonplace in the churches of Western Christendom during the fourteenth and fifteenth centuries. This was the religious art that the earliest Protestant reformers grew up staring at during the Mass. Perhaps this played some role in provoking iconoclasm in the more radical among them.

An example of such a painting, completed just a year before Martin Luther issued the *Ninety-Five Theses,* is the Isenheim Altarpiece of Grunewald. It was finished in 1516, but like many before it—especially from the middle of the fourteenth century—it depicts the crucified Christ with sores resembling those of plague victims. It is therefore a type known as a "plague cross." And its imagery of death is as ghastly as that of the Kaufmann Crucifixion, if not more so. Christ's mangled and withered body bears no sign, symbolical or otherwise, of divinity. It is the color of a cadaver. His ribs protrude under the skin. His arms are pulled up above His slumped body, and the fingers of each hand twist upward in a gruesome

---

20   Anselm of Canterbury, *Why God Became Man*, in *The Major Works*, edited by Brian Davies and G. R. Evans, translated by Janet Fairweather (Oxford: Oxford University Press, 1998), 287.

The Kaufmann Crucifixion

display of rigor mortis. His head hangs downward, and His mouth gapes wide in death.

The death of the Savior had set men free, but Western men used their freedom to contemplate the most gruesome details of death. During this time a tidal wave of morbidity arose, and as it broke upon the foundations of Christendom, it weakened them further.

A heightened anticipation of personal mortality led to what many called "the art of dying." This practice had a lineage more ancient than the Great Division, as early Christian monasticism had stressed the importance of a sober recognition of one's mortality as a safeguard against delusion. But as a cultural theme, springing beyond the walls of the cloister (where, it should be noted, the inmates were comparatively better equipped to practice it sanely), it awaited the Papal Reformation of the eleventh century. It was then, as we have seen, that a monasticization of the laity (as well as the parish clergy) was imposed on all from the clerical heights.

One of the most influential expressions of this morbidity was a treatise by Innocent III, penned before his election, entitled *The Misery of the Human Condition*. It was a ceaseless lament about being alive in a world as wretched as this one. In it the future pope complained about the fact that man is conceived in the slime of sexual intercourse and destined for every kind of hardship and sorrow. It is better to be dead, the future pope concluded. He expressed the intention of writing a sequel on the theme of human dignity but, significantly, never found the time or interest to make it happen.

Preparing for death came to be seen as the most valuable way to spend one's life. Suso's *Little Book* dedicated an entire chapter to it. But far more influential was an anonymous volume entitled *The Art of Dying*, which appeared in the fifteenth century and became another of the most copied books of the period. Its popularity was due in part to the use of graphic woodcut illustrations showing the horrors of purgatory and hell beyond the grave. Another example was the miracle play *Everyman*, which appeared in England during the same century. In it, the protagonist—who explicitly stands for every man watching the drama—is suddenly confronted by death and forced to reflect on his wasted life in one final effort to evade hell.

A morbid preoccupation with death influenced the appearance, at about the same time, of tombs decorated with sculptures depicting the remains of the deceased. These "cadaver tombs" were even more graphic than the woodcuts or plague crosses, in part because they were three-dimensional. But they also showed the body of the person—often recognizable to those who knew him—in an advanced state of putrefaction. One in the Belgian town of Boussu featured a spinal cord emerging through a cavity in the belly, a gaping rib cage, and a skull encased in the last vestiges of decaying skin.

If one wanted to identify the geographical center of what was becoming a cult of morbidity, it would have to be the Cemetery of the Innocents in Paris. Since numerous parishes in the city used this cemetery for burials—especially during the Black Death—its capacity was soon exceeded. During the fifteenth century, then, charnel houses were built to receive bones disinterred as graves were reused. Because of this, Parisians would visit the site out of fascination with the spectacle of death and to cultivate a fear of the judgment that would follow. To focus their thoughts, a mural was painted on one of the charnel houses depicting what came to be called the "dance of death" (or *danse macabre*). It was an image of people—including rich and poor, kings and peasants, young and old—being led inexorably toward the grave by a skeletal specter known simply as Death. This image—by no means an icon in the traditional sense—was soon reproduced throughout the West.

In the village of Hrastovlje, Slovenia, such an image appeared on the interior south wall of a fifteenth-century church dedicated to the Holy Trinity. From the front of the temple to the rear, the image depicted a procession of Christians being led to their deaths by skeletal figures marching westward away from the altar. The effect is one of intense and literal disorientation; it presents a striking contrast with Christendom's traditional iconography and eastward orientation. An interesting point of contrast, located only two hundred miles away on the opposite side of the Adriatic, is the sixth-century church of Sant'Apollinare Nuovo in Ravenna. There a mosaic along the south wall also depicts a procession of men, but in this case they are oriented, that is, they face eastward toward the paradisiacal symbol of the altar. In the case of Hrastovlje, the dance of death had come to direct the penitents' attention—even liturgically—toward a ghastly and terrifying judgment. Along with the plague cross, this image was a monument to the disintegrating culture of paradise.

The cult of morbidity was not the product of a spiritual revival. Traditional Christian piety, as we have seen, had always been focused on the Resurrection. As Johan Huizinga observed,

> *a thought which so strongly attaches to the earthly side of death can hardly be called truly pious. It would rather seem a kind of spasmodic reaction against an excessive sensuality. In exhibiting the horrors awaiting all human beauty . . . these preachers of contempt for the world express, indeed, a very materialistic sentiment, namely, that all beauty and all happiness are worthless because they are bound to end soon. Renunciation founded on disgust does not spring from Christian wisdom.*[21]

The Eleventh Hour

NEVERTHELESS, A SPIRITUAL REVIVAL WAS soon to arise in the West on the eve of the Protestant Reformation. Its character, significantly, was actually one of counter-reformation. That is to say, the revival took as its starting point the institutions and practices introduced by the Papal Reformation and sought to reform them. It was in this sense a reaction to the new Christendom.

The revival took a variety of forms, one of them being heresy. The overbearing effects of papal supremacy, with its clericalism and sacerdotal authoritarianism, provoked numerous reactions that went well beyond the boundaries of traditional Christianity. We have already considered the case of the Albigensians. They were closely related to another sect in France and Italy called the Waldensians. The inquisition failed to exterminate this movement the way it did the Albigensians. It did, however, nip various other heretical groups in the bud. One was called the Free Spirits. Their beliefs consisted of largely anticlerical and mystical ideas that the

---

21   J. Huizinga, *The Waning of the Middle Ages* (New York: Doubleday, 1954), 141.

inquisitors deemed dangerous to the new church order.

Significantly, many holding such views were women who chose to live in quasi-monastic seclusion in towns. These "beguines," as they came to be known (the word may be related to *Albigenisan*), did not adhere to any of the officially prescribed religious orders. But they proved to be fervent reformers. Marie of Oignies (d. 1213), for instance, exuded such piety that a future cardinal, Jacques of Vitry, became her lifelong spiritual disciple. (Awkwardly, he also served as her father confessor.) Marie was an extreme advocate of the new piety pioneered by Bernard of Clairvaux. Her devotional rule was centered on imagining the Passion of Christ and participating emotionally in His sufferings. But she was also known to enact those sufferings physically. She not only fasted and wore a tight rope around her waist, she practiced self-flagellation and other acts of self-harm. According to the life written by Jacques of Vitry, on one occasion she even cut off a piece of her flesh in imitation of Christ's wounds and then buried it in the earth. Whether the mutilation was intended to form the stigmata that Francis of Assisi had recently been the first to receive is not clear. However, other mystics of the time did manifest stigmata, and the vast majority of them were women.

The clerical establishment was never comfortable with the beguines and suspected them of harboring the errors of the Free Spirits. In 1310 one of their members, Marguerite Porete, was actually burned at the stake as a heretic. In 1312 the Council of Vienne banned them outright. Interestingly, one of the heresies they were said to hold was that the human being, joined mystically with Christ, can attain even in this life an experience of paradise like that the saints enjoy in eternity. Since the days of Makarios of Egypt, this is what Eastern theologians had also been claiming. However, the anthropological pessimism that had come to pervade Western piety after the Great Division had made such a claim appear heretical. Such pessimism had also led to its association with acts of self-harm. In the end, after the Council of Vienne, many of the beguines were compelled to enter established monastic orders. Others continued to pursue a life of mysticism within lay society, but in greater obscurity than before.

Not all efforts at counter-reform were heretical, however. A less disruptive response to the disintegration of Western Christendom was a movement known as the "modern devotion" (*devotio moderna*). As with the "modern art" of Giotto and the "modern way" of Occam, its leaders were profoundly conscious that they belonged to a new age. Geert Groote (d. 1384), their founder, was, like the beguines, profoundly unhappy with the state of the new Christendom. After studying theology and canon law at Paris he abandoned the life of a scholastic. He then entered a Carthusian monastery, but after several years abandoned it as well. He resolved to preach instead, bringing his vision of mystical piety to the laity of Holland and Germany. His sermons' anticlerical themes aroused the suspicion of the inquisition but ultimately led to no more than a revocation of his license to preach. This mattered little, however, for he died the following year after passing his prophetic mantle to devoted followers. They now organized networks of laymen and laywomen to institutionalize the movement. Assuming the names of the Brethren and Sisters of the Common Life, they were little different from professed monks. Like monastics, they held property in common, and they practiced strict fasting, liturgical prayer, and celibacy. However, they never took vows and so evaded what they considered to be the oppressive atmosphere of contemporary monasticism.

The modern devotion is most famous for *The Imitation of Christ*, a work written by a member of the Brethren named Thomas à Kempis (d. 1471). In the tradition of Groote, it is an intensely individual meditation on the Christian life. While the work conforms to the same mold created by Bernard three hundred years earlier, it also caused cracks in it. For the *Imitation* no longer recognizes the legitimacy of a division between the clergy and the laity. Written in the vernacular, it appealed to the latter as much as the former. The bifurcation of Christian society was itself now subject to reform for the better.

Nevertheless, the *Imitation* bears much in common with the piety of the new Christendom. It is thoroughly Augustinian in its grim view of the human condition and the world. "Living on earth is a misery," Thomas declares. "The more a man desires spiritual life, the more bitter the present becomes to him, because he understands better and sees more clearly the defects, the corruption of human nature."²² Such cosmological contempt, advanced by Augustinianism and articulated by a long line of writers since the time of Pope Innocent III, prevents the author from experiencing the kingdom of heaven in its immediacy. Thomas even contributed to the new cult of morbidity. "How happy and prudent," he writes, "is he who tries now in life to be what he wants to be found in death. Perfect contempt of the world, a lively desire to advance in every virtue, a love for discipline, the works of penance, readiness to obey, self-denial, and the endurance of every hardship for the love of Christ, these will give a man great expectations of a happy death."²³

But while the *Imitation* dismisses the potential of experiencing paradise in this world, it places great value on eucharistic communion. Its deep piety, which attracted one of the largest readerships of the time, is directed toward an experience that Groote and other contemporaries clearly believed was in decline. And so it is no surprise that Thomas concludes the book with an extended reflection on the Eucharist. Like others seeking spiritual revival, he brought attention to the fact that in his day the laity continued, as it had for centuries, to avoid communion. "It is lamentable," he remarks, "that many pay so little heed to the salutary Mystery which fills the heavens with joy and maintains the whole universe in being."²⁴

Thomas concludes the *Imitation* by calling his contemporaries back to an appreciation of Christendom's greatest treasure. Offering his own words as the voice of his generation, he declares penitently to Christ:

> When I think how some devout persons come to Your Sacrament with the greatest devotion and love, I am frequently ashamed and confused that I approach Your altar and the table of Holy Communion so coldly and indifferently; that I remain so dry and devoid of heartfelt affection; that I am not completely inflamed in Your presence, O my God.²⁵

---

22 Thomas à Kempis, *The Imitation of Christ*, translated by Aloysius Croft and Harold Bolton (Mineola, NY: Dover Publications, 2003), 20.
23 Ibid., 22.
24 Ibid., 118.
25 Ibid., 134–135.

Thomas's sense of awe at the Eucharist was consistent with the earliest piety of the West. His lamentation at the indifference of so many toward participation in it was a prophetic sign that the West's paradisiacal culture was disintegrating.

In the contemporary East, lay participation in the Eucharist was equally rare. But there was no reformation to lament this deficiency, no vigorous pattern of reform and counter-reform as there now was in the West. With only one exception, Orthodox Christendom had never been inclined toward reform movements. The exception was the iconoclastic reformation of the eighth century, and that had proved to everyone how dangerous such movements can be. By the end of the fourteenth century, Byzantium was on the brink of collapse. Yet the culture of paradise was as strong as ever.

An example of this was the work of Nicholas Cabasilas. He was introduced in the previous chapter as the author of a commentary that placed eucharistic communion at the center of the Divine Liturgy. Even more significant is a book he wrote entitled *The Life in Christ*. Written as the Byzantine state continued to disintegrate, this work provides an interesting contrast to the *Imitation of Christ*. Without lamentation, without despondency about the condition of life in this world, Nicholas expresses sublime confidence in man's spiritual transformation through the sacramental life of the Church.

Nicholas was a hesychast, and the opening sentence of his book expresses the basic conviction of the old Christendom: that the kingdom of heaven is not of this world, but that it has come into the world to provoke a spiritual transformation:

> *The life in Christ originates in this life and arises from it. It is perfected, however, in the life to come, when we shall have reached that last day. It cannot attain perfection in men's souls in this life, nor even in that which is to come without already having begun here.*[26]

---

26 Nicholas Cabasilas, *The Life in Christ*, translated by Carmino J. DeCatanzaro (Crestwood, NY: St. Vladimir's Seminary Press, 1974), 43.

This was the ancient conviction of Eastern Christendom. It was now restated by Nicholas even as the world long shaped by it was swallowed up by Islam.

Nicholas presented a view radically distinct from Augustinianism. Man, he argues, actively participates in salvation. This is due in part to a soteriology that is defined primarily not by original sin, but by the sacraments. Sin is a disease more than a crime in the legal sense. The Christian life is one of therapy rather than justification. "If, then, one speaks of our condition as a disease in need of a cure, Christ did not merely go to the patient and deign to look at him and touch him, but with His own hand wrought what was needed for healing, and even became Himself our medicine and diet and whatever else is conducive to health."[27] It is participation in the life of Christ and not merely the satisfaction of guilt that saves. "Human effort," Nicholas insists, "also has a contribution to make."[28]

The life in Christ is not preoccupied with the Passion, as had become the case in the new Christendom. It looks to the entire range of Christ's divine actions, especially the Incarnation and the Resurrection.

He who seeks to be united with [Christ] must therefore share with Him in His flesh, partake of deification, and share in His death and resurrection. So we are baptized in order that we may die that death and rise again in that resurrection. We are chrismated in order that we may become partakers of the royal anointing of His deification. By feeding on the most sacred bread and drinking the most divine cup we share in the very Flesh and Blood which the Saviour assumed. In this way we are joined to him who for our sake was incarnate and who deified our nature, who died and rose again.[29]

Nicholas expresses a metamorphocentric piety grounded in the sacramental life of the Church. It is this life that sustains the world and transforms it, even now. It replaces the primordial paradise lost to Adam and Eve with the eschatological paradise opened by Christ.

27 Ibid., 141.
28 Ibid., 63.
29 Ibid., 65–66.

The gates of the mysteries [that is, the sacraments] are far more august and beneficial than the gates of Paradise. The latter will not be opened to anyone who has not first entered through the gates of the Mysteries, but these were opened when the gates of Paradise had been closed. The latter were able to let out those within, while the former only lead inside and let no one out. It was possible to shut the gates of Paradise and so they were shut; in the case of the Mysteries the curtain and the dividing wall were entirely destroyed and taken away. It is impossible to raise a barrier anew and for the gates to be closed again and these worlds to be divided from each other by a wall.[30]

Through the sacramental life of Christ, these "worlds"—the cosmos and paradise—will never suffer division.

But division was looming ever more ominously in the West, where theologians worked to counteract the effects of the Papal Reformation. One of the boldest of these was the Oxford scholastic John Wycliffe (d. 1384). His radical views came to be known as Lollardy. In many ways they represented a sort of proto-Protestantism, producing a wish list of later reforms. These included the elimination of clericalism; the preeminence of scripture over papal decretals and canon law; the rendering of the Scriptures and liturgy in the vernacular; the repudiation of the doctrine of transubstantiation; the abolition of mendicant orders; the demonasticization of normative spiritual life; and, of course, an end to papal supremacy. Needless to say, such views were ahead of their time. Or, put differently, they were a return to an earlier time before the millennium. And so they came to nothing.

But Lollardy did inspire other reformers. The most influential was a Prague theologian named Jan Hus (d. 1415). With the Papal Schism as a backdrop, his reform of the Czech Church was at first quite formidable. He assumed most of Wycliffe's criticisms of Roman Catholicism, with the exception of transubstantiation (which he endorsed). But on certain points he went further. He declared, in agreement with the early Greek fathers, that the apostles shared equally in their ministries and that Peter was not preeminent over them. Scripture revealed that "not one of the apostles ever

---

30 Ibid., 56–57.

presumed to claim that he was the head or the bridegroom of the Church."[31] It therefore goes without saying that like the Orthodox of his day, he denied to the papacy primacy over the universal Church, insisting that only Christ Himself could be assigned such status. In short, many of Hus's views were simply those of the ancient Church, which continued in the contemporary East to practice conciliarity and reject the innovation of papal supremacy.

Hus also attacked the papacy's practice of issuing indulgences. As we have seen, this was something new to Western Christendom. After the Great Division, a juridical understanding of penance had come to prevail, and popes had used their "plenitude of power" to issue, from time to time, releases from such penances in the form of plenary indulgences. Their argument for doing so was that the pope, as the Vicar of Christ, has access to merits amassed by Christ and His saints. He therefore possesses unique and exclusive power to distribute those merits when occasion arises. The crusades, with their initial goal of recovering the Holy Sepulcher, were the earliest such occasion. The jubilee of 1300, which brought pilgrims to the relics of Saint Peter, had been another. By the fifteenth century, however, so many other opportunities had begun to present themselves that the practice of granting indulgences entered, as Richard Southern aptly put it, an "inflationary spiral." For "once the bottomless treasure had been opened up there could be no restraining its distribution."[32]

In 1411 one of the three rival popes, John XXIII, issued an indulgence to all who made financial contributions to a crusade against one of his rivals. When papal legates arrived in Prague to enlist subscribers, Hus rallied his supporters to oppose them. Citing the scriptures alone, he claimed that the very institution of plenary indulgences is wrong and that true penance depends exclusively on heartfelt repentance. What is more, he attacked the papacy for organizing bloodshed, even when it considered war necessary, by citing the Sermon on the Mount's call to love one's enemies and turn the other cheek. In one of his most audacious acts, Hus composed a list of six

---

31   Daniel DiDomizio, "Jan Hus's De Ecclesia, Precursor of Vatican II?," *Theological Studies* 60 (1999), 247–260.

32   Southern, *Western Society and the Church*, 139.

The execution of Jan Hus

errors that demanded reform and publicly fixed it to the wall of the church where he regularly preached in Prague. Like the objections nailed to the church door of Wittenberg a century later, they were all ultimately directed toward the sale of indulgences.[33]

In 1415, Hus was burned at the stake as a heretic. The occasion for his condemnation was the same Council of Constance that asserted conciliarity against the papacy and brought the Papal Schism to an end. This was ironic, for Hus had been called to the council by the future emperor Sigismund with a pledge of safe conduct. More ironic still was the fact that Gerson and the other conciliarists in attendance urged the decision to execute him. His stand against papal supremacy would seem to have made him their ally. In fact, they were truly appalled by his other reform demands. Most importantly, they were eager to demonstrate a zero-tolerance policy toward heresy in order to rob their papal adversaries of the doctrinal high ground. Religious violence, it turned out, begat religious violence.

The consequences of Hus's execution were not limited to the moral subversion of Western conciliarity. When Czech reformers learned of it, Bohemia exploded in rebellion. Led by a brilliant commander named Jan Zizka (d. 1424), himself a follower of Hus, their forces quickly gained control of the

---

33 The six errors were not obviously related, though several deal with the problems of clericalism. Nevertheless, as a recent historian has noted, they "are linked and are a polemical response to the positions taken by his adversaries in the controversy over indulgences." C. Colt Anderson, "The Six Errors: Hus on Simony," in *Reassessing Reform: A Historical Investigation into Church Renewal*, edited by Christopher M. Bellitto and David Zachariah Flanagin (Washington, D.C.: Catholic University of America Press, 2012), 105–123.

region. The Czechs fought with the conviction that the Hussite reformation was the only way Christendom could be saved from disintegration. Some even turned to apocalypticism, establishing an armed commune in a mountaintop town called Tabor. The papacy, now restored to a single occupant by the Council of Constance, resolved to crush the reformation by force. Pope Martin V (r. 1417–1431) launched no fewer than four international crusades against the Hussites, and his successor instigated a fifth. None was successful.

The writing was now on the wall. Czech Christendom—having been founded in the ninth century by Byzantine missionaries Cyril and Methodios, but, more recently, subjected to Rome—would not go back to the *status quo ante*. The Hussite Wars were a turning point. With victory on their side and Jan Hus in their memory, reformers negotiated partial autonomy for the Bohemian Church in 1436.

In itself, the agreement was but a tremor in the cultural tectonics of the West, but it warned of an earthquake yet to come.

The Northern Thebaid

IN THE EAST, A LONG way from Bohemia, Russian Christendom was also in ferment. There the changes were not reformatory, however, for Orthodoxy had never been subjected to a papal reformation and therefore had no need to counter it.

Russian spiritual revival was primarily monastic. The Mongol invasions had not only destroyed towns, they had wiped out most of the two hundred or so monasteries that had been established since the time of Feodosy. But the invaders had only been interested in suppressing political independence, not spiritual life. In fact, they were inclined to leave the monasteries alone and even granted them freedom from tribute. This changed somewhat when their khan Uzbek (r. 1313–1341) converted to Islam, but for the most part monks were free to do as they pleased, provided they did not inspire political independence or impede taxation.

By the middle of the fourteenth century, Russians were again building monastic settlements and continued doing so on a large scale well into the fifteenth century. Many of these were located in the deep north beyond the reach of the khans. A pattern arose whereby monks seeking solitude founded hermitages that attracted more monks, who then began to develop the land by clearing forests and planting fields. This in turn attracted lay-people seeking relief from life under the Mongol yoke, and with time villages and even towns began to appear. The cycle of this monastic colonization of the wilderness was completed when monks in the settlement would tire of the burdens of community life and set off to establish new hermitages in the limitless expanse that came to be known, referencing the hermitages of the early desert fathers near Thebes, as "the Northern Thebaid."

The most important example of this process was Holy Trinity Monastery north of Moscow. It was founded by Sergy of Radonezh (d. 1392), whose holy way of life both expressed the revival's values and inspired its further expansion. Sergy was guided by hesychasm, the tradition of prayer of the heart that had been defended by Gregory Palamas and elaborated by Nicholas Cabasilas. The Russian monk never traveled to Byzantium, but he did correspond with Ecumenical Patriarch Philotheos (d. 1379), who was a friend of Gregory and a fellow advocate of hesychasm. There can be no doubt that the way of life at Holy Trinity Monastery was hesychastic. As such it united

Holy Trinity Monastery at Sergiev Posad, near Moscow

the heights of Athonite prayer with the depths of native Russian kenoticism.

Sergy himself is an example of this union. He received a vision of the Uncreated Light more than once. One such occasion occurred in the middle of the night. While gazing out of his window, he beheld the divine presence radiating from the night sky. After another such vision, he was "so filled with ecstasy that his face glowed therewith."[34] This metamorphic sign was, as we have noted, a characteristically Eastern Christian experience, the closest equivalent in the West being the stavrocentric stigmata of a figure like Francis. This sign linked Sergy to a lineage stretching back through Byzantine ascetics to Moses himself. But such exaltation came through humility. According to a Life composed soon after his death, Sergy was said to practice the same gentleness when correcting aberrant monks that we observed in the life of Feodosy. Also kenotic was his reluctance to exercise authority over them. On one occasion, as he stood in the altar before a service, he overheard a conversation in which the brotherhood was grumbling about his leadership. After the service was over, without revealing his knowledge of the remarks, he meekly asked their forgiveness and disappeared through the monastery gate in search of a new place to establish a hermitage. Needless to say, the brothers soon pursued him and ultimately persuaded him to return.

Sergy left behind a community that continued to grow and disseminate hesychasm throughout the Northern Thebaid. It has been calculated that beyond the nine monasteries founded by him directly, another fifty were founded by monks from Holy Trinity Monastery and from these forty more were founded in turn.[35] Some of these monasteries also became centers for the transmission of Christianity to pagans. Stefan of Perm (d. 1396), a friend of Sergy, spent years studying languages so that he might translate the Scriptures and the divine services into the Finno-Ugric tongue of the Zyrians. He also built beautiful temples to attract them to Christianity. His was a decidedly paradisiacal form of missionary work in which the world, with its natural beauty and vernacular languages, came to radiate God's presence.

---

34   Quoted from Epifany's life of St. Sergy contained in *Medieval Russia's Epics*, 287.
35   Sergius Bolshakoff, *Russian Mystics* (Kalamazoo, MI: Cistercian Publications, 1980), 15.

Holy Trinity Monastery had become a kind of Russian Athos, a source for the continued growth of asceticism in Russia. This asceticism flowed to the south into Moscow and its environs. Simonov Monastery was established there under one of Sergy's disciples. Its streams also flowed northward, into the dense and largely uninhabited forests. Among the habitations it fed were some that grew into large-scale centers of asceticism, charity, and art. These include Kirillo-Belozersky Monastery (1397), Ferapontov Monastery (1398), and, on an inhospitable island in the distant reaches of the White Sea, Solovetsky Monastery (1436). These large-scale monasteries started as sketes (monastic settlements of only a handful of monks) but grew as more monks and peasants learned of their existence and settled near them. Boyars began to visit, too, and some endowed the monasteries with rich gifts of money and land.

Because of their size and resources, these monasteries became centers for copying, architecture, and hymnography. Monks copied manuscripts and composed chronicles. Protected by defensive walls, they raised magnificent temples featuring uniquely Russian elements such as the elongated onion dome and the pyramidal tent roof. Celebrating the fullness of the divine services, they developed melodies that carried hymnography beyond Byzantine monophony and into a form of polyphony. But by far the most creative activity of the monasteries was iconography.

This too was the result of contact with and influence from Byzantium. A case in point is Feofan the Greek (d. 1410). Having studied hesychasm in Constantinople as a youth, he traveled to Novgorod to create frescoes in the many churches there. His icon of Saint Makarios of Egypt at the Church of the Savior not only depicts one of the earliest desert fathers to practice the prayer of the heart, but also vividly represents the hesychastic vision of divine participation by showing the saint's hands raised in prayer and his fingertips illumined like fire, as were those of Abba Joseph (whose example of spiritual transformation we discussed briefly in the previous chapter). Feofan also painted icons in the Moscow region, such as a Transfiguration that depicts the brilliance of the Uncreated Light through symbolic imagery. Feofan's contribution to the culture of Christendom also consisted in training a monk of Holy Trinity Monastery who would become arguably the greatest iconographer in history.

Andrey Rublev (d. 1430) brought the hesychastic style of Feofan to its highest level of development. He, more than any other painter, succeeded in depicting with form and color the transfiguration of matter within the sacramental life of the Church. This can be seen in an icon of the Theotokos executed for Dormition Cathedral in Vladimir, in which Mary's body is unnaturally elongated (a mark of Feofan's influence) to represent deification. Her head is subtly bowed toward Christ (who would have appeared in an adjoining icon), and her hands are extended in supplication. Her fingers seem to reach outward toward the God-Man, who is the source of her, and all human, dignity. The faces of all the saints depicted by Andrey consistently show the deified state of the human being. There is no remnant in them of the sinful passions. His icon of Christ Pantocrator is perhaps the most serene image of divinity made human. The Almighty looks piercingly into the face of the believer, stirring repentance through His kenotic love.

Most famous of all is Andrey's representation of the Old Testament Trinity. It was modeled on the "hospitality of Abraham," in which the patriarch unwittingly entertained three angels who represent the Holy Trinity (Gen. 18:1–3). The icon was commissioned for Holy Trinity Monastery and ultimately found a place in the temple where Sergy's incorrupt relics were kept. Here especially, colors are used to express the sanctification of matter. Andrey's three angels, each representing a person of the Godhead, sit around an altar table on which stands a chalice containing the Eucharist, the material body of the eternal Word. Having centered the icon on this representation of heavenly immanence, Andrey expresses the unity of the Trinity by emphasizing the personhood of each member—Father, Son, and Holy Spirit. He does this by setting the gaze of each angel on the face of the others, causing the believer's eyes to move from one to the other until finally the last angel guides his gaze into chalice itself. Visually, then, Andrey's icon of the Holy Trinity proclaims the hesychastic doctrine of sacramental communion, with its assertion that man does not merely behold God, in the Western sense, but actually participates in His divine energies.

The objectively deifying experience of the Incarnation thus proved an inspiration for Russian iconography in the way the subjectively emotional experience of the Crucifixion did in the West. But the Russians did not of course ignore Christ's Passion. Perhaps one of the most striking examples of its depiction was an icon created by another painter of the Northern Thebaid, Dionisy (d. 1502). Though he was most famous for the dazzling frescoes that cover every surface of the interior walls of Ferapontov Monastery, his icon of the Crucifixion belongs to a monastery dedicated to the Holy Trinity near the town of Vologda. In it, Christ is represented in the traditional Byzantine way, full of beauty and dignity even in death. Unlike the Isenheim Altarpiece, this icon shows His body as beautifully curved and elongated. Unlike the Kaufmann Crucifixion, it depicts no trace of bloodletting. The icon was a proclamation, as traditional iconography had always been, of the Incarnation and the Resurrection. Because the man hanging dead on the cross was also God, His body would rise from the dead.

By the end of the fifteenth century, Russian monasticism had been renewed after the ravages of the Mongol invasion. As scores of monasteries were founded, many coalesced into major centers of cultural, economic, and social life. Kirillo-Belozersky Monastery, for instance, fed more than five hundred people a day during famines as part of its charity work. But asceticism and prayer could prove difficult within monasteries of such scale. Hesychasm, with its goal of mystical "stillness" (*hesychia*), had always favored the lonely hermitage over the richly endowed and crowded cenobium.

In fact, it was a monk from Kirillo-Belozersky named Nil Sorsky (d. 1508) who offered an alternative to such "super-monasticism." Disappointed by his monastery's burgeoning endowments of land, he departed for Mount Athos to live as a hermit. There he studied Athonite asceticism under the supervision of a hesychastic elder. Upon his return to Russia, Nil established a skete on the banks of the remote Sora River (for which he is named). There he spent the rest of his life in the company of only a handful of fellow monks, making up to three thousand prostrations a day and praying without ceasing.

Nil also made time to translate the works of the Greek fathers and to compose a handful of works himself. The most significant was a Rule he composed for his brotherhood (actually more of an ascetic treatise than a conventional list of monastic regulations). Intentionally unoriginal, it is made up largely of quotes from the Scriptures and the fathers. Especially in evidence are hesychastic writers of the East such as Symeon the New Theologian and Gregory of Sinai. But occasionally Western saints like Pope Gregory of Rome are also quoted. This lack of originality was Nil's stated goal. "I have written a teaching," he states in the opening,

> for the profit both of my soul and the souls of my lords, who are truly related to me in the brotherhood of one spirit. I therefore call you brothers instead of disciples. We have but one teacher, our Lord Jesus Christ, Who gave us the Scriptures and sent the holy apostles and the venerable fathers to teach the way of salvation to the human race. These saints began by doing good, only afterwards did they teach. As for me, I have done nothing good whatsoever, but I expound the teaching of the Holy Scriptures for those who desire salvation.[36]

With this kenotic statement, Nil launched Russian Christendom's first ascetic treatise.

The work echoes many others that had been written over the centuries, both in the East and the West. But its attention to the principle of mental stillness, drawn from the hesychasts, makes for a striking contrast with Heinrich Suso's *Little Book of Eternal Wisdom*. The latter, as we have seen, was an effort to revive mystical prayer in the face of scholasticism. It advocated a highly emotional meditation on Christ's Passion. Drawing on the legacy of Bernard of Clairvaux, Suso's path to divine union involved mental exertion to imagine the suffering of Christ and the Virgin Mary. Nil, drawing on the asceticism of the old Christendom, advocated a very different approach. For him, the silencing of the imagination and its emotions was the path that leads to union. The monk, he writes, should aim at "keeping his heart silent and aloof from any thought whatever, even if it be a good one." Only the

---

36   Nilus Sorsky, *The Monastic Rule*, in *A Treasury of Russian Spirituality*, edited by
      G.P. Fedotov (London: Sheed and Ward, 1950), 90.

Jesus Prayer ("Lord Jesus Christ, Son of God, have mercy on me a sinner") avails to acquire this stillness or hesychia. Otherwise, Nil warned, our experience of divine communion becomes something of our own making and not the action of the transcendent God working deification in us.[37]

Stillness is thus transformative and is the only true path toward the ecstasy of union with God. "The fathers call such a condition prayer," he states,

> because this great gift has its wellspring in prayer and is bestowed on the saints during prayer, but no man knows the real name for it. For when, by this spiritual operation, the soul is drawn to what is divine, and through this ineffable union becomes like God, being illumined in its movements by the light from on high, and when the mind is thus allowed a foretaste of beatitude, then it forgets itself and all earthly things and is affected by nothing. . . . When a man is conscious of this sweetness flooding his entire being, he thinks that this indeed is the kingdom of heaven and can be nothing else.[38]

Needless to say, it was for this experience of paradise that Nil maintained his distance from the large monasteries of his day, leaving the seclusion of his cell only on Sundays for fellowship with the brotherhood at the Divine Liturgy.

At the beginning of the sixteenth century, then, Russia had become a very different place than she had been under the Mongol yoke. The monastic transformation of the north was one of the reasons for this.

Political reunification was another. But as the princes of Moscow reassembled the Russian state, questions were raised about the validity of hesychasm. Its call to poverty and its mystical detachment from society appeared counterproductive to the formation of a powerful centralized state. Furthermore, the affiliation of hesychasm with the international culture of Athos seemed dangerously unpatriotic.

Not that this latter point mattered much. For by now Byzantium had ceased to exist.

---

37 Ibid., 100.
38 Ibid., 104.

"Better a Fez than the Tiara"

FROM THE DAYS OF SULTAN Alp Arslan, the Turkish march through East-ern Christendom had never come to a halt. Nearly four centuries had now elapsed since the fateful Battle of Manzikert. The crusades, with their relent-less but futile campaigns against the Arabs, had only made jihad a more compelling doctrine for the new bearers of Islam. And when Constantinople was itself finally freed of the Latin yoke, there was very little an impover-ished and diminished Byzantium could do to stay the final onslaught.

The Turks by this time were ruled by the Ottoman dynasty, which orig-inated with an obscure figure from northern Anatolia named Osman (d. 1324). He was a ghazi, a Muslim raider who used the doctrine of jihad to inspire followers to participate in the conquest of Christendom and to enrich themselves in the process. His son and successor continued the strug-gle by carrying Turkish power across the Dardanelles and capturing Galli-poli in 1354. With this campaign, the Turks finally established a foothold in Europe.

During the century that followed, they continued their conquest with ruthless purpose. In 1362 Adrianople was conquered and became the capital of an emerging Ottoman Empire. The Turks advanced in an arc around Con-stantinople to eliminate the Balkan kingdoms and other potential allies of Byzantium. In 1389 they annihilated the Serbian army and its leader, Prince Lazar, at the Battle of Kosovo Field. The state of Serbia, which had long fought to defend its independence from neighboring Byzantium, ceased to exist. Thoroughly alarmed by these developments, King Sigismund of Hun-gary raised a crusade that, with the help of the Bulgarians, met the Turks at the town of Nicopolis in 1396. This was the same Sigismund who would later become Holy Roman Emperor and issue a worthless writ of safe conduct to Jan Hus. In this case, he kept his word and a fierce battle ensued. But the Turks were again victorious, and now the Bulgarian state ceased to be.

In an effort to form a dependent and loyal political class, and to demor-alize the Christian population, the Turks introduced an infamous slave tax called the *devshirme*. According to this ordinance, squads of Turkish scouts were sent through the countryside to abduct Christian boys of about ten years of age. Literally torn in many cases from the arms of horrified parents, the boys were taken off to the sultan's court at Adrianople. There they were forced to convert to Islam. Over the course of years, trained to retain little memory of their native families, land, or faith, they became the empire's fiercest warriors, known as janissaries.

The first half of the fifteenth century saw a lull in Turkish conquests. One reason for this was that the armies of Tamerlane (d. 1405) attacked the Turks in Anatolia, causing the redirection of military resources to the east. During the decades that followed, Byzantine hopes for rescuing Constantinople from the inevitable attached themselves to a council sponsored by the papacy and being held in the West. As we saw above, Pope Eugene IV was deposed by conciliarists at the Council of Basel in 1439. In response he convened a countercouncil to defend papal supremacy. Opening initially in the town of Ferrara, the council was soon moved to Florence. Eugene saw an opportunity of delegitimizing the conciliarist movement by arranging a new reunion treaty with the Orthodox Church.

However, the eleventh hour had already sounded in Byzantium. Greek advocates for a reunion council that would ensure military assistance were not difficult to find. But many of those who greeted Eugene's offer were motivated by more than the fear of Turkish conquest. In recent decades, two more or less distinct theological parties had appeared in Byzantium, and both sought reunion of a sort. Each had its own interests. One party represented the dominant influence of hesychasm in the East and the other a more recent interest in scholasticism.

Both can be traced to the astonishing intellectual creativity of the empire's final decades, largely born from the broad-minded patronage of the former emperor John Kantakouzenos (r. 1347–1354). In 1351 he had presided at the Council of Constantinople, which definitively confirmed hesychasm. Then, after abdicating the throne, he spent nearly three decades in monastic retirement, acting as a patron of theology and intellectual life. Kantakouzenos was a friend and supporter of the lay hesychast Nicholas Cabasilas, whose *Life in Christ* we discussed above. But he also supported the study of Western scholasticism and encouraged the translation of Thomas Aquinas into Greek.

Above all, Kantakouzenos had supported efforts to lay the groundwork for a council that would finally bring the Great Division to an end.

By the time the Council of Florence was announced, both hesychasts and scholastics were eager to contribute to it. The former party, represented by Metropolitan Mark of Ephesus (d. 1444), truly believed deviations by Roman Catholics since the Great Division would finally be refuted and Orthodoxy restored throughout Christendom. The scholastic party, however, looked to the council as an opportunity to advance the cause of Western theology within the Orthodox Church. Their numbers included Metropolitan Bessarion of Nicaea (d. 1472) and Metropolitan Isidore of Kiev. This party also included lay intellectuals George Scholarios, a Thomist at heart, and George Plethon, whose Christian faith was actually giving way to neopaganism.

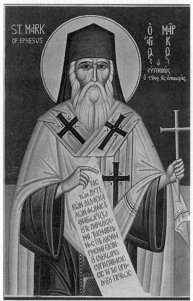

Metropolitan Mark of Ephesus

Emperor John VIII (r. 1425–1448) personally led this theologically mixed delegation to Italy. In Florence, the Orthodox were given a real opportunity to speak, in contrast to the largely passive role played by their predecessors at Lyons in 1274. But their arguments had no measurable impact on the Roman Catholic delegation. Mark's ability to get to the point of why the Orthodox could never accept Western innovations served to electrify debate but not resolve it, much to the annoyance of both pope and emperor. For his part, Bessarion was a paragon of flexibility and in any case was already accustomed to the logical and juridical categories of Latin reasoning. After months of discussion, a treaty of union was finally produced that satisfied almost everyone. And so *almost everyone* signed it.

The document proclaimed the same Roman Catholic positions that had come into existence since the time of Cardinal Humbert. First, papal supremacy was asserted, and the pope, as successor to Saint Peter and Vicar of Christ, was assigned universal rule over the entire Christian Church.[39] Second, purgatory was established dogmatically as the way in which souls undergo necessary postmortem punishment and suffering prior to experiencing the joy of paradise. And third, the filioque was confirmed. For good measure, the assertion was even made that early Greek fathers had envisioned this clause when they spoke of the Spirit proceeding "through the Son." Centuries of theological objections to the innovation since the time of Patriarch Photios were passed over in silence.

The only accommodation to Orthodoxy the council made was in that bedeviling question that had consumed Greeks and Latins in 1054. The eucharistic bread, the treaty conceded, could be offered in either unleavened or leavened form.

The treaty of union was a complete and unequivocal victory for the Roman Catholic Church. It was not a victory for the counter-reformation that had roiled her for nearly half a century. The conciliarists in Basel realized that by obtaining the submission of Constantinople, Pope Eugene had captured the holy grail of ecclesiastical politics. He had outwitted them. Though the conciliarists declared Eugene deposed and elected a contender (briefly renewing the Papal Schism), their international support soon collapsed, and they were forced to surrender. The restoration of papal ecclesiology, therefore, was the ultimate and only lasting achievement of Florence. The tragedy of Western conciliarism, which had stumbled along for decades in blind ignorance of Orthodoxy, was now complete. Its obituary only awaited the Protestant reformers.

The papal bull that declared the end of the schism was entitled *Let the Heavens Rejoice* (*Laetentur Caeli*). But, as Norwich notes, "the heavens, it soon

---

39   In defense of this the *Donation of Constantine* was invoked yet again, though, as it turned out, for the last time. Only a year later it was definitively exposed by Lorenzo Valla as the fraud that it was. It was fitting. Having entered use in 1054 as Exhibit A in Humbert's legal case against conciliar ecclesiology, now, four centuries later, its pernicious and divisive influence was consummated when Bessarion ceded the argument for papal supremacy.

became clear, had precious little reason to do so."⁴⁰ It is true that almost everyone in the Orthodox delegation had signed his name to the document. But one had not. Metropolitan Mark of Ephesus, the leading representative of hesychasm, declared that the agreement deviated from the faith that had, to quote the Synodikon of Orthodoxy, "established the universe." And so he refused to sign. He departed Florence and returned to an East that was threatened with destruction. But he remained Orthodox. Pope Eugene, on seeing Mark's resolve, reportedly responded with the cry, "So we have accomplished nothing!"

Indeed, the reaction to the treaty in Constantinople was nearly revolutionary. When the emperor and his loyal supporters returned, they were greeted with widespread outrage. Public disturbances broke out, and some of the signatories were attacked in the streets. In Kiev, Isidore was thrown in prison. Bessarion, disgusted with his countrymen and now a dedicated scholastic, renounced Orthodoxy and emigrated to the West (where he became a cardinal). George Scholarios, on the other hand, repented of his support and joined Mark in calling for the repudiation of the union treaty.

None of this prevented Pope Eugene from ordering the crusade he had promised in exchange for reunion. But like other Western efforts, it came to nothing. At the Battle of Varna in 1444, an army of Roman Catholic Hungarians and Poles was wiped out by the Turks. Powerless and undefended, ruled by an apostate emperor, Constantinople now awaited her end.

It soon came. Sultan Mehmet II, the namesake of Islam's founder, had been raised with only one purpose: the final annihilation of Byzantium. He identified with his ghazi ancestors and was strongly influenced by the jihadist vision of his tutor Akshamsaddin, who claimed to discover in the vicinity of Constantinople the tomb of an original companion to Muhammad who had perished during the first Muslim siege of the city in the seventh century. One of the sayings of Muhammad, the youthful sultan was told, was that the army that conquers the capital of Christendom will surely enter paradise. All of this inflamed Mehmet's military imagination. In 1453, he assembled

40   John Julius Norwich, *Byzantium: Decline and Fall* (New York: Alfred A. Knopf, 1996), 402.

his warriors in Adrianople. For centuries, he reminded them, Islam had been fighting for the city without success. Now it was time for one final, relentless assault on its walls.

The people of Constantinople knew what was coming. At the end of the previous year, the desperation of the last emperor, Constantine XI (r. 1449–1453), had been revealed when he had the papal bull of reunion proclaimed from the ambo of Hagia Sophia. The bishop who proclaimed it was Isidore of Kiev, who, having escaped prison in Moscow and been made a cardinal in Rome, was sent by the pope to make one final push for papal supremacy. Very few of the fifty thousand or so Orthodox who made up the population of Constantinople responded. Their religious convictions were too strong and the memory of an earlier conquest at the hands of Roman Catholics too grim to welcome reunion. As one remarked, it would be better to live under the fez of the Turk than the papal tiara of Rome.

The siege began on April 6. The Turkish force was staggering. Mehmet commanded at least a hundred thousand men, though more than twice that figure was reported by the terrified Greeks. The army was coordinated with a huge navy consisting of hundreds of vessels that formed an impassible barrier across the entire Bosphorus. Finally, Mehmet commissioned a Hungarian cannon founder named Orban to forge a siege weapon unlike any previously known. The result was a monster of iron whose maw measured more than two feet in diameter. It was so heavy it required sixty oxen to haul it to the base of the city's famous Theodosian Walls.

When the cannon let loose, little in its range remained standing. At first, the Byzantines were able to repair the walls almost as quickly as they were knocked down. But eventually they could not keep pace with the weapon's destruction. In the early morning of May 29, Mehmet ordered all his remaining soldiers to charge.

It was still dark when this murderous wave crashed against the city's walls. The Byzantines did their best, but within a few hours, as additional surges of Turks attacked, they could no longer resist. As the enemy began to pour through the wall, Emperor Constantine—the namesake of the city's founder—courageously threw himself into the breach and was never seen

The fall of Constantinople

again. His body was never recovered. The city fell.

Mehmet's soldiers were now given leave to do as they pleased with Constantinople's people and wealth. Churches were desecrated and houses were robbed. Some thirty thousand Christians, the remainder of the population after the casualties of the siege, were either murdered or sold into slavery. In either case, most of the women were first raped. Mehmet himself ordered the seizure of the most beautiful girls and handsome boys to be sent back as sex slaves to his generals in Anatolia.

With the queen of Christian cities now lying at his feet, the twenty-one-year-old successor to and namesake of Muhammad made his way directly to the one building he most wanted to visit. By the time he arrived, Hagia Sophia had become a charnel house for the clergy and laity who had steadfastly continued serving Matins throughout the disaster. Some were beheaded, others were impaled. Before entering, Mehmet gathered some dust from the ground on the square to pour over his head in a quaint and incongruous ritual of humility. Perhaps he stood on the same spot where Cardinal Humbert had paused on his way out of the cathedral in 1054, and the dust was the same that he had shaken from his feet. In any case, the sultan then marched into what had once been the greatest Christian temple on earth to declare that it would henceforth be a mosque. An ulama ascended the ambo to proclaim the fundamental beliefs of Islam, and the order was given to knock down the cross that had stood victoriously above the exterior of the central dome.

That cross was eventually replaced by a crescent moon. One legend states that before the sun rose on that fateful day, when the cry went out that the city had fallen, Mehmet had taken notice of the faint sliver of moon shining in the dark sky above. Whether this is true or not, the moonlike crescent came to be used by the Ottoman Empire in the centuries ahead, and it was gradually adopted as the standard symbol of Islam.

CHAPTER SIX

The Fall of Paradise

A S HE REACHED THE TOP of the famous Holy Stairs (*Scala sancti*)—the very ones Christ had ascended before being flayed and condemned by Pontius Pilate—a German monk named Martin Luther suddenly had a doubt. "What if," he exclaimed aloud among the throng of pilgrims that surrounded him, "it is not true?"

The question he asked was not whether Jesus had really trod the same marble stairs, by then located in the Lateran Palace, though by the beginning of the sixteenth century skepticism of such relics was common. Luther's doubt was whether his act of laboring up them on his knees had accomplished anything.

For in 1510 he had come on a pilgrimage to Rome, not only for his own salvation but for that of his family.[1] He could do little for his parents, for they were still alive and mostly responsible for their own salvation. But his grandfather was another matter. He had died years earlier, and Luther assumed he was languishing in a place of misery. To comfort his suffering relative, the young monk had obtained an indulgence from the pope that required him to crawl up the venerable staircase saying the Our Father on

---

1   Strictly speaking, Luther was visiting the city on monastic business. But he treated the journey as a pilgrimage, visiting as many of its holy places as possible.

Martin Luther

each of its twenty-eight steps, kissing them as he advanced. These were the terms of his grandfather's release from torment, and Luther had readily submitted to them. But by the time he reached the landing, the entire ritual suddenly seemed profoundly hollow.

Luther had been taught—and all fellow Roman Catholics believed—that beyond the grave awaited a far greater pain than the one now raging in his knees. This place of punishment was not hell, though it was rumored to tear the soul no less. It was called purgatory. Many authorities claimed its agonies would last thousands of years—though what exactly a "year" outside the time and space of this world was, not even the most proficient scholastic claimed exactly to know. What was certain was that only the saints were exempt from it. The general consensus—from village priest to university theologian—was that nearly everyone else must enter purgatory upon death and languish there a very, very long time before entering paradise.

Only two paths provided shortcuts around the agonies of purgatory. One was the fulfillment of a lifetime of penances, the accumulated punishment imposed by priests through the sacrament of confession. The other was an indulgence, an automatic remittance of such penances. Like so much in the new Christendom, this path was also managed by the clergy. And entry to it was permitted only through the agency of that highest of all priests on earth, the pope.

Could direct communion with God, which had nourished Christian civilization since Pentecost, depend so entirely on such a heavy-handed system of penance? Could that system really be so punitive and legalistic? Could paradise be divided from this world by millennia of suffering?

Luther looked down at the hobbling pilgrims ascending toward him and had his doubts.

The Curse of Penitential Pessimism

DURING THE FIVE CENTURIES THAT elapsed between Cardinal Humbert's strolls in the Lateran Palace and Martin Luther's pilgrimage to it, Western Christendom had been changed by a new, stavrocentric piety. As we saw in chapter four, this piety looked beyond the traditional view of repentance—that it consisted exclusively of spiritual transformation—and began to see it as the act of satisfying God with acts of suffering. Anselm had presented the salvation of the world in terms of satisfaction—that which the crucified Christ provided before an offended and wrathful God. The Incarnation and Resurrection were thus displaced by the Crucifixion, and Western soteriology came inevitably to focus almost exclusively on the suffering of Christ. Nurtured by the writings of Bernard, inspired by the preaching of the mendicants, stunned by the imagery of Giotto—people began to ponder as never before the awful specter of an impending judgment. As they did, penance became a way not only of turning toward God but of satisfying His anger.

The earliest evidence of this stavrocentric shift is found in the ascetical teaching of Humbert's contemporary and fellow reformer, Peter Damian. He was the first major writer to advance the practice of corporal self-harm known as "the discipline." He believed that repentance was not only—as it was in the East—a "change of heart" that restored the penitent to a life of paradisiacal communion with God. More than this, sin, even if forgiven, must be punished.

"What benefit is derived from ceasing to commit sins," he asked, "if one does not strive to wash away those already committed by the satisfaction of rigorous penance?"[2] In his view, divine punishment for one's sins could only be averted through self-punishment. Such a piety can be summarized with one of his aphorisms: "There is no choice between penance and the kingdom of heaven."[3] Heaven, in other words, could not be attained without punishment. The awesome scale of paradise demanded an awesome means of acquiring it.

---

2   Quoted in Blum, *St. Peter Damian*, 78.
3   Quoted in ibid., 105.

Hence self-flagellation. If Christ suffered the laceration of His body, Peter reasoned, so must any monastic seeking union with Him. Rachel Fulton has noted that in Peter's concept of redemption, "pain was currency." He could thus declare:

> *O what a delightful, what a wonderful sight, when the celestial Judge looks forth from heaven, and man punishes (sacrifices) himself below for his sins! There the accused himself, presiding over the tribunal of his inmost being, holds a three-fold office: in his heart he constitutes himself the judge, in his body the accused, and with his hands he rejoices to hold forth as executioner, as if the holy penitent were saying to God: "There is no need, Lord, for you to order your officer to punish me, nor is it necessary for you to strike me with the fear of your vengeance of a just trial. I have laid hands upon myself, I have taken up my own defense, and I have offered myself in place of my sins."*[4]

Peter and his fellow monks at the Monastery of the Cross at Fonte Avellana were hardly alone in holding such convictions. During the centuries that followed, the discipline became widely used by monks and even laymen. Indeed, groups of flagellants appeared from time to time, especially in periods of anxiety such as the Black Death.

The door to this momentous development had been opened by the new system of tariff penance, by which satisfaction for one's sins had been separated from forgiveness. With the rise of private confession and its clerical institutionalization now in place (something we discussed in chapter four), penances were understood more as punishments than medicines. For scholastics like Duns Scotus, the sacrament of priestly absolution stood on its own and was therefore divided from the penitent's healing contrition.

This created a technical distinction between guilt (*culpa*), which was forgiven by absolution, and punishment (*poena*), which was still necessary, even after the granting of forgiveness. Penance (*poenitentia*) was now the principal way of satisfying this divine requirement. It could take all sorts of

---

4   Fulton, *From Judgment to Passion*, 103.

forms—prayer, alms, pilgrimages, and even (as we have seen) holy warfare during a crusade. But if it was not completed, the debt of punishment would have to be satisfied after death.

Thus was born the Roman Catholic doctrine of purgatory, which identified a place to which most saved Christians must go immediately after death to be purged through punishment until they are made worthy of entering paradise.

It is highly significant that this doctrine had never appeared during the first millennium. It only took dogmatic form in the wake of the Great Division. Prior to that time, a handful of church fathers had spoken of a process of purification that would occur between death and the Last Judgment. The most significant among them was Augustine, who wrote of "purgatorial punishments" that would be needed to cleanse some people of minor sins.[5] This greatest of Latin fathers also emphasized that the pain of such punishments would far exceed anything experienced in this world. But only after the system of tariff penance had introduced the need for penitential satisfaction following absolution was a place called "purgatory" named and elaborated by scholastic authorities.

The first to do so, according to historian Jacques Le Goff, was a theologian in Paris named Peter the Chanter (d. 1197).[6] The doctrine ignited swiftly within the heated atmosphere of early scholasticism, and in less than a century it was proclaimed a dogma of the Roman Catholic Church. Aquinas helped define it. According to him, postmortem satisfaction of sin

is made by punishments, just as in this life their purgation would have been completed by punishments which satisfy the debt; otherwise, the negligent would be better off than the solicitous, if the punishment which they do not

---

5   The very earliest authority cited by later advocates of purgatory was Paul, who in a single verse had spoken obliquely of some being saved "by fire" (1 Cor. 3:15).

6   The author makes a strong distinction here between the innovative noun *purgatorium*, denoting a specific place, and earlier uses of the adjective "purgatorial" such as those by Augustine. Jacques Le Goff, *The Birth of Purgatory*, translated by Arthur Goldhammer (Chicago: University of Chicago, 1984), 165.

complete for their sins here need not be undergone in the future. Therefore, if the souls of the good have something capable of purgation in this world, they are held back from the achievement of their reward while they undergo cleansing punishments. And this is the reason we hold that there is a purgatory.[7]

In other words, divine justice demands a legalistic reckoning for each and every sin, and it would be an offense to such justice to allow "negligent" sinners into paradise on the same terms as the saintly or otherwise "solicitous."

It is interesting that Aquinas died on his way to the Second Council of Lyons, to which he had been called by the pope to make the case against the Orthodox on doctrines such as purgatory.

Byzantine bishops had also been invited to attend this council. They had been all but compelled to do so by their emperor, Michael Paleologos, who had only recently wrested Constantinople back from the Latins. Michael's motivation for reunion was purely political. He wanted an assurance that the crusaders would not return, as well as military support against the ever-menacing Turks. In exchange, Pope Gregory X (r. 1271–1276) demanded the usual submission to Rome and the adoption of the filioque. But on this occasion he introduced a new standard of unity—or rather of division—with the doctrine of purgatory. In the end, the imperial will prevailed and the complaisant bishops signed the treaty of union and returned home, where, to no one's surprise, their capitulation was soon repudiated by Orthodox clergy and laity alike. When the same caesaropapist reunion scenario played itself out two centuries later in Florence, however, Mark of Ephesus, as we saw in the previous chapter, actually refused to sign. And he did so in part because to him, as a hesychast, the punitive logic of purgatory contradicted traditional Christianity's principles of divine participation and heavenly immanence. To the Orthodox, purgatory and paradise were incompatible.

In the meantime, however, the new doctrine had reconfigured the culture of the West. Within a century of the Great Division, literature from Italy to

---

7   Quoted in Jerry L. Walls, *Purgatory: The Logic of Total Transformation* (Oxford: Oxford University Press, 2012), 62.

Ireland was describing a place of postmortem punishment in rich and harrowing detail. Some accounts located it within the very bowels of the earth. One even claimed it was accessible to the living through a cave located on a lake island in a remote part of northern Ireland. The work was entitled *Saint Patrick's Purgatory*, and it became one of the most widely disseminated accounts of the doctrine. It told of a penitent named Owain who traveled on pilgrimage to the site voluntarily to endure three nights of penance in the darkest hole on earth. There he was subjected to agonies on the scale of those experienced only by the damned in hell. Augustine had warned that purgatorial punishment was more excruciating than anything imaginable on earth, and Owain got his fill. He survived the ordeal, barely, and returned to his home to advocate to friends and family similar acts of penance.

A more encouraging, and by far the most famous, expression of the doctrine was rendered by Dante (d. 1321). His *Divine Comedy* appropriated the new conception of a tripartite afterlife consisting of hell, purgatory, and paradise to produce one of the most exquisite reflections on salvation ever. For him purgatory was definitely a place, located on an island in the southern hemisphere and accessed, somewhat like Saint Patrick's purgatory, by traveling into the center of the earth. In this case the subterranean journey led through hell (recorded in the poem's first volume) and then out of the earth to Mount Purgatory, which had to be ascended to reach paradise (the subject of volume three).

Throughout this second volume of the work, the poet described the excruciating torments of purgatory that lead the elect upward to paradise. What he conveyed, however, is the ancient conviction that penance is therapeutic in character. Those suffering on the ledges of Mount Purgatory do so willingly, with the knowledge that they are being improved and transformed by their hardships. What is more, the process was so filled with confidence in the ultimate attainment of paradise that one penitent who had been suffering for five hundred years could delight in the fact that

> *when some spirit, feeling purged and sound,*
> *Leaps up or moves to seek a loftier station,*

The whole mount quakes and the great shouts resound.[8]

Dante's optimistic vision of purgatory was less common than Owain's, but it was not unique. Luther's contemporary Catherine of Genoa (d. 1510) also taught that postmortem punishment would be transformed by an ever-growing experience of divine communion. "I do not believe it would be possible to find any joy," she wrote,

> comparable to that of a soul in purgatory, except the joy of the blessed in paradise—a joy which goes on increasing day by day, as God more and more flows in upon the soul, which he does abundantly in proportion as every hindrance to His entrance is consumed away. The hindrance is the rust of sin; the fire consumes the rust, and thus the soul goes on laying itself open to the Divine inflowing.[9]

The experience of joy in this beautiful vision radically contradicts that of *Saint Patrick's Purgatory*, and like Dante's it was not typical. Nevertheless, it was little different in its outcome: postmortem suffering led the soul inevitably closer to communion with God. Like the rest of Christendom, then, even purgatory was oriented toward paradise.

But that did not prevent the living from dreading it. So harrowing was purgatory in the popular imagination that the pious lived in awful expectation of it. Indeed, life became little more than an opportunity to evade purgatory, a hedge of never-ending acts of penal satisfaction in the hope of avoiding it. This overwhelming pessimism encouraged, and in turn was supported by, the emotional piety of modern art, especially images of Christ's suffering like those inspired by Giotto. Its ultimate symbol was Christ's mangled and bleeding body during His Passion, not His transfigured body on Mount Tabor or His resurrected body at His Ascension.

---

8   Dante, *The Divine Comedy 2: Purgatory*, translated by Dorothy L. Sayers (New York: Penguin, 1955), 236.

9   Catherine of Genoa, *Treatise on Purgatory*, translated by Cardinal Manning (London: Burns and Oates, 1858), 5–6.

But the new Christendom remained creative even in its pessimism, and before long an important evolution of doctrine had occurred. Predictably, it was announced by the papacy. As we noted in the previous chapter, Boniface VIII had declared in 1300 the first-ever jubilee, a year of plenary indulgences to all who made their way to one of the pilgrimage sites of Rome. Historians estimate that perhaps as many as two million people took advantage of the expiatory boon.[10] But history's most imperious pope went further. Knowing many pilgrims had perished during their journey, he granted the indulgence even to them in order to free them from purgatory. With this precedent in place, subsequent popes began offering indulgences for the dead with almost cheerful liberality. And when Pope Sixtus IV (r. 1471–1484) formalized the practice with a papal bull, the floodgates of automatic expiation were thrown open.

This new penitential conception—a serious blow to Christendom's paradisiacal culture because of its almost mechanical approach to penance—became embedded in the feast known as All Souls Day. During the first millennium, prayers for the departed had been linked—both in the West and the East—to worship during fasting seasons. Both halves of Christendom practiced intercessory prayer for the sake of the departed. In the middle of the eleventh century, however, the reforming Abbot Odilo of Cluny designated November 2—the day following the Western commemoration of All Saints—as a special "day of the dead" throughout the largest single network of monasteries. As the doctrine of purgatory was elaborated in the century that followed, All Souls Day became an opportunity for the living to undertake intercessions for the departed with the understanding that doing so would reduce the amount of punishment they were obligated to endure beyond the grave.

By now scholasticism had actually begun to reduce postmortem suffering to a rationalized system. Alexander of Hales (d. 1245), when reflecting on the sufferings of the saints, had concluded that "just as specific pain entails

---

10   According to some of these historians, Boniface in turn took advantage of them. The pope had been in dire financial troubles, and the influx of pilgrims brought welcome increase in papal revenue.

satisfaction for the sin [of the individual], so the common pain of the universal Church, crying for the sins of dead believers, praying and lamenting for them, is an aid to [their] satisfaction."[11] More explicit and accessible was *The Golden Legend*, a widely read collection of saints' lives written by Bishop Jacobus of Voragine (d. 1298). It provided a sort of calculus of salvific pain. The entry for the feast of All Souls Day encouraged the living to add to the sufferings of the dead their own intercessions (or "suffrages"), because, as Jacobus put it, "God counts both payments as one sum total."

> *Thus if the person owed a penance of two months in purgatory he could, due to suffrages offered by others, be freed in one month; but he is never released from purgatory until the debt is paid in full. Once it is fully paid, the payment belongs to the one who made it and is credited to him. If he does not need it, it goes into the Church's treasury or benefits the souls in purgatory.*[12]

By the end of the fifteenth century, even more audacious claims about the mystery of penance were being made. Frederick the Wise of Saxony (r. 1486–1525), under whose patronage Luther became professor of the Bible at Wittenberg, boasted one of Europe's largest reliquaries. Its contents included articles such as a twig from the Burning Bush and a hair from Jesus' beard. When venerated collectively, these holy objects were said by one calculation to have the effect of eliminating nothing less than 1,902,202 years in purgatory![13]

The confidence of such a calculus is breathtaking, and not only to modern skeptics. Contemporaries spent their lives gaining access to these spiritual treasuries because they were awed by them. But it was an experience profoundly different from that of pilgrims in the old Christendom. A sense of wonder was common to both, but in the East it was caused exclusively by the perception that a relic manifested God's presence on earth. In the West,

11 Le Goff, *Birth of Purgatory*, 249.

12 Jacobus de Voragine, *The Golden Legend*, translated by William Granger Ryan (Princeton: Princeton University Press, 2012), 667.

13 Roland Bainton, *Here I Stand: A Life of Martin Luther* (New York: Mentor Books, 1950), 53.

this perception was mixed with its near opposite—that the relic was a means toward an end, an instrument of expiation, a defense against the very presence of an otherwise unappeased and threatening God.

With such pessimism about the human condition, it is hard to see how the West could sustain its paradisiacal culture in the long run. Christendom had been built on the conviction that the kingdom of heaven had come into this world and that through the sacramental life of the Church, man enjoyed a communion with God that was as enduring as it was immediate. Relics of sanctified matter and pilgrimages to sanctified places were manifestations of paradise here in this world, even now. How this was possible was left as a mystery. But purgatory and the penitential system to which it gave birth had come to erect between paradise and this world a wall of suffering—the framework of which was mathematics and the penal logic of scholasticism.

Martin Luther's Agony

MARTIN LUTHER MAY HAVE BEEN thinking such thoughts as he returned from his disillusioned pilgrimage to Rome. But they were still a long way from resolution. In the meantime, he was soon transferred to the town of Wittenberg, where he lived in the Augustinian priory and taught scripture at the university to which it was attached. He made for a very highly strung monk, priest, and professor. His prior, Johann von Staupitz, frequently observed in him paralyzing moods of despair.

Indeed, Luther had only become a monk after going to pieces in fear during a thunderstorm, vowing to enter a cloister if by the prayers of Saint Anne he were spared. Two years later, while serving his first Mass as a newly ordained priest, he nearly had a nervous breakdown when it came time to read the canon (the Latin equivalent of the Byzantine anaphora). He was so tormented by a sense of sinfulness and doom that he had to be assisted by the attending clergy. His condition did not improve in Wittenberg.

There he undertook the severest discipline of asceticism and confession. He was forever nervous of omitting some small sin, knowing that it would add inescapably to his future time in purgatory. One of his confessions was so scrupulous that he spent six hours making it. And on more than one occasion he would return to the confessional within the hour after recalling a sin he had neglected to name. His confessors naturally despaired when they saw him approaching. One acutely observed, "Man, it is not God who is angry with you. You are angry with God."[14]

And indeed it was true. As Luther recalled later, his anxiety was the result of a highly sensitive mind seeking communion with God in an environment of overwhelmingly penitential pessimism. His agony represented an indictment of the state into which Western Christendom had fallen:

> *Is it not against all natural reason that God out of his mere whim deserts men, hardens them, damns them, as if he delighted in sins and in such torments of the wretched for eternity, he who is said to be of such mercy and goodness? This appears iniquitous, cruel, and intolerable in God, by which very many have been offended in all ages. And who would not be? I was myself more than once driven to the very abyss of despair so that I wished I had never been born. Love God? I hated him!*[15]

Instead of communion with God, Western culture had brought Luther to a state of alienation from God. Standing outside the gates of paradise, as it were, he could only gaze ruefully within at an inaccessible tree of life.

Luther searched desperately for a means of entry. Contemporary reform movements drew his interest. He fell under the influence of nominalistic individualism. He raved about German mysticism. And, in his restless need for change, he even resonated with the ideals of the modern devotion. But nothing satisfied him for very long. He could never be a follower. He was too brilliant and too unstable for that.

Finally, his spiritual ferment reached its peak when one night, sitting in the monastery library, he had an illumination. Meditating on Paul's Epistle to the Romans, he suddenly concluded that the God he had hated—the God who had erected a labyrinthine system of penances overseen by a clerical hierarchy—did

---

14   Ibid., 41.
15   Ibid., 44.

not exist. In other words, the God of second-millennium Roman Catholicism was a fiction, invented by the clergy, justified by the scholastics, and sustained by the superstitions of the non-communicating masses.

But God could be found, Luther was convinced, if one bypassed the past five centuries of accumulated falsehood and looked to the Scriptures. And there, in Romans (and Galatians), was a teaching that sharply contrasted faith with the penitential works in which, as a pious Roman Catholic, he had come to place such futile hope. The key phrase was Paul's declaration "The just shall live by faith" (Rom. 1:17). Instantly, Luther felt as if shackles had been removed from him. "Now I felt," he later recalled, "as if I had been born again: the gates had been opened and I had entered Paradise itself."[16]

Yet as the German monk was reaching this "reformation breakthrough" (as some historians like to call it), back in Rome his soon-to-be adversary the pope was instituting yet another round of indulgences—forging, as it were, new shackles to place on the souls of penitents.

After its return from Avignon, the papal court had abandoned the now decrepit Lateran Palace and made a new headquarters across the Tiber River in the Vatican. There Saint Peter's Basilica stood. But it too was in sorry shape, a poor monument to a papacy that had just defeated the conciliar movement and reestablished its supremacy.

This was the age of the "Renaissance popes," and in imitation of Italian princes like the Medicis of Florence, they spent vast sums on public works that would display the power of the papacy. Pope Sixtus IV, who had written the bull formally assigning to the papacy the power of indulgences for the dead, had set an example by building the Sistine Chapel (which he named after himself). Indeed, Michelangelo was at work on the chapel's ceiling when another Vicar of Saint Peter, Leo X (r. 1513–1521), resolved to move ahead with a long-delayed plan to rebuild Saint Peter's Basilica. To fund this project, Leo ordered the sale of an indulgence.

In Germany, a cardinal by the name of Albrecht of Mainz saw an opportunity. Having purchased his lucrative office with loans, he needed money

---

16   Heiko A. Oberman, *Luther: Man between God and the Devil*, translated by Eileen Walliser-Schwarzbart (New York: Image Books, 1992), 165.

to pay them off. He therefore proposed to Leo that he be permitted to sell the Saint Peter's indulgence in his realms (which bordered Saxony where Wittenberg lay) and keep half the proceeds for himself. In exchange, Leo X appears to have ignored the fact that Albrecht's troubles arose from simony—that greatest of ecclesiastical blasphemies, the practice of which had once provoked his namesake Leo IX to launch the Papal Reformation in the first place. What a difference five centuries and two Leos could make! So a deal was struck, and early in 1517 Cardinal Albrecht dispatched Johann Tetzel, the most enterprising vendor of indulgences in history, to get the job done.

And he did. By the end of the year, funding for Saint Peter's Basilica was accumulating rapidly. But as it did, unlettered peasants were streaming into Wittenberg's confessionals declaring that they had purchased automatic

remission of sins for themselves and their deceased family members. They even had certificates signed by Tetzel to show as proof. In their enthusiasm, they repeated the friar's melodious sales pitch:

> As soon as your coin into the
>   coffer rings,
> The soul from purgatory springs.

Martin Luther had had enough. On the eve of All Saints Day and two days before All Souls Day, he walked to the church door of Wittenberg and nailed to it ninety-five theses against the sale of indulgences for all of Christendom to see.

Johann Tetzel with his coffer

The Protestant Counter-Reformation

THIS EVENT HAS ALWAYS BEEN taken as the beginning of the Protestant Reformation. Indeed it was. However, it was also the outcome of a long-term development that, as this book has tried to show, had its origins in the eleventh century. That development was itself a reformation. For this reason, the great upheaval that followed Luther's public attack on indulgences might just as well be called a counter-reformation.[17]

For in the end Luther's action was a reaction to the changes brought to the West by the Papal Reformation. To call the movement he started simply "the Reformation" and to leave it at that suggests it was a correction of abuses and errors that had almost always existed. This is certainly how its advocates have presented it. But the most immediate problems Luther addressed were in fact rather new. They were almost entirely absent from Western Christendom during the first millennium. And, significantly, they continued to be absent from Eastern Christendom after the great cultural turning point that was the Great Division.

One need only consider the list of Roman Catholic practices rejected by Protestant reformers and the dates when those practices had become more or less officially established. The list began, as we have seen, with indulgences. These had first been introduced by Pope Urban II when calling the First Crusade in 1095. The list was immediately broadened to include the dogma of purgatory, which had been proclaimed at the Second Council of Lyons in 1274. (Purgatory was, after all, a precondition for indulgences as they had come to be defined by the sixteenth century.) Third, Protestants condemned the requirement that all priests be celibate, a practice at the heart of the Papal Reformation that was first advocated insistently by Peter Damian, who died in 1072. Protestants also rejected the restriction of the Scriptures and liturgy to Latin, which had been demanded on occasions

---

17 The term "counter-reformation" is of modern origin and has been used exclusively, to my knowledge, for the Roman Catholic response to Protestantism during the sixteenth century. This response included energetic and sincere efforts at reform, such as those contained in the activities of the Council of Trent and the newly created Society of Jesus.

such as the condemnation of John Wycliffe's English Bible at the Council of
Constance in 1415. Finally, and most emphatically, the Protestants attacked
the institution of papal supremacy, which dated to the pontificate of Leo IX
and was documented in Cardinal Humbert's excommunication of Patriarch
Michael Cerularius in 1054.

These five practices of Roman Catholicism that Protestants "protested"
(hence their name) were the direct result of changes that had occurred since
the Great Division. Other more positive points in their protest, such as the
famous formulas "faith alone" (*sola fide*), "scripture alone" (*sola scriptura*), and
"grace alone" (*sola gratia*), were closely related to these innovations and cannot really be understood apart from them. In fact, their urgent, minimalistic
formulation ("only this, and nothing more!") expressed the reactionary character of the movement. But even reactionaries can be revolutionaries, as we
saw in the case of that great innovator, Pope Gregory VII.

So Protestantism had its start as a counter-reformation designed to confront and in many cases reverse an earlier reformation that had not only
altered the character of Christendom in the West but separated it from the
East. It is therefore remarkable that so little attention has been given by historians to the "common cause" the reformers naturally had with the Orthodox Church. At the same time, the small amount of research that has been
done into the reformers' interest in Orthodoxy has revealed how very little
understanding they had of it. This is to some extent understandable in that
Byzantium, with its rich theological legacy, had been wiped out only decades
earlier by the Turks. There were no Greek fathers with whom to discuss doctrine. And, as we shall see below, the Russians, since the time of the Mongol
invasions, had been able to do very little in terms of building a cosmopolitan
center for theological exchange. During the sixteenth century, in fact, their
national complacency was even subverting ties to the Greeks.

A few gestures toward the East were made by Protestant leaders, such
as a famous exchange of letters between Lutheran divines at Tuebingen
and Patriarch Jeremias of Constantinople, which began in 1573. But it came
to nothing. Interestingly, as much as the Protestant party desired support
against its Roman Catholic adversaries, they sided with Rome against the

Orthodox on matters such as the filioque and the use of unleavened bread.

This brings attention to another detail often ignored by historians. While representing a real counter-reformation against the innovations of Roman Catholicism, Protestantism also retained many of the practices and much of the ethos it had inherited from its rival. It was, from the Orthodox point of view, the opposite side of the same coin. This was especially true (as we shall see) in Protestantism's dependency on Augustinianism. Its leaders, in attacking the new Christendom, were not restoring the old Christendom to the West. They were in fact perpetuating the new.

As they did so, there was a tendency to venture ever further away from Christendom's paradisiacal source, its "tree of life." Without intending it, the most fearless among them even reached the frontiers of a post-Christian Christendom.

The Labyrinth and the Abyss

NOWHERE WAS THIS MORE EVIDENT than in the tendency to choke off the two ancient springs of Christendom, heavenly immanence and divine participation. We have seen how fundamental these were for a civilization with a supporting culture that directs its members toward heavenly transformation. While in Byzantium and Russia these two sources continued to be accessible through liturgical life and hesychasm, in the West they had been choked off by the effects of the Papal Reformation. The Protestant Reformation went further and all but blocked them entirely. By the time the Reformation had run its course, the garden of Christendom was wilted and ready to fall.

This may explain the apocalyptic desperation of some early Protestants. We have noted the messianic expectation stirred centuries earlier by Joachim of Fiore. Radical Protestants revived it on a massive scale, and in so doing brought attention to a need for unity between heaven and earth. Torn by the forces of division, some were so indignant that they called for the total transformation of the world.

For Thomas Muentzer (d. 1525), for instance, heaven and earth became fused in one great millenarian explosion of hope and violence. The German theologian had stood side by side with Luther in Wittenberg at the posting of the *Ninety-Five Theses,* but soon fell out with him because of Muentzer's taste for political revolution. Luther, a rebel in theology, was the staunchest of reactionaries when it came to civil disobedience. The radical Muentzer was driven from Saxony by Frederick the Wise and began to earn a living as an itinerant preacher of the apocalypse. Against both "papists" and Lutherans, he promised divine retribution through a radical plan for institutional reform for the better. "God speaks clearly," he declared, "about the transformation of the world. He will prepare it in the last days in order that his name may be rightly praised. . . . The pitiable corruption of holy Christendom has become so great that at the present time no tongue can tell it at all. . . . For the godless person has no right to live when he is in the way of the pious."[18] Acting on this conviction, he helped raise the hopes of impoverished peasants weary of living under the oppressive conditions imposed by ecclesiastical princes and noblemen. In 1525, the resulting German Peasants' War killed a hundred thousand rebels, including Muentzer (who was captured and beheaded).

Another example of Protestant millennialism was the early Anabaptist movement. Like Muentzer, its prophets hated the politically conservative Luther as much as they hated the pope. As one leader named Bernard Rothmann declared, "previously there has been no true understanding of the glory of the kingdom of Christ on earth. . . . We know, however, that his kingdom must be fulfilled during our generation, and that the scriptural reference to the kingdom of Christ must be awaited here on earth."[19] Rothmann's followers did not wait long. In 1535 they seized the German town of Muenster and there created a theocracy of terror they called the New Jerusalem. Books were burned, Old Testament polygamy was restored, and a multitude of the insufficiently reformed were put to death. Finally, a combined army of Roman Catholics and Lutherans stormed the urban

---

18 *A Reformation Reader*, edited by Denis R. Janz (Minneapolis, MN: Fortress Press, 2008), 166–167.
19 Ibid., 223.

madhouse and massacred its inhabitants. As a grim warning to other cities, iron cages containing the corpses of the town's leaders were suspended from the Gothic belltower, where they remain to this day.

Protestants with revolutionary inclinations got the message. They realized the cause of reform could not be fulfilled in acts of millennialism. In fact, the idea of establishing the kingdom of God on earth came to seem fundamentally anti-Christian. After all, Jesus had declared that His kingdom is not of this world. Until He returned in glory, it was therefore necessary to submit to earthly authority.

Luther had endorsed this view in an important tract entitled *The Freedom of the Christian* (1520). He also applied the principle of submission to a hair-raising manifesto of political reaction entitled *Against the Murderous Thieving Hordes of Peasants* (1525). In this latter work he called on all able-bodied and law-abiding Germans to "smite, slay, and stab" the rebels of the Peasants' War. Echoing in certain ways the justification of religious violence we noted in Bernard's *New Knighthood*, Luther was confident that by suppressing peasant insurrection the righteous would be serving God. They would be acting to restore order to a world in which the kingdom of heaven is kept where it belongs: heaven.

Political conservatism need not entail contempt of the world and man's condition within it, but in Luther's case it did. In his political statements he often fell back on the Augustinianism he had inherited from the Roman Catholic Church. He had been a member of the Augustinian order of monks, and his thinking was profoundly shaped by the father of Christian dualism.

Augustinianism was behind the starkly pessimistic account of the human condition embraced by Luther. He called his view a "theology of the cross" and opposed it to a pejoratively named "theology of glory." He insisted his view was revealed by Scripture alone—especially 1 Corinthians 1:18—but to the historian its origin is also clearly visible in the recent culture of the West. This was in fact the triumph of stavrocentrism. But in the absence of a healthy metamorphocentric alternative, it fulfilled the curse of penitential pessimism. Luther claimed knowledge of God is not participatory or cooperative but submissive and even passive. It is not grounded in an experience of divine glory, but in faith alone. This was in some ways the outcome of his study of nominalism, with its categorical rejection of the optimistic epistemology of scholastics like Thomas Aquinas.

Luther's stavrocentric theology also presents a very different understanding of divine knowledge from that upheld in the East by Gregory Palamas. Indeed, as its antithesis Luther presented a derogatory "theology of glory," by which he meant knowledge of God that emphasizes man's capacity to participate mystically in the divine life. For Luther, efforts at working with God (known in traditional Christianity as *synergy*) inevitably rob God of His transcendent sovereignty. It is impossible not to see in such a claim Luther's preoccupation with contemporary Roman Catholicism and his need to resolve its system of penance. But in advancing this idea he and other Protestants drew ever further away from a view of salvation that emphasizes deification. As long as salvation was defined as satisfaction, it could be achieved only through the renunciation of hope in divine participation.

But the "theology of the cross" enabled Luther to assert an either-or doctrine of justification by faith alone against penitential works. This assertion became extremely liberating to Protestants of the time and continues to inspire many non-Protestant Christians today. Man's paltry efforts to obey the law or fulfill elaborate penances will not be the basis of judgment. His inner transformation will. The problem was that in addition to ignoring certain passages in the Scriptures that speak of the necessity of works (especially James 2:17 and Revelation 20:13)—as well as the fact that nowhere in Scripture is the expression "faith alone" ever used—such dualism foundered on the deeply submerged doctrine, also inherited from Augustine, of original sin.

For in attacking the misplaced optimism they saw in scholasticism, Protestant theologians tore down all remaining convictions about the innate goodness of humanity. In his commentary on Galatians, for instance, Luther declared that everything considered good and beautiful in man is but an arsenal in the hands of Satan.

All that is in the world is subject to the devil's malice, for he reigns over the entire world. This is why the world is also called the devil's kingdom. . . . No matter how many people there may be in this world, they are all subject to sin and to the devil. They are all the devil's subjects, for his tyranny holds all men captive. . . . When Christ is absent, then the evil world and the devil's kingdom are present. All the spiritual and bodily gifts you profess—be they wisdom, justice, holiness, eloquence, power, beauty, or riches—are therefore but the instruments and slavish weapons of the devil's infernal tyranny. These he uses to make you serve him, to promote his reign and to increase his power.[20]

Virtually every other Protestant father concurred. And so, as Jean Delumeau wrote, "it was therefore in the sixteenth century, and specifically in Protestant theology, that the accusation of man and the world reached its climax in Western civilization."[21]

And it was John Calvin (d. 1564) that brought it there. His main contribution to the desiccation of paradise was a withering doctrine of "total depravity." This was, of course, a variation of the doctrine of original sin and reminds us of the Augustinian basis of the new Christendom.

Yet Augustine himself would probably have dissented from the idea of total depravity. For despite his pessimism about the human condition, it was he who once compiled an eloquent catalog of blessings enjoyed by man in the world. This catalog of course included the image of God—a "spark" that "has not been utterly put out"—and the many godly virtues that flow from it.[22] But it also included the goodness of the cosmos itself, which, "even though mankind has been condemned and cast out of paradise," continues to surround him and assure him of divine favor. These blessings, for instance, consisted of

---

20   Quoted in Jean Delumeau, *Sin and Fear: The Emergence of a Western Guilt Culture*, translated by Eric Nicholson (New York: St. Martin's Press, 1990), 28.
21   Ibid., 27.
22   Augustine, *City of God*, translated by Bettenson, 1071.

the manifold diversity of beauty in sky and earth and sea; the abundance of light, and its miraculous loveliness, in sun and moon and stars; the dark shades of woods, the colour and fragrance of flowers; the multitudinous varieties of birds, with their songs and their bright plumage; the countless different species of living creatures of all shapes and sizes, amongst whom it is the smallest in bulk that moves our greatest wonder—for we are more astonished at the activities of the tiny ants and bees than at the immense bulk of whales. Then there is the mighty spectacle of the sea itself, putting on its changing colours like different garments, now green, with all the many varied shades, now purple, now blue.[23]

And so the catalog of blessings went on, page after page, as the saintly Latin father approached the conclusion of his *City of God*. It was, in this sense, his final cosmological and anthropological word.

Calvin did not harbor even such a reserved affirmation of man and the cosmos. This was due in part to the overwhelmingly distressing circum-

John Calvin

stances of his time. Christendom had gone to war, and he was in effect a theological combatant. But it was also due, it seems, to a remarkably resilient disposition to pessimism. William Bouwsma attributed this disposition to a pair of interconnected fears from which Calvin suffered throughout his life: what the reformer called the "labyrinth" and the "abyss."[24] The first was associated with the same penitential system of salvation from which Luther, too, found it so difficult to escape. The second was the limitless transgression into which the human being, freed from a strict system

---

23   Ibid., 1075.
24   William J. Bouwsma, *John Calvin* (Oxford: Oxford University, 1988), 45.

of discipline, would inevitably fall. One produced a state of claustrophobia, the second "the absence of boundaries and the unintelligibility of things, the void, nothingness, disintegration of the self."[25] Both anxieties, when purged of Christian hope by secularization, would one day haunt the civilization Calvin now so profoundly began to reshape.

His starting point was human depravity. Calvin proved even more Augustinian in this than Augustine. In his *Institutes of the Christian Religion*, he reminded his readers, after reviewing Augustine's famous conflict with Pelagius, that every human being is subject to original sin. This by itself was what Christians had always believed in the West. However, Calvin advanced his argument to a level of extremity that surpassed by far all previous theologians.

> Original sin [is] an hereditary pravity and corruption of our nature, diffused through all the parts of our soul, rendering us obnoxious to the Divine wrath. . . . Our nature being so totally vitiated and depraved, we are, on account of this very corruption, considered as convicted and justly condemned in the sight of God. . . . For when it is said that the sin of Adam renders us obnoxious [reprobate] to the Divine judgment, it is not to be understood as if we, though innocent, were undeservedly loaded with the guilt of his sin; but, because we are all subject to a curse, in consequence of his transgression, he is therefore said to involve us in guilt. . . . Therefore infants themselves, as they bring their condemnation into the world with them, are rendered obnoxious to punishment by their own sinfulness, not by the sinfulness of another. . . . Their whole nature is as it were a seed of sin, and therefore cannot but be odious and abominable to God. . . . This depravity never ceases in us, but is perpetually producing new fruits. . . . For our nature is not only destitute of all good, but is so fertile in all evils that it cannot remain inactive.[26]

This was an anthropologically pessimistic tour de force, and it would permanently alter the culture of the new Christendom.

---

25 Ibid., 46.

26 John Calvin, *Institutes of the Christian Religion*, vol. 1, translated by John Allen (Philadelphia: Presbyterian Board of Publication, 1921), 229–230.

"In Heaven and Not Here"

MIRED IN DEPRAVITY, CHRISTENDOM COULD hope to offer little more to its people than unrestricted access to the Word of God through Scripture. Accordingly, divine worship was to be radically reformed by two principles. The first was graphological, that is, worship must conform exactly to what is recorded in the Scriptures (*graphi* in Greek). If an element of worship could not be demonstrably located in the Bible, it was to be eliminated. By applying such a radical principle of "Scripture alone," Calvin went beyond the Lutherans, who retained much of the Roman Catholic Mass. He also revealed the incoherence of sola scriptura. Calvin was opposed fundamentally (later adherents would call themselves "fundamentalists") to anything regarded as "tradition." By this word—which was, it might be noted, perfectly biblical— the Protestant counter-reformers primarily meant Roman Catholicism and not, significantly, traditional Christianity as it had been known before the Great Division. Yet the principle of "Scripture alone" ignored the fact that the New Testament had been written decades after the faith was given at Pentecost and was therefore the product of tradition. Scripture itself bore witness to the priority of tradition over Scripture (Acts 2:42) and to the need to remain faithful to tradition (2 Thess. 2:15). But the furious way in which the counter-reformation was advanced frequently resulted in disregard for such subtleties.

The second principle of Reformed worship, as Calvin came to define it, was even more harmful to the paradisiacal culture. It demanded that worship involve nothing of this world that is material or physical. In this sense Calvinism resonated with and took a step further in the new aesthetic of Gothic dematerialization. This antimaterial dictum was, in fact, a step toward liturgical gnosticism, reviving a contempt for the body condemned by early fathers like Irenaeus. It was also a child of Augustinianism, though a disfigured one, and was basically dualistic. It assumed the opposition of two realities, spirit and matter. Reflecting on Christ's encounter with the Samaritan Woman, Calvin concluded that since "God is Spirit" (John 4:24), it is improper to use anything material in His worship. That God became material in the Incarnation seems to have had no direct impact on Calvin's bleak cosmology.

No doubt Calvin was using the principle of nonmaterial worship to combat perceived errors and superstitions in contemporary Roman Catholicism. Like Luther, for instance, he was appalled at the ongoing traffic in relics. The frantic rush of the non-communing laity to "see God" during the elevation of the eucharistic Host also disturbed him. But in reaction Calvin went to an extreme. He declared that "whatever holds down and confines the senses to the earth is contrary to the covenant of God; in which, inviting us to Himself, He permits us to think of nothing but what is spiritual."[27] The bodily humanity that Christ assimilated to His divinity and which contained all five of the senses was, it appears, almost meaningless.

It is no surprise, then, to read in the *Institutes* page after page of attacks on the idolatry of icons. Calvin scarcely launches the great treatise before being drawn, before the gloomy account of human depravity, to this epitome of human blasphemy. Three chapters of Book I are dedicated to it. After an erudite retelling of Old Testament injunctions against images, especially the Second Commandment, Calvin comes finally to the "papists." He shows little knowledge of Eastern fathers such as John of Damascus when discussing the topic, but he condemns as a "subterfuge" Gregory the Great's claim that icons communicate the Scriptures to the illiterate. However, Calvin seems most perturbed by recent developments in Western painting.

The early naturalism of Giotto had by now developed into lavishly sensual representations such as those adorning the ceiling of the Sistine Chapel. In the Creation of Adam, Michelangelo's God looks more like the pagan Zeus than Christ does in the equivalent icon at Monreale discussed in chapter three. More remarkably, the Last Judgment in the sanctuary behind the altar (itself a radical innovation of subject matter) depicted a cacophony of naked bodies.[28] The sour Calvin was, as always, keen in his contempt: "But what

---

27 Quoted in Carlos M. N. Eire, *War against the Idols: The Reformation of Worship from Erasmus to Calvin* (Cambridge: Cambridge University Press, 1986), 201.

28 Indeed, the celebration of the human body in it deviated so radically from tradition that the papal chancellor in charge of overseeing Michelangelo's work ordered that at least loincloths be added to obscure the genitalia. Though the artist was forced to submit, he took revenge by depicting one of the damned

they call the pictures or statues of their saints—what are they but examples of the most abandoned luxury and obscenity? . . . Even prostitutes in brothels are to be seen in more chaste and modest attire, than those images in their temples."[29] Again, one cannot help feeling that the intensity of Protestantism was due to the fact that it was a counter-reformation set against the perceived errors of the new Christendom, not the old.

Calvin was not completely oblivious to the East, though he had little to say about Greek patristic reflections on iconography. What he did say about Orthodoxy was characteristically vitriolic. Some of his polemic was aimed at the fathers of the Seventh Ecumenical Council. In rejecting iconoclasm, they had made a distinction between the "worship" (*latrea*) due to God alone and the "veneration" (*proskynesis*) of icons. Calvin dismissed this out of hand as another subterfuge. Interestingly, in his account of the council's proceedings he admits to depending on a document composed in the West during the reign of Emperor Charlemagne. It appears that even though he was perfectly competent in Greek, Calvin was using the infamous eighth-century Latin translation of the proceedings, which grossly mischaracterized the actual ruling. If this is true, then it is understandable that he would find in the most authoritative sanction for icons in history statements "so disgusting, that I am quite ashamed to repeat them."[30]

One thing is certain. The fundamental principle in the conciliar ratification of icons was the doctrine of the Incarnation, which had been elaborated earlier by John of Damascus. The Second Commandment that preoccupied Calvin's legalistic mind had not been absolute, the Greek father noted, for after giving it (Ex. 20:4) God commanded that icons be made for worship in the tabernacle (Ex. 25:18). Along with specific and highly detailed statements about the material composition of this, the heart of Old Testament worship before the temple (species of wood, types of precious metals, physical dimensions), God commanded its Holy of Holies contain a material work of human hands. This was called the Ark of the Covenant, and on it were to

---

with the chancellor's face.

29   Calvin, *Institutes*, vol. 1, 103.

30   Ibid., 111.

be fashioned icons of the cherubim—those very "things of heaven" that the Second Commandment had forbidden.

But John of Damascus's defense of icons was not grounded, as Calvin's attacks were, in the Old Covenant. The Incarnation was its center. When God became man, the human image was filled with a glory and beauty that should not be suppressed. In Christ, the material creation had been sanctified. "I do not venerate the creation over the Creator," John wrote,

> but I venerate the Creator who became creation like me, and came down into creation without humiliation and without being debased in order to glorify my nature and make me to be a partaker of the divine nature. . . . Thus, taking courage I represent God, the invisible, not as invisible, but insofar as he has become visible for us by participation in flesh and blood. I do not represent the invisible deity but I represent the flesh of God which has been seen.

This was simply a theological language that Calvin, the student of human depravity, was unable to speak. And so the otherwise magisterial presentation of Protestant theology in his *Institutes* has nothing of substance to say about the early patristic affirmation of icons.

But the masses of discontented Roman Catholics who joined the Reformation were no longer familiar with Eastern Christianity. And so, under Protestant influence they unleashed a wave of iconoclasm such as had not been seen since the days of Emperor Leo III. Like its eighth-century antecedent, this movement wiped out centuries of accumulated Christian piety.

Its earliest stirrings were in Wittenberg, where another of Luther's restless disciples named Andreas Karlstadt (d. 1541) advocated the destruction of all Roman Catholic images in the town. He was nonplussed when his mentor dismissed him as a fanatic and publicly opposed the plan. Ultimately Karlstadt fled Saxony and took up the iconoclastic cause in Switzerland. There he was joined in the movement by Zwingli, who oversaw the destruction of statues and images. In 1528, Bern Cathedral became the site of one of the most telling signs of what was to come. After three weeks of public debates about every innovation Western Christendom had come to stand for since the Great Division, from clerical celibacy to transubstantiation, the riots began. Protestants ripped out altars and tore down every image they could find. Their children danced in the streets singing songs about liberation from the worship of "a baked god"—that is, a false god who is said to be present among His people in the Eucharist.[31] As a mountain of shattered stained glass and pieces of statuary ascended toward the ceiling of the cathedral, Zwingli mounted the pulpit to proclaim the victory of true worship.

But the greatest upheaval was yet to come. Called the Icon Storm (*Bildersturm*), it occurred in Holland and northern Germany. In 1566, crowds of people inspired by Calvinist preaching swarmed across the countryside and through the towns, smashing stained glass windows and toppling statues. Since anticlericalism was fundamental to their agenda, they also looted monasteries and ransacked the homes of priests. When this greatest of the counter-reformation's iconoclastic spasms subsided, it was as if a fire had gutted an entire region of Western Christendom. Hundreds of churches had been stripped of their beauty. All that was left, in many cases, was the Reformed architectural ideal of "four bare walls and a pulpit."

But by this time, even the Roman Catholic Church had brought ruin to the iconographical tradition of the West. It did so not through iconoclasm but through what can be called *iconotorsion,* that is, the twisting or distortion of iconography. The most celebrated painters of the day—Botticelli (d. 1510), Leonardo da Vinci (d. 1519), Raphael (d. 1520), Michelangelo (d. 1564)—contributed to it. The exquisite work of these iconotorts was coveted everywhere Italian churches were built or redecorated. These painters were especially patronized by the popes, whose need to reestablish supremacy in the wake of the conciliar movement led them to erect ecclesiastical monuments featuring modern art.

In the East, by contrast, icons were not painted in the naturalistic style but in an anagogic style paralleling the heavenly symbolism of the liturgy. As naturalism became the dominant approach to painting in the West, the iconographical experience of heavenly immanence was completely undermined. Hideous images like the Isenheim Altarpiece, on the one hand, and

---

31   Eire, *War against the Idols*, 111.

voluptuous images like the Sistine Chapel ceiling on the other, assured that this experience was all but choked out of Western culture.

And as a result the long history of Western iconography came to an end. What this meant was that revealing the presence of God in the world was no longer the purpose of art. Demonstrating the ingenious presence of the artist was. In the words of Hans Belting, "the new presence *of* the work succeeds the former presence of the sacred *in* the work."[32] Though this transition had been underway for centuries, the Protestant attack on icons precipitated it. "As [iconographical] images fell from favor" through events like the Icon Storm, Belting concluded, "they began to be justified as [secular] works of art."[33] In other words, as paradise fell, a secular civilization that can be called utopia took its place.

But perhaps the most noxious effect of Calvinism on the West's paradisiacal culture was the rejection of Christ's physical presence in the Eucharist. Since the first century, Christendom had depended on doctrinal integrity, adherence to the apostolic tradition. According to the apostle Luke, the first Christians "continued steadfastly" beyond Pentecost "in the breaking of the bread," that is, in eucharistic communion (Acts 2:42). This was always understood within church tradition as the real, actual, and physically perceptible body and blood of Christ. The Apostle Matthew joined Luke and Mark in relating Jesus' statements at the Last Supper that "this is my body" and "this is my blood" (Matt. 26:26–28). The apostle John had added Christ's statement that "unless you eat the flesh of the Son of Man and drink His blood, you have no life in you" (John 6:53). The apostle Paul revealed the early Church's liturgical practice of the mystical supper, warning of the danger of communing in the Eucharist in an "unworthy" way and "not discerning the Lord's body" (1 Cor. 11:29). The real bodily presence of Christ in the Eucharist was unquestionably a part of apostolic doctrine.

As a biblically attested tradition of the Church it had scarcely ever been challenged. One exception was the ninth-century Frankish theologian

---

32 Belting, *Likeness and Presence*, 459.
33 Ibid., 470.

Ratramnus of Corbie, a self-declared opponent of Patriarch Photios and critic of the Eastern fathers. He proposed a symbolical understanding of the Eucharist. His view was revived after the Great Division by Berengar, whose views, as we have seen, were rejected by the papacy as heretical in 1059. Even so, a rationalistic rather than patristic method of interpreting tradition had now been established, and it remained at the heart of scholastic and post-scholastic theology. As part of the Protestant assault on Roman Catholicism, Scripture was now joined to logic in the Protestant effort to replace tradition. Luther rejected the doctrine of transubstantiation on scriptural grounds, but retained, with an alternative he called "consubstantiation," a belief in the bodily presence of Christ. Not so Zwingli. He asserted that Christ was not present at all in the Eucharist, and that the liturgical rite was no more than a symbolic recollection of the historical Last Supper. The two reformers fought it out at the Marburg Colloquy of 1529, but not surprisingly, on this most important of sacramental doctrines, they continued thereafter in a state of division.

Calvin positioned himself somewhere in the middle of this debate. Luther's doctrine appeared dangerously close to transubstantiation, and he therefore regarded it as a concession to superstition. It certainly violated the French reformer's principle of nonmaterial worship. Preoccupied with man's total depravity, Calvin claimed that a corrupt "seed of religion" causes all men to tend toward a material rather than spiritual understanding of worship. This view was embraced by contemporary Reformed churches and reduced to the theological principle "the finite cannot contain the infinite" (*finitum non capax infiniti*).

This was particularly true with the Eucharist. And though Calvin concluded that Zwingli's argument could not withstand the scriptural evidence discussed above, he could not bring himself to accept that the body and blood of Christ are physically present in the eucharistic elements. How could a completely transcendent God suffer such dishonor? So he settled on a doctrine of "spiritual presence," whereby Christ is present only in the mind of the believer, but not in the physical world itself. In fact, this was little more than a doctrine of spiritual absence.

And among the more radical of the Protestants this doctrine caught on. It spread in Calvin's native Paris and resulted in the Placards Affair of 1534, when radical Protestants surreptitiously distributed pamphlets in the dark of the night declaring that "the world will be completely destroyed" if the real presence of Christ in the Eucharist is not renounced.[34] The scandal caused in the city of Saint Louis, Saint Thomas Aquinas, and Saint Bonaventure was overwhelming. Even King Francis came out to find a pamphlet on his bedroom door in the morning.

We have already seen how attacks on the real presence mingled with iconoclasm in the rage of Protestants during the Reformation riots in Switzerland. Indeed, it was to Geneva that Calvin soon emigrated with William Farel (d. 1565), the agitator responsible for the placards. From this "protestant Rome" (as a contemporary called it) Calvin directed the formation of an international Reformed church. Here, after decades of tireless effort, he finally completed his life's work of abolishing Roman Catholicism and every element of traditional Christianity—save Scripture—with which he could associate it.

But it was in a land far from Geneva that Calvin's greatest work was accomplished. Britain had initially taken the course of moderate reform, more inclined to follow the example of Luther than that of Calvin. However, the Geneva reformers had something of a special agent across the English Channel. His name was John Knox, and he tirelessly advanced the Reformed cause in his native Scotland. In 1560, the Presbyterian Church of Scotland was established along Calvinist lines. But Knox did not stop there. Traveling to England, he gained the confidence of reformers such as Archbishop Thomas Cranmer (d. 1556), who, like him, embraced Calvin's eucharistic doctrine of the real absence. In 1552 the Book of Common Prayer, which now governed the English liturgy, was revised under Knox's influence to include a statement called the "black rubric." It spoke for the desiccated state of paradisiacal culture. Expressing concern that people would continue to kneel while receiving the Eucharist, it declared that by doing so they must not under any circumstances infer Christ's material presence in the sacrament.

---

34   Eire, *War against the Idols*, 190.

Contrary to the convictions of a millennium and a half of piety, the black rubric pedantically insisted that Christ is "in heaven and not here."

The Tower and the Kremlin

NOT ONLY WAS CHRISTENDOM LOSING its sacramental experience of paradise, but its political culture, long shaped by the ideal of ecclesiopolitical symphony, was also changing. We have seen how the state maintained a close relationship to the bishops long after the conversion of Emperor Constantine in the fourth century. In the sixteenth century, however, while states remained officially committed to Christianity, some began to restructure themselves in such a way as to subvert the transformative values of the gospel. The city-states of Italy commended in Machiavelli's amoral political treatise *The Prince* (1532) are a good example, and they foresee the complete collapse of Christian statecraft. More immediately, however, kingdoms in northern Europe were also subverting traditional political culture by using religion as an instrument with which to destroy their enemies. Their priority, clearly, was the formation of the modern national state.

One important example is England. On the heels of the Hundred Years' War, she had suffered a dynastic civil conflict known as the Wars of the Roses (1455–1487). The house of Tudor ultimately prevailed in this, and it produced its most important king in the person of Henry VIII (r. 1509–1547). Within a few years of his accession, however, he found himself in the midst of the Reformation upheaval. Domestically, demands to join the Protestants grew, especially from communities long influenced by the memory of Lollardy. There was also much anticlericalism, which found an easy target in Archbishop Thomas Wolsey (d. 1530) of Canterbury. This prelate, simultaneously a papal legate and the chancellor of the realm, surrounded himself with palatial luxury and was reputed to be thoroughly corrupt. Henry for his part had no sympathy for England's Protestants, and his initial opposition to the Reformation moved him to write a treatise defending papal supremacy—an act that represented, as we saw in chapter three, the ultimate standard of Christian monarchy. Indeed, the treatise earned him a

Henry VIII of England

commendation by the pope as a "defender of the faith." However, political concerns soon came to outweigh religious ones.

Henry had married a Spanish princess named Catherine of Aragon. In the course of twenty years, she had given him only one surviving child, a girl named Mary. Henry had during this time kept numerous mistresses in his court, and now he settled on replacing Catherine with the sister of one of them, a beautiful girl named Anne Boleyn. He sent Cardinal Wolsey to Rome to argue the case for annulment, the technical and legalistic means by which popes in the past had granted rulers a second chance at marriage. But the pope balked. The unsuccessful Wolsey returned to England to find himself condemned as a traitor, and he soon died while awaiting trial. His fate was a sign of what was to come for any who stood in the way of Henry's ambitions, or merely failed to advance them.

Henry decided that in the absence of a papal annulment, he would simply order a divorce himself. His choice for Wolsey's successor as English primate had been the Calvinist Archbishop Thomas Cranmer, who was himself secretly married. He declared Henry's union with Catherine null and void. He also blessed Henry's swift remarriage to Anne, who was already pregnant. However, she too soon proved a disappointment, for the child she bore was a daughter, Elizabeth.

As Henry began to think of yet new alternatives for gaining an heir, he assigned his chief minister, Thomas Cromwell (d. 1540), the task of arranging a complete break from Rome. Cromwell faithfully fulfilled the commission, reorganizing the English government so that the king would have unprecedented control over it. Cromwell masterminded the wholesale dissolution of Britain's monasteries, at once crushing the center of opposition to Protestantism and assuring, through redistribution of monastic lands, the complete dependence of the aristocracy on Henry. The act provoked an uprising in 1536 known as the Pilgrimage of Grace. But though it involved tens of thousands of opponents to the Reformation, the uprising was ruthlessly put down.

Cromwell also carried out Henry's orders to destroy the shrine of Thomas Becket at Canterbury Cathedral. Since the twelfth century, the shrine had attracted millions of pilgrims from throughout Europe. One of these was

Geoffrey Chaucer (d. 1400), who set his famous *Canterbury Tales* in the context of a pilgrimage to it. But Cromwell's greatest achievement in the service of Henry was the Act of Supremacy issued by Parliament in 1534. The lords that dominated Parliament had been the beneficiaries of the monastery dissolution, and they were happy to declare their now Protestant king the "supreme head" of the Church of England. Five centuries of papal supremacy were thereby reversed, and English Christendom, formerly subject to the pope, was now in the hands of its king.

This had, indeed, been the goal of Henry II during the twelfth century. But as we saw in chapter three, Henry VIII's namesake had been thwarted by the power of Rome. And he had been thwarted most dramatically by the very Becket whose shrine had now been desecrated. The symbolism was probably not lost on the guards of the Tower of London, a castle on the Thames that served as a political prison. They realized the reversal of history was not complete yet.

A fourth Thomas now fell under the malignant gaze of the cynical king. Thomas More (d. 1535) was a renowned scholar and the author of *Utopia*, a reflection on the shortcomings of contemporary Christendom. After the fall of Wolsey, More had been appointed chancellor by Henry. But he was scrupulous enough to resign in objection to the Act of Supremacy. Henry would not abide even a hint of disapproval from his subjects, even when they kept their silence. More was sent to the Tower of London. The charges of treason

The Tower of London today

were patently spurious. When he was publicly beheaded, it was for the crime of having a conscience. And to terrorize those who might likewise place truth before power, Henry had his head impaled on a pike over the Tower Bridge for all of London to see.

The only surviving Thomas at the top of Henry VIII's religious terror-state was the Archbishop of Canterbury, Thomas Cranmer. He lived to see Henry's long-awaited male heir ascend the throne as Edward VI (r. 1547–1553). But as the dates of Edward's reign indicate, he did not last long. A sickly child-king, he acquiesced as supreme head of the Church to Calvinists like Cranmer. Accordingly, the Reformation gained rapid momentum. It was only checked during the reign of Mary (r. 1553–1558), when Roman Catholicism was briefly reimposed. Mary's reign signaled the end for Cranmer. With other Protestants, he was arrested and condemned for heresy. Though he issued a complete retraction of his views—even declaring adherence to papal supremacy—on the day of his execution he retracted his retraction. As the fire began to consume him on the gallows, he famously placed his right hand into it first to punish the limb that, by writing the initial retraction of his Reformed faith, had caused offense.

Reformation England was a monstrous deviation from the Christendom that had given it birth. Perhaps the best example of this was the marriage record of its initial ruler. After divorcing Catherine, Henry remained in wedlock with Anne Boleyn for only three years before he got rid of her as well. Like her successors, she had a grim fate. Denounced by Cromwell as an adulteress and a traitor, she was thrown into the Tower and publicly beheaded. Another of Henry's mistresses named Jane Seymour was next, but she died after only a year due to complications in bearing Edward, Henry's only son. Jane was replaced by Anne of Cleves, whose appearance, not living up to Henry's expectations, led not only to her divorce (in six months) but to the downfall of Cromwell himself, since he had arranged the marriage. Catherine Howard lasted a year and a half, and like Anne Boleyn was beheaded for adultery in the Tower. Only wife number six, Catherine Parr, survived, due entirely to the fact that she had the good fortune (or good sense) to marry a dying king.

The religious terror-state of Henry VIII was not the only case in which political ambition overwhelmed paradisiacal culture. Russia, which had almost no contact with Tudor England, was another example. By the end of the fifteenth century, the Mongol yoke was becoming nothing more than a bad memory among the Eastern Slavs. The grand prince of Moscow, Dmitry Donskoy, had raised an army in 1380 and defeated the Golden Horde at the Battle of Kulikovo Field. A century later, his successor Ivan III (r. 1462–1505), who earned the title "the Great," formally terminated Russia's tribute obligations to the former oppressors. Under Ivan's ambitious leadership, eastern Russia was unified into a militarily strong national state.

Western Russia, on the other hand, remained outside Moscow's orbit. Since the time of the Mongols, Kiev and other territories west of the Dnieper River had fallen under Polish and Lithuanian political domination. A growing distinction between the descendants of Kievan Russia thus began to manifest itself. This would eventually lead to the formation of distinct ethnic groups among the Eastern Slavs, including the "Great Russians" affiliated with Moscow, the "Little Russians" (known in modern times as Ukrainians), and the "White Russians" (or Belarusians). In the meantime, the nobility living under Poland and Lithuania were pressured to convert to Roman Catholicism, leaving an Orthodox peasantry to fend for itself.

Ivan the Great, to strengthen the national state now reemerging in the east under Muscovite rule, did what his distant Kievan predecessor Andrey Bogolyubsky had been unable to do: he suppressed the independence of the boyars and established a centralized autocracy. He also suppressed the autonomy of the various Russian city-states in the east. Like Andrey, he went to war against the northwestern principality of Novgorod. But he was victorious. The proud democratic city-state was now incorporated into the Muscovite autocracy.

To mark these and other political achievements, Ivan married a Byzantine princess named Sophia Paleologos who had survived the fall of Constantinople. He also began to use the title *tsar*, which was the Slavic variant of the Byzantine emperors' title of *caesar*.

The ambitions of Muscovite rulers, combined with Russia's status as the only independent Orthodox power in the world after 1453, had a disruptive effect on the old culture. Since her baptism under Vladimir, Russia had maintained close ties with Byzantium. Her princes even established marital alliances with the royalty of the West. The Mongol invasions reduced foreign contacts, but these had resumed as the state began the process of national liberation during the fourteenth century. The flowering of hesychastic monasticism in the northern Thebaid had been a sign of continued participation in the larger Byzantine commonwealth. With the rise of Moscow, this began to change.

The earliest evidence of the shift was the loss of respect for the patriarchate of Constantinople after the sham union of Florence in 1439. Russians had rioted upon Metropolitan Isidore's return from the council as a Roman Catholic cardinal. After Isidore was driven out of Moscow, the metropolitanate was transferred permanently from Kiev to the new capital, and it was no longer subject to approval from abroad. After the fall of Constantinople, an obscure monk named Filofey wrote a treatise arguing that the Greeks had been conquered because they were apostate. Three Romes now marked the history of Christendom, he claimed: the first had fallen away in 1054; the second had done so in 1439; and the third, Moscow, would and could never fall until the end of time. This Third Rome doctrine, as it came to be known, was never officially endorsed. But it did illustrate the isolated mentality of Russia as she entered the sixteenth century.

Growing confidence in the Muscovite state and disregard for the universal Church also led to strong religious disagreements. Nil Sorsky, as we noted in the previous chapter, had been inspired by Sergy of Radonezh and followed his example in spreading hesychasm throughout northern Russia. The Athonite model of asceticism he and his disciples practiced had little need for wealthy monasteries and even less for an alliance with the Muscovite state. They were rugged hermits living in the wilderness. But another form of monasticism, also inspired by Sergy, sought to build vast cloisters in which large numbers of monks would live. These monasteries would be centers of national life, building beautiful temples and amassing the large treasuries needed to finance them. They were content to own large tracts of land with the peasants that were attached to them, and to use their resources to provide alms to the poor. Such monasticism was represented by Joseph of Volokolamsk (d. 1515). He formed a party known as the "possessors," which eventually came into conflict with Nil and other "non-possessors." Paradoxically, both tendencies flowed from the same source—Holy Trinity Monastery, where Sergy had been abbot. However, the spirit of division, which had largely left Russian Christendom in peace during the dark years of the Mongol yoke, now rose up within her.

In 1503 Ivan the Great called a council in Moscow, which both Joseph and Nil attended. The council condemned the non-possessors. From that moment, the Russian Church lost the ability to withstand political intrusion. Ironically, Joseph considered himself a defender of monastic autonomy. But as the sketes of the north were closed in the decades that followed (the very time the monasteries of England were being dissolved), the richly endowed monasteries he defended became financial dependencies of the state and, as a result, agents of political compliance. Furthermore, after Joseph died, a disciple of his named Daniel became metropolitan and initiated a more radical possessor policy founded on the premise of subservience to the state. Daniel intervened in the succession of Ivan's son Vasily III (r. 1505–1547). When the new ruler launched a purge of rival princes, he assisted in it. Then, when Vasily decided without canonical justification to divorce his wife, Daniel blessed a second marriage.

The possessor capitulation to Muscovite autocracy accelerated Russia's estrangement from the universal Church. Ties with the post-Byzantine Greek East were gradually allowed to lapse. A particularly tragic example of this was the case of Maxim the Greek (d. 1556), an Athonite scholar who came to Moscow to assist in the translation of Byzantine patristic writings and liturgical books. The Mongols' destruction of Kiev and other cultural centers had severely stunted intellectual life, and theological reflection was all but absent in the self-proclaimed heir to Byzantium. Maxim was a rare shaft of light from the source of Eastern patristics, and he might have laid a foundation for a brilliant future. However, as a foreigner he was treated with suspicion and contempt.

Maxim's habit of criticizing the government and the possessors' mistreatment of peasants did not help. By sympathizing with the non-possessors, he earned the hostility of radicalized possessors under Daniel. In fact, Maxim actually went on record as an opponent of Vasily's second marriage. This provoked Daniel to move against him, and in 1521 Maxim was condemned as a heretic and consigned to a monastic prison as punishment. There he lived in prayer and research for three more decades, while outside his cloister the Muscovite ecclesiological vision grew ever more myopic. The last great hope of living contact with the Byzantine fathers faded, opening the way for the radical Westernization of the Russian Orthodox Church a century later.

Into this environment was born Ivan the Terrible (r. 1533–1584). He had been raised within the Moscow Kremlin. During his minority there he had been brutally mistreated by boyar chaperones, and he spent his youth preparing for vengeance. But the violent reign that followed was set in motion by the much more basic ambition, shared with his contemporary Henry VIII, of asserting himself over every authority in society, whether civil or ecclesiastical.

Some of Ivan's policies were beneficial to Russia, especially in the first years of his reign. In 1552 he conquered the Muslim city of Kazan, securing the eastern borders for the first time since the Mongol invasions. He oversaw the continued development of an independent national Church, presiding over the Stoglav Council of 1551. This council subordinated Greek liturgical practices whenever they conflicted with those prevalent in Russia.

The council also used the principle of ecclesiopolitical symphony to defend Ivan's power to direct the affairs of bishops, which would prove no benefit to Russia in the future. Going beyond what even the most caesaropapist Byzantine emperors believed, Ivan declared himself the ruler of the Church and accountable only to God. In the absence of other legitimate witnesses to God's will, this meant in practice that he was totally unconstrained.

The "good" period of Ivan's reign came to an end in 1560, when his wife Anastasia suddenly died. He was convinced she had been poisoned by the boyars, and in his grief (he had loved her intensely) he unleashed policies that were destructive and irrational. Thus began the "bad" period of his rule.

Ivan the Terrible

This period was dominated by an institution Ivan created called the *oprichnina*. It represented a radical reorganization of the state that gave the tsar direct control over its military and economic resources. Thousands of loyal *oprichniky* administered it, and did so with the use of terror. In a bizarre parody of ecclesiastical administration, Ivan ordered these men to dress in black uniforms resembling cassocks. As he unleashed them on Russia, thousands of innocent people were put to death, often for treason. Almost all of Novgorod was destroyed and thousands of its people massacred by these demon-like hordes.

Back in Moscow, Red Square became the site of regular public executions.[35] There, in sight of the Kremlin, Ivan placed a block of stone known as the *Lobnoe Mesto*, or "place of the skull." It was here that proclamations were made and condemnations announced. One explanation of its name was that it was modeled on the place of public execution in Jerusalem where Jesus Himself was crucified. This would have been in keeping with Ivan's character. Increasingly sadistic in his efforts to destroy perceived enemies, he nevertheless maintained a strong attachment to Christianity and infused his terror-state with its symbols. It was said that after watching with fascination the interminable executions beneath the Kremlin, he would prostrate himself for hours begging God to have mercy on the souls of his innocent victims.

Ivan's reaction to criticism was complex. On the one hand, as the divinely appointed punisher of sedition, he had no patience for clerical witnesses to the gospel of love and forgiveness. An example of this was Metropolitan Philip of Moscow (d. 1569). Russia's primate had been recruited from one of the wealthiest monasteries, Solovky in the White Sea. Exercising the kenotic ministry of intercession, Philip placed himself between the tsar and the people he was savaging. One day at the Kremlin's Dormition Cathedral, Philip refused Ivan the blessing cross that is customarily kissed at the conclusion of the Divine Liturgy. Instead, like Ambrose before Emperor Theodosios, he subjected the tsar to a public rebuke for his unrestrained bloodletting. Ivan,

---

35 It was named not for the blood spilled there, but for the fact that it was considered "beautiful," the old Russian word for which also meant "red."

who always carried a staff with him, smashed it down next to the metropolitan and departed the scene in a rage. Soon after, he ordered the oprichniky to arrest the metropolitan and murder him in a monastery. Like Thomas More in England, Philip went to his death a martyr for Christian conscience in the face of a Christian state that no longer had one.

On the other hand, Ivan welcomed criticism from powerless witnesses to Christian piety. In particular, he was said to tolerate holy fools—those ascetics who, instead of pursuing monastic reclusion, place themselves in the midst of society to provoke repentance. According to legend, one of these figures confronted Ivan one day by hurling a piece of horseflesh at him as a sign of the violence he was inflicting on the innocent. Instead of having the man arrested, Ivan was said to ask for his blessing and cheerfully send him on his way. It was a bad sign for Russia's paradisiacal culture that such outcasts were becoming the only witnesses to Christendom's transformational imperative.

The most famous of the holy fools by far was Basil the Blessed (d. 1557), a fact confirmed by the eventual dedication of the colorful and multitextured cathedral on Red Square to his memory. His ministry to the people of Moscow included smashing the windows of the rich and making prostrations before prostitutes. Bizarre actions like these were seen as prophetically living out Paul's teaching about folly (or feigned idiocy) for the sake of Christ. In a spiritually poetic way, each act was designed to provoke repentance and spiritual transformation in the Christians who observed it. On Great and Holy Friday, for instance, Basil was said to position himself at the entrance to the Kremlin's Dormition Cathedral, gnawing on a sausage and winking at people as they filed in for worship. His point seems to have been that though many might be fasting from food on the day Christ died for their sins, they were continuing unrepentantly to live in those sins.

Ivan certainly was. And because of those sins, the state over which he ruled was veering toward a precipice. Separated from Latin heretics in the West and Greek apostates to the south, Russia was not only divided from the rest of Christendom, her government was divided from its people. The oprichniky ravaged the land, killing thousands without resistance. As the

The Cathedral of Basil the Blessed in Red Square

late Nicholas Riasanovsky noted, the growing upheaval was a case of "civil massacre, not civil war."[36]

Ivan resembled Henry VIII in another way: he married and then brutalized a long succession of wives. He appears to have had a total of seven, outdoing his English contemporary by one. However, after the third wife, the clergy, following Orthodox canons, refused to recognize any more (a problem the supreme head of the Church of England never faced). Some wives were therefore illegitimate, and at least a couple may have been no more than legendary. The first, Anastasia, Ivan loved with great affection. But as we have seen, her sudden death unbalanced him and set him on the course of despotism. Among the other wives, some lasted only a matter of days before they were sent packing to a monastery or died mysteriously, probably from the effects of poison.

---

36 Nicholas V. Riasanovsky and Mark D. Steinberg, *A History of Russia* (New York: Oxford University Press, 2005), 142.

Despite this succession of consorts, Ivan—like Henry—failed to produce a healthy and long-lived male heir. This was largely his own fault. For a promising eldest son had been set to succeed him, but one day the tsar flew into one of his rages and beat the youth to death with his staff. After that, the Kremlin was empty of competent heirs.

Thus, when the Christian tyrant finally died, he left Russia divided and confused. His only heir was a half-wit named Fyodor (r. 1584–1589), whose greatest ambition was to call the faithful to worship by personally ringing the enormous bells of the Kremlin. After Fyodor's death, the long dynasty to which Vladimir himself had belonged became extinct. Lacking political leadership, Russia would soon be faced with a national catastrophe not seen since the Mongol invasions. It was a period known as the Time of Troubles.

The Division of Russian Christianity

BY THE TIME OF IVAN'S death, many Russians were becoming accustomed to thinking about their land as "Holy Russia" (*svyataya Rus*), a nation defined by her adherence to the Christian faith. The term was in fact first used in written form by one of Ivan's chief adversaries, a boyar by the name of Ivan Kurbsky. It gained currency in the century that followed, giving expression to the conviction that Russia, alone among the nations in her freedom from foreigners and her adherence to Orthodoxy, was a chosen people—or New Israel (another epithet enjoyed by her people)—destined to preserve Christendom in its most perfect form.

This made the national cataclysm known as the Time of Troubles particularly painful for Russians to endure. Its origins lie as much with foreign aggressions as domestic delusions. The Protestant Reformation had recently rent Western Christendom in half, pitting Roman Catholics in the south against Protestants in the north. In fact, the early territorial lines drawn by the schism in the West would not change much in the centuries ahead. To compensate, the papacy renewed its hopes of drawing the Orthodox to itself, whether through negotiation or force of arms.

The first approach guided the policies that led to the Union of Brest. Ever since the Mongol invasions of Russia, Orthodox Slavs to the west of Kiev had lived under the rule of Roman Catholic kings in Poland and Lithuania. Much of the intervening three centuries had seen the degradation of parish life. Orthodox bishops, frequently harried by the authorities, found it difficult to maintain good order in their dioceses. This made them, more than the peasantry, amenable to overtures from papal representatives who promised freedom of worship in exchange for submission to the papacy. In these negotiations the newly formed Society of Jesus played an important role. Though they had very little support from their flocks, a group of four bishops finally agreed to sign the treaty of union in 1596.

The treaty's terms were similar to those of the Union of Florence, with the exception that the filioque was now made optional in the East. Purgatory and papal supremacy were not. Leavened bread, as in the case of Florence, was allowed for those local churches accustomed to using it. In general, the agreement allowed the formerly Orthodox signatories freedom to continue Eastern Christian liturgical practices while demanding they adhere to Roman Catholic standards of doctrine and ecclesiology. This was acceptable to the papacy, as the treaty, without bloodshed or financial investment, had done what the crusades never could. The creation of the Uniate church, as Eastern-rite Roman Catholics now came to be known, effectively reversed at least part of the division precipitated by Cardinal Humbert in 1054. And it did so at a time when the heirs to the Papal Reformation were hemorrhaging profusely in the West.

Since the East Slavic lands in question were not part of the Muscovite state, the Union of Brest had little immediate impact on the Russians. The second approach to union pursued by Rome, however, did.

The extinction of the Rurik dynasty in the years following Ivan the Terrible's death—along with the rise of civil conflict, much of it a consequence of the oprichnina's depradations—greatly weakened the monarchy. In 1598 a boyar named Boris Godunov usurped the throne in the absence of any legitimate heir. He had ensured none would be found by ordering the murder of Ivan's youngest son, Dmitry. When Godunov died in 1605, no uncontested successor could be found.

A renegade Russian monk now appeared at the Polish court and, incredibly, claimed to be the deceased Dmitry. Known to historians as the First False Dmitry (for others would soon follow), the monk convinced King Sigismund III to place a small army under his leadership, and he would return to Russia at the head of it to claim the throne. The Roman Catholic ruler consented, especially after being counseled by Jesuits sent from Rome. Pope Paul V was eager to follow the success of Brest with an even more ambitious union, the wholesale conversion of Orthodox Russia.

False Dmitry proved an effective commander, and with the Russian state in disarray he soon captured Moscow. True to his word, he established a Polish court there and began to advance the interests of the Roman Catholic Church. The mother of the real Dmitry even made an appearance claiming him as her son.

But all of this proved too much for the Russians. In less than a year they overthrew the pretender. So disgusted were they at the aggression of Poland and Rome that they burned his body to ashes and sent them back to the West by firing them from a cannon. Two more False Dmitrys would appear in the years that followed, and the conflict with Roman Catholic Poland only intensified. Polish soldiers invaded Russia in 1606, besieging Holy Trinity Monastery and persecuting one of Moscow's first patriarchs, Germogen. King Sigismund's son Wladyslaw was proclaimed tsar, and Russia became in effect a puppet state of Poland. Jesuit advisors appeared from Rome and began discussing the path toward conversion.

But the Polish occupation did not extend much beyond the region of Moscow, and in 1613 a Russian army under Michael Romanov brought it to an end. The monarchy was restored under a new dynasty that would govern for three more centuries until the Revolution.

An event that led toward that catastrophe, and brought the age of division to a kind of culmination in Russia, was the Old Believer Schism. For centuries, Russians had been almost totally cut off from the broader population of the Orthodox Church. The fall of Constantinople had ensured this. Beyond that, the Union of Florence had caused deep estrangement from the leadership of doomed Byzantium. The superstitious belief that Russia represented the only and last bastion of piety in a world on the eve of the apocalypse had taken hold of many hearts during the century that followed. The Third Rome doctrine discussed above was the most remarkable expression of this.

With a conviction that Russian Orthodoxy possessed superiority over all other forms of Christianity—even the Orthodoxy of Greeks, Serbians, or Arabs—the Russian Church had little openness to traditional Christianity's transformational imperative. Though this is a metric of limited value, the fact that few Russians were canonized as saints during the century following Maxim the Greek is telling. The Russian Church, it seems, was becoming complacent.

In 1653, Patriarch Nikon of Moscow introduced reforms of the Orthodox Church in Russia. The goal was to align her more perfectly with the Orthodox Church beyond her borders, especially in Greece. The changes addressed largely secondary, non-doctrinal matters. They included the use of three rather than two fingers in making the sign of the cross and the spelling of the name Jesus. But the changes provoked a hornet's nest of resistance—especially from a group known as the Zealots of Piety, led by a priest named Avvakum.

Nikon had, it seems, been inspired by the example of the Papal Reformation in the Roman Catholic Church. This was a period when popes faced unprecedented challenges to their authority from Protestants, and the Council of Trent had only recently reasserted papal supremacy with majestic dignity. Nikon's exchanges with Tsar Alexey indicate that he too sought the subjugation of political authority to his office. He certainly sought the subjugation of the Russian Orthodox Church to it.

The scheme would prove, over centuries, to be a failure of catastrophic proportions on not only the religious but the political and social fronts. Avvakum soon led a movement of resistance to the reforms, embracing what his followers considered the honorable label of "Old Believers" (*starovertsy*). To Nikon and the broader Church, they were simply schismatics (*raskolniky*). But they were numerous, and as the state stepped in to enforce the reforms, they withdrew to Russia's limitless forests to live out the Christian faith in their own way. When the government sent soldiers to arrest them, they chose to fight rather than surrender to what they regarded as the church of the Antichrist. In some cases, when confronted by the state, they chose self-immolation over submission to an Orthodox Church that seemed to betray the native Russian faith.

By the end of the seventeenth century, many of Russia's most zealous Christians had chosen division over unity. The stage was set for the introduction of a new, secular vision of Russian Christendom.

Pagans, Witches, and Heretics

THE TIME OF TROUBLES HAD been a calamity for Russia, but it was mild in comparison to what was about to befall Western Christendom. The Protestant Reformation proved unstoppable, despite the vast coercive powers accumulated by the Roman Catholic Church during its five centuries of existence. In fact, the armies of Protestant Christendom would be more than a match for the inquisitors and crusaders sent against them from Rome.

Before the violence broke out in Europe, however, Roman Catholics were forcing their way into a New World discovered by Christopher Columbus in 1492. The discovery had been funded by the Spanish crown and was seen by many as a form of crusading. Soon Portugal was also involved, and it became necessary to obtain arbitration from Pope Alexander VI (r. 1492–1503) to delimit the territories each power was entitled to colonize. The division of the world along a longitudinal meridian running through modern Brazil was the result. With the lion's share of territories granted it, the Spanish crown led the way in colonizing America's pagan population. Conquistadors like Hernando Cortés (d. 1547) and Francisco Pizarro (d. 1541) respectively wiped out the civilizations of Mexico and Peru, opening the way for Franciscan and Dominican missionaries. Disease brought by the Europeans soon decimated the entire population, killing tens of millions. To maintain the profitability of their colonies, Europeans therefore resorted to the importation of slaves from Africa. While in recent centuries certain forms of slavery had been restricted by popes in their effort to speak the moral voice of

Christendom, Alexander's bull granting colonial territories to the Europeans opened the way to enslavement by mandating that "barbarous nations be overthrown and brought to the faith."

The riches extracted from the New World were considerable, and they helped Spain expand into a global power. But the costs to the native population were indescribable. And while many pagans sincerely converted to Christianity, so much suffering was visited on them in the exchange as to stagger even the least sensitive missionary. One who was particularly sensitive was a former colonist named Bartolomé de las Casas (d. 1566). After repenting of the evils to which he had contributed, he entered the Dominican order and dedicated the remainder of his life to defending Native Americans from European rapacity.

In 1550 Bartolomé found himself back in Valladolid, Spain, participating in a debate, almost unbelievably, about whether the violent colonization of the Indians was just or not. His opponent, a theologian named Sepúlveda, drew upon Augustinianism to argue that wars of conquest against Spain's helpless subjects were just because of the end they served, namely, Christianization. This was a return to the same argument that had been used to justify the crusades, and the argument's scholastic logic all but ignored the gospel of peace. The fact that the jurors of the debate—all of whom were professional theologians—required months to reach a decision, and that once they did it was inconclusive, indicates vividly how far Christendom had slipped from its vision of paradisiacal love and harmony. Nevertheless, Pope Paul III (r. 1534–1549) was impressed with the Dominican's zeal and subsequently revoked his predecessor's earlier provisions for enslavement. This, perhaps, was the first step toward a papacy of moral conscience that, freed

Bartolomé de las Casas

from baggage of Gregory VII, would produce modern luminaries like John Paul II.

Back in Europe, religious divisions were exacerbating fears of demonic interference in Christian society. Though belief in witches was relatively uncommon in earlier centuries, crusades against heretics and the introduction of the inquisition had greatly heightened such fears. It also established a precedent for dealing with them. Occasional trials and the execution of sorcerers were the result. But it was only at the height of the Protestant Reformation that a veritable "witch craze" overtook much of Western Christendom. (No such phenomenon occurred in the East.) Tens of thousands of people—both Roman Catholic and Protestant—were charged with holding communion with the devil and in many cases were executed. There was widespread support for the persecutions among both theologians and the unlettered. But there was also much skepticism, expressed especially by inquisitors, whose professional training in religious subversion seems to have inoculated them against this particular spiritual pathogen.

And in Spain, inquisitors had other perceived dangers to attend to in any case. There, the inquisition, an institution introduced by Pope Gregory IX during the thirteenth century, had been transferred to the crown when King Ferdinand (r. 1479–1516) and Queen Isabella (r. 1474–1504) obtained papal approval for a uniquely Iberian variant. The Spanish inquisition was initially dedicated to the prosecution of Muslim and Jewish recidivism. Under the direction of Grand Inquisitor Thomas of Torquemada (d. 1498), a Dominican friar of Jewish ancestry, it was preoccupied with cleansing Christendom of religious heterogeneity. The Spanish inquisition got to work in earnest after the Moors were ejected from Granada in 1492. That same year, the Jews themselves were formally expelled from Spain, and those who were allowed to remain on condition of submitting to obligatory baptism were carefully monitored—and punished when lapses occurred. It was under Torquemada's leadership that the infamous *auto-da-fe* was introduced, by which the condemned were forced to play out a ritual public penance prior to being burned at the stake. The macabre sacramental character of the spectacle was enhanced by the fact that it began formally with the celebration of the Eucharist. Within a century, the Spanish inquisition had grown into a bureaucracy so strong that "it provided," according to one historian, "nothing less than the first seeds of totalitarian government."[37]

Yet it must be remembered that the inquisition was a sign of how much Christendom had changed since the Great Division. Furthermore, in light of the post-totalitarian sensitivity of scholars today, it should be remembered that the death toll of the Spanish inquisition was modest. After two centuries of existence, it had placed fewer than 150,000 persons on trial, and of that figure fewer than ten percent had been executed. For a terror of scale, Christendom would have to await the coming of secularization.

"The Righteous Judgment of God"

IF NEITHER WITCH HUNTERS NOR inquisitors produced a death toll that was truly cataclysmic, the same cannot be said of armies. Historians are used to speaking in textbooks about "the wars of religion." However, the conflicts that erupted during the sixteenth and seventeenth centuries are more properly called the "wars of Western religion," for they only involved Roman Catholics and Protestants, both the products of the Great Division and quite distinct, as this book has shown, from the Church of the first millennium. No Orthodox Christian fought against other Christians for the faith. This is significant, because the religious wars' spectacle of hypocrisy would, in centuries to come, cause intelligent and morally concerned intellectuals great scandal. If such minds were more conscious of the Christian East— where missionary conquests, witch hunts, inquisitorial executions, and confessional wars were almost totally absent—the modern prejudice against a civilization with a supporting culture that directs its members toward the heavenly transformation of the world might indeed be less virulent.

The wars of Western religion began almost as soon as a viable alternative to Roman Catholicism appeared. We have already noted the German Peasants' War, which pitted the Protestant poor against the Protestant nobility. This was not a confessional conflict as such. Only in 1530, when Luther and

---

37 Toby Green, *Inquisition: The Reign of Fear* (New York: St. Martin's Press, 2007), 8.

his chief collaborator Philip Melanchthon issued the Augsburg Confession, was a formal statement defining a new Christian polity created. This was the formal beginning of Lutheranism.

While Emperor Charles V had initially been reluctant to use force against Luther and other Protestants, the formation of an alliance of German princes called the Schmalkaldic League, which adopted the Augsburg Confession, compelled him finally to act. The Schmalkaldic Wars followed. They concluded in 1555 with the Peace of Augsburg, by which princes of any given territory within the Holy Roman Empire were awarded the power to determine the religion of their realm. The formula for this was "his region, his religion" (*cuius regio, eius religio*). In other words, after the first large-scale war between Protestants and Roman Catholics, nothing had been resolved except a return to the *status quo ante*. Equally futile but far greater conflicts were yet to come.

As we enter this, the final phase in the age of division, we might pause to consider a striking though somewhat fanciful portent. In 1631, Mount Vesuvius suddenly erupted. The volcano had a long history of activity dating back to the first century, when it totally destroyed the pagan city of Pompeii. But the seventeenth-century event, occurring during the course of the religious wars, can serve as a metaphor for them. The topography of Western Christendom had by now became so volatile that it can be likened to the great stratovolcano in Italy. Its cone had been forced to higher and higher elevations by the accumulated layers of reform and counter-reform. It was, as volcanologists like to say, ready to blow.

Five centuries of internal pressures had never really been resolved. They had been building ever since Pope Leo IX led the first papal army to war against the Normans at Civitate in 1053. Since that time, institutional reform for the better—the bastard child of the transformational imperative—had been ravaging Christendom's paradisiacal culture. Sincere as they were, these acts only had the cumulative effect of increasing the mountain's internal pressures. The Schmalkaldic Wars were but a whiff of steam and ash that briefly topped its summit, signaling ominously that time had finally run out.

The eruption was terrible. After the brief silence that followed the Peace of Augsburg, fissures exploded throughout Western Christendom. Like secondary vents on the side of a volcano, they were spectacular in their release of energy. But as destructive as they were, they were only triggers for the truly vesuvian Thirty Years' War.

One of the secondary vents was France. There, in 1562, war broke out between Roman Catholics and native Calvinists known as the Huguenots. The war's most atrocious single event occurred in 1572 with the Saint Bartholomew's Day Massacre. On the feast of the holy apostle, the queen mother Catherine of Medici arranged the murder of thousands of defenseless Huguenots in Paris and other towns. Only with the conversion to Roman Catholicism of Henry of Navarre (who cynically grumbled that "Paris is worth a Mass") did the violence finally subside. The Edict of Nantes that formally ended the conflict in 1598 did little more than recognize an irreconcilable religious division, granting grudging toleration to the Huguenots. A stunning three million people had been killed by the violence, but the pressures of division had scarcely been reduced.

Indeed, they had already burst out in another secondary vent located in Holland. The Dutch Revolt began in 1568 with the suppression of Protestantism by the Spanish Duke of Alba, who executed thousands and sparked a popular rebellion that simmered for the next eight decades. The death toll in this outburst was more than half a million. And the mountain's destabilization continued.

In 1642, English Protestants known as Puritans launched the English Civil War. It was a reaction by Calvinists against the high-church tendencies of Archbishop Laud of Canterbury, who had deviated from a *via media* charted by Queen Elizabeth (r. 1558–1603) in which the divisive pressures of Protestantism and Roman Catholicism were kept in temporary containment. The Puritans, quite literally, wanted violently to "purify" the Church of England of virtually all remnants of traditional Christianity. When Charles I (r. 1625–1649) signaled a return to tradition, Parliament, largely in the hands of Protestant beneficiaries of Henry VIII, launched a civil war. Led by the Calvinist zealot Oliver Cromwell (d. 1658), the Puritans prevailed and executed Charles, creating a Christian Commonwealth.

In some ways, it was at this moment that Western Christianity, in the form of Calvinism, finally ran its course as the basis for a Christian civilization. Its demand for reform for the better, measured institutionally since the Papal Reformation, had now morphed into a secular ideology in which the gospel was almost secondary. As the political scientist Michael Walzer has argued when discussing the Puritans during the Civil War,

Oliver Cromwell

The power of an ideology . . . lies in its capacity to activate its adherents and to change the world. Its content is necessarily a description of contemporary experience as unacceptable and unnecessary and a rejection of any merely personal transcendence or salvation. Its practical effect is to generate organization and cooperative activity. Calvinist ideology can be briefly summarized in these terms.[38]

So might the Roman Catholicism of Pope Gregory VII five centuries earlier. The only difference was the fall of paradise that had resulted. For whereas eleventh-century reformers were still influenced by the anthropological optimism and cosmological reverence of traditional Christianity, the seventeenth-century ones, as we have seen, were not. "The permanent, inescapable estrangement of man from God," Walzer reminds us, "is the starting point of Calvin's politics."[39]

---

38 Michael Walzer, *The Revolution of the Saints: A Study of the Origins of Radical Politics* (New York: Atheneum, 1970), 27.

39 Ibid.

A new reign of religious terror descended on England with the ascendancy of the Puritans. After being named Lord Protector in 1653, Cromwell reorganized England into a series of military districts. The Church of England was subjected to a new reformation, often by force and with oppressive results. Liturgy was despoiled and Calvinist preaching enforced. The annual celebration of the Incarnation at Christmas was outlawed, but Sunday was upheld as an obligatory day of rest. Moral legislation proliferated. It threatened not only to land adulterers and blasphemers in jail but to punish those who failed to show up for church.

And while violence simmered in England and Scotland, in Ireland it exploded. The long-term cause was Irish weariness of English domination. The short-term cause was the Puritans' hatred of Roman Catholicism.

England's island neighbor, as we saw in chapter three, had been conquered by Henry II with papal approval. The forced union was a bitter one for the Irish. Centuries earlier they had filled England and Scotland with the paradisiacal culture of Celtic monasticism. The English Church had assented to Roman leadership at an early stage, and after the Norman displacement of Saxon clergy her episcopate had been an advocate of the Papal Reformation. Ireland had as a result been firmly placed under the papacy. It is ironic, then, that when England revolted against papal authority it was now the Irish who were targeted as "papists." Parliament was dominated by Puritan radicals who viewed Ireland's continued loyalty to Rome as sign of barbarity and superstition.

Fresh from the execution of his former king, Cromwell led an expeditionary army across the Irish Sea to suppress uprisings throughout Ireland. As with the recent Civil War, he was possessed by a certainty that he was exacting divine vengeance on the enemies of God. His letters from the time exude the Old Testament's pre-incarnational imagery of righteous warfare. One of his first actions was the siege of Drogheda late in 1649. When the town's defenders realized they had no chance against Cromwell's army, they offered their surrender. The Puritan warlord, however, refused to accept it. Instead, he ordered his soldiers to burn Drogheda to the ground, giving no quarter to the men, women, and children it contained. After details of the massacre were reported back to him, Cromwell hailed the massacre as "the righteous judgment of God." In all, the English Civil War and its Cromwellian outcome cost about five hundred thousand lives, most of them Irish.

But the French, Dutch, and English wars of religion were only secondary vents for the groaning hatred that was welling up within the volcano of Western Christendom. The main eruption occurred in Germany. In 1618, a group of Protestant soldiers threw a pair of Roman Catholic agents of the Holy Roman Emperor out of a castle window in Prague. This act was known thereafter as the "defenestration of Prague." It ignited the Thirty Years' War, a conflict so calamitous that were it not for the world wars of the twentieth century it might have been the worst in the history of Christendom. It too was a Great War.

As with the wars that preceded it, the battle lines were drawn, with one exception, between Roman Catholics and Protestants. The former were limited to the Holy Roman Empire and Spain; while Protestant combatants included Bohemians, Saxons, Prussians, the Dutch, English, Scots, and, famously, the Swedes under the command of King Gustavus Adolphus (r. 1611–1632). During pitched battles the Swedes employed, for the first significant time in history, the power of the musket. Volley fire, by which lines of musketeers coordinated loading and firing in a never-ending hail of lead, reduced entire armies—foot soldiers, archers, and mounted knights—to a pile of corpses. The history of warfare in which battles were decided by hand-to-hand combat and sheer muscular strength was now over.

Nearly every state in Western Christendom participated in the war. But one initially remained aloof. France, firmly Roman Catholic, would have been expected to leap in on the side of the Empire and Spain. But the age of division had taken its toll. King Louis XIII (r. 1610–1643) had different priorities. Guided by his chief minister Cardinal Richelieu (d. 1642), he adhered to a policy of "state logic" (*raison d'etat*) by which political interests took precedence over spiritual ones. As a result, the heir to the zealous crusader Saint Louis ordered his armies to attack the defenders of the papacy. French national interests had turned in a decidedly secular direction.

The Thirty Years' War marked the near total dereliction of Western

Christendom. No previous event, no abomination of desolation, had so tarnished its history as the spectacle of Christians murdering each other in the name of the God of love. The war ended with the Peace of Westphalia (1648), in which the same principle of "his region, his religion" was renewed (though this time Calvinists were included). But by this time, some ten million corpses littered its volcanic crater. In Germany, where most of the battlefields lay, up to half the population had been killed. Not the intrigues of the Byzantine court; not the crusades; not the bloodletting of Ivan the Terrible; not the execution of heretics by the inquisition—no evil done in the name of Christ during the course of a millennium and a half had ever done so much to discredit Christendom as this meaningless bloodbath. A civilization with a supporting culture that directs its members toward the heavenly transformation of the world no longer existed. Paradise had fallen.

Among the countless images kept alive in the West by those who survived the Thirty Years' War was that of Magdeburg, a town on the Elbe River in central Germany. In 1631—the year Vesuvius erupted—Roman Catholic armies besieged Magdeburg, and when it finally fell they subjected it to unspeakable cruelty. Of its twenty-five thousand Protestant inhabitants, only a few hundred survived. As churches burned to the ground, the Christian conquerors pillaged and raped for days. In one episode a group of women was said to have been cornered by soldiers at the top of a castle overlooking the river, and rather than fall into the hands of their assailants, they decided in desperation to leap over the palisades to their deaths. Theirs were some of the thousands of bloated bodies that clogged the Elbe for weeks thereafter. The infamous rape of Magdeburg, as this microcosm of the war came to be known, was never forgotten. And the town itself never really recovered.

But more importantly, Christendom never recovered. The wars of Western religion had taken something from it that could never be restored. Though memories of the war's victims were soon forgotten, the memory of its hypocrisy could not be.

Voltaire the deist could not forget. Writing a century later, he used the spectacle of Christian violence in the Thirty Years' War as the context for

The rape of Magdeburg

the conversion of his hero Candide to deism. Bertolt Brecht the atheist could not forget. Writing in the twentieth century, he used the sack of Magdeburg as the context for *Mother Courage,* in which the superiority of Marxism over Christianity is asserted. Nietzsche the nihilist could not forget. He dated the degeneration of Western morals to the era of confessional warfare.

But the fall of paradise was expressed with even more poignant nihilism in popular culture. In a film set during the Thirty Years' War called *The Last Valley* (1971), the character of a war-weary captain, played by Michael Caine, is asked about the God for whom all the West is currently fighting. "Don't talk to me of God," he responds. "We killed God at Magdeburg."

As he surveyed the carnage of Drogheda, Oliver Cromwell had spoken of "the righteous judgment of God." The moral basis for such a statement was mournfully defective, and his words were an abomination. But like Caiaphas among the Sanhedrin, he may have unintentionally uttered a word of truth. For the new Christendom he so well represented, it would seem, now stood irrevocably judged by God.

EPILOGUE

Toward Utopian Horizons

T HE PROTESTANT REFORMATION—OR, AS I have argued, counter-reformation—marked a turning point in the rise and fall of what the West once was. Prior to it the new Christendom, formed in the aftermath of the Great Division, had been struggling heroically but with increasing desperation to fulfill its ancient imperative toward the paradisiacal transformation of the world. After the Reformation, the transformational imperative was recalibrated, as it were, toward a very different goal. Instead of paradise, Western Christendom set its course for utopian horizons.

Historians are agreed on the importance of the Protestant Reformation in the making of the modern world. Not all see it in the same light, however.

Protestants have long considered its effects beneficial, for obvious reasons. The prevailing narrative for them is of a church (defined by individual faith rather than sacramental unity) rescued from the darkness of clericalism and ignorance. But they are joined in their interpretation by a great number of secular historians, who see in the same pattern of enlightenment a decisive move toward rationalism. Indeed, the atheist Max Weber traced the rise of a scientific understanding of the cosmos to Calvinism. In part, he based his famous thesis about the modern "disenchantment of the world" on the French reformer's repudiation of heavenly immanence.[1]

Roman Catholic historians have naturally been more circumspect about the benefits of the Protestant Reformation. Acknowledging many of the problems that led to it, they point to the loss of religious unity that resulted. For them the cure was more harmful than the illness. Echoing secular historians, some have also attributed the decline of a Christian culture in modern times to Protestantism. According to Brad Gregory, for instance, the movement's "unintended consequences" include postmodernism's totally subjective and mutually exclusive beliefs and values—something he aptly calls "the Kingdom of Whatever." For him, "the Reformation is the most important distant historical source for contemporary Western hyperpluralism with respect to the truth claims about meaning, morality, values, priorities, and purpose."[2]

As insightful as these interpretations of the Protestant Reformation are, however, they fail on one very significant point. They all view it largely as an event in itself, a sudden and unprecedented reaction to contemporary historical circumstances. In fact, the Protestant Reformation was, as its name suggests, part of a much longer process that began with the Papal Reformation five centuries earlier. It was the culminating event—and consummation—of an age that began with division and ended with it as well.

Seeing it this way requires a perspective different from that of most modern historians. It requires a knowledge and appreciation of the old Christendom, to which the West became increasingly blind after the Great Division. A fuller understanding of the Protestant Reformation's place in history therefore benefits from insights offered by the Orthodox Church.

The most important of these insights is that Western Christendom proved incapable of preserving the paradisiacal culture that had sustained it during the first millennium. Instead of pursuing heavenly transformation, the West became preoccupied with the institutional project of reform for the better.

---

1   Weber's sociological research also led him to Calvinism in discerning the origins of industrialization, a topic he addressed in his famous book *The Protestant Ethic and the Spirit of Capitalism.*

2   Brad S. Gregory, *The Unintended Reformation: How a Religious Revolution Secularized Society* (Cambridge, MA: Harvard University Press, 2012), 369.

The East had no share in the reformation projects of popes or Protestants and passed through the age of division with its paradisiacal culture intact. True, Byzantium fell to the Muslim Turks in 1453, and its culture was thereafter forced underground. But this disruption was the result of external forces and had little to do with Orthodoxy. In the case of Russia, the old Christendom continued to flourish until national isolation (a development not unrelated to the trauma of Constantinople's fall) made the Muscovite state appear as the solitary bearer of the true faith. Once this happened, Tsar Ivan the Terrible could harbor the delusion that acts of terror were a legitimate part of pious statecraft. A century later, the Old Believers could rush into schism with a similar conviction that paradise and Holy Russia were one. At the end of the seventeenth century, the East had not been deprived of a paradisiacal culture. If anything, it had become supersaturated with it.

Not so the West. More than five centuries had elapsed since the Great Division, and in that time first the Papal Reformation and then accretions resulting from it had gradually choked off the cultural streams that once watered Western Christendom. Desiccated and withered, paradise finally fell amid the vesuvian destruction of religious warfare.

But Christendom was more than a *culture* shaped by paradisiacal beliefs and values. It was also a *civilization* with institutions of governance, social organization, and art.[3] This civilization survived the age of division and, for a long time afterward, even remained Christian. It consisted of things like divinely established monarchy; liturgically initiated, heterosexual, monogamous, lifelong marriage; and the use of painting, music, and architecture to enhance worship. Above all, this civilization was founded on the glorious legacy of Christian anthropology: that the human being, male or female, is a creature with innate dignity made in the image and likeness of God.

---

3   Without making too fine a point of it, I distinguish conceptually between culture and civilization. The first, sometimes likened to the soul, animates the latter by providing it with beliefs and values. Civilization, on the other hand, can be likened to a body that possesses individual parts or institutions that mark its individuality. For a summary of the relationship between culture and civilization using Oswald Spengler's model, see the introduction to *Age of Paradise*, 15–18.

Nevertheless, beneath the civilization of the new Christendom appeared new beliefs and values very different from those nourishing the old Christendom. Together they can be called secular humanism, and with time they supplanted traditional Christianity. The result was a new culture, that of utopia.

The word *utopia*, as I noted in the introduction to *The Age of Paradise*, was coined precisely during the Protestant Reformation. It was intended by Thomas More, who wrote a book by that title, to denote a civilization in which the heavenly vision of traditional Christianity was actually realized in this world. His use of the word was intentionally ironic, for in Greek *utopia* literally means "nowhere." More's work expressed the author's indignation about the failure, as he perceived it, of Western Christendom's transformational imperative. The irony was amplified by the fact that More was sent to his death for refusing to recognize the right of Henry VIII to rule the Church of England. What was most ironic about the origins of utopia was the fact that it became, in the hands of More's humanist successors, a concept of civilization in which secular values replaced the heavenly ones for which More was martyred.

But as a model of civilization, utopia was closely related to paradise. There is no way to understand its appearance outside of this cultural context. The idea of utopia sprang from the frustrations of seeking the kingdom of heaven in a civilization oriented toward heaven but tragically denying the experience thereof. Utopia did not replace Christendom's paradisiacal culture. It distorted it.

During the half-millennium considered in this book, we have traced the manifold ways in which the original culture of the West was systematically stifled by forces such as clericalism, penitential pessimism, and the rejection of Christ's sacramental presence. During the age of division, the doctrinal integrity of traditional Christianity was progressively subverted, leading to innovations that included papal supremacy, purgatory, and the total depravity of man. These innovations, while appearing historically necessary and even "traditional" to their advocates, undermined the experiences that lay at the heart of a paradisiacal culture. As we have seen, they attenuated divine participation and heavenly immanence.

As a result, Christendom's transformational imperative underwent a painful but inevitable recalibration. By the end of the period in question, the former orientation toward the kingdom of heaven was in disarray. The West, from the point of view of the old Christendom, had become *disoriented*. It was becoming a civilization with a supporting culture that directed its members toward the *secular* transformation of the world.

By the time Martin Luther nailed his *Ninety-Five Theses* to the church door of Wittenberg, the process of cultural recalibration had been underway for some time. It began among the intellectual leadership least inclined toward the cerebral quarrels of scholasticism. Italians, far from the universities of the north, were the first to lead the way.

The result is commonly called the Renaissance, and it represented a sea change in the history of Western beliefs and values. To explain it, the assertion is often made that during the fourteenth century Italian intellectuals rediscovered the culture of ancient pagandom, and, falling in love with it, began to replace Christianity with it. The term *renaissance* means "rebirth." After its initial use in the sixteenth century by Giorgio Vasari, the term was widely adopted in the nineteenth by a sympathetic secular professorate eager to distance itself from the religious past.[4] To support this narrative of rebirth, modern scholarship required the invention of a "medieval" interval between classical antiquity and the secular present, a period during which men under the spell of traditional Christianity were assumed to have had little knowledge of or interest in the worldly values of ancient art and literature.

I might pause to note here that nowhere in the pages of this book have variants of the term "medieval" been used—a detail over which readers familiar with conventional Western historiography may have puzzled. This term—indispensable as it may seem in our prevailing narrative about the origins of modernity—is of doubtful historiographical value. In fact, it does

---

4   Vasari's use of the term appears in his *Lives of the Artists* (1550). In the nineteenth century, the view that modernity arose because of a Renaissance breakthrough was most authoritatively established by Jacob Burckhardt's *The Civilization of the Renaissance in Italy* (1860).

little more than perpetuate ignorance about the history of Christendom and the role of Orthodoxy in shaping it.

For it is a fact that there was never a time when the achievements of pagan antiquity were unknown in Eastern Christendom. The Greek fathers read and were familiar with Homer, Sophocles, and Plato. But such authors were of extremely limited interest to them. Compared to the beauty of paradise—whether experienced through hesychastic prayer of the heart, liturgical anagogy, or "joy-making mourning"—pagan literature simply wasn't that attractive.

Nor was it in the West, until the age of division. Only in the fourteenth century did pagan culture begin to attract the hearts and minds of intellectuals there. And it did so not because the culture of Christendom "lost out" to the more optimistic worldliness of pagandom. Pagan culture gained in popularity because the West had drifted away from the culture of the old Christendom, and because Western intellectuals were exhausted by the pessimistic culture of the new Christendom. It was precisely at this time, when Barlaam suffered discomfiture in Constantinople, that the paradisiacal culture of the old Christendom was beginning to falter.

Highly sensitive writers such as Petrarch, who studied under Barlaam, simply could not square the exalted values of paradise with the increasingly stavrocentric piety that surrounded them. So they began to look beyond Christendom for a way of sustaining their civilization's irrepressible transformational imperative. Though they might have turned to the old Christendom of the East, prejudice against it had become too great since the time of Cardinal Humbert. Barlaam's experience in Constantinople was, as we saw, not only a repetition but a reinforcement of 1054. Instead, these writers turned for answers to pagandom.

Terms like "medieval" and "renaissance," therefore, not only obscure the broader history of Christendom in the East; they perpetuate confusion about the real origins of modernity. The disintegration and fall of a paradisiacal culture in the aftermath of the Great Division—and not a spontaneous rediscovery of classical pagandom some thirteen centuries after Pentecost—is what best explains the first step toward the secularization of the West.

A second important step toward modernity occurred in France during what is often called the Enlightenment. This period might more properly be considered, with a nod to the old Christendom, the "benightenment." For what had once been the true light of the world—the gospel of Jesus Christ—became for the secular humanists of the eighteenth century nothing more than ignorance, superstition, and hypocrisy. But these so-called *philosophes* were not above using a Christian vocabulary, even if they audaciously transposed its imagery of light. Enlightenment for them came from natural science and rationalistic philosophy, not the incarnate God and His apostles. The French philosophes harnessed secular humanism even more effectively than their Italian predecessors, using it to fill the sails of a West carried ever closer to the coasts of utopia.

But such a quest required spiritual provisions, and having now jettisoned Christianity (something their Italian predecessors could not have brought themselves to do) the philosophes were compelled to invent an alternative religion, known as deism. Deism is a belief that a deity exists but has no salvific relationship with the world. Having created everything that exists, the deity has abandoned the world, leaving it solely in the hands of men. Miracles, which defy the empirical certainties of nature, are only illusions.

This was a liberating faith (and it was a faith, in that none of its claims could be "proven"). It empowered those who held it—the new Christendom's privileged and educated elite—to assume ever greater control of the world around them. Among those to embrace it was the American statesman Thomas Jefferson. He rewrote the life of Jesus to separate, as "diamonds from the dunghill," only those moral teachings of the gospel that conformed to his secular definition of reason. The Incarnation and all other miracles were systematically dismissed.[5]

Deism was, in the absence of a compelling experience of paradise, a way of restoring to the West an optimistic view of man and an affirmative view of the cosmos in which he lived. In this sense it filled a void left in the wake

---

5   The work was never published due to its radically anti-Christian character. But it was distributed to friends and eventually became known as the Jefferson Bible.

of the age of division. Being born within about a half-century of the Treaty of Westphalia, philosophes like Voltaire considered the wars of Western religion as only the most recent example of moral bankruptcy in a civilization with a supporting culture that directed its members toward the heavenly transformation of the world. In their view, the world was in need of transformation, but not on the heavenly terms offered by traditional Christianity. It needed a savior, but in the form of man and not the God-Man. Voltaire concluded his novel *Candide* with the protagonist, having abandoned hope in a God who seeks communion with man in the world, calling on those around him to take sole responsibility for the world, and by doing so to "cultivate our garden."

Deism would eventually fade from Western culture, being superseded after the French Revolution by first romanticism and then atheism. These later expressions of utopian culture produced additional projects directed toward the secular transformation of the world. They would find their most ambitious and uncompromising expression in the Russian Revolution of the twentieth century.

But by then the age of utopia was reaching its end. Fired by indignation, secular humanism had become more than a light to the new Christendom, dispelling its bleak cosmology. It was becoming a noxious fire, consuming the very civilization that had given birth to it. Friedrich Nietzsche had already attacked rationalism and progress as illusions. The First World War seemed to confirm such newfound pessimism. The primacy of nationalist hegemony, the manipulation of knowledge, and the mass production of new weapons such as the machine gun and poison gas all marked the beginning of an age of nihilism.

Christendom had become post-Christian. And in doing so, it forfeited the cosmological and anthropological legacy of paradise. The world had ceased to be a means of communion with God, beautified by heavenly immanence. It had become nothing more than a means of satisfying earthly needs. Man himself, once dignified as *imago dei* (the "image of God"), was no longer a "partaker of the divine nature." He was now reduced to the status of an animal species designated in zoological terms as *homo sapiens*.

In Russia, which had joined the new Christendom through the western-izing policies of Peter the Great, the Communists were the first to act ideo-logically on such nihilistic convictions. Under Stalin, they destroyed human lives by the millions in the name of socialism. The Nazis were quick to follow suit. Under Hitler, they destroyed human lives by the millions in the name of nationalism. And even in the more "humane" post-Christian Christen-dom that emerged after the Second World War—the deadliest war in his-tory—liberal democracy has destroyed and continues to destroy unborn human lives by the millions in the name of individualism.

Alexander Schmemann once called secularism the "stepchild" of Christi-anity.[6] By way of conclusion, we might reflect on this insight and embellish it a bit. Secular humanism was indeed not the *natural* offspring of a faith in the Incarnation. How could it be? For we have seen in this book how tradi-tional Christianity redeemed the world by filling it with paradise, not by abandoning it to utopia. But in the divided household of the new Christen-dom, secularism was given a home. There it was nurtured, and there it came of age. And when the age of division had finally run its course and paradise, like an ancient family estate, lay in ruins, the jealous stepchild emerged from obscurity to claim Christendom's inheritance as its own.

The stage was set for the tragedy of secularization.

---

6   Alexander Schmemann, *For the Life of the World* (Crestwood, NY: St. Vladimir's
     Seminary Press, 1973), 127.

Index

Illustrations indicated by page numbers in italics

A

Abbo of Fleury, 41
Abelard, Peter, 154–55, 189, 236
Acre, 96, 97
Agilbert (bishop), 196
Agnes (Holy Roman empress), 42, 67, 87
Albert Magnus, 155
Albigensian (Cathar) Crusade, 97–98, 147
Albrecht of Mainz, 287–88
Alcuin of York, 49, 92n27, 151, 216
Alexander Nevsky, 113
Alexander of Hales, 283–84
Alexander II (pope), 85, 87, 93
Alexander III (pope), 123
Alexander VI (pope), 323
Alexios Komnenos (Byzantine emperor), 94, 96
Alexios III (Byzantine emperor), 103
Alexios IV Angelos (Byzantine emperor), 103–4
Alexios V (Byzantine emperor), 104
Al-Hakim (Fatimid caliph), 72
al-Kamil, Malik (Ayyubid sultan), 132, 135
Alleumes of Clari, 104–5
All Souls Day, 283–84
Alp Arslan (Seljuk sultan), 71–72, 73, 75–76, 77, 79
Amalar of Metz, 177, 179, 180
Ambrose of Milan, 49, 98, 130
Americas, 323–24
Anabaptism, 292–93
Andrey Bogolyubsky, 108–10
Andrey Rublev, 263
Anonymous of York, 124–25
Anselm of Canterbury, 152–53, 153, 154, 199–200, 201, 235, 245–46, 277
Anselm of Havelberg, 127
Anselm of Lucca, 93
Anthony of Kiev, 142

Anthony the Great, 140
anthropology, Christian, 17–18, 337, 342
Antioch, 96, 97, 99–100
apocalypticism, 225–26, 259, 291–93
apophaticism, 159
Arabs, 70–71, 243
architecture
    Gothic, 186–94
    Romanesque, 184, 185–86, 189
Aries, Philippe, 197
Aristotle, 93, 153–54, 155, 164, 234
Arius, 98
Armenia, 48, 73
Arnauld Aimery, 97–98, 147
art, modern, 212–13, 302. *See also* iconography
art of dying, 248
Ash Wednesday, 219
Athanasios of Athos, 141
Athanasius of Alexandria, 26, 119, 199, 201
atheism, 342
Augsburg Confession, 326–27
Augustine of Hippo
    The City of God, 36–38, 86, 119, 296
    dualism of, 37–38, 119
    on Eucharist, 49
    on faith and reason, 152
    on just war, 93
    on paradisiacal nature of the Church, 223
    on penance, 213n47
    portrait, 37
    on purgatorial punishments, 279
    on reformation, 38–39
    theological context of, 151
    vs. total depravity, 295–96
    Western Christendom and, 17, 39–40
Augustinianism
    adoption by Franks, 18, 119–20

clerical celibacy and, 84
cosmology of, 85–86
Gothic architecture and, 189
pessimism of, 17
Protestants and, 291, 293–94, 298
scholasticism and, 152
on theology, 155–56
Thomas a Kempis and, 252–53
Avignon papacy, 229, 229–31
Avvakum (Old Believer), 322

B

Baldwin (Latin emperor), 136–37
Baldwin, John, 153, 236
Barlaam of Calabria, 158–59, 162, 163–64,
    165, 166, 167–68, 340
Basil the Blessed, 317
Basil the Great, 17, 73, 119, 140, 236, 236n65
Basil II (Byzantine emperor), 25, 73, 74
beguines, 240, 251
Beihammer, Alexander, 72
Bellitto, Christopher, 144
Belting, Hans, 183, 303
Benedict of Aniane, 31
Benedict of Nursia, 140, 172
Benedict VIII (pope), 28, 29, 101
Benedict X (antipope), 67–68, 69
Berengar, 153, 235, 304
Bernard of Clairvaux
    against Cluny, 145, 150
    critique of papal court, 123
    crusades, recruitment for, 148
    iconoclasm of, 188–89, 190
    Knights Templar and, 148–49
    legacy of, 251, 252, 265
    portrait, 145
    against scholastic rationalism, 155,
    235–36
    stavrocentric piety of, 200–201
Bessarion of Nicaea, 269, 270n93, 271
Black Death, 243, 243, 244, 249, 278
Boersma, Hans, 120–21
Bohemia, 258–59
Bonaventure, 155–56
Boniface VIII (pope), 137, 138, 138–39,
    226–27, 228, 229, 283, 283n10

Boris and Gleb (passionbearers), 22, 108,
    110, 113, 203
Bouwsma, William, 296
Brecht, Bertolt, 333
Brethren and Sisters of the Common Life,
    252
Britain, see England
Burckhardt, Jacob, 339n4
Byzantine Empire
    Christianization of, 25–26
    conquest by Ottomans, 267–68, 271–74
    defeat by Seljuks, 73–77
    defense against Arabs, 71
    First Crusade and, 95–96
    Italian peninsula and, 9–10, 69–70
    reunion attempts with West and, 90–91,
    94, 127–28, 235, 268–71, 280
    See also Constantinople; Eastern
    Christendom

C

Cabasilas, Nicholas, 80, 80n17, 180, 268
    The Life in Christ, 254–56
Cabié, Robert, 179
Cadaver Synod (897), 28
cadaver tombs, 249
Caesarea (Cappadocia), 73
caesaropapism, 62–63
Calixtus II (pope), 144
Calvin, John (Calvinism)
    on Eucharist, 299, 303, 304
    iconoclasm of, 298–300, 301
    as ideology, 329
    portrait, 296
    Reformed church, development of, 305
    on total depravity, 295, 296–97
    Weber on, 335–36, 336n1
canon law, 64–66, 124, 137, 217
Canute of England (king), 27
Carolingian Empire, 18, 26, 27–28, 31, 117.
    See also Franks
Carroll, Warren, 131
Casas, Bartolome de las, 324, 324
Cassiani, 195–96
Cathar (Albigensian) Crusade, 97–98, 147
Catherine of Genoa, 282

Celestine V (pope), 224–25, 226
celibacy, clerical, 13–14, 81–85, 100, 289
Celtic Christianity, 69, 125, 129, 215–16, 330
Cemetery of the Innocents (Paris), 249
Charlemagne (Holy Roman emperor), 31,
    62, 92n27, 184
Charles of Anjou, 136–37
Charles I (English king), 328–29
Charles V (Holy Roman emperor), 327
Chartres Cathedral, 191, *192*
Christendom
    as civilization, 337
    division within, 17–18, 51, 59
    in first millennium, 19–21
    Great Schism, 51–58
    reunion attempts, 90–91, 94, 127–28,
        235, 268–71, 280, 319–20
    See also Eastern Christendom; papacy;
        Protestant Reformation; Russia; West-
        ern Christendom
Christmas, 202, 330
Christ the Sufferer (*Christus patiens*),
    208–11, 210n46, *211*
Christ the Victor (*Christus victor*), 205–8,
    207, 209
church, vs. state, 122
churches
    Gothic architecture, 186–94
    iconostasis, 183–84
    orientation of, 33, 186
    role in worship, 176, 181
    Romanesque architecture, 184, 185–86,
        189
Church of the Holy Sepulcher (Anastasis),
    72, 95, 196
Cistercians, 144–46, 188
civilization, 337–38, 337n3
Clement V (pope), 126, 229–30
Clement VI (pope), 230–31
Clement VII (antipope), 231, 232
clerical celibacy, 13–14, 81–85, 100, 289
clericalism
    clerical celibacy and, 121
    development of, 79–80
    diminished role for laity, 80–81, 121–22,
        168, 169, 174

Divine Liturgy as safeguard against,
    169–71
    in East, 169
    iconostasis and, 184
    liturgical language and, 173–74
    penance and, 216–17
    privatization of Mass and, 172–73
    unleavened bread for Eucharist and,
        171–72
    in West, 168–69
Cluny (monastery)
    Cistercians against, 144–45, 188
    Cluny III church, 94, *185*, 185–86,
        186n23
    Henry III and, 42
    influence of, 80, 92
    liturgical development at, 33, 143–44
    monastic reform by, 30–31, 32
Collection in Seventy-Four Titles, 64–65
college of cardinals, 69, 92, 123, 230
colonialism, ecclesiastical, 99–100, 106
Columbanus, 216
Columbus, Christopher, 323
Communion, *see* Eucharist
communism, 343
conciliarism, 233–35, 240, 270
conciliarity (synodality), 18, 227–28, 232–33
confession, 214, 216, 217
Congar, Yves, 120
Conrad of Gelnhausen, 234
Constantine Monomachos (Byzantine
    emperor), 48, 51, 56, 169
Constantine the Great (Byzantine emperor),
    19, 60, 61
Constantine XI (Byzantine emperor),
    272–73
Constantinople
    fall of, 272–74, *273*
    Fourth Crusade and, 103–6, *107*
    Hagia Sophia, *21*, 21–22, 105, 176, 182,
        273–74
    papal attempts to control, 137
    unrest against Venetians, 102–3
    See also Byzantine Empire; Eastern
        Christendom
Corpus Christi, feast of, 175

cosmology
    Augustinian, 36–38, 39–40, 85–86
    division within, 17–18
    Islamic, 71
    laity within, 80–81
    nominalism and, 239
    politics and, 62–63
Council of Clermont (1095), 94
Council of Constance (1414–1418), 232–33, 258, 290
Council of Florence (1439), 235, 268–71, 280, 312, 321
Council of Pisa (1409), 232
Council of Rheims (1049), 45
Council of Trullo (692), 13–14, 81
Council of Vienne (1312), 251
Council of Worms (1122), 128
counter-reformation
    heretical approaches, 250–51
    Hus, 256–58, 258, 258n87
    Hussite Wars, 258–59
    modern devotion (*devotio moderna*), 252–54
    Protestant Reformation as, 289–91
    use of term, 289n17
    Wycliffe, 256
Cousins, Ewert, 201, 203–4, 205
Cranmer, Thomas, 305, 308, 310
Cromwell, Oliver, 328–29, 329, 330–31, 333
Cromwell, Thomas, 308–9, 310
cross and Crucifixion
    Christ the Sufferer depictions, 208–11, 210n46, 211
    Christ the Victor depictions, 205–8, 207, 209
    Luther's "theology of the cross," 293–94
    naturalistic depictions, 211–12, 245–48, 247
    in Russian iconography, 264
    stavrocentrism, 197–205, 277
    True Cross, 72, 97
crusades
    First Crusade, 94–96, 131–32, 147
    Second Crusade, 96
    Third Crusade, 96
    Fourth Crusade, 102–6, 107

    Fifth Crusade, 132, 133
    Sixth Crusade, 133, 134–35
    Seventh Crusade, 136
    Eighth Crusade, 136–37
    Albigensian (Cathar) Crusade, 97–98, 147
    Crusader States, 96
    ecclesiastical colonialism from, 99–100, 106
    Gregory VII's dreams of, 90–92, 131
    holy war/just war and, 92–93, 92n27
    monastic support for, 147–48
    papal supremacy and, 131–32, 134–36
    against Russia, 112–13, 113
    violence of, 96–97
    Wendish Crusade, 107
culture, vs. civilization, 337n3
Cyprian of Carthage, 124
Cyril and Methodios (missionaries), 173
Cyril of Alexandria, 151, 204

D

Dallen, James, 213
dance of death, 249–50
Dandolo, Enrico, 106
Daniel (metropolitan of Moscow), 313, 314
Dante, *Divine Comedy*, 203, 281–82
Dawson, Christopher, 39–40, 61, 80, 150
death, 243–50
    art of dying, 248
    Black Death, 243, *243*, 244, 249, 278
    cadaver tombs, 249
    Crucifixion, naturalistic depictions of, 211–12, 245–48, 247
    culture of dread and, 243–44
    dance of death, 249–50
Decretals, 124
deification (*theosis*), 26, 54–55, 238, 240–41. *See also* hesychasm
deism, 341–42
Delumeau, Jean, 295
Demus, Otto, 185
The Descent of the Virgin into Hell, 202–3
devshirme, 267–68
dhimmis, 71, 72
Dies irae ("Day of Wrath") hymn, 244

Dionisy (Russian iconographer), 264
Dionysios the Areopagite, 159, 176, 180
Divine Liturgy of John Chrystostom, 39n20,
    169–71. *See also* liturgy
divine participation, 84, 167–68, 238–39,
    280, 291, 338. *See also* deification;
    hesychasm
Dix, Gregory, 174, 176
Dmitry Donskoy (Mowcow grand prince),
    311
Dominicans, 147, 151
Donation of Constantine, 53, 63–64, 234,
    270n93
Donatism, 122
Doukas, Andronikos, 75, 76, 77
Doukas, John, 74, 77
dread, culture of, 197, 243–44
The Dream of the Rood, 208
dualism, Augustinian, 37–38, 80, 119–20
Duns Scotus, 217, 278
Durand, William, 126
Dutch Revolt, 328

E

Eastern Christendom
    Christianization of, 25–26
    clericalism, 169
    conflict with papacy, 11, 13–14, 18, 46,
        47–50
    ecclesiastical colonialism of, 99–100, 106
    Ecumenical Patriarch, title of, 46
    Great Schism, 51–58
    influences on West, fading, 32–36
    Lent in, 219–20
    metamorphocentrism of, 199, 202–3
    monasticism in, 140–41
    penance in, 214–15
    preservation of paradise in, 337
    Protestants and, 290, 300
    reform movements, lack of, 254
    reunion attempts with West, 90–91, 94,
        127–28, 235, 268–71, 280, 319–20
    theology in, 119, 151
    See also Byzantine Empire; Constantino-
        ple; Russia
Eastern-rite Roman Catholics, 319–20

ecclesiastical colonialism, 99–100, 106
Eckhart, Meister, 240–41
ecumenical councils
    First Council of Nicaea (325), 81, 227–28
    Fourth Ecumenical Council (451), 204,
        238
    Sixth Ecumenical Council (681), 50
    Seventh Ecumenical Council (787), 300
    in West, 227
Ecumenical Patriarch, title of, 46
Edessa, 96
Edict of Nantes (1598), 328
Edward Longshanks (English king), 138
Edward VI (English king), 310
Eighth Crusade, 136–37
Eleanor of Aquitaine, 96, 128–29
England
    conquest by Normans, 69, 93
    English Civil War, 328–29, 330
    Henry II and Thomas Becket, 128–31
    Papal Schism and, 232
    Protestant Reformation in, 305–10
    war with France, 129, 138
Enlightenment, 341–42
Epistle to Diognetus, 19
Erlembald, 85, 93
Eucharist
    adoration of (feast of Corpus Christi),
        175, 175n8
    apostles on, 303
    consecration of, 174–75
    individualistic piety and, 175–76
    infrequent communion, 168
    Protestants on, 303–6
    Thomas a Kempis on, 253–54
    transubstantiation controversy, 153–54
    unleavened bread controversy, 13,
        48–50, 55–56, 170–71, 270
Eugene III (pope), 96, 123, 148
Eugene IV (pope), 234–35, 268, 270, 271
Eusebius of Caesarea, 36, 120, 130
Everyman (miracle play), 179, 248
excommunication, 87

F

False Dmitry, First, 321

Farel, William, 305
Fatimid Caliphate, 71–72
Fedotov, George, 23, 110
Feodosy of Kiev, 23, 23–25, 142, 196, 203
Feofan the Greek, 262–63
Ferdinand (Spanish king), 325
feudalism, 27–28
Fifth Crusade, 132, 133
filioque, 18, 28–29, 35, 101, 156–57, 228, 270
First Council of Nicaea (325), 81, 227–28
First Crusade, 94–96, 131–32, 147
First World War, 342
flagellation, self-, 198, 241, 251, 277–78
Folcrad, 86
Forgiveness Sunday, 219–20
Formosus (pope), 28
Fourth Crusade, 102–6, 107
Fourth Ecumenical Council (451), 204, 238
Fourth Lateran Council (1215), 100, 150,
    217, 227
France
    Albigensian (Cathar) Crusade, 97–98,
    147
    Avignon papacy, 229, 229–31
    feudalism in, 27–28
    Gothic architecture, 186–94
    Papal Schism and, 232
    papal visits, 45n24
    Saint Bartholomew's Day Massacre, 328
    Thirty Years War and, 331
    war with England, 129, 138
Franciscans, 146–47, 151, 201–2
Franciscan Spirituals, 226, 230
Francis of Assisi, 146, 201, 202
Franks, 18, 35–36, 49, 71, 119–20, 173, 215.
    See also Carolingian Empire
Frederick Barbarossa (Holy Roman empe-
    ror), 96
Frederick of Lorraine (future Pope Stephen
    IX), 52, 67
Frederick the Wise (Saxony elector), 284,
    292
Frederick II (Holy Roman emperor), 133,
    133, 134–36, 226
Free Spirits, 250–51
Fulton, Rachel, 197, 278

Fyodor (Russian tsar), 319

G
Germanos of Constantinople, 177, 179, 180
German Peasants War, 292, 293, 326
Germany, see Holy Roman Empire
Germogen (patriarch of Moscow), 321
Gero Crucifix, 209, 211
Gerson, Jean, 233–34, 239–40, 258
Giotto, 211–13, 245
Glaber, Rudolfus, 42
Gleb and Boris (passionbearers), 22, 108,
    110, 113, 203
Godunov, Boris, 320
The Golden Legend, 284
Gothic architecture and art, 186–94
    Crucifixion depictions, 208–9
    cultural effects of, 193–94
    development, 186
    influences on, 187–89
    vs. Romanesque, 187
    transcendence focus, 189–91, 193
Gratian, 124, 217
Great Schism, 51–58
    bull of excommunication, 57–58
    failure to reverse, 59
    impetus for, 13–14
    Leo IX's death and, 54
    Michael Cerularius's evasion, 56–57
    opportunity to prevent, 51–52
    papal supremacy claims and, 52–53
    unleavened bread controversy and,
    54–56
Gregory Akindynos, 165
Gregory, Brad, 336
Gregory of Nyssa, 17, 119
Gregory Palamas, 159–60, 160, 162–63, 165,
    202n39, 236, 236n65
Gregory the Great (pope), 46, 299
Gregory the Theologian, 119
Gregory VI (pope), 42, 44
Gregory VII (pope; formerly Hildebrand)
    clerical celibacy and, 81, 82, 83, 84–85
    crusade dreams, 90–92, 131
    destruction of Rome and death of,
    89–90

investiture conflict, 85–89, 128, 139
Papal Dictate, 77n12, 78–79, 87, 88, 124, 126, 227
papal supremacy and, 44, 77–79, 233
Pope Nicholas II and, 67, 68
portrait, *80*
warfare and, 93
Gregory VIII (pope), 96
Gregory IX (pope), 98, 112, 124, 132–33, 134, 135, 151–52
Gregory X (pope), 127, 280
Gregory XI (pope), 231
Groote, Geert, 252
Guido (archbishop of Milan), 85, 87
guilt, 213. *See also* penance
Guiscard, Robert, 10, 69, 89, 90
Gustavus Adolphus (Swedish king), 331

H

Hagia Sophia, *21*, 21–22, 105, 176, 182, 273–74
heavenly immanence, 101, 102, 120–21, 167–68, 239, 291, 338
Henry of Navarre, 328
Henry II (English king), 96, 128–31, 309
Henry II (Holy Roman emperor), 18, 29
Henry III (Holy Roman emperor), 10, 40–42, *41*, 44, 60, 67, 86
Henry IV (Holy Roman emperor), 85, 87–89, *91*, 139
Henry VIII (English king), 306–8, *307*, 309–10
Heraklios (Byzantine emperor), 92n27
heresy, 98
Herman of Reichenau, *On Contempt for the World*, 35
hesychasm, 159–66
Christocentric asceticism and, 160–62
defense by Gregory Palamas, 159–60, 162–63
objections to, 162, 163–64
in Russia, 260–61, 265–66
victory of, 165–66
See also deification (*theosis*)
Hilandar Monastery, 142, 183
Hildebrand, *see* Gregory VII (pope)

Holland, Tom, 46
holy fools, 317
Holy Roman Empire
Byzantine Empire and, 184–85
feudalism in, 28
investiture conflict, 85–89, 128
papacy and, 28–29, 40–42
Peace of Augsburg (1555), 327
Thirty Years War, 331–33
Wendish Crusade, 107
Holy Trinity Monastery (Russia), 260–61, 262, 313
holy war, 92–93, 92n27. *See also* crusades; wars of Western religion
Honorius I (pope), 50
Honorius II (antipope), 87
Honorius III (pope), 132, 147
Honorius of Autun, 178
Hosios Loukas (church), *182*, 182–83, 190
Hrabanus Maurus, 49
Hubert of Therouanne, 84–85
Hugh the Great (Cluny abbot), 32
Huguenots, 328
Huizinga, Johan, 250
humanism, secular, 165–66, 338, 341, 342, 343. *See also* secularization
Humbert (cardinal)
on Christ the Sufferer depictions, 210n46
comparison to Barlaam of Calabria, 167
death, 77
on *filioque*, 101
Great Schism and, 13–14, 49, 50, 51, 52, 53, 54, 55–56, 57–58
papal elections and, 77
papal reformation and supremacy, 44, 46, 47, 60–64
transubstantiation controversy and, 154
Hus, Jan, 256–58, *258*, 258n87
Hussite Wars, 258–59
hypostatic union, 19–20, 238

I

iconography
Bernard of Clairvaux on, 188–89
Calvin on, 299–300, 301

Christ the Sufferer depictions, 208–12, 210n46, *211*
Christ the Victor depictions, 205–8, *207, 209*
development of, 181–83
Franks against, 35
iconotorsion, 302–3
John of Damascus on, 300–301
vs. naturalistic depictions, 211–12, 245–48, *247,* 299
Protestant iconoclasm, 301–2
in Russia, 262–64
iconostasis, 183–84
Ignatius of Antioch, 124, 172
Igor of Novgorod-Seversk, 110
Ilarion of Kiev (metropolitan), 108
imagination, 198–99, 265
Incarnation, 19–20, 26, 101, 163, 200–201, 300–301
Indigenous peoples, 324
indignation, 60, 94, 118, 120, 167, 224, 342
indulgences, 95, 104, 257, 275–76, 283, 287–88, 289
Innocent III (pope)
    Albigensian Crusade, 97, 98
    confession and, 217
    crusades and, 132, 147
    Fourth Crusade, 102–3, 105–6
    Franciscans and, 146
    juridical authority of, 123
    The Misery of the Human Condition, 248
    portrait, *103*
    vestments and, 178
    Vicar of Christ title, 100
    Wendish Crusade, 107
Innocent IV (pope), 136
inquisition, papal, 98, 124, 147, 250
inquisition, Spanish, 325–26
investiture
    ban on lay investiture, 100
    investiture conflict, 85–89, 128, 139
Ireland, 69, 129, 215, 281, 330–31
Isabella (Spanish queen), 325
Isenheim Altarpiece, 246, 248
Isidore of Kiev, 269, 271, 272, 312
Islam, 70–71

Ivan the Terrible (Russian tsar), 314–19, *315,* 337
Ivan III the Great (Moscow grand prince), 311, 313

J

Jacobus of Voragine, *The Golden Legend,* 284
Jacques of Vitry, 251
janissaries, 267–68
Jefferson, Thomas, 341, 341n5
Jeremias (patriarch of Constantinople), 290
Jerusalem, 72, 95, 96, 97, 100, 132, 135, 218
Jerusalem Council, 44, 228
Jesuits (Society of Jesus), 320, 321
Jesus Christ, 19, 92, 101, 293
Jesus Prayer, 162
Jews, 97, 138, 325
jihad, 70–71, 72–73, 267
Joachim of Fiore, 225–26, 230
Joanna of Naples, 231
John Cassian, 215
John Chrystostom, 214
John Italos, 164
John Kantakouzenos (Byzantine emperor), 268–69
John of Brienne, 132
John of Damascus, 151, 159, 299, 300–301
John of Fecamp, 35
John of the Ladder, 213–14, 215
John the Theologian (apostle), 26, 55, 303
John II (Byzantine emperor), 80
John IV (patriarch of Antioch), 100
John VI (Byzantine emperor), 165
John VIII (Byzantine emperor), 269
John VIII (pope), 18, 29
John X (patriarch of Constantinople), 106
John XII (pope), 11, 28
John XXII (pope), 230, 241
John XXIII (pope), 257
Joseph, Abba, 214–15, 262
Joseph of Volokolamsk, 313
jubilee, 283
Jungmann, Joseph, 175
juridical authority, 122–24
Justin Martyr, 172

just war, 93. *See also* crusades; wars of Western religion

K

Kaldellis, Anthony, 56
Karlstadt, Andreas, 301
Kaufmann Crucifixion, 246, 247
kenoticism, 23, 202–3, 261
Kiev, 108, 112, 271
Kiev Caves Monastery, 24, 142
Kirillo-Belozersky Monastery, 262, 264
Kirill of Turov, 196
Klauser, Theodor, 170
Knights Hospitaller, 148
Knights Templar, 138, 148–49
Knox, John, 305
Kurbsky, Ivan, 319

L

Ladder of Divine Ascent, 140
Ladner, Gerhart, 38–39, 39n20
laity, 80–81, 168, 169, 171–72, 173–74. *See also* piety
Lanfranc, 153, 235
Lateran Palace, 28, 60, 61–62, 65, 92, 123, 287
Lazar (Serbian prince), 267
legal authority, 122–24
Le Goff, Jacques, 279, 279n6
Lent (Great Fast), 214, 219–20
Leo of Ohrid, 13, 49, 50
Leo I the Great (pope), 11, 43, 66, 81, 151, 204
Leo III (pope), 28, 61–62
Leo IX (pope; formerly Bruno of Toul)
   death, 54
   election as pope, 42–43
   Great Schism and, 13–14, 47, 49, 50, 51, 53
   papal reformation and supremacy, 11–12, 42–43, 44–46
   portraits, 43, 46
   war against Normans, 9, 10, 12–13, 93
Leo X (pope), 287–88
Light, Uncreated, 162, 202, 202n38, 261
liturgy
   allegorical interpretation of, 176–77

churches, role in, 176, 181
clericalism and, 169–71
dramatization of, 177–79, 202
eucharistic approach to, 180
iconostasis and, 183–84
language of, 173–74, 289–90
privatization of, 172–73
resurrectional and transfigured approach, 179–80, 181, 184, 194–97
See also Eucharist; iconography
Lollardy, 256
Lombard, Peter, 217, 225
Lossky, Vladimir, 204
Louis the Fat (French king), 187, 193
Louis the Pious (Holy Roman emperor), 31
Louis VII (French king), 96, 129
Louis IX (French king), *136*, 136–37
Louis XIII (French king), 331
Louth, Andrew, 66
Luke (apostle), 303
Luther, Martin
   Augsburg Confession, 326–27
   Augustinianism of, 293–94
   civil conservatism of, 292
   as counter-reformation, 289
   on Eucharist, 304
   ninety-five theses, 288
   portrait, 276
   spiritual crisis, 275–76, 275n1, 285–87

M

Machiavelli, Niccolò, *The Prince*, 306
Magdeburg, 332, 333
Maiolus of Cluny, 32
Makarios of Egypt, 23, 23n3
   Spiritual Homilies, 160–61
Marie of Oignies, 251
Mark of Ephesus, 269, 269, 271, 280
marriage, 83–84. *See also* clerical celibacy
Martimort, A. G., 49
Martin of Tours, 98
Martin V (pope), 259
Mary (English queen), 310
Matthew (apostle), 303
Maximos the Confessor, 18, 26, 151, 159, 176, 180

Maxim the Greek, 313–14
medieval, use of term, 339–40
Mehmet II (Ottoman sultan), 271–72, 273–74
Melanchthon, Philip, 327
metamorphocentrism, 199, 202–3
Methodios and Cyril (missionaries), 173
Meyendorff, John, 51, 160–61
Michael Cerularius (patriarch of Constantinople)
    Ecumenical Patriarch title, 11, 46
    Great Schism and, 13, 51–52, 52n31, 53, 56–57, 58
    portrait, 46
    religious assimilationist approach by, 48–49, 73
Michael Paleologos (Byzantine emperor), 280
Michael VII (Byzantine emperor), 90
Michael VIII (Byzantine emperor), 127–28
Michelangelo, 287, 299, 299n28, 302
Milan, 85, 87
modern devotion (devotio moderna), 252–54
modernity, 213, 339n4, 340–41
monasticism
    Athonite monasticism, 141, 141–43
    Benedict of Aniane reforms, 31
    Cistercians, 144–46, 188
    Cluniac reforms, 30–31, 32, 33, 143–44
    crusades, support for, 147–49
    Dominicans, 147, 151
    Eastern influences, 33–35
    Franciscans, 146–47, 151, 201–2
    itinerant orders, 146–50
    monastic orders, 144, 150
    origins of, 140
    papal supremacy from, 139–40
    penitential basis, 140–41, 143
    proprietary church and, 29–30
    rivalry within, 188
    in Russia, 259–62, 264–66, 312–13
Mongols, 110–12, 243, 259, 311
Monreale Cathedral, 133–34
More, Thomas, 309–10, 338
Morosini, Thomas, 106
Morris, Colin, 175

Moses (prophet), 202
Mount Athos, 141, 141–43
Mount Vesuvius, 327
Muentzer, Thomas, 291–92
Muhammad, 71, 72

N

Native Americans, 324
naturalism, 209–10, 211–12, 245, 299, 302
natural theology, 156
Neoplatonism, 160, 163, 240–41
Nestor the Chronicler, 23
New World, 323–24
Nicene Creed, and filioque, 18, 28–29, 35, 101, 156–57, 228, 270
Nicholas I (pope), 11, 18
Nicholas II (pope), 67–68, 69
Nichols, Aidan, 52n32
Nicolaitan Schism, 11, 11n2, 18
Nietzsche, Friedrich, 194, 333, 342
nihilism, 194, 342–43
Niketas of Nicomedia, 127
Niketas Stethatos, 54–56, 141, 169, 184
Nikon (patriarch of Moscow), 322
Nilos of Rossano, 33
Nil Sorsky, 264–66, 312
nominalism, 236–39
Normans, 9–11, 12, 13, 27, 68–70, 89–90
Northern Thebaid, 259–62, 264–66, 312–13
Norwich, John Julius, 89, 230, 270–71
Notre Dame Cathedral (Paris), 191, 191n27

O

Occam's Razor, 237
Odilo of Cluny, 32, 283
Odo of Cluny, 32, 82
Olaf II of Norway (king), 27
Old Believer Schism, 321–23, 337
orientation, church, 33, 186
original sin, 18, 82, 197, 294–95, 297
Orthodox Church, see Eastern Christendom
Otto of Constance, 85
Otto the Great (Holy Roman emperor), 28
Otto III (Holy Roman emperor), 184–85
Ottoman Turks, 267–68, 271–74
Ozment, Steven, 157

P

pagan philosophy, 26, 155–56, 164, 236, 236n65, 340
pain, asceticism of, 198–99, 241–43, 251, 277–78
Pange Lingua (hymn), 208
papacy
    apocalypticism in, 225–26
    Avignon papacy, 229, 229–31
    Cadaver Synod, 28
    canon law, 64–66, 124, 137, 217
    "city of God" conception, 102
    clerical celibacy, 13–14, 81–85, 100, 289
    clericalism, 79–81, 121–22, 168–69, 171–74
    college of cardinals, 69, 92, 123, 230
    conciliarism and, 233–35, 240, 270
    conflict with East, 11, 13–14, 18, 46, 47–50
    Constantinople and, 137
    curia (papal court), 92, 117–18, 122–24
    Great Schism, 51–58
    Holy Roman Empire and, 28–29, 40–42
    indulgences, 95, 104, 257, 275–76, 283, 287–88, 289
    inquisition, 98, 124, 147, 250
    institutionalization of, 117–18, 139–40
    investiture conflict, 85–89, 128, 139
    moral decay, 28, 30–31, 230–31
    Normans and, 9–10, 12, 68–69
    origin of term, 66, 117
    papal elections, 69, 77, 86
    Papal Schism, 231–33
    papal supremacy, challenges to, 124–27, 128–31, 137–39
    papal supremacy, development of, 18, 43–46, 60–66, 67–69, 77–79, 227–29
    reformation of, 10–12, 42–43, 44–45, 59, 118–19
    secuarlization and, 120–21
    universities and, 151–52
    Vicar of Christ title, 100–102, 122, 228, 257
    See also crusades
Papadakis, Aristeides, 77, 77n12, 80n17, 99, 149, 151, 157

Papal Dictate (*Dictatus papae*), 77–78, 77n12, 87, 88, 124, 126, 227
Paphnutios of Thebes, 81
Paris, 27, 249, 305
Passion Week, 177–78, 195–96
Patarenes, 85, 87, 93
Paul (apostle), 20, 38, 44, 124, 215, 279n5, 303
Paul III (pope), 324
Paul V (pope), 321
Peace of Augsburg (1555), 327
Peace of Westphalia (1648), 332
Pelagius (cardinal), 132, 135
penance, 213–20
    canonical penance, 213–14, 213n47
    confession and, 214, 216, 217
    juridical approach, 215–18, 278–79
    Lent, 214, 219–20
    pilgrimage and, 218
    private penance, 214
    therapeutic approach, 214–15, 219–20
Peter Damian
    on clerical celibacy, 82–83, 289
    papal reformation and, 44, 64, 77
    pessimism and dread of, 33–35, 197–99
    portrait, 34
    privatization of Mass and, 172–73
    on self-flagellation, 198, 241, 277–78
    on stigmata, 198, 202
Peter of Amalfi, 52
Peter the Chanter, 279
Peter the Hermit, 147
Peter the Venerable (Cluny abbot), 145
Petrarch, 166, 340
Philip of Moscow (metropolitan), 316–17
Philip the Fair (French king), 137–39, 227, 229
Philip II (French king), 96
Philips, Jonathan, 105–6
philosophy, and theology, 156, 235–36, 236n65. *See also* pagan philosophy
Philotheos (patriarch of Constantinople), 260
Photios (patriarch of Constantinople), 11, 18, 151, 182

piety
  allegorical interpretations of liturgy,
    176–77
  Christ the Sufferer depictions, 208–12,
    210n46, 211
  Christ the Victor depictions, 205–8, 207,
    209
  death, focus on, 243–50
  Eucharist, unleavened bread, and,
    171–72
  Eucharistic adoration, 175, 175n8
  Eucharistic consecration, 174–75
  individualization of, 175–76
  liturgical dramatization and, 177–79
  modern devotion (devotio moderna),
    252–54
  mystical approaches, 240–41, 250–51
  pain, asceticism of, 198–99, 241–43, 251,
    277–78
  penance, 213–20
  privatization of Mass, 172–73
  resurrectional and transfigured
    approach to liturgy, 179–80, 181, 184,
    194–97
  stavrocentrism, 197–205, 277
pilgrimage, 218
Pisano, Giunta, 209–10
Placards Affair, 305
Plato, 164, 189
Plethon, George, 269
politics, 306. See also caesaropapism;
    symphony
Porete, Marguerite, 251
priests, see clerical celibacy; clericalism
Priscillian, 98
proprietary church, 29–30, 86
Protestant Reformation
  apocalypticism in, 291–93
  assessments of, 335–36
  clerical celibacy and, 84
  as counter-reformation, 289–91
  in England, 305–10
  on Eucharist, 303–6
  iconoclasm of, 298–300, 301–2
  Luther, 275–76, 285–87, 288
  Orthodox and, 290, 300

paradiasical decay, 291
  pessimism of, 293–95, 296–97
  sola scriptura, 298
Psellos, Michael, 52, 74, 77, 80, 164–65,
    210n46
Pseudo-Isidorian Decretals, 64
purgatory, 279–86
  development, 270, 279–80
  dread of, 282
  freedom from, 283–85
  literature on, 280–82
  Orthodox on, 280
  overview, 276
  Protestants against, 289
Puritans, 328–29, 330–31

R
rationalism, see nominalism; scholasticism
Ratramnus of Corbie, 304
Ravenna, 33–34, 250
reformation, vs. transfiguration, 38–39
Regino of Pruem, 216
relics, 106, 284–85, 299
religious persecution, 98. See also
    inquisition
religious wars, see wars of Western religion
Renaissance, 339, 339n4, 340
repentance, 140–41, 143, 214. See also
    penance
Requiem Mass, 244
revealed theology, 156
Riasanovsky, Nicholas, 318
Richard the Lionheart (English king), 96,
    97
Richelieu (cardinal), 331
Rollo (Norman warlord), 27, 27
Romanesque architecture and art, 184,
    185–86, 189, 208–9
Romanos IV (Byzantine emperor), 69,
    74–77, 79
Romanov, Michael (Russian tsar), 321
romanticism, 342
Rome, 89–90, 218, 229
Romuald, 34
rose window, 191
Rothmann, Bernard, 292

Rule of Saint Basil, 31, 33
Rule of Saint Benedict, 31, 144
Runciman, Steven, 55, 58
Russia
    centralization of, 108–10, 311–12
    conversion and Christianization, 22–25, 107–8
    crusade against, 112–13, *113*
    holy fools, 317
    as Holy Russia, 319
    iconography in, 262–64
    Ivan the Terrible, 314–19, *315*
    metamorphocentrism in, 202–3
    monasticism in, 259–62, 264–66, 312–13
    Mongols and, 110–12, 259, 311
    Old Believer Schism, 321–23
    resurrectional focus, 196
    spiritual isolation, 313–14
    Third Rome doctrine, 312, 322
    Time of Troubles, 319–21
    western Russia, 311
Ryazan, 111–12

S

Saint Bartholomew's Day Massacre, 328
Sainte Chapelle (Paris), 193
Saint John Lateran (basilica), 33, 60
Saint Patrick's Purgatory, 281
Saint Peter's Basilica, 287–88
Saint Sophia Cathedral (Kiev), 108
Saint Sophia Monastery (Serbia), 183
Saladin, 96, 97
Sant'Apollinare Nuovo (Ravenna), 250
Sava of Serbia, 142–43, *143*
Schmalkaldic Wars, 327
Schmemann, Alexander, 343
Scholarios, George, 269, 271
scholasticism, 152–58
    Anselm of Canterbury and, 152–54
    apophaticism and, 159
    Bernard of Clairvaux against, 155, 235–36
    confession and, 217
    Gothic architecture and, 189
    impacts of, 157–58
    nominalist critique of, 240

    Peter Abelard and, 154–55
    on priestly role, 122
    rationalism in, 235
    Thomas Aquinas and, 155–57
Schulz, Hans-Joachim, 181
Scotland, 232, 305
Second Council of Lyons (1274), 127, 280, 289
Second Crusade, 96
Second World War, 343
secularization, 120–21, 157, 163–64, 297, 326, 340, 343. *See also* humanism, secular
Seljuk Turks, 70, 71–73, 75–77
Serbia, 142–43, 267
Sergy of Radonezh, 260–61, 312
Seventh Crusade, 136
Seventh Ecumenical Council (787), 300
Sicily, 47, 133
Sigismund (Holy Roman emperor), 258, 267
Sigismund III (Polish king), 321
Simonov Monastery, 262
simony, 45, 100, 126, 288
Siricius (pope), 98
Sistine Chapel, 287, 299, 299n28
Sixth Crusade, 133, 134–35
Sixth Ecumenical Council (681), 50
Sixtus IV (pope), 283, 287
slavery, 323–24
Society of Jesus (Jesuits), 320, 321
Socrates Skolastikos, 81
sola scriptura, 298
soteriology, 26, 199, 245–46, 255, 277
Southern, Richard, 79, 228, 257
Spain, 323–24, 325–26
stained glass windows, 190–91, 193
state, vs. church, 122
stavrocentrism, 197–205
    development, 197–99, 277
    Franciscans and, 201–2
    Luther and, 293–94
    vs. metamorphocentrism, 202–3
    piety implications, 200–201
    problems from, 204–5
    See also penance
St. Denis (basilica), *189*, 189–91, 243–44
Stefan of Perm, 261

Stephen II (pope), 53, 63
Stephen VI (pope), 28
Stephen IX (pope; formerly Frederick of
    Lorraine), 52, 67
stigmata, 198, 202, 251
Stoglav Council (1551), 314
Studion Monastery, 24, 54, 141
Suger (abbot), *187*, 187–88, 189–90, 193
Suso, Heinrich, 241–43, 245, 265
Sweden, 331
Sweeney, Jon, 225, 226
Symeon of Thessaloniki, 181
Symeon the New Theologian, 34, 54, 151,
    169n2, 202n38, 265
Symeon the Stylite, 198
sympathy, 200
symphony, 62, 80, 125, 130
Synodikon of Orthodoxy, 165, 271
Synod of Sutri (1046), 42
Synod of Whitby (664), 125
Synod of Worms (1076), 88

T

Taft, Robert, 176
Tamerlane, 268
tariff penance, 216, 278
Tauler, Johannes, 241
Taylor, Charles, 239
Tellenbach, Gerd, 61, 79
Tetzel, Johann, 288, *288*
Teutonic Knights, 112–13, 148
Theodore the Studite, 206
Theodosius I (Byzantine emperor), 130
Theodulf of Orléans, 35, 151
theology
    apophaticism, 159
    hesychasm, 159–66
    natural vs. revealed, 156
    nominalism, 236–39
    philosophy and, 156, 235–36, 236n65
    scholasticism, 152–58
    traditional understanding of, 119, 151
    universities and, 151–52
theosis (deification), 26, 54–55, 238, 240–41.
    See also hesychasm
Third Crusade, 96

Third Rome doctrine, 312, 322
Thirty Years War, 331–33
Thomas a Kempis, *The Imitation of Christ,*
    252–54
Thomas Aquinas
    on confession, 217
    Dionysios the Areopagite and, 159
    Greek translation of, 268
    hesychasm and, 158
    portrait, *156*
    on purgatory, 279–80
    scholasticism and, 155, 156–57, 236, 237
Thomas Becket, 129–31, *130*, 308–9
Thomas of Celano, 244
Thomas of Torquemada, 325
Time of Troubles, 319–21
total depravity, 295, 296–97
transcendence, 188, 189–91, 193
transfiguration, 38–39, 179–80, 204–5
Treaty of Verdun (843), 26
Turks
    Ottoman, 267–68, 271–74
    Seljuk, 70, 71–73, 75–77
Tyerman, Christopher, 93, 134

U

Uncreated Light, 162, 202, 202n38, 261
Union of Brest (Uniate church), 319–20
universities, 151–52
Unum sanctum, 139, 228
Urban II (pope), 92, 94–95, *95*, 99, 122, 131,
    147, 150, 185, 289
Urban IV (pope), 137, 175
Urban VI (pope), 231, 232
utopia, 335, 338–40, 341–42

V

Vasari, Giorgio, 339, 339n4
Vasily III (Russian tsar), 313, 314
Venice, 102–3, 106
vestments, 178
Vicar of Christ (title), 100–102, 122, 228, 257
Vikings, 26–27. See also Normans
Viladesau, Richard, 209
Vladimir (city), 109, 112
Vladimir (grand prince), 22, *22*, 107, 203

Vladimir Icon of the Mother of God, 108–9
Vladimir Monomakh, *Testament*, 108
Voltaire, 332–33, 342
von Simson, Otto, 187, 188, 193
Votive Masses, 173

W

Waldensians, 250
Walzer, Michael, 329
war, holy/just, 92–93, 92n27. *See also* cru-
  sades; wars of Western religion
Ward, Benedicta, 199
wars of Western religion, 326–33
  about, 326
  English Civil War, 328–29, 330–31
  German Peasants War, 292, 293, 326
  Saint Bartholomew's Day Massacre, 328
  Schmalkaldic Wars, 327
  Thirty Years War, 331–33
Weber, Max, 335–36, 336n1
Wendish Crusade, 107
Western Christendom
  Augustinianism, 17–18, 36–40, 119–20
  Christianization of, 26–27
  clericalism, 79–81, 121–22, 168–69,
    171–74
  counter-reformation, 250–54, 256–59
  Eastern influences on, 32–36
  ecclesiastical colonialism by, 99–100,
    106
  feudalism, 27–28
  Great Schism, 51–58
  humanism, secular, 166, 338, 341, 342,
    343

modernity, 213, 339n4, 340–41
nihilism, 342–43
nominalism, 236–39
paradiasical decay, 167–68, 223–24, 329,
  336, 337, 338–39
proprietary church, 29–30, 86
Renaissance, 339, 339n4, 340
reunion attempts with East, 90–91, 94,
  127–28, 235, 268–71, 280, 319–20
scholasticism, 152–58
secularization, 120–21, 157, 163–64, 297,
  326, 340, 343
stavrocentrism, 197–205, 277
theology in, 119, 151
utopian orientation, 335, 338–39, 340–42
wars of Western religion, 326–33
  See also crusades; monasticism; papacy;
  piety; Protestant Reformation
William of Occam, 236, 237, 237–38, 239n67
William of Sabina, 113
William the Conqueror, 69, 91, 93, 128
windows, stained glass, 190–91, 193
witch trials, 325
Wolsey, Thomas, 306, 308
worship, *see* Eucharist; iconography; liturgy
Wycliffe, John, 256, 290

Y

Yaroslav the Wise, 107–8
Yury Dologoruky, 108

Z

Zizka, Jan, 258–59
Zwingli, Ulrich, 301–2, 304

About the Author

J OHN STRICKLAND IS AN ORTHODOX priest and former college professor. His first book, *The Making of Holy Russia*, is a study of the resilience
of Christianity in the modern world. An active blogger and podcaster, he
brings to the present work a lifetime of reflection on the religious background of the West. He lives in western Puget Sound with his wife and five
children.